2,000 YEARS OF CHRIST'S POWER

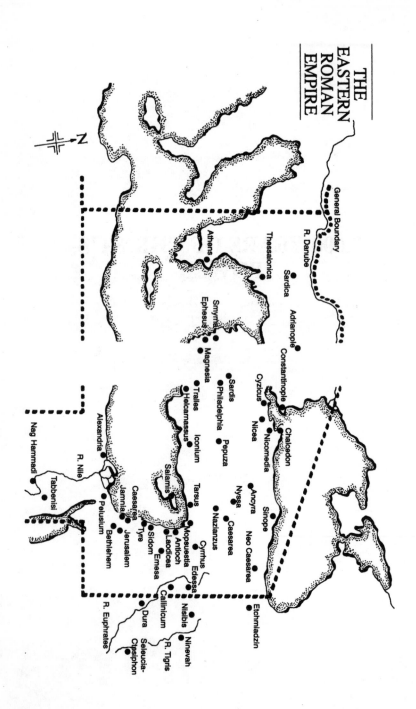

THE EASTERN ROMAN EMPIRE

N

General Boundary

R. Danube

Sardica
Thessalonica
Adrianople
Athens
Constantinople
Smyrna
Ephesus
Magnesia
Cyzicus
Nicea
Sardis
Nicomedia
Chalcedon
Philadelphia
Tralles
Pepuza
Halicarnassus
Iconium
Sinope
Nyssa
Ancyra
Neo Caesarea
Caesarea
Nazianzus
Etchmiadzin
Alexandria
Salamis
Tarsus
Nag Hammadi
R. Nile
Caesarea
Mopsuestia
Cyrrhus
Tabbenisi
Jamnia
Sidom
Antioch
Edessa
Nisibis
Pelusium
Jerusalem
Tyre
Emesa
Laodicea
Callinicum
Nineveh
Bethlehem
Dura
R. Tigris
Seleucia-
Ctesiphon
R. Euphrates

2,000 YEARS OF CHRIST'S POWER
PART ONE: THE AGE OF THE EARLY CHURCH FATHERS

Dr N. R. Needham

GRACE PUBLICATIONS TRUST
175 Tower Bridge Road
London SE1 2AH
England
e-mail: AGBCSE@AOL.com

Managing Editors:
J. P. Arthur M. A.
H. J. Appleby

ISBN 0946462 496

Distributed by
EVANGELICAL PRESS
Faverdale North Industrial Estate
Darlington
Co Durham DL3 OPH
England

Printed in Great Britain by
Creative Print and Design Group
Ebbw Vale
Gwent
NP3 5SD

Dedication

To Professor Alec Cheyne, Dr David Wright, Dr Peter Matheson, and Dr Andrew Ross, the Church history tutors at New College, Edinburgh University, from 1978 to 1982, when I was an undergraduate student there. Their excellence as teachers inspired me to specialise in Church history.

Contents

Illustrations

Acknowledgements

I would like to pay my debt of thanks to the following:

The Samuel Bill Theological College in Abak, Nigeria, whose students inspired this work; John Appleby of Grace Publications who seized on the idea when I mentioned to him that I was thinking of writing something like this; Dr David Wright of New College, Edinburgh University, one of my first and most effective teachers of Church history, who kindly read through the first draught of this book, and made numerous helpful comments; Phil Arthur of Grace Publications, who read through the next two draughts, and made even more numerous and helpful comments; the St Edward Brotherhood of Brookwood near Woking, Surrey, who let me use their library, overflowing with works by and about the early Church fathers, and also provided generous hospitality; the Evangelical Library in Chiltern Street, London, another invaluable resource and place of study; Stephen Rees of Stockport, who tracked down a much-sought-after quotation; and all the noble souls who kept me going by continually asking me when this book was coming out (now it's out, you'd better buy it).

A very special note of thanks to the Eastern Orthodox monks of Holy Transfiguration Monastery (Brookline, Boston, Massachusetts 02146-5997, USA), who supplied all but one of the pictures of the early Church fathers, and kindly gave permission for us to use them. Thanks to the Evangelical Library, Chiltern Street, London, for supplying the picture of Augustine of Hippo.

Many thanks to John Noble of Aberystwyth for providing the indices, and to Joyce Bell of Lancaster for helping with the proof-reading.

Christians normally attribute all their virtues to God and all their vices to themselves. In that spirit, I gratefully ascribe whatever virtues this book enjoys to the influence and advice of others. I alone remain responsible for whatever defects it contains.

Preface

Though the learning and power of the Roman Empire were so great, and both were employed to the utmost against Christianity, yet all was in vain. They could neither root it out, nor stop its progress. In spite of all, the kingdom of Christ wonderfully prevailed, and Satan's heathen kingdom mouldered and consumed away before it, agreeable to the text, "The moth shall eat them up like a garment, and the worm shall eat them like wool" (**Isaiah 51:8**). And it was very observable that, for the most part, the more they persecuted the Church, the more it increased; insomuch that it became a common saying, "The blood of the martyrs is the seed of the Church." Herein the Church of Christ proved to be like a palm-tree; of which it is remarked, that the greater weight is hung to its branches, the more it grows and flourishes. On this account probably the Church is compared to a palm-tree, "This thy stature is like to a palm-tree" (**Song of Solomon 7:7**). Justin Martyr, an eminent father in the Christian Church, says that in his days there was no part of mankind, whether Greeks or barbarians, or by what name soever they were called, even the most rude and unpolished nations, where prayers and thanksgivings were not made to the great Creator of the world, through the name of the crucified Jesus.

Jonathan Edwards (1703-58), *A History of the Work of Redemption,* **in** *Works,* **volume 1, p.591.**

Introduction

This is not a book for academics or professional historians. I wrote this for "ordinary Christians". The term may sound patronising. All I mean is Christian people who don't have any great intellectual training (who make up the majority of our church members), who love Jesus Christ, see Him as the Lord of time and history, and want to know something about the history of His Church. Frequently the question in their minds is, "How did the Church get to be in the state that it's in today? Where did this, that, or the other doctrine, practice, or denomination come from?" These are very valid questions. Curiosity is the mother of knowledge. The problem for such folk is that most books on Church history tend to fall into one of two categories:

(i) Academic works produced for the benefit of other academics, written in a complex and demanding language, which most non-academics find it hard to struggle through.

(ii) Popular works written in much simpler language, which can sometimes be rather careless about their historical facts, and often approach the subject from a very narrow theological point of view, which doesn't really do justice to the human beings or circumstances they are describing.

I faced this problem when I was teaching Church history in Nigeria. The students were highly motivated to study the subject. But their command of English was at a fairly simple level. I found myself quite stuck when they asked me to recommend textbooks. It seemed that practically all the good ones fell into category (i), while practically all the readable ones fell into category (ii). After puzzling over this, it dawned on me that maybe I should try to turn my own lectures into a textbook, which would (hopefully) combine the historical depth and accuracy of the first category with the popular readable style of the second.

And that was the genesis of this work. Whether I've succeeded I'll have to leave the reader to judge. But if you've been looking for an introduction to Church history - something which won't blind you with science, but won't reduce the story to the level of a children's tale either - you are the person I had in mind when I wrote this book.

If all goes according to plan, this will be Part One of a four part series. Part Two will cover the "Middle Ages"; Part Three will look at the Reformation and its aftermath; and Part Four will trace the story from the "Enlightenment" to the 20th Century.

Happy and fruitful reading.

A note on the design and style of this work

When an important character receives his first significant mention in a Chapter, his name is printed in bold type and italics. Each Chapter ends with a list of these characters, together with the dates of their births and deaths. Then follow some quotations which I thought would helpfully illustrate the characters and topics dealt with in that Chapter. All quotations from Greek and Latin originals are my own renderings of what that person or document said.

Whenever I use the word "Church" with a capital "C", I mean either the universal Church, or a particular branch of it (*e.g.* the English Church), or a famous ecclesiastical building (*e.g.* the Church of the Holy Wisdom). When I use the word church with a small "c", I am referring to a local church (*e.g.* the church in Antioch).

The footnotes usually contain cross-references or more detailed explanations of points discussed in the main text. Occasionally they contain humorous remarks by myself in my more irreverent moods.

Semi-circular brackets ( ) within a quotation are part of the quotation. Square brackets [ ] contain my own comments.

The glossary at the end of the book contains brief definitions of most of the historical and theological terms which might baffle the newcomer to Church history. For example, if you have already encountered Sabellianism in an earlier Chapter, but can't remember what this mysterious entity was, the easiest remedy is to look it up in the glossary.

Apart from the portrait of Augustine of Hippo, all the illustrations are copies of traditional "icons" of the early Church fathers. These icons give us the long-established historical picture of what the fathers looked like. Readers should therefore regard these icons as themselves part of Church history. Sensitive Protestants will dislike the circular halo and the word "saint" found in some of the icons; it may help them to overcome their revulsion if they treat these features as historical in nature. Here, in these icons, is how past generations of Christian people learned to visualise and love the early Church fathers (halo, sainthood and all).

One of my most zealously Evangelical friends is always protesting against the name "early Church fathers", since the Lord appears to command us to call no man "father" in a religious sense: "for One is your Father, He Who is in heaven" (**Matthew 23:9**). Deferring to my friend's scruples, in his presence I speak about "the early Church pioneers". However, "early Church fathers" is the normal and accepted name for these illustrious persons, and that is what I have called them in this book. After all, the Lord in **Matthew** went on to say, "Do not be called teachers, for One is your Teacher, the Christ" (verse 10), but Reformed Christians are happy enough to refer to "teaching elders". And Christ is our one true Shepherd, but again, many Evangelical Christians call their ministers "pastor" (shepherd) without thereby detracting from the glory of Christ.

As for "father", the apostle Paul claimed to be the spiritual father of the Corinthian believers (**1 Corinthians 4:15**) without any intended disobedience to his Saviour. And whether we realise it or not, the great men of the early Church are indeed *our* spiritual fathers; they shaped much of the worship and theology (especially the doctrine of the Trinity and the incarnation) which we accept and confess today. "Early Church fathers", then, is what I call them, with a child's love and reverence for his parents in the faith. If we think we now see further than they did in some points, it is only because we are standing on their shoulders.[1]

I have striven throughout these pages to be objective and impartial, and not to let my own theology interfere (or not *too* much anyway) with the way I describe and assess people and events. As I study the colourful panorama of Church history, I hope I can appreciate the reality of the Lord Jesus Christ's gracious presence with His people in spite of what I would regard as sins and errors.

---

[1] Here is the exposition of Christ's words in **Matthew 23** offered by the Puritan Matthew Poole: "It is most certain that our Saviour doth not here forbid the giving of the titles of masters and fathers to His ministers, for then Paul would not have given himself the title of father, 1 Cor.4:15, nor called the Galatians his little children, Gal. 4:19, nor called Timothy his son, and himself his father, Phil.2:22, nor called himself a doctor [teacher] of the Gentiles, 1 Tim.2:7, 2 Tim.1:11. That which He forbids is, 1. An affection of such titles, and hunting after them. 2. The exercise of an absolute mastership, or a paternal absolute power, so as to require any to believe things because *they* said them, or to do things because *they* bid them, without seeing the things asserted, or first commanded, in the Word of God. For in that sense, God alone is men's Father, Christ alone their Master. Pastors and teachers in the church are all but ministers - ministers of Christ to publish *His* will and to enjoin *His* laws; nor must any be owned as masters or fathers to impose *their* laws and doctrines."

A Chapter on TIME

(Note: This chapter is written for readers who may find it difficult to understand the BC - AD dating system and other ways in which historians describe time.)

This book is about Church history. But what exactly do we mean by "Church history"? Think about your own life. You were born on a certain day some time in the past. When you were born, you were not a full-grown adult, but a baby. Then you began to grow up. The baby became a child; the child became a teenager; the teenager became an adult. So you could picture your life as a sort of "time line":

Birth: Baby > Child > Teenager > Adult

This line is the history of your life. In this book, we are going to look at the history of the Christian Church. Like your own life, the Church too has a history; it has passed through different stages, just as you passed through the stages of being a baby, a child, a teenager, an adult. If we think of the Christian Church as being born on the day of Pentecost, we could picture its life as a sort of line, like this:

Birth: Early Church > Middle Ages > Reformation > Present Day

Historians usually divide up the life-story of the Church into these different stages. We begin with the "early Church" period, which began with the birth of the Church on the day of Pentecost, and lasted for some 600 years. Next we have the "Middle Ages" period, which covered (roughly) the next thousand years. Then we have the

"Reformation", which saw the birth of Protestantism. And if we count from the Reformation to the present day, that is almost another 500 years.

So if we think of the Church as if it were a human being, we can see that it has a life-story of its own: born as a baby at Pentecost, its childhood was the "early Church" period, its teenage years were the "Middle Ages", and its adulthood was the time from the "Reformation" to the present day. In these books, we are going to follow this life-story of the Christian Church, from its birth to its adulthood. (Whether the Church today is "adult" in a *spiritual* sense is a different question.)

BC and AD dates

This series of books is full of dates - naturally enough, since it is a history book. Most of the dates are years. For example, the city of Rome was founded in the year 753 BC. The first Roman emperor, Augustus, ruled from the year 31 BC to the year AD 14. The first ever "ecumenical Council" of the Church, the Council of Nicaea, met in the year AD 325. The Byzantine Empire, the stronghold of Christian civilisation in the East for a thousand years, fell in the year AD 1453. The French Revolution, which introduced modern secular democracy to the world, began in the year AD 1789.

The letters *BC,* which we attach to some of these years, stand for *Before Christ.* When we say that Augustus ruled the Roman Empire from 31 *BC*, we mean that he began his reign 31 years *before the birth of Christ*. These BC numbers get bigger the further back in time we go. The city of Rome was founded, according to Roman tradition, in 753 BC - that is, 753 years before the birth of Christ. Compare these two dates:

        Augustus began his reign 31   BC
        Rome was founded 753   BC

Which of these dates is closer to us today? The answer is 31 BC - the smaller number. The *smaller* a BC number is, the *nearer* it is to us today. The *larger* a BC number is, the *further away* it is from us.

However, the opposite is true of AD numbers. *AD* stands for *Anno Domini* (Latin for "in the year of our Lord"). Compare these two dates:

The Council of Nicaea met ...... AD   325
The Byzantine Empire fell .... AD 1453

Here, the larger number 1453 is nearer to us today. The Byzantine Empire fell 1453 years after the birth of Christ, but the Council of Nicaea met much earlier, only 325 years after Christ was born. So with AD numbers, the *smaller* it is, the *further away* it is from us; the *larger* it is, the *nearer* it is to us.

But *any* BC number, whatever its size, is further away from us than any AD number: or, to put it differently, *any* AD number, whatever its size, is closer to us than any BC number.

We can see this more clearly if we look at the time-line below:

<u>Birth of Christ</u>

BC———|————————|————**X**——|————————|————**AD**
      753 BC   31 BC   AD 325   AD 1453   Today
   Rome founded   Augustus's   Council   Byzantine
                   reign starts   of Nicaea   Empire falls

From the BC end of the time-line, the year numbers get smaller and smaller as they approach the birth of Christ. But *after* the birth of Christ, the year numbers get larger and larger as they approach our own time.

We do not usually bother to put the letters AD in front of a year which comes after Christ's birth. For instance, we do not say that the 2nd World War broke out in AD 1939; we just say 1939. So all years in this book which do not have either BC or AD attached to them are in fact AD years. For the first four Chapters of Part One, I have put AD in front of all the AD years, but from Chapter 5 onwards I have left it out. However, we *always* put BC at the end of a year which comes before Christ's birth.

Centuries

Another important feature of this time-system is the division of the years into *centuries*. A century is *one hundred years*. So when we refer to the *1st* Century AD, we mean the *first hundred years after Christ's birth* - that is, from the year AD 1 to the year AD 100. The *2nd* Century AD is the *second* hundred-year period after Christ's birth, from the year AD 101 to the year AD 200. The *3rd* Century AD is the *third* hundred-year period after Christ's birth, from the year AD 201 to the year AD 300. And so on.

Notice how the number of the *century* is always 1 greater than the number of the *years* which it contains:

The *3rd* Century AD contains the years that begin with the number *2* - the years 201, 202, 203, *etc.*

The *4th* Century AD contains the years that begin with the number *3* - the years 301, 302, 303, *etc.*

The *5th* Century AD contains the years that begin with the number *4* - the years 401, 402, 403, *etc.*

So if we want to know which century a year is in, we simply *add 1 to the first number of the year*. To give an example, Gregory the Great became pope in the year 590. That was in the *6th* Century - add 1 to the "5" of 590, which gives 6. Or again, the great Eastern monk, Theodore of Studium, died in the year 826. That was in the *9th* Century - add 1 to the "8" of 826, which gives 9.

When we get to years that have *four* figures instead of three, we have to add 1 to the first *two* numbers to find out the century. The previous examples were with three-figure years - 590 and 826. Let us now take a four-figure year. The great Italian theologian, Thomas Aquinas, was born in the year 1225. That was in the *13th* Century - add 1 to the "12" of 1225, which gives 13. Or again, the great Russian Orthodox novelist, Dostoyevsky, died in the year 1881. That was in the *19th* Century - add 1 to the "18" of 1881, which gives 19.

There is one exception to this rule, and that is where *a year ends in two zeroes* - for example, the year 800. This was the year when Charlemagne was crowned as the first Holy Roman emperor. But the year 800 was not, as we might have thought, in the 9th Century. It was the last year of the 8th Century. *A year ending in TWO ZEROES is the LAST year of the SAME century as the number which the year begins with.* So the year 500 is the last year of the 5th Century, the year 1200 the last year of the 12th Century, the year 1600 the last year of the 16th Century, and so on.

At the time of writing these words, we are living in the 20th Century, the twentieth hundred-year period after the birth of Christ, from the year AD 1901 to the year AD 2000. We will soon be entering the 21st Century.

Where did it come from?

Who created this method of counting the years? Its inventor was *Dionysius Exiguus,* a Scythian monk who lived in Italy (Scythia was the ancient name for the area of southern Russia around the Black Sea). We do not know when Dionysius was born, but he was active in the year 500 and died some time after 525. Using the historical evidence at his disposal, Dionysius worked out that Christ must have been born 753 years after the city of Rome had been founded. So he called this "year 1" - or the year AD 1, the first year *Anno Domini,* "in the year of our Lord", after Christ was born. Everything before that was BC - before Christ.

Unfortunately, Dionysius was probably wrong in his dating of Christ's birth. Historians today think that Christ was born several years earlier than Dionysius thought (between four and seven years earlier). However, since Dionysius's date became the accepted one, it means that we today use his dating system, with the odd result that today's historians have to say that Christ was born in about 4 BC. This does not mean that Christ was born four years before His birth (which would be rather silly); it merely means He was born four years before *Dionysius* thought He was born. In fact, other early scholars seriously questioned Dionysius's date for Christ's birth.

The Venerable Bede[1] a great English Church historian, disputed Dionysius's date in the 8th Century, and a German monk, Regino of Prum, rejected it in the 9th Century. Nevertheless, Dionysius's date became the norm.

It took a long time (a thousand years!) before the whole Christian world accepted Dionysius's dating system - his method of dividing up time from the birth of Christ onwards. Dionysius did not actually think very highly of his own system, and himself used a quite different dating system - the system known as the *indiction*. This was the most widely used dating system in the Christian world until the 13th Century. An "indiction" was a period of 15 years, based on the intervals between each new tax assessment in the Roman and Byzantine Empires (the Byzantine Empire was the Roman Empire in Eastern Europe and the Middle East, after the fall of the Roman Empire in the Western world). In Christian Europe, the indiction system was dated from the beginning of the reign of the emperor Constantine, the first of the Christian emperors, who became emperor of Rome in the year AD 312. Each succeeding year in the 15 year indiction period was named according to its numerical place in the period; so the first year was called "the first indiction", the second year was called "the second indiction", and so on, up to the "the fifteenth indiction" - and then the cycle would start over again. To fix the time of each indiction, government officials and historians referred to the Roman or Byzantine emperor who was then reigning. For example, "The 23rd year of emperor Constantine, the eighth indiction" (which is AD 335 in the Dionysian system).[2] This combination of the indiction year with the year of a Roman or Byzantine emperor's reign was for a long time the prevailing method of counting the years in the Christian world.

---

1   For Bede, see Part One, Chapter 12, section 3.
2   If you find number-games interesting, you can work out which indiction any AD year is by a simple method: take the AD year, add three, and divide by 15; the number left over is the indiction for that particular 15 year period.

Dionysius's system made very slow headway against the indiction system. England adopted the Dionysian system at the synod of Whitby in 664. In Rome, the papacy accepted it under pope John XIII (pope from 965 to 972). By the 11th Century, most of Europe had embraced the Dionysian system; the last European country to adopt it was Spain, which went over to Dionysius's system only in the 14th Century. It was not until the 15th Century that it was accepted in the Greek-speaking Eastern world of the Byzantine Empire.

Dates in brackets

Throughout this series of books, you will often see dates in brackets. For example: **Martin Luther (1483-1546)**. This means that Martin Luther was born in the year 1483, and died in the year 1546. Whenever dates appear in brackets after a person's name, that is usually what they mean: the years of that person's birth and death. Sometimes the second date has only two figures. For example, **John Bunyan (1628-88)**. Bunyan was born in 1628. But because the year of his death also begins with 16 (he died in 1688), people often do not repeat the 16. So instead of writing 1628-1688, we write 1628-88.

However, if the person is a secular ruler - an emperor, a king, a prince, a president - then the dates in brackets after that person's name refer to the years of his *period of rule*, rather than his birth and death. For example, **Otto III (1039-56)**. This means that the Holy Roman emperor Otto III *reigned* from 1039 to 1056.

In the case of popes or patriarchs, the dates in brackets after their names also refer to the years of their reign. For example, **pope Pius IX (1846-78)**. This means that Pius IX was pope from 1846 to 1878. If it is important that a pope or patriarch's date of birth should be known, that will be separately noted inside the brackets.

Roman numbers.

Rulers both in Church and state often have Roman numbers after their names, as in the two examples above - **Otto III** and **Pius IX**.

These Roman numbers tell us that Otto was the third (III) Holy
Roman emperor to be called "Otto", and Pius was the ninth (IX)
pope to be called "Pius". The following table gives the meaning of
these Roman numbers:

I 1st	XI 11th	XXI 21st
II 2nd	XII 12th	XXII 22nd
III 3rd	XIII 13th	XXIII 23rd
IV 4th	XIV 14th	XXIV 24th
V 5th	XV 15th	XXV 25th
VI 6th	XVI 16th	XXVI 26th
VII 7th	XVII 17th	XXVII 27th
VIII 8th	XVIII 18th	XXVIII.......... 28th
IX 9th	XIX 19th	XXIX 29th
X 10th	XX........... 20th	XXX 30th

(I = 1, V=5, X=10. If a "I" comes *after* a "V" or "X", it increases
its value; so VII stands for 7, and XIII for 14. But if a "I" comes
before a V or X, it lessens its value by 1; so IV stands for 4, and IX
stands for 9.)

Chapter 1.

THE HISTORICAL BACK-GROUND: ROME AND ISRAEL

We are familiar with the kind of world in which Christians today live their lives and seek to serve their Master. All we have to do is look around us, read a newspaper and watch the television. But what exactly was the world like when the Christian faith entered it for the first time, two thousand years ago? What sort of society acted as home to the very first followers of Christ - men and women who actually saw Him, who read the Gospels and Paul's letters as fresh productions which had only just been written? What kind of world did they live in?

To answer this question, we need to consider two basic factors: the Roman Empire and the history of Israel.

1. The Roman Empire.

At the time of Jesus in the 1st Century AD, the Roman Empire controlled the whole of Mediterranean Europe, North Africa and the Middle East. The Empire was made up of a vast variety of ethnic and religious groups, and three main forces held it together:

(a) A common political loyalty. One man ruled the Empire: the emperor, whose government was based in the capital city of Rome, in central Italy, from which the whole Empire had grown. The city of Rome was founded in the 8th Century BC - the year 753 BC, according to tradition. This was around the same time that the Old Testament prophets Isaiah and Hosea lived. After two centuries of being governed by kings, in 510 BC a political revolution transformed Rome into a "Republic", with aristocratic and democratic elements blended in its government, and a deep hostility to monarchy or rule by one man. Power now rested in the hands of the Senate, a sort of parliament dominated by the upper classes. From the 3rd Century BC onward, Rome's dominion grew steadily, through conflicts and diplomatic alliances, until it stretched across the whole of the Mediterranean world. And then disaster struck: a series of devastating civil wars in the 1st Century BC blew the Republic to fragments, as well as spreading bloodshed and destruction across Europe, North Africa and the Middle East, making it necessary for a single strong ruler to restore order.

At first, it seemed that this ruler would be *Julius Caesar* (born 102 BC) - the most celebrated soldier and politician in Roman history. However, at the height of his military and political success, Julius was assassinated in 44 BC by a group of Senators who still believed in the Republic; the Republicans were led by Brutus and Cassius, probably the most famous conspirators and assassins of all time. But the death of Julius Caesar did not restore the Republic. It simply unleashed a fresh series of civil wars. Julius's young nephew and adopted son, Octavius Caesar, took up his murdered uncle's cause, and proved more than equal to the task. After defeating Brutus and Cassius and all other rivals, Octavius assumed supreme power over the Roman world in 31 BC, and in 27 BC the Senate gave him the title *Augustus*, which means "the exalted one". History refers to him by this title. (Our month of August is named after him.)

Augustus was the first and perhaps the greatest of all the Roman emperors; his 45 years of government restored peace, stability, justice and civilisation to a war-torn world. It is little wonder that grateful millions looked on him as a divine saviour sent from heaven (see the quotations at the end of the chapter). Augustus's personality, too, was quite as remarkable as his political achievement; starting out as a ruthless power-seeker who would murder his opponents without any qualms of conscience, he matured into a wise, moderate, generous ruler, certainly a far more decent and upright character than most of the emperors who came after him. His reign lasted from 31 BC to AD 14. This means that, Augustus was emperor at the time of Jesus's birth. **Luke 2:1** mentions him: "And it came to pass in those days that a decree went out from Caesar Augustus that all the world should be registered." It was

Augustus who ordered the census which took the Virgin Mary and Joseph on their fateful journey to Bethlehem, where their special Child was born.

Augustus was such a successful ruler that the principle of government by a single supreme figure, the emperor, became the established pattern for most of the rest of Rome's long history. The Roman Empire depended on the emperor and his armies for maintaining peace and security within the Empire, and also for defending the Empire against aggression from outside, especially from two great enemies: (i) the mighty Parthian (Persian) Empire in the East;[1] (ii) the Germanic tribes who lived across the Rhine and Danube rivers in the North. Rome represented the principle of order against the threat of chaos.

(b) A common economy. The sea-coast cities of the Mediterranean, especially the large ones such as Rome itself in the West and Alexandria in the East, depended on trade and commerce for the basic necessities of life. For example, grain from North Africa fed the population of Rome, and the wines of Italy were exported throughout the Mediterranean. So a great network of trade bound together the coastal cities of the Empire into a single shared economy.

(c) A common intellectual culture. The dominant culture in the Roman Empire was not Roman but Greek. At the end of the 4th Century BC, the language and values of Greek civilisation had spread out from Greece itself across the whole of the Eastern world - the Balkans, Asia Minor, Syria, Persia, Palestine and Egypt - through the amazing conquests of *Alexander the Great* (336-323 BC), king of the Greek state of Macedonia. Alexander's empire broke up after his death, but it left throughout the East an enduring legacy of *Hellenism* - the term historians use for Greek culture (from the word *Hellas*, which is Greek for "Greece"). When the

---

1 Persia (present-day Iran) became known as the "Parthian" Empire in 247 BC, when the nomadic Parthian people took it over. In AD 224, the Sassanians overthrew Parthian rule, and Persia became known as the "Sassanid" Empire.

Romans began to gain control of the Eastern world, they came into
contact with Hellenism, and found it immensely attractive. The
armies of Rome vanquished the East, but Eastern culture vanquished
Rome. By the 1st Century BC, the Greek language, Greek methods
of education, Greek art and literature, and Greek philosophy and
science had taken root across the entire Roman Empire. Everyone
in the Eastern half of the Empire who lived in a city spoke Greek as
his first language. In the Western half of the Empire, Latin was the
first language, but most educated people would have spoken Greek
as their second language.

This social and political setting into which Christianity was born was
also a world where religion flourished - indeed, in the everyday lives
of people throughout the Roman Empire, religion was a pervasive
and powerful force. At the time of Jesus and the apostles, there were
four main forms of religion in the Empire (apart from Judaism, which
we will look at in section 2):

(a) Traditional pagan religion. This involved the worship of a
family of gods headed by the chief god whose Greek name was Zeus
(Jupiter or Jove in Latin). There were different gods for different
aspects of life: Poseidon (or in Latin, Neptune) was the god of the
sea, Ares (Mars) the god of war, Aphrodite (Venus) the goddess of
love, and so on. People tried to obtain the blessing of the gods in all
the affairs of life: in agriculture, business, marriage, politics, war.
Pagan worship involved such things as animal sacrifices, prayer, and
various ways of trying to find out the will of the gods (*e.g.* through
divination, dreams and prophecy). This traditional pagan religion was
the official faith of the Roman Empire, funded and upheld by the
state, and regarded as essential to its survival and prosperity. The
emperor himself was the high priest ("pontifex maximus") of
traditional paganism. Family heads and elected city leaders were
expected to carry out its ceremonies as part of their normal duties.
Traditional pagan religion was also part of the wonderful literary and
artistic culture of the Empire, because it formed the religious
background of the two great epic poems, the *Iliad* and the *Odyssey*.
These had been written several centuries before the birth of Christ
and were usually ascribed to the Greek poet *Homer* (active around
750 BC). Another important poem was the *Aeneid*, written by the
Roman poet *Virgil* (70-19 BC), which told the story of how the first

Romans settled in Italy. The *Iliad, Odyssey* and *Aeneid* were the most admired works of literature in the Greek and Roman world, and often depicted the characters and activities of the traditional pagan gods.

(b) Emperor-worship. The amazing growth of Rome's dominion over the Mediterranean world encouraged the Romans to believe that there was a special divine power at work, creating the Empire, and that this power was especially connected with the emperor. Hellenism gave a powerful stimulus to this belief; Hellenistic culture already saw kings as divine figures, gods incarnate. When the ideals of Hellenism flowed into the Roman world, they gave rise to the practice of worshipping the emperor. In the Eastern half of the Empire, where Hellenistic values were more deeply rooted, people worshipped the emperor in his own lifetime as a living god. In the West, however, emperor-worship was less open and obvious; people normally worshipped, not the emperor himself, but the *genius* of the emperor (the divine power that stood behind him). The Senate raised some emperors, such as Augustus, to the ranks of the gods after they had died, and people then prayed to them throughout East and West.

(c) The Eastern mystery cults. These were forms of religion which had a more recent origin than traditional Roman paganism. The most popular cults at the time of Jesus were those of the goddess Cybele (which arose in Asia Minor), the goddess Isis and the god Serapis (originated in Egypt), and the god Mithras (originated in Persia). Mithraism became especially popular in the Roman armies, and in the 4th Century it was for a time the chief rival to Christianity. These cults had spread across the Empire from the East, and were much more intimate and emotional faiths than traditional paganism or emperor-worship. A mystery cult involved the worshipper in a close personal relationship with his god or goddess. The worship of the cult deities made an overpowering appeal to the physical senses and feelings of the worshipper, involving song, dance, musical instruments, public processions, religious feasting, ritualistic animal sacrifices, and (especially in the Isis cult) group acts of sexual immorality. Worshippers often fell into ecstatic states of trance and prophecy as they took part in the worship.

The cults were also much more like the Christian Church than the other types of religion were, in the sense that a worshipper had to join a mystery cult by a personal decision of his own, and be initiated into membership by special ceremonies. The very name "mystery" comes from the Greek word *mystes*, which means "the initiated ones". The most common initiation rite was the *taurobolium*, practised in both Cybele-worship and Mithraism. The person being initiated into the cult climbed down into a pit and a wooden grating was placed across the top. Those above the pit then sacrificed a bull over the grating, cutting off the animal's genitals and placing them in a special vessel. The bull's blood poured down through the grating over the person in the pit, who turned his face upwards so that he could open his mouth and drink the blood, as it came streaming down over his head, shoulders and body. He had to make sure that the bull's blood soaked every part of him. The claim of the mystery cult was that this "blood-baptism" bestowed a new birth and the gift of immortality on the believer. All the cults promised eternal life after death to their followers; indeed, this was their greatest appeal - traditional paganism and emperor-worship offered no such consolations in the face of death.

(d) Philosophy. In the Roman Empire, philosophy was not just an academic subject taught in universities. It was a total way of life which promised peace and fulfilment to those who practised it. However, it was not a mass movement; philosophers came almost exclusively from the educated classes. At the time of Jesus, there were three chief types or "schools" of philosophy competing for people's allegiance, all originating from the Greek city of Athens, the birthplace of European thought:

Platonism, named after the great Athenian philosopher *Plato* (427-347 BC). As far as his historical influence is concerned, Plato was the greatest philosopher who ever lived; historians have often said that all European philosophy is just "a series of footnotes to Plato"! His outlook, Platonism, was the most religious of the philosophies that emerged from Greece. After a period of decline, it had undergone a revival in the 1st Century BC. This new revived Platonism was known as "Middle Platonism".[2] It combined Plato's fundamental

---

2   It was called "Middle" Platonism because it came between the old Platonism of Plato himself, and the new Platonism of Plotinus in the 3rd Century. See Chapter 6, section 2 for Plotinus.

teaching with some of the ideas of another outstanding Greek philosopher, *Aristotle* (384-322 BC).

Middle Platonism had a profound belief in God as the Supreme Being, and taught that the eternal "ideas" in God's mind were the source of everything in the universe. Reality could be found only in the eternal realm of these divine ideas. In the world of space and time, Platonists said, everything is constantly changing; nothing stays exactly as it is, but is always in the process of becoming something else. Rather than simply *being*, everything in this world is *becoming*. By contrast, the eternal world of God's ideas is unchanging; it possesses true and permanent being. An individual human person might change in many ways; but the idea (or perfect form) of "humanity" in God's mind is fixed and eternal - and, therefore, more real than any individual man or woman on earth. The true destiny of human beings, Platonists taught, was to be found by rising above the changing and unreal world of time, and contemplating the eternal ideas in the mind of God, especially the idea of Goodness. The human soul, according to Platonists, was itself eternal in its essence (that is, the soul had existed from all eternity, and was by nature immortal and incapable of being destroyed), and therefore the soul had more in common with God than with the world. By contemplating God, the philosopher will become like God - and that is his ultimate goal.

Many of the early Church fathers[3] were converts from Platonism, and its general religious outlook continued to exert a strong influence on them, especially in two areas: (i) The thinking of many early theologians was strongly coloured by Platonism's extreme emphasis on the sheer gulf between the changing realm of time and the eternal unchanging God. This made it difficult for some Christian thinkers to understand how an unchanging God could have entered the world of time by becoming a man in Jesus Christ; to solve the problem, they were tempted to say that Christ was something less than absolutely divine. It was not until the Arian controversy of the 4th Century that the Church finally purged this "temptation" out of its theology.[4] (ii) Platonism's teaching on the superiority of the soul and the spiritual

---

3   For the title "early Church fathers", see Chapter 3, section 1.
4   For the Arian controversy, see Chapter 8.

life over the body and physical life held powerful attractions for many Christians. It produced a tendency in some of them to interpret the spiritual life as a war between body and soul. Taken to its logical conclusion, this resulted in the belief-system known as Gnosticism.[5]

Epicureanism, named after **Epicurus** (342-270 BC), who founded a school of philosophy in Athens in about 307 BC. Epicurus taught that pleasure was the supremely desirable quality. However, he did not define pleasure in terms of physical self-indulgence. According to Epicurus, people could achieve true happiness only by a life of quietness, retirement, peace and self-control. Unlike Platonism, Epicureanism was an anti-religious philosophy: Epicurus said that fear of the gods and of what happened after death was one of the main causes of human anxiety. But in reality, the gods took no interest in humanity or human affairs, and there was no life after death. People must recognise this, Epicurus held, if they were to be free from fear and live happy and peaceful lives. Epicureans formed themselves into small communities where they practised their philosophy together, using various counselling techniques for guiding each other into the peaceful life.

Stoicism. This school of philosophy did not have a single founder. Its main thinkers were three Greek philosophers, **Zeno** (334-262 BC), **Cleanthes** (died 232 BC) and **Chrysippus** (280-207 BC). The name "Stoic" comes from the Stoa, a hall in Athens where Zeno taught. Stoics were materialists; they held that everything was ultimately made of matter. They defined the matter from which everything is made as a kind of fire. Even the soul, they said, is a very refined form of this fire. They also taught that the universe was controlled by a power to which they gave different names - God, Fate, Providence, Reason. According to Stoics, the human soul was a tiny portion or fragment of this divine Reason, and humanity could find true fulfilment only by living in harmony with Reason. This involved controlling, disciplining and suppressing the passions or emotions. Some of the best and most virtuous Romans were Stoics, *e.g.* Cato the Younger (95-46 BC) and the emperor Marcus Aurelius (reigned AD 161-80). The great Stoic philosophers of the 1st Century AD,

---

5   For Gnosticism, see Chapter 4, sections 1 and 2.

Seneca 6 (4 BC - AD 65) and *Epictetus* (AD 55-135), often spoke in an almost Christian way in their writings about morality, and Christians read them with admiration. Stoicism was quite influential on early Christian thinking about ethical issues and ideas of divine providence.

Luke mentions Stoic and Epicurean philosophers in **Acts 17:18**; they argued with the apostle Paul when he preached in Athens.

2. The Jewish background.

The Romans had first come in contact with the Jews in 161 BC, when Rome and Judaea made a military alliance against the Seleucid Empire, one of the smaller kingdoms into which Alexander the Great's empire had broken up (the Seleucid Empire controlled present-day Iran, Iraq and Syria). In 88 BC, Roman forces began a long war with king Mithridates IV in Asia Minor (modern Turkey). Rome finally won the war in 66 BC under their leading general, *Pompey the Great* (106-48 BC). At the same time, a civil war had broken out in Judaea between two rival claimants to the Jewish throne, the brothers Hyrcanus and Aristobulus. Both sides appealed to Pompey for military asistance. Pompey entered Jerusalem in 63 BC with the help of Hyrcanus and his party, and the Romans confirmed Hyrcanus as high priest and political leader of Judaea, but would not let him take the title "king". They placed Judaea under the supervision of the Roman governor of Syria. However, in 57 BC Aristobulus's son Alexander raised a rebellion against Rome in Judaea. The rebellion was crushed and Rome reorganised the Judaean structure of government, depriving Hyrcanus of all political power and leaving him only as high priest.

After further rebellions and wars, including the civil wars within the Roman Empire which eventually brought Augustus to power, the Romans placed *Herod Antipater* (37-4 BC) on the throne of Jerusalem, but with Judaea as a Roman province. This is the Herod of **Matthew** chapter 2, who tried to kill the infant Jesus. (The Herod who executed John the Baptist, and before whom Jesus was brought

---

6   Seneca's brother Gallio is mentioned in **Acts 18:12-17.**

after His arrest, was the son of Herod Antipater. He is known as
Herod Antipas, and he ruled only Galilee and Peraea in the northern
part of Judaea, until the emperor Caligula deposed and exiled him in
AD 39.) Because of the friendly relations Rome had enjoyed with
Judaea up till then, Jews gained all sorts of special privileges within
the Empire. For instance, they were exempt from military service,
and did not have to take part in any pagan rituals, not even emperor-
worship.

In AD 6, there was a Jewish rebellion against Rome, led by Judas the
Galilean (mentioned in **Acts 5:37**). Roman armies defeated the
revolt. The emperor, Augustus, now placed Judaea under direct
Roman rule. A Roman governor (a "procurator") was put in charge
of Palestine; he was immediately responsible to the emperor.
Pontius Pilate was, of course, the governor at the time of Jesus's
public ministry (Pilate ruled from AD 26 to 36). The governor
controlled three main aspects of Palestinian life:

(a) Military affairs and public order. There was a Roman army
stationed in Palestine at Caesarea (on the coast of Samaria, south of
Mount Carmel).[7]

(b) Taxation. By the time of Jesus, Rome taxed some 30-40% of
people's income. There was also a highly unpopular poll tax (a tax
not based on property or wealth - every person paid the same
amount).

(c) The administration of justice. The governor had very wide
powers. He could sentence to death or pardon at will.

Even though Rome now exercised this direct control over Judaea,
the Jews still had some degree of local independence. They had their
own Jewish courts of justice outside of Palestine. Within Palestine,
they had the **Sanhedrin**, often mentioned in the **Gospels** and **Acts**.
This was the supreme governing council of the Jews; it had 70
members, drawn from among the priests, lawyers and elders of the

---

7   There were two Caesareas in the Roman Empire, one in Palestine, the
     other in the province of Cappadocia in Asia Minor. Cappadocian
     Caesarea was more important in early Church history.

Jewish aristocracy. The Sanhedrin possessed the power to try all kinds of legal cases, but not to inflict the death penalty. It had its own police force.

At the time of Jesus, the religious life of the Jews was divided among a number of groups or parties. There were four outstanding groups:

The Sadducees. They were a small party whose power-base was centred on Jerusalem and the temple. Sadducees were almost all priests and members of the Jewish aristocracy, and were the strongest group in the Sanhedrin. In religious matters, they accepted the authority of the Pentateuch alone (the first five books of the Old Testament). They rejected any notion of life after death, denied the existence of angels and spirits, and did not believe in the resurrection of the dead (see **Matthew 22:23, Acts 23:8**). No-one is sure how the name "Sadducees" originated or what it means.

The Pharisees. They were the largest group, emerging after Israel's exile in Babylon, and they exercised the greatest influence over ordinary Jewish people. They were also the main enemies of Jesus. The name "Pharisees" means "the separated ones" or "the pure ones". This refers to the high moral code of conduct the Pharisees observed. They were chiefly concerned with obedience to God's law in everyday life, personal holiness, rather than with temple worship. Pharisees believed that Israel's conquest by the Roman Empire was a punishment by God for Jewish disobedience. The proper Jewish response was repentance and a return to individual and national obedience to God's will. In matters of theology, Pharisees were deeply opposed to the Sadducees; they accepted the whole of the Old Testament, and believed in the reality of the spiritual world, life after death and the resurrection of the body.

The Zealots. The Zealots ("zealous ones") were a party of terrorists or freedom-fighters, perhaps founded by Judas the Galilean, who wanted to liberate Judaea from Roman rule by the use of violence. They thought it was sinful to pay taxes to the Roman emperor, because God alone was the true King of Israel. Zealots often acted as assassins, killing those whom they regarded as national enemies. One of Jesus's twelve apostles, Simon the Canaanite, was (or had been) a Zealot (**Luke 6:15**).

The Essenes. These were Jews who broke away from ordinary life and lived together in small religious communities. The great Jewish theologian and historian **Philo of Alexandria** (20 BC - AD 45) estimated that there were about 4,000 Essenes altogether. Their community at Qumran, north-west of the Dead Sea, is the most well-known to us today, because of a large number of ancient writings discovered there in 1947 and the years following (these writings are called "the Dead Sea Scrolls"). Essenes had no private property, but shared everything in their communities. They practised celibacy, refused to swear oaths, underwent frequent ritual washings, and devoted much time to studying the Old Testament prophets. They expected God to intervene in world history through one or more Messiah figures. Some Essenes were also Zealots. The name Essenes may come from an Aramaic word meaning "healers".

Most Jews did not in fact live in Palestine. The great majority, some 6 million, were scattered throughout other parts of the Roman Empire and beyond. They are referred to as the *diaspora* (Greek for "dispersion" - those dispersed or scattered from Palestine). There was a huge Jewish community of 1 million in Alexandria, and other large communities in Antioch, Ephesus and Rome. The diaspora Jews tended to live together in special Jewish areas of a city, and there was little social contact between them and Gentiles. Jewish dietary laws made it almost impossible for Jews and Gentiles to eat together. This made Jews very unpopular with Gentiles, because they seemed anti-social. Some Jews, however, especially in Alexandria, tried to bring together and blend their Judaism with Hellenistic culture. The greatest of these was Philo, who in his writings endeavoured to reinterpret the Jewish faith in the light of Greek philosophy. This attempt led Philo to combine the Old Testament idea of "God's Word" with the Greek philosophical concept of Reason (both "Word" and "Reason" are *logos* in Greek). For many Greek philosophers, Reason was divine, yet distinct from God, and was God's agent in creating the universe.[8] Philo's fusion

---

8   For more about the philosophical concept of reason or *logos*, and how it influenced early Christian theology, see Chapter 3, section 4, under **Justin Martyr**.

of Reason with God's Word produced a notion of the Word remarkably similar to the New Testament doctrine of Christ as God's eternal Son (see the quotation at the end of the Chapter). This fact prompted some early Christians to claim that Philo had been converted to the Christian faith. There is, however, no evidence for this, and Philo nowhere mentions Jesus of Nazareth.

Much more common than Hellenising Jews like Philo were Gentile converts to Judaism. They were called "God-fearers" (see **Acts 10:2, 10:22, 13:43, 17:4, 17:17**). A considerable number of Gentiles were attracted to Judaism because of its belief in one God and the purity of its moral code. However, they were put off by the ceremonial aspects of Judaism, especially circumcision. So they would attach themselves to the local synagogue but refuse to be circumcised. They were looked on as still being pagan by true circumcised Jews. The most obvious New Testament example of a God-fearer is the centurion Cornelius of **Acts 10**.

At the time of Jesus, relations between Rome and the Jews were getting progressively worse. The Parthian Empire in Persia, on Rome's Eastern frontier, was a constant threat to Roman power; and there was a large Jewish community in the Parthian city of Babylon, which made Rome suspicious of the political loyalty of Jews in Palestine. Jewish sympathies at this point did tend to be more favourable to Parthia than to Rome. The growing tensions between Rome and Judaea would finally explode into the great Jewish War of AD 66-73 (see next Chapter).

Important people:

Greeks and Romans	*Jews*
Political and military leaders:	Herod Antipater (37-4 BC)
Alexander the Great (336-323 BC)	Herod Antipas (deposed
Pompey the Great (106-48 BC)	AD 39)
Julius Caesar (born 102 BC, died 44 BC)	Philo of Alexandria (20 BC - 45)
Emperor Augustus (31 BC - AD 14)	
Pontius Pilate (governor of Judaea, (AD 26-36)	

Poets:
Homer (active around 750 BC)
Virgil (70-19 BC)

Philosophers:
Plato (427-347 BC)
Aristotle (384-322 BC)
Epicurus (342-270 BC)
Zeno (334-262 BC)
Cleanthes (died 232 BC)
Chrysippus (280-207 BC)
Seneca (4 BC - AD 65)
Epictetus (AD 55-135)

Platonist religion: Plato

To discover the Maker and Father of the universe is a difficult task, and having found Him it would be impossible to tell everyone about Him. Let us go back to our question, and ask what model the Maker of the universe used in making it. Did He make the universe in the image of something eternal and unchanging, or in the image of something that has come into being? If the universe is beautiful, and if its Maker is good, clearly His gaze was fixed on something eternal when He made the universe. The alternative, that He made the universe in the image of something changeable, is blasphemous. Beyond doubt, then, God's eyes were gazing on the eternal; for the universe is the fairest of all things that have come into being, and God is the best of causes. [Plato means that the universe is so beautiful because it is a divinely created image of eternity; but it is *only* an image, so while eternity is unchanging, the universe is full of change]....

Let us then state the reason why the Builder of our changing universe built it in the first place. He is good; and goodness has no trace of jealousy in it. Therefore, being without jealousy, God wanted everything to be as like Himself as possible. This is the best principle we can discover from human wisdom concerning the origin of our changing universe, and we should accept it. So then, since God wanted everything to be good, and (as far as possible) perfect, and since He found the visible universe in a state of unrest, full of chaotic and disorderly movement, He brought order into its disorder, because He judged that order was in every way better than disorder. The best can only ever produce the highest. So God considered that in the entire realm of visible nature, things that possess intelligence are always superior to things that lack it, and that intelligence can be found only in soul. Therefore, in fashioning the universe, He planted reason within soul, and soul within body, and thus made sure that His work should be highest and best in its nature. And so the most likely story we can tell is that by God's providence, this universe of ours came into existence as a living thing with soul and intelligence.

Plato, *Timaeus* **28-30**

Stoic religion: Seneca

God is near you, with you, within you. Yes, Lucilius, there dwells within us a divine spirit, guarding us and watching us in everything we do, both our good and evil deeds. As we treat Him, so He will treat us. Indeed, no-one is good without God. Can anyone possibly rise above the chances and changes of life unless God helps him? It is God Who inspires us to noble and high-minded endeavours. In each and every good person, "A god dwells, though we are not sure who he is" (as Virgil says).

If you have ever come across a thick wood of ancient trees that have grown to a fantastic height, blocking out the sky with a mass of branches, then the height of the forest, the loneliness of the place, and your sense of wonder at finding such a deep and solid gloom in the outdoors, will convince you that a deity dwells there. A cave which has penetrated deep into the mountain that rests over it, creating a hollow of amazing extent - not by human labours, but by the process of nature - will strike into your soul some sense of the divine. We venerate the sources of important streams; we build altars at spots where a mighty river bursts forth suddenly from the earth; we worship hot springs; we consider holy the dark or bottomless waters of pools. And if you come across a human being who is never terrified by dangers, never influenced by cravings, happy in the midst of adversity, calm amid the storm, viewing the human race from a higher standpoint and the gods from their own standpoint, do you not think that a feeling of veneration for this person will arise within you?

Do you not think you will say to yourself, "Here is a mind so great, so awesome, that it cannot be placed on the same level as the feeble body it dwells in"? A divine power has descended into that body. A soul that is lifted up above the things of earth and is well-ordered, passing through any experience with a proper view of its littleness, simply smiling at all the things we fear or pray for - that soul is moved by a heavenly energy. A soul so uplifted cannot stand at such a height unless it is upheld by a deity.

Seneca, *Moral Epistles to Lucilius***, Epistle 41**

The first emperor, Augustus, as divine Messiah

Behold the man - the promised one, of whom you know -
Caesar Augustus, son of a god, predestined to rule
And to restore the Golden Age to Latium,
Where Saturn used to rule. His empire will extend
Beyond the Garamants and Indians, over lands
In the far north and south of the stars of the zodiac
And the yearly path of the sun....

Virgil, *The Aeneid***, Book 6, lines 791-96**

We live in the crowning era, long prophesied:
Born of time, a great new cycle of centuries
Begins. Justice returns to the earth! The Golden Age
Returns! Its First-born [Augustus] descends from heaven above!
Look kindly on this Infant's birth, O chaste Lucina [goddess of birth];
For with Him, hearts of iron will cease, and hearts of gold
Will inherit the earth. Yes, the reign of Apollo [god of light] has begun!
And this glorious ages dawns, and the march of its great months begins, during your time in office as consul, O Pollio:
With you at the forefront, humanity will be set free from its age-long fear,
And all the stains of our past wickedness will be washed away.
This Child will enter into the life of the gods,
And will see them walking with the heroes of old,
And He will rule a world made peaceful by His father's virtuous deeds.

O Child, Your first birthday-gifts will come from wild nature -
Small gifts! Earth will shower you with romping ivy, fox-gloves,
Bouquets of gipsy lilies, and sweetly-smiling acanthus.
Goats will walk home without anyone herding them,
Their udders full of milk. The ox will no longer fear the lion.
Blossom, soft as silk, will grow from your cradle to form a bed.
Snakes will die, along with all lovely but poisonous plants.
The fields everywhere will breathe spice and incense.

Virgil, *The Fourth Eclogue*

I am not sure whether we should observe the birthday of Augustus
more for the joy of it or for the profit of it. It is a day which we might
justly regard as equal to the beginning of all things - equal in the
benefits it has brought, if not in reality. For he has restored everything
that was ruined and had fallen into a miserable condition. He has
given a fresh look to the universe, which was ready to perish if
Caesar had not been born as a blessing to all mankind. Each
individual may therefore look on Augustus's birthday as the
beginning of his own life and physical being. Now that he has been
born, we can no longer feel that life is a burden.

As proposed by the high priest Apollonius, son of Menophilus, of
Azani, the Greeks of the province of Asia resolve: That because the
providence which orders all human life has shown a special concern
and zeal, and has conferred upon life its most perfect adornment by
giving us Augustus, whom it equipped for his benevolent work among
mankind by filling him with virtue, and sending him as a Saviour for
us and our descendants, the one who causes wars to cease and sets
all things in beautiful order; and because Caesar by appearing made
the hopes of those who predicted a better future look poor compared
with what he has actually done, for he not only surpassed all previous
benefactors, but left no chance for future ones to go beyond him; and
because the gospel which went forth into the world through him
arose on the birthday of this god....

Part of a letter of the proconsul of Asia to the cities of Asia

Essenes, Pharisees and Sadducees: The view of a Jewish historian of the 1st Century AD

There are three schools of thought among the Jews, known as the Pharisees, Sadducees and Essenes. The Essenes have the strictest way of life. Jews by birth, they have a strong sense of brotherhood with each other. They shun the seeking of pleasure as a vice, and praise self-control and the mastery of one's passions as virtue. They reject marriage, and choose the children of others while they are still young and teachable, training them to live as Essenes. They do not actually wish to do away with marriage as the method of increasing the human race, but they fear the sexual immorality of women, being convinced that no woman ever remains faithful to one man. They despise money, and are communists as far as property is concerned; no Essene has more than any other. When men join their sect, they have to give up all their property to the common ownership of the community, so that you will not see among the Essenes either degrading poverty or excessive wealth. Each man's possessions become part of the common fund, and like a group of brothers their entire property belongs equally to all....9

Of the other two schools of thought, people regard the Pharisees as the most authoritative interpreters of the Law. They are the leading Jewish sect. They teach that everything happens according to destiny, or the will of God; the actual decision to do good or evil rests chiefly with human beings, they say - but even so, in every human act, destiny takes a hand. They hold that every soul is immortal, but only the souls of good people receive new bodies, while the souls of evil people go to eternal punishment. The Sadducees, the other sect, deny the existence of destiny in any form, and teach that God can neither decree sin nor have any involvement with it. People are absolutely free, they say, to choose between good and evil; each individual must decide solely for himself. The Sadducees utterly deny the immortality of the soul, punishments in hell, and heavenly rewards. The Pharisees are bound together by a common spirit of friendship and seek to promote harmony with the common people. But the

---

9   This is similar to the early Church in Jerusalem - **Acts 2:44-45**.

Sadducees are disagreeable, even towards each other; they treat one another with the harshness that people usually reserve for foreigners.

Josephus, *The Jewish War*, Book 2, chapter 7

A Hellenising Jew: Philo of Alexandria on the Word of God

The Father of the universe has granted the office of Mediator to His supreme messenger and most ancient Word, who regulates matters between the Creator and His creatures. The Word is the intercessor on behalf of perishing mortals in relation to the Unchangeable Being; he is the ambassador of the Sovereign to His subjects. The Word glories in this gift, and declares, "I have stood between the Lord and you. For I am not unbegotten, as God is, nor am I begotten, as you are, but I stand in the middle of these extremes, pledging myself for both. I pledge to the Creator that the human race shall not prefer chaos to beauty and fall entirely into ruin and apostasy. And I pledge to creation that I will maintain the joyful hope that God in His mercy will not despise His own handiwork. For I announce to creation God's message of peace, that He can purge away hostilities and is the perpetual preserver of peace."

Philo on Exodus 14:19

Chapter 2.

THE JESUS MOVEMENT

1. Jews and Gentiles in the early Church.

We must leave to our New Testament studies an account of the life
and ministry of Jesus of Nazareth. What we will be looking at here
is the impact which that life and ministry had on men and women in
the 1st Century AD - the beginnings of Church history. Our primary
source is, of course, the book of **Acts**.

Early Christianity and the early Church were what we could call a
Jesus movement. In its first years, this was a religious movement
which blossomed exclusively within the confines of Judaism, and
revolved around Jerusalem as its spiritual home. The original
followers of Jesus were all Jews, and they had no intention of being
anything other than faithful and pious Jews. They continued to
worship in the Jerusalem temple, to obey the law of Moses, and to
have a negative attitude towards Gentiles. The living heart of their
faith was not so much the death as the resurrection of Jesus of
Nazareth. When Jesus was executed, despair had engulfed His
followers: they seemed to have a dead leader and a lost cause. It was
Jesus's resurrection from the dead that transformed these broken
and despairing people into the fiery apostles and martyrs of a new
faith - a faith which, within three centuries, and despite vigorous
persecution, would conquer the whole Roman Empire. In the thought
and preaching of the early Church, the resurrection was seen as
God's mighty vindication of all Jesus's claims: He really was the
long-promised Messiah of Israel, the Son of God, the Saviour of
sinners, the source of God's gift of the Holy Spirit to all who obeyed
Him (see, for example, **Acts 2:33-6, 4:10-12, 13:30-39, 17:30-**

32, and **Romans 1:3-4**). So whichever period of Church history we are studying, it is always worth pausing and reminding ourselves of this: *the entire history of the Christian Church is rooted in one central reality - the resurrection of Jesus Christ from the dead.* If Jesus of Nazareth had not risen, there would be no Church history. The rest of the story told in these pages flows out of the resurrection.

The early Church, then, started its life as a purely Jewish movement, a sect within Judaism. Yet by the end of the 1st Century, events had transplanted the Church from its original Jewish soil into the Gentile world, where it became an almost exclusively Gentile movement. How did this astonishing change take place? We find some clues in **Acts**.

The process of transition began when tensions arose within the early Christian community in Jerusalem between Palestinian Jews, and Jews from a more Hellenistic background ("Hellenism" means Greek culture - see previous Chapter, section 1, under **A common intellectual culture**). We find this tension described in **Acts 6**, where Luke refers to the two parties as, literally, "the Hebrews" and "the Hellenists". Many Jews, as we saw in Chapter 1, lived outside Palestine in lands where Hellenistic culture was dominant, such as Egypt and Asia Minor. So the "Hellenists" of **Acts 6** were Jews who had been born in a Hellenistic country and grown up in a Hellenistic culture, speaking Greek as their first language. They had then either moved into Palestine and settled there, or (perhaps) were there as pilgrims for the passover feast. The chief language spoken in Palestine was Aramaic, not Greek, and Hellenistic Jews would have known little or no Aramaic. The "Hebrews", by contrast, were the Jews native to Palestine. They knew some Greek, but Aramaic was their first language, and they had little or no contact with Hellenistic culture, which in any case they despised as pagan.

This cultural divide between Palestinian and Hellenistic Jews would already have produced friction between them before any of them became Christians. The problem was that the Palestinians thought of themselves as the true Jews, born and brought up in the Jewish homeland which God had given to their ancestors, and they looked on Hellenistic Jews as partly foreign, perhaps corrupted by contact with pagan society. On the other hand, Hellenistic Jews tended to think of themselves as being more cultured and civilised than their Palestinian cousins. They regarded Palestinian Jews as rather narrow-minded, too traditional, not aware enough of the outside world. (This description of Palestinian and Hellenistic Jews applies only in a general way to what most of them tended to be like. There were exceptions. The most notable exception was the apostle Paul, who was brought up in the Hellenistic city of Tarsus in Asia Minor, but surpassed even the Palestinian Jews in his intolerant zeal for traditional Judaism, before his Damascus road experience convinced him that Jesus was the Messiah.)

These existing problems between Palestinian and Hellenistic Jews carried over into the Jesus movement. Jesus of Nazareth had followers from both the Hellenistic and Palestinian sections of the Jewish people, and the friction between them continued, despite their common faith in the risen Messiah. **Acts 2:44-5** relates how the early Christian community in Jerusalem cared for its poorer members; the provision of food for Christian widows was part of that system of care, since widows were unable to support themselves economically and depended on others. However, the Hellenists felt (rightly or wrongly) that the widows from their section of the community were not getting a fair deal. Luke records in **Acts 6** how the Hellenists complained that their widows were being overlooked in the distribution of food. This particular problem was resolved by the appointment of seven deacons whose names are all Greek - an indication that they were elected from the Hellenistic group within the Jesus movement. But the underlying tensions between Palestinian and Hellenistic believers remained.

The non-traditional attitudes and outlook of the Hellenistic Jewish Christians surfaced in a dangerous way when they began to take a more openly negative, critical stance towards the history and traditions of Israel. It seems that they started to view these things afresh in the light of their new faith in Jesus, and to show less respect for the temple and the law of Moses than was customary. Their spokesman was the Hellenistic deacon Stephen, and his lengthy speech recorded in **Acts 7** shows us the sort of criticisms that Hellenistic believers could make of Jewish history and tradition. This provoked and outraged the Jewish authorities, and led to the first great persecution of the Church. Stephen was stoned to death, and many believers were forced to flee from Jerusalem. This persecution, however, seems mainly to have affected the Hellenistic section of the Church. The more traditionally-minded Palestinian believers, represented by the apostles, were mostly left alone by the Jewish authorities; Luke makes it clear in **Acts 8:1** that the apostles were not affected by the persecution. Ordinary Palestinian believers who were scattered from Jerusalem would have dispersed into other parts of Palestine, and then reassembled in Jerusalem after the trouble had died down, as **Acts 11:1** indicates. Hellenistic believers, however, appear to have left Palestine entirely.

From this point onwards the Christian community in Jerusalem was purified of its Hellenistic elements, and became entirely Hebrew and Palestinian in character. It was led by *James*, known as "the Lord's brother" (**Galatians 1:19, 2:9**), who remained so faithful to Jewish tradition that even unbelieving Jews admired him. Much debate has centred on the identity of James. Some think he was the same person as James the apostle, son of Alphaeus (**Matthew 10:3, Acts 1:13**). If so, his title "the Lord's brother" must mean "the Lord's kinsman" or "cousin", otherwise the apostle James would be called "son of Joseph" rather than "son of Alphaeus". (The word "brother" can be used in the Bible in this more general sense of "kinsman", rather than strictly "brother".) Whether or not James the Lord's brother was the same person as James the apostle, he clearly played a dominant role in the Jerusalem church - see **Acts 15**. Also known as James the Righteous, he was martyred in AD 62 by the Pharisees. According to early Church tradition, James was appointed by the apostles as the first bishop of the church in Jerusalem (see next Chapter, section 2 for bishops in the early Church, and the end of this Chapter for the story of James's martyrdom).

The scattering of the Hellenistic believers from Palestine was the event which first took the Jesus movement into the non-Jewish world. First, the Hellenistic Christians broke through the age-old divide between Jews and Samaritans, as Luke narrates in **Acts 8**. Philip, one of the Hellenistic deacons, was responsible for this bold venture. The Samaritans were of mixed Jewish and Gentile descent, existing on the borderlands between Judaism and the Gentile world. **Acts 10** then relates how the centurion Cornelius and his kinsmen became the first Gentile converts in Palestine; but Cornelius had already embraced most of the teachings of Judaism - he was a "God-fearer".

The first largely Gentile church from a pagan background was founded outside of Palestine in the Roman province of Syria, in the great Eastern city of Antioch. Although Antioch had a big Jewish community, it was basically a vast throbbing centre of Gentile Hellenistic civilisation. Some of the Hellenistic Christian refugees from Jerusalem made their way to Antioch and began preaching the Gospel, not only to Jews, but to pagan Gentiles as well. Luke records the momentous event in **Acts 11:20-21:** "Now those who were scattered after the persecution that arose over Stephen travelled as far as Phoenicia, Cyprus and Antioch, preaching the word to no-one but the Jews only. But some of them were men from Cyprus and Cyrene, who, when they had come to Antioch, spoke to the Hellenists, preaching the Lord Jesus. And the hand of the Lord was with them, and a great number believed and turned to the Lord." In this way the first mainly Gentile church, made up of converts from paganism, was established in Antioch through the preaching of the scattered Hellenistic believers of Jerusalem.

The term *Christian* was also first used in Antioch: "And the disciples were first called Christians in Antioch" (**Acts 11:26**). This makes sense, because in a Gentile city like Antioch, where the followers of Jesus were mostly pagan converts, they would have seemed to the Gentile population to be something other than a Jewish sect. The label *Christians* (in Greek, *Christianoi*) may have been formed by a process derived from the Latin language. In Latin, a plural word ending in *-iani* could describe the troops of a particular general. For example, *Galbiani* would mean "Galba's troops", "Galba's men". So *Christiani*, or in Greek *Christianoi*, may have meant "Christ's men", "followers of Christ". By the AD 60's the word was widely accepted by all believers in Jesus as a suitable name for themselves; **1 Peter 4:16** uses the term. Prior to this, Christians called themselves by labels such as "followers of the Way" (**Acts 9:2, 22:4**); their Jewish enemies called them "the sect of the Nazarenes" (**Acts 24:5**).

It was from the Gentile church in Antioch that the first organised Christian mission went out, headed by the apostle *Paul* (**Acts 13**).

From this point onwards, Paul dominates the story of the Jesus movement. From fanatical Jewish opponent and foremost persecutor of Jesus's followers, he became through his encounter with the risen Lord on the Damascus road (**Acts 9**) Jesus's most ardent convert and apostle. It was through Paul's missionary activities that the Jesus movement went West into Europe, rather than staying in Palestine and the Middle East. As more and more Gentiles became Christians, it was Paul who insisted against the more traditional Jewish believers of Palestine that Gentile converts did not have to accept the law of Moses or be circumcised in order to be true followers of Jesus. More than any other individual, the apostle Paul was the man who made it possible for the Jesus movement to turn from being a purely Jewish sect into a largely Gentile body.

Paul was also the supreme thinker and theologian of the early Church. His letters form the largest single ingredient of the New Testament, and throughout the history of the Church they have provided a unique source of spiritual and doctrinal renewal for theologians and preachers. Many great movements of reform or revival in the Church can be traced to a fresh appreciation of Paul's writings. Next after Jesus Himself, Paul has had the greatest historical impact on the life and thought of the Christian Church over the past 2,000 years.

2. The persecution under Nero.

In the days of the apostles, the authorities of the Roman Empire were generally friendly or at least neutral towards the Jesus movement. Opposition and persecution came mainly from unbelieving Jews, and sometimes from ordinary pagan Gentiles (**Acts 19:21-41**), but not usually from government officials. The apostle Paul certainly gives a very positive view of the Roman government in **Romans 13**.

However, this was not always to be the case. In AD 64, the emperor *Nero* (AD 54-68) launched the first great official persecution of Christians by the Roman government. In that year, the worst fire that Rome had ever known swept through the city and destroyed 10 of its 14 districts. Many people suspected that Nero himself had started the fire so that he could rebuild Rome in a grander style. In order to divert popular anger away from himself, Nero decided to blame the

fire on the Christian community in Rome. The Roman historian
Tacitus (AD 55-117), who was alive at the time, tells us what
happened:

> "To kill the rumours [that he had started the fire] Nero
> charged and tortured some people hated for their evil
> practices - the group popularly known as Christians. The
> founder of this sect, Christ, had been put to death by the
> governor of Judaea, Pontius Pilate, when Tiberius was
> emperor. Their deadly superstition had been suppressed
> temporarily, but was beginning to spring up again - not now
> just in Judaea, but even in Rome itself, where all kinds of
> sordid and shameful activities are attracted and catch on.
> First, the authorities arrested those who confessed to being
> Christians. Then, on information obtained from them, the
> courts convicted hundreds more, not so much for starting the
> fire as for their anti-social beliefs. In their deaths they were
> made a mockery. They were covered in the skins of wild
> animals, torn to death by dogs, crucified, or set on fire - so that
> when darkness fell they burned like torches in the night. Nero
> opened up his own gardens for this spectacle and gave a
> show in the arena, where he mixed with the crowd, or stood
> dressed as a charioteer on a chariot. As a result, although
> they were guilty of being Christians and deserved to die,
> people began to feel sorry for them. For they realised that
> they were being killed, not for the public good, but to satisfy
> one man's madness."

Nero's persecution shows that by the AD 60's the Roman
authorities recognised Christians as a distinct group, separate from
the Jews. Christians were obviously unpopular with the ordinary
inhabitants of Rome; people looked on Christians as being rather
strange and suspicious folk who did not mix with non-Christians. The
authorities may have regarded them as a secret illegal society.
Tacitus's reference to Christ being crucified under Pontius Pilate is
the first known evidence we possess of a pagan writing testifying to
the events recorded in the New Testament. (Tacitus wrote in the
opening years of the 2nd Century AD.) The great Jewish historian
Flavius Josephus (born AD 37, died after 100) also mentions these
events in his **Antiquities of the Jews**, written in AD 93-94 (see the
end of the Chapter for a quotation).

The persecution was limited in scope to the city of Rome. It did not extend throughout the Empire. However, it claimed two great victims. The apostles Peter and Paul were probably both in Rome during Nero's persecution, and it seems likely that they were both executed at this time. Tradition says that imperial soldiers beheaded Paul and crucified Peter upside-down. As a Roman citizen, Paul could not be subjected to the humiliation of death by crucifixion. According to tradition, Peter thought he was unworthy to die in the same way as his Lord, and so to humour his scruples the authorities agreed to crucify him head-downwards.[1]

Nero was the first Roman emperor to persecute Christians. Others were to follow in his footsteps. In the 1st Century, the emperor **Domitian** (AD 81-96) also unleashed his fury on the Church in the final year of his reign, AD 96; it was Domitian who banished the apostle John (by then an old man and the last surviving apostle) to the island of Patmos, just off the west coast of Asia Minor (see the end of the Chapter).

3. The Jewish War.

The Jewish War (or Jewish Revolt) had a far greater effect on the future of the Jesus movement than Nero's persecution in Rome did. The War came about through the final triumph of Zealot opinion in Israel; the Zealots led a mighty nationalist uprising against the Roman Empire, lasting from AD 66 to 73. After the most appalling bloodshed, Rome's armies totally crushed the revolt, almost completely destroyed Jerusalem, and reduced the temple to a pile of smouldering ruins. The loss of Jewish life was horrific; the Jewish historian Josephus, who was alive at the time and wrote a history of the Jewish War, estimated that 1,100,000 Jews were killed in the fighting, and 97,000 taken captive and then sold into slavery or put to death for sport in the Roman arenas.[2] The Jewish Palestinian

---

1   Another tradition says that Peter and Paul survived Nero's persecution and were executed a few years later in about AD 67. If this is correct, Nero was still persecuting Christians even after the affair of the great fire in Rome in AD 64.

2   An arena was a sort of sports stadium. Roman sports were quite violent, *e.g.* fighters known as "gladiators" who fought each other to the death for the amusement of the crowd.

Christians, however, took no part in the War; in obedience to the prophetic words of Jesus in **Luke 21:20-24**, they left Judaea before the serious fighting started, and took refuge in the Gentile town of Pella, in northern Peraea, east of the Jordan (near the brook Cherith - **1 Kings 17:3-5**).

The Jewish War had a number of far-reaching consequences:

(i) The fall of Jerusalem meant that both Judaism and the Jesus movement lost their spiritual home. Jerusalem, once the "mother church" of apostolic Christianity, ceased to have any importance in the life of the early Church for the next 300 years. This geographical separation of the Jesus movement from its Palestinian roots quickened the Church's drift away from a Jewish to a Gentile membership.

(ii) The refusal of Jewish Palestinian Christians to help their fellow Jews in the revolt against Rome meant that they were regarded as traitors in Jewish eyes. This helped to widen the gap between the Christian faith and the Jewish people.

(iii) The crushing of the Jewish Revolt by Rome meant that the Pharisees became the controlling force within Judaism. The failure of the great Zealot rebellion destroyed the influence of the Zealots as a national party. The fall of Jerusalem and the destruction of the temple removed the power-base of the priestly, aristocratic Sadducees. The War also wiped out the Essenes, because they too had joined in the revolt against Rome; their community at Qumran (the one we know most about) was destroyed by the Romans in AD 68. So only the Pharisees were left to offer spiritual leadership to the Jewish people and guide their future; and the Pharisees had always been the most determined Jewish enemies of Jesus and His followers. Gathering together after the War in the city of Jamnia (or in Hebrew, Jabneh) on the southern coast of Palestine, the Pharisees re-established the Sanhedrin, and rallied the shattered forces of Judaism around their own strict interpretation of the Old Testament and the Mosaic law. They placed a curse on all Christians ("the Nazarenes") in the Jewish liturgy (the prayer-book used in worship); this made it impossible for Jewish Christians to worship any longer in the synagogue.

The ultimate effect of the Jewish War was to cut Christianity off almost completely from its Jewish origins. From now on, the future of the Jesus movement rested in the Gentile world.

Important people:

The Church
James the Lord's brother (died
   AD 62)
Peter (died AD 64 or 67)
Paul (died AD 64 or 67)
John (died end of 1st Century)

Political and military
Emperor Nero (AD 54-68)
Emperor Domitian (AD 81-
   96)

Others
Flavius Josephus (born AD
   37, died after 100)
Tacitus (AD 55-117)

Josephus's testimony to John the Baptist and Jesus

Some Jews thought that the destruction of king Herod's army [in AD 36 by an Arabian king] was a righteous punishment from God, on account of the way Herod had treated John who was called the Baptist. For Herod killed him, and John had been a good man who had exhorted the Jews to train themselves in virtue, to be fair towards each other and holy towards God, and to come together for baptism. God would accept their baptism, John said, on condition that they received it, not to escape the punishment their sins deserved, but to purify the body, as the soul had already been purified by righteousness. When crowds gathered around John, aroused by his words, Herod became afraid that John's amazing power over the people would lead to a rebellion, since the people seemed ready to do anything John said. So Herod decided to prevent any movement towards revolution which John might inspire, by getting rid of John, rather than waiting for a revolt to happen and then blame himself when it was too late. So because of Herod's suspicions, he sent John in chains to the fortress of Machaerus and had him executed there....

At this time Jesus appeared, a highly gifted man, if we can call him a mere man; for he was a miracle-worker, a teacher of those who loved to hear the truth, and he gained many followers from among the Jews and even the Gentiles too. He was the Messiah. The most important men in Israel prompted Pontius Pilate to condemn him to death on a cross; but those who loved him from the beginning did not stop loving him, for on the third day he appeared to them alive again. The inspired prophets foretold this and many other wonderful things about him. Even today the group of people named after him, the "Christians", have still not died out.[3]

Josephus, *Antiquities of the Jews*, Book 18, chapter 2

The martyrdom of James the Lord's brother

Guidance of the Church passed to the apostles, together with the Lord's brother James. From the Lord's time until our own, everyone has called him "James the Righteous". There were many people called James, but this one was holy from his birth; he drank no wine or intoxicating liquor, and ate no animal food; no razor came near his head; he did not smear himself with oil and he took no baths. He alone was allowed to enter the Holy Place, for his garments were not made of wool, but of linen. He used to go into the sanctuary alone, and was often found there on his knees, beseeching forgiveness for the people, so that his knees grew hard like a camel's from his continually bending them before God in worship and praying for forgiveness for the people. Because of his righteousness which no-one surpassed, he was called "James the Righteous" and *Oblias* (in our own language, "Bulwark of the people, and Righteousness"), fulfilling the prophecies which had been made about him....

Since many even of the ruling classes believed in Jesus, the Jews and scribes and Pharisees were greatly agitated; they said there was a

---

3　Some scholars have disputed whether Josephus, a non-Christian Jew, could have written such a "Christian" testimony about Jesus; they suggest that this part of Josephus's *Antiquities* was inserted into the book by Christians. However, every single copy of the *Antiquities* which we possess contains this passage, and modern scholars have defended its reliability. And perhaps Josephus's positive statements about Jesus are not his own opinion but his record of what Christians believed. "He was the Messiah" - that is, He claimed to be, and His followers believed Him to be, the Messiah.

danger that the whole people would expect Jesus to return as the Messiah. So they gathered together and said to James: "Be good enough to restrain the people, for they have gone astray after Jesus, believing that He is the Messiah. Please make the facts about Jesus plain to all who come for the passover day. We all accept what you say; we can confirm, and so can all the people, that you are a righteous man and do not judge according to appearances. So make it clear to the crowd that they must not go astray concerning Jesus; everyone, including us, accepts your judgment. So take your stand on the parapet of the temple, so that from that height you may be seen easily, and your words be heard by everyone. Because of the passover, all the tribes of Israel have gathered here, and the Gentiles too."

So the scribes and Pharisees made James stand on the sanctuary parapet and shouted to him: "Righteous one, you whose words we are all bound to accept, the people are going astray after Jesus Who was crucified. So tell us, what is meant by 'the door of Jesus'?"[4] James replied as loudly as he could: "Why do you ask me about the Son of Man? I tell you, He is sitting in heaven at the right hand of the great Power, and He will come on the clouds of heaven." Many were convinced and gloried in James's testimony, crying out, "Hosanna to the Son of David!" But the scribes and Pharisees said to each other, "We've made a bad mistake here, giving such an opportunity of testimony to Jesus. We had better go up and throw James off the parapet, to frighten the people and stop them believing him." So they called out, "Well, well! So even the Righteous one has gone astray!"....

So they went up and threw the Righteous one off the parapet. Then they said to one another, "Let's stone James the Righteous!" So they began stoning him - for despite his fall, he was still alive. But he turned and knelt and said, "O Lord God and Father, I beseech you to forgive them; they do not know what they are doing." While they pelted him with stones, one of the descendants of Rechab the son of Rachabim (the priestly family to which Jeremiah the prophet bore witness[5]) called out, "Stop! What are you doing? The Righteous one is praying for you!" But one of them, whose job was to cleanse and bleach

---

4   "The door of Jesus" refers to **John 10:9.**
5   **Jeremiah 35.**

cloth, picked up his club with which he beat out the clothes, and crushed the head of the Righteous one. And thus James was martyred. They buried him on that very spot, by the sanctuary, and his headstone is still there by the sanctuary. He proved a faithful witness to Jews and Gentiles alike that Jesus is the Messiah.

Eusebius of Caesarea's *History of the Church*, Book 2, chapter 23

The martyrdom of Peter and Paul

So it happened that Nero, the first man to stand out as a notable fighter against God, was led on to murder the apostles. In his reign (so it is recorded) Paul was beheaded in Rome itself, and Peter too was crucified. This record is confirmed by the fact that the cemeteries in Rome are even today named after Peter and Paul. It is also confirmed by a Churchman called Gaius, who lived when Zephyrinus was bishop of Rome [AD 199-217]. In his book *Dialogue* with Proclus, a leader of the Montanist heretics,[6] Gaius says this about the place where the bodies of the two apostles have been reverently laid: "I can point out the monuments of the triumphant apostles. If you go as far as the Vatican or the Ostian Way, you will find the monuments of the men who founded this church [in Rome]."

Eusebius of Caesarea's *History of the Church*, Book 2, chapter 25

The persecution by emperor Domitian and the exile of John to Patmos

Domitian's horrible cruelty struck down many victims. In Rome, he put to death large numbers of distinguished, high-born men of great achievements, without a fair trial. He banished countless other eminent men for no reason at all and seized their property. And then at last Domitian showed himself to be an emperor who walked in the steps of Nero for his hatred and hostility towards God. Indeed, he was the second emperor to organise a persecution of us Christians, although his father Vespasian had harboured no evil designs against

---

6   For the Montanists, see Chapter 4, section 3.

us. There is abundant evidence that the apostle and Gospel-writer John was still alive at that time, and because of his testimony to God's Word he was sentenced to exile on the island of Patmos (**Revelation 1:9**).... In fact, our faith shone out so brightly at that time, that even historians who rejected our beliefs wrote down without hesitation in their history books both the persecution and the martyrdoms it produced. They also recorded the exact date of the persecution, that it was in the 15th year of Domitian [AD 96]. Flavia Domitilla, who was a niece of Flavius Clemens, one of Rome's consuls [chief magistrates] that year, was banished to the island of Pontia, along with many others, as a punishment for their testimony to Christ....

After 15 years of Domitian's rule, Nerva became emperor. The Roman senate voted to strip the dead Domitian of his honours, and to return to their homes all whom he had unjustly banished, restoring their property to them. The historians of the time record this. At the same time the apostle John, after his exile on Patmos, went back to live once more in his home at Ephesus, as early Christian tradition says.

Eusebius of Caesarea's *History of the Church*, Book 3, chapters 17-20

Chapter 3.

THE APOSTOLIC FATHERS, PERSECUTION AND APOLOGETICS

1. Christian leaders after the apostles.

The period in Church history just after the death of the apostles is known as the age of the *apostolic fathers*. This is the name we give to the authors of the earliest Christian writings which came next after the New Testament. The name was invented in the 17th Century, when scholars believed that these early Christian writers all had direct personal contact with the apostles; most historians today think that only a few of them did. Christian writers and teachers who lived after the apostles in the first five or six centuries of Church history are generally known as the *early Church fathers*. Historians and theologians often refer to these centuries as the *patristic* age (from the Greek and Latin *pater*, "father" - the age of the fathers). However, we must not confuse the *early Church* fathers with the *apostolic* fathers; the apostolic fathers were simply the *first* generation of early Church fathers. The age of the apostolic fathers stretched only from about AD 95 to 140.

The main Christian writings which have survived from the age of the apostolic fathers are:

The Letter of Clement. This was written in about AD 96 by *Clement of Rome*, a presbyter (elder) or bishop of the church in Rome. He wrote the letter to try to settle a dispute in the Corinthian church. In a conflict between the older and younger generations, the Corinthian Christians had dismissed all their presbyters and replaced them by new youthful leaders. Clement's response was to emphasise the need for good order in the Church. He argued that

God's purpose of salvation revealed a sort of "chain of command": God the Father sent the Lord Jesus Christ, Christ sent the apostles, the apostles appointed bishops (or presbyters) and deacons in the churches, and they in turn appoint their successors. A church must not disturb this chain of command by dismissing its officers without just cause, which did not exist in the case of the Corinthian presbyters. Clement therefore entreated the Corinthians to restore their deposed leaders back into office.

The Letters of Ignatius of Antioch. Ignatius was the bishop of the church in Antioch at the beginning of the 2nd Century. Arrested for being a Christian, he was taken to Rome by a military escort, where the authorities executed him in about AD 110. As Ignatius journeyed to Rome, he wrote seven letters - to the churches of Ephesus, Magnesia, Tralles, Philadelphia and Smyrna (all in Asia Minor), and the church of Rome, and a personal letter to Polycarp, bishop of the church in Smyrna. In these letters Ignatius strongly urged the supreme importance of unity in the local church, arguing that this unity depended on having one bishop in charge of each congregation. Ignatius's letters reveal a deep spiritual devotion to Christ and an enthusiastic longing to sacrifice his life for Christ's sake.

The Didache (Greek for "teaching" - pronounced "did-a-kee"). This is the oldest surviving handbook of church discipline, dating from about AD 100. It originated from Syria, and its full title is *The Teaching of the Lord to the Gentiles through the Twelve Apostles*. It is divided into two parts. Part One concerns doctrinal teaching to be given to Christians, based on a contrast between the "Way of Life" and the "Way of Death". Part Two is about various church practices: prayer, fasting, baptism, the Lord's supper, church leadership, how to handle visiting prophets.

The fragments of Papias (AD 110-30). Papias was bishop of the church in Hierapolis in Phrygia, Asia Minor. He set out to preserve as much as he could of the deeds and sayings of Christ which had not been recorded in the Gospels, collecting accounts of these deeds and sayings from Jewish Christians who had been dispersed from Jerusalem, who in turn claimed they had received them from the apostles. Many of these alleged sayings of Christ are very strange; the Church as a whole did not recognise them as genuine, although some Christians accepted some of them.

Ignatius of Antioch (Died AD 110)

The Letter of Barnabas (about AD 120). This was probably written in Alexandria. It is an essay on how to interpret the Old Testament in a Christian way. The **Letter** is quite anti-Jewish in tone, claiming that the Jews misunderstood God by taking certain parts of the Old Testament law literally, where God meant them to be understood in a symbolic or spiritual sense. The anti-Jewish spirit of the **Letter of Barnabas** shows how quickly events had cut the Church off from its Jewish roots. For most Christians, "the Jews" now simply meant those who had crucified Christ and continued to reject Him - a lost, blind people. This attitude produced among many Christians a mindless hostility to Jews.

The Shepherd of Hermas (AD 100-140). Written in Rome, this was said to be the work of a Christian prophet called Hermas. In the **Shepherd**, Hermas claimed to have received a series of revelations from two heavenly figures, an old woman and an angel dressed as a shepherd. Hermas's main concern was with the moral purity of the Church, and the question of whether Christians can be forgiven for committing serious sins after baptism. He argued that serious post-baptismal sin could be forgiven only once.

The Letter of Polycarp to the Philippians (about AD 110). Polycarp (AD 70-160) was bishop of the church of Smyrna in Asia Minor and one of the most famous martyrs of the 2nd Century (see section 3). His **Letter** to the church in Philippi is, perhaps, the best document from the age of the apostolic fathers for giving us a feeling of what typical, mainstream Christianity was like in this period. Polycarp's letter was mostly made up of quotations from the New Testament. He warned the Philippians against departing from apostolic doctrine, and especially against the heresy of Docetism (see next section). He also exhorted them to live upright Christian lives, admonishing them against the sin of greed, and urged on them the duty of submitting to their presbyters.

The Letter to Diognetus (AD 100-150). No-one knows who wrote this letter, or who Diognetus was. The letter set out to show the falsehood of paganism and Judaism, and the superior teaching of Christianity. Many readers have found it to be the most noble and beautiful of all Christian writings from this earliest period.

2. The development of Christianity in the age of the apostolic fathers.

If the age of the apostles was a time of pioneering enthusiasm and freshness, then the age of the apostolic fathers was a time of settling down, consolidating, and preserving the teachings and traditions of the apostles. We will look at four important areas of Christian development in this period: Church organisation, Church teaching, Church worship, and the relationship between Church and society.

Church organisation

The main issue the Christian community had to decide in the age of the apostolic fathers was the question of leadership: who was to govern and guide the churches now that the apostles were all dead? The pattern of church leadership that emerged after the apostolic age was a threefold ministry of *bishop, presbyters* and *deacons*. This took some time to develop itself fully, but by around AD 180 it was universally accepted throughout the Church. In the New Testament itself, the words "bishop" and "presbyter" do not refer to two distinct offices; they are simply different names for the same office. In the *Letter of Clement*, bishop and presbyter are also identical. However, in the writings of Ignatius of Antioch (about AD 110) we see these two words being used to refer to distinct offices. Ignatius argued vigorously for a single leader of each church, whom he called the "bishop", and under the bishop a team of secondary leaders, whom he called "presbyters" (and, next after them, the deacons). Ignatius saw the bishop as the centre or focus of unity in the local church. In his *Letter to Smyrna* he says: "Shun divisions as the beginning of evil. Follow your bishop as Jesus Christ followed the Father, and follow your presbyters as the apostles; and respect the deacons as you would respect God's commandment. Let no-one do anything in the church apart from the bishop. Holy communion is valid when celebrated by the bishop or by someone the bishop authorises. Where the bishop is present, there let the congregation gather, just as where Jesus Christ is, there is the Church."

It is important for us to understand that the bishops were not seen as new apostles. The early Church fathers counted the apostles as unique, and constantly referred back to them, quoting their writings and teachings as the final authority. It is true that the early Church did see some of the *functions* of the apostles continuing in and through the Church's bishops, especially the functions of teaching and Church discipline; but the bishops were still not apostles in *status* - they could not claim personal infallibility, proclaim new doctrines, or write new Scriptures.

Great obscurity veils the way that the threefold ministry of bishop, presbyter and deacon developed in early Church organisation. Part of the problem is the confusion that the terms "bishop" and "presbyter" can cause. As we have seen, Christians came to apply the title "bishop" to the single leader of a church, and "presbyter" to the secondary leaders who functioned under him. However, it is still possible that a pattern of one-man-leadership existed before the leader was *called* a bishop. Justin Martyr, for example (see below), in the mid-2nd Century, clearly taught a pattern of church government with one single leader at the top, but he called the leader "the president of the brothers" rather than "bishop". So in the earliest years, churches may have been led ultimately by one paramount leader, even though he was not actually given the title "bishop"; he and his team of secondary leaders may all have been called "bishops" and "presbyters" without distinction. It is the separation of the term "bishop" from "presbyter" that causes difficulty in interpreting what happened in early Church organisation. Much controversy has raged around this matter. The view which this book is about to offer should, therefore, not be seen as the only possible interpretation, but as one that appears to make sense of the evidence:

Originally, the bishop was probably the senior presbyter, the most respected elder who presided over his fellow elders as a "first among equals". It is likely that this pattern of leadership was based on the Jewish synagogue, which had a body of elders led by one senior elder, the "president" or "ruler of the synagogue" (**Luke 13:14, Acts 18:8** - this was true of the larger synagogues, at any rate). The Christian bishop seems to have begun as the president of the Christian body of elders in each local church. From that position, the status of the "president" gradually increased in importance throughout the 2nd Century. This growth in the president's status was what caused the Church to apply the title "bishop" exclusively to him, in distinction from the other elders who were simply called "presbyters". (To add to the confusion, Christians still sometimes called the bishop a "presbyter", but no longer called the presbyters "bishops".)

The *bishop* was the man[1] who conducted the services of worship, oversaw church discipline, and had the sole power to ordain, baptise and preside at the Lord's supper (although he could delegate to his presbyters the act of baptising and celebrating communion). Every local church had its own bishop, and no bishop had authority over any other church. In his own church, he became bishop through a two-part process: (i) he was elected by the votes of the congregation; (ii) he was then ordained by other bishops through the laying on of hands. Because the bishop alone could ordain another bishop, this gave rise (from the end of the 2nd Century) to the doctrine of "apostolic succession". According to this understanding of Church government, the apostles ordained the first bishops by the laying on of hands; these bishops then ordained their successors, transmitting apostolic authority to them by the laying on of their hands; and so on. Therefore, a true bishop could trace his authority directly back to the apostles through this "family tree" of ordinations. Modern readers should, however, realise that this view of apostolic succession did not give any kind of absolute authority or infallibility to bishops in the early Church. If bishops fell into heresy (as many did during the Arian controversy of the 4th Century - see Chapter 8), it became the duty of all orthodox Christians not to recognise them any longer. Apostolic succession included *holding the faith which the apostles had taught*, as well as being ordained by bishops who could trace their own ordination back to the apostles. For above all else, the bishop in the early Church was the guardian of apostolic doctrine, the congregation's official teacher - a function he carried out through preaching. The bishop was first and foremost a preacher, and the reputation of great bishops derived largely from their preaching abilities.

This elevation of the office of bishop to central importance did not mean that the *presbyters* no longer had any influence in the local

---

[1] Women were not allowed to be bishops or presbyters in the early Church, but they were equally eligible with men to be chosen as deacons.

church. Presbyters were not the bishop's servants, appointed by him to carry out his will; they were his colleagues, elected by the people, helping the bishop to provide leadership and discipline within the church. The *deacons* were responsible for visiting the sick and distributing food, clothing, and other necessities of life to the poorer members of the congregation. They also assisted the bishop in the service of worship, especially the Lord's supper, where they distributed the bread and wine.

Church teaching

In the age of the apostolic fathers, the Church had an extremely narrow, conservative, traditional attitude towards doctrine. Christian teachers tended simply to repeat what the New Testament says, without necessarily having any deep understanding of what it meant. However, two forms of teaching developed which the Church regarded as deviating from apostolic doctrine and therefore as heretical. The first was called *Docetism* (from the Greek *dokeo*, "to seem").[2] Docetic views were widespread in Asia Minor. According to Docetism, Jesus Christ was not a true human being. Christ only *seemed* to be a man; in fact, He was a purely heavenly being, Who could not have had any real contact with the inferior world of flesh. Therefore He did not physically suffer or die, and did not physically rise again. Ignatius of Antioch condemned Docetism with special vigour, seeing it as a betrayal of apostolic teaching and a threat to the unity of the Church. We can see the beginnings of Docetism recorded in the New Testament itself; the apostle John attacks it in **1 John 4:1-3**. The Docetic concept of Christ grew out of the Greek philosophical idea that flesh and physical matter hindered and corrupted the spirit, so that God, the supreme spiritual being, could not have direct involvement in the physical world.

The second form of heretical teaching developed among what was left of the Jewish Christian community, and was called *Ebionism*. Ebionites were traditional Jewish Christians who looked back to the earliest days of the Jerusalem church, and continued to practise the

---

2 Docetism is pronounced "Doss-eh-tizzum". Docetic is pronounced "Doh-see-tik".

Old Testament law, *e.g.* circumcision. They regarded Jesus, not as God in the flesh, but simply as the supreme prophet, the one man who had perfectly obeyed God's law. He became the Son of God by adoption at His baptism, and would return one day as the heavenly Son of Man to reign over the nations of the earth from Jerusalem. Ebionites rejected the writings of the apostle Paul; to them, Paul was a traitor to the Jewish faith and a heretic. (*Ebionism* comes from the Hebrew *ebionim*, "the poor ones", perhaps referring to their practice of voluntary poverty.)

Church worship

What was a Christian service of worship like in the 2nd Century? We are fortunate in having a good description of a normal Christian gathering for worship in the writings of the 2nd Century theologian, Justin Martyr (see section 4 for Justin's life). In his *First Apology*, Justin says:

> "On the day called Sunday there is a meeting of all believers who live in the town or the country, and the memoirs of the apostles, or the writings of the prophets, are read for as long as time will permit. When the reader has finished, the president in a sermon urges and invites the people to base their lives on these noble things. Then we all stand up[3] and offer prayers. When our prayer is concluded, bread and wine and water are brought; and the president offers up prayers and thanksgivings to the best of his ability, and the people assent with Amen. Then follows the distribution of the things over which thanks have been offered, and the partaking of them by all; and the deacons take them to those who are absent.... We hold our common assembly on Sunday because it is the first day, on which God put to flight darkness and chaos and made the world; and on the same day, Jesus Christ our Saviour rose from the dead."

---

3   Justin does not mean that prayers were the only part of worship which the church offered in a standing posture. He means that when the "president of the brothers" led everyone in corporate prayer, anyone who may have been sitting and resting had to join the rest of the congregation in standing for prayer. See below for standing in worship.

The "president" of the assembly, who expounded the Scriptures and oversaw holy communion, was the senior presiding elder - that is, as Church organisation developed in the 2nd Century, the bishop. In another place, Justin gives a more detailed account of the Lord's supper or *eucharist* (from the Greek *eucharisteo*, "to give thanks"), which Justin describes like this:

> "Then bread and a cup of wine mixed with water are brought to the president of the brothers. He takes them and offers up praise and glory to the Father of the universe, through the name of the Son and of the Holy Spirit. He gives thanks at considerable length for our being counted worthy to receive these things from His hands. When he has finished the prayers and thanksgivings, all the people present express their joyful agreement by saying Amen. ('Amen' means 'Let it be so' in Hebrew).... Then those whom we call deacons give to each of those present the bread and the wine mixed with water over which the thanksgiving was pronounced, and carry away a portion to those who are absent."

> "We call this food 'eucharist', which no-one is allowed to share unless he believes that the things we teach are true, and has been washed with the washing that is for the forgiveness of sins and a second birth, and is living as Christ has commanded. For we do not receive them as common bread and common drink. But as Jesus Christ our Saviour became flesh by the word of God, and clothed Himself in our flesh and blood to save us, so also we have been taught that the food which is blessed by the word of prayer handed down from Christ, by which our blood and flesh are nourished as the food becomes part of ourselves, is the flesh and blood of the same Jesus Who became flesh. For the apostles, in the memoirs composed by themselves called 'Gospels', have delivered to us what was commanded to them: that Jesus took bread, and when He had given thanks said, 'Do this in remembrance of Me, this is My body'; and in a similar way, after taking the cup and giving thanks, He said, 'This is My blood,' and gave it only to them."

From Justin's account, we learn that the main ingredients of Christian worship in the 2nd Century were (i) the reading and expounding of Scripture, (ii) prayer, and (iii) the celebration of the Lord's supper. Indeed, compared with many Churches today, the Lord's supper held a remarkably high place in early Christian worship. The local church celebrated it every Sunday and it formed a large part of the service. Singing, which for many modern Christians is such a central part of worship, was not so important in the early Church; in fact, Justin does not mention it here at all. However, he does mention it elsewhere, and we know from other accounts that singing and chanting were a widespread practice in the worship of the early Christians. In the 2nd Century, the most common form of singing and chanting was "responsive". This means that one person (a Scripture reader or a clergyman) would sing or chant a passage, usually from a psalm, and the congregation would then make a response - either a single word, such as "Alleluia", or a chorus. There was also solo singing and full congregational singing, although the latter did not really become popular until the 4th Century.

What the early Christians chanted and sang were the **Psalms** of the Old Testament, and some of the poetic parts of the New Testament (*e.g.* the Virgin Mary's praise of God in **Luke 1:46-55**). It was probably not until the 4th Century that the singing of hymns written by ordinary Christians began to become common. However, one of the greatest patristic hymns, the *Gloria in excelsis* ("Glory in the highest", based on **Luke 2:14**), dates from the 2nd or 3rd Century (see the end of the Chapter). No musical instruments accompanied the chanting and singing; Christians did not use instruments in their worship in the 2nd Century, or indeed for many centuries afterwards. The early Church looked on musical instruments as being part of Jewish or pagan worship, but not part of the apostolic tradition of Christian worship. In one of the writings of Theodoret of Cyrrhus, an eminent Church father who lived in the early 5th Century, we find the following typical statement:

"Question: If songs were invented by unbelievers with a purpose of deceiving (**Genesis 4:21**), and were appointed under the Jewish Law because of the childishness of their minds, why do Christians who have received the perfect teachings of grace (which are quite contrary to pagan and Jewish customs) still sing in the churches, like the Jews who were children under the Law? Answer: Simple singing is not childish. What is childish is singing with lifeless organs, dancing, cymbals, *etc.* Therefore we Christians put aside the use of such instruments and other things fit for children, and we retain only simple singing."

Modern Western readers should also note that standing throughout worship was the traditional practice in the early Church period, and for centuries afterwards. The Western Church only began to introduce pews (fixed seats in the main part of the church building) in the 14th Century - quite a late development. The Eastern Church never introduced pews into Eastern church buildings. People who were tired during early Church worship could sit around the edges of the building, but everyone had to stand to pray; the early Christians considered standing the only proper posture for public spoken prayer. Early Christian art also shows us that when praying, Christians spread out their arms with upturned palms, and kept their eyes open, looking upwards to heaven.

As Justin's account shows us, early Christian worship was (generally speaking) simple in form and fixed in structure. The pattern Justin describes would not have varied greatly in any church throughout the Roman Empire. An important point which does not come out so clearly from Justin is that the service of worship was divided into two distinct parts. The first part, known as "the service of the Word" (singing, reading and sermon), was open to baptised believers, those who were receiving instruction in the Christian faith, and probably also to those who were simply curious about Christianity. The second part, the prayers and the eucharist (the Lord's supper), was only for those who had been baptised; the rest had to leave. From descriptions and instructions in the writings of the early Church fathers, we can say that a fairly typical service of worship in any congregation of the 2nd Century would have been structured something like this:

Part One: Service of the Word

1. Opening greeting by bishop and response by congregation. Usually the bishop said, "The Lord be with you," and the congregation responded, "And with your spirit".

2. Scripture reading: Old Testament. A deacon gave the readings. In larger congregations, the deacon chanted the Scripture passage rather than simply read it - a practice probably derived from Jewish synagogue worship.

3. Psalm or hymn.

4. Scripture reading: New Testament. The first New Testament reading was from any book between **Acts** and **Revelation**.

5. Psalm or hymn.

6. Scripture reading: New Testament. The second New Testament reading was from one of the four **Gospels.** This pattern of three readings, from Old Testament, **Acts-Revelation,** and **Gospels,** goes back to the earliest times. From the 3rd Century, "lectionaries" were drawn up which specified exactly which passages of Scripture should be read on each Sunday of the year.

7. Sermon. The bishop preached this in a sitting posture. Sitting was the accepted posture for preaching and teaching in the early Church. See **Matthew 5:1-2, Luke 4:21-23 & 5:3, John 8:2, Acts 16:13**.

8. Dismissal of all but baptised believers.

Part Two: The eucharist

1. Prayers. The "prayer leader" - in the West, the bishop; in the East, the senior deacon - announced a topic for prayer. The congregation knelt and prayed silently for a time. Then they were exhorted to stand up; and the leader, with a spoken prayer, summed up the congregation's petitions on that topic. (As we saw, the early Church regarded standing as the proper posture for public spoken prayer; so the rest of the church had to stand in order to take part spiritually in the spoken prayers of the bishop or senior deacon.) The leader then announced another topic; the congregation knelt and prayed silently; then they stood as the leader summed up again with a spoken prayer. And so on, for quite a lengthy time.

2. Holy communion. This happened in the following order: (i) Greeting by the bishop, response by the congregation, and the "kiss of peace" - the men kissed the other men, the women kissed the other women. (ii) The "offertory". Each church member brought a small loaf and a flask of wine to communion; the deacons took these gifts and spread them out on the Lord's table. The flasks of wine were all emptied into one large silver cup. (iii) The bishop and congregation engaged in a "dialogue" with each other - see the example from Hippolytus recorded below. The bishop then led the congregation in prayer. (iv) The bishop and deacons broke the loaves. (v) The bishop and deacons distributed the bread and offered the cup to the congregation. Something would be said to each person as he received the bread and wine - for example, in the Roman church, the deacon said, "The bread of heaven in Christ Jesus" as he offered the bread; the church member replied with "Amen." Communion was always received in a standing posture. Church members took home the bread and wine that had not been consumed, and used them on weekdays for the celebration of communion in the home.

3. Benediction. A phrase such as "Depart in peace" was spoken by a deacon.

The whole service would have lasted about 3 hours.

For many modern Christians, two aspects of this early Church worship will stand out as quite striking. (i) The first is the fact that the early Church did not allow unbelievers to be present when the congregation prayed. This was because, in early Church thinking, the congregation at prayer was participating by the Holy Spirit in the glorified Christ's own heavenly ministry of prayer. This was something in which unbelievers could not share, for they lacked the Spirit. (ii) The second is the way that all church members brought their own bread and wine to be used in communion. The early Christians attached great significance to this provision of the communion bread and wine by every church member: it was the whole church offering itself to God, as together all its members presented to Him the fruits of His creation. When the deacons placed the loaves and wine on the Lord's table, they were (in a symbolic sense) laying the congregation itself on the table through its gifts, thus consecrating the people to Christ. As the great early Church father

Augustine[4] told his people at communion, "There you are, on the table; there you are, in the cup."

The use of "liturgy" - fixed, written prayers and exhortations to be read out by the bishop and congregation - is found from a very early date in Christian worship. The oldest known example of a church's liturgy for holy communion occurs in the writings of *Hippolytus*. He was a presbyter in the church at Rome who fell out with its bishop Callistus (AD 217-22), set himself up as a rival bishop, but was later reconciled with the Roman congregation and died a martyr's death in AD 236. Hippolytus's *Church Order* contains the communion liturgy from the church in Rome. After the "offertory" (see above), the bishop and congregation recited the following dialogue and prayer:

> Bishop: The Lord be with you.
> Congregation: And with your spirit.
> Bishop: Lift up your hearts.
> Congregation: We lift them to the Lord.
> Bishop: Let us give thanks to the Lord.
> Congregation: It is fitting and right.
> Bishop: We thank You, O God, through Your beloved

Servant Jesus Christ, Whom in these last times You have sent to us as Saviour, Redeemer, and Messenger of Your counsel, the Logos[5] Who comes from You, through Whom You have made all things, Whom You were pleased to send from heaven into the womb of the Virgin, and in her body He became flesh, and was revealed as Your Son, born of the Holy Spirit and the Virgin. To fulfil Your will and prepare a holy people for You, He stretched out His hands [on the cross] when He suffered, so that He might release from suffering those who have believed in You.

And when He delivered Himself willingly to suffering, to loose the bonds of death and break the chains of the devil, to tread down hell and enlighten the righteous, to set up the boundary stone and manifest the resurrection, He took a loaf, gave thanks and said, "Take, eat, this is My body which is

---

4   For Augustine, see Chapter 9, section 3.
5   For "the Logos" as a title of Christ, see section 4 under Justin Martyr.

given for You." In the same way He took the cup and said, "This is My blood which is poured out for you. Whenever you do this, you remember Me."

Remembering, therefore, His death and resurrection, we offer to You the loaf and the cup, and give thanks to You that You have counted us worthy to stand before You and serve You as priests.[6] And we pray to You, that You will send down Your Holy Spirit on this offering of the church.[7] Unite it, and grant to all the saints who partake of it that we may be filled with the Holy Spirit and strengthened in our faith in the truth, so that we may praise and glorify You through Your Servant Jesus Christ, through Whom be glory and honour to You in Your Church, now and for ever. Amen.

Hippolytus wrote in the early 3rd Century, but since he was recording the established tradition in the Roman church, this communion liturgy certainly goes back to the 2nd Century. In the first few centuries of Christian worship, each individual church tended to have its own liturgy; it was much later that liturgy became "standardised", so that all churches in the West eventually followed the Roman church's liturgy, and all in the East followed that of Constantinople. It is also important to realise that in the early centuries, liturgy did not rule out "free prayer" by the bishop (praying his own prayers not written in the liturgy); there was a mixture of both elements. Again, it was only later that liturgy became all-important to the exclusion of free prayer.[8]

Christian worship revolved around Sunday, or "the Lord's day" as the early Church called it - the day on which the Lord Jesus had risen from the dead. However, this weekly pattern of worship was allied to a yearly pattern which revolved around Easter. (Christmas was a later development - see Chapter 7, section 3). Easter was the Christian equivalent of the Jewish Passover. Christ had died at the same time that the Passover lamb was sacrificed; so Christians

---

6   The liturgy is referring here to the entire congregation as priests.
7   The "offering of the church" refers to the gifts of bread and wine brought by the whole church to communion and laid on the Lord's table.
8   See Chapter 7, section 3.

celebrated their Saviour's death at Easter, when Jews were celebrating the Passover. The churches of Asia Minor observed Easter on the precise day of Passover, the 14th of Nisan (in the Hebrew calendar), which was not necessarily a Sunday. But the churches of Palestine, Alexandria and Rome always observed Easter on a Sunday, the one that fell just after the 14th of Nisan. This caused a serious controversy in the 2nd Century, the *Quartodeciman* controversy (from the Latin word for "four-teenth"), but at the Council of Nicaea in the 4th Century the custom of Palestine, Alexandria and Rome triumphed.[9]

Church and society

The moral and social values of the early Christians brought them into sharp conflict with the pagan society in which they lived. In part, this was because of the way that pagan *religion* was present in so many of the Empire's social practices and institutions. For example, Christians could not take part in official state occasions, holidays or celebrations, because these always involved worshipping the gods. Public entertainment, e.g. in circus and theatre, was accompanied by sacrifices to the gods, and stage plays usually portrayed pagan religion and sexual immorality; the Church therefore shunned these things. Christians had scruples about going to a pagan hospital, because hospitals employed priests of the god Aesculapius, the god of healing, to pray over the patients. Many Christians would not send their children to Roman schools where pagan religion was taught. A Christian artist could do little or no work for pagan customers, since it almost always involved drawing, painting, carving or weaving pagan religious symbols. Various careers were either completely closed or highly dangerous to the believer, because they involved pagan religion; the most notable were politics, the army, and teaching. Magistrates conducted pagan worship as part of their ordinary duties; soldiers had to attend sacrifices to Rome's gods as a sign of their allegiance to the Empire; and teachers instructed pupils about the gods from the "sacred books" of Greece and Rome, especially Homer's *Iliad*.

There were other aspects of Roman society that Christians opposed

---

9   For the Council of Nicaea, see Chapter 7, section 3, and Chapter 8, section 1.

on *ethical* grounds. For example, Christians condemned the most popular form of Roman entertainment, the gladiatorial arena, where men fought each other to the death; the Church rejected such violence, and the enjoyment of watching it, as utterly contrary to Christ Who came to give life, not to destroy it. Christians also rejected the widespread Roman custom of abortion (killing unwanted unborn children) and infanticide (killing unwanted newly-born children).[10] They opposed easy divorce, which was at that time the normal Roman practice; a great early Church father of the 3rd Century, Tertullian,[11] remarked that Roman women "long for divorce as if it were the natural consequence of marriage". The Christian view was that the only causes which could justify a divorce were adultery and the desertion of a believer by an unbelieving partner. Even then, the vast majority of Christians would not permit a divorced person to remarry - and many disapproved of widows and widowers remarrying.

Not surprisingly, this rejection by Christians of so many areas of Roman life made them highly unpopular with their pagan neighbours, who accused Christians of being self-righteous and anti-social.[12]

The early Church's attitude to the army was especially complicated. Many Christian leaders opposed the idea of Christians being soldiers, not just because it involved pagan worship, but also because they did not think Christians should ever kill a human being for any reason. However, many Christians did in fact serve in the Roman army; they managed to avoid committing idolatry, and could often live the life of

---

10   In a letter written by a loving pagan Roman husband to his pregnant wife, the husband says: "If you give birth to a boy, let it live. If it is a girl, throw it away." Unwanted babies were simply thrown on the nearest rubbish-heap and left there to die.

11   See Chapter 5, section 2 for Tertullian.

12   Contrary to what many people think, the early Church did not oppose slavery, which was not abolished when the Empire became Christian in the 4th Century. However, Christian teaching and practice did improve the conditions in which slaves lived. For example, the sanctity of marriage between slaves was recognised by the Church (not by the Empire), and Church funds were often used to buy the freedom of slaves from cruel masters.

a soldier without having to kill anyone, since in the Roman Empire the army acted as a police, prison and fire service, as well as a strictly military force. Christian soldiers spread the Gospel as they did tours of duty in different parts of the Empire; some famous Christians, *e.g.* Pachomius,[13] were converted by Christian soldier-evangelists. During times of persecution, Christian soldiers were often the first to suffer: picked out and put to death for their known faith. Even so, it was not until the 4th Century, when the emperors became Christians, that Christian leaders began to accept that Christians could take part in actual warfare. The first Christian to write in defence of war was Athanasius,[14] the great 4th Century bishop of Alexandria, who wrote that "it is lawful and praiseworthy to destroy an enemy" in a "just war" (usually a war of national self-defence against invasion).

3. Persecution.

Most people know that the Roman Empire persecuted Christians. But *why* were the early Christians persecuted? Some of the early Church fathers, such as Tertullian, tried to argue that it was only the bad emperors who persecuted the Church; good emperors left the Church in peace. Unfortunately, this is not true! Some bad emperors, such as Nero (AD 54-68) and Domitian (AD 81-96) did persecute Christians. But other bad emperors like Commodus (AD 180-92) were tolerant. And some good emperors such as Trajan (AD 98-117), and the virtuous philosopher-emperor Marcus Aurelius (AD 161-80), were persecutors. In any case, persecution came not so much from the emperors themselves, as from the governors of the Empire's provinces and from popular hatred of the Christians.[15]

Another important factor is that the Roman state assumed the right to control the religious life of its subjects. It classified religions into two simple categories, *licita* ("permitted") and *illicita* ("not permitted"). Once it had become clear to Roman magistrates that

---

13   For Pachomius, see Chapter 7, section 3.

14   For Athanasius, see Chapter 8, sections 2 and 3.

15   By "good" and "bad" emperors, I mean emperors whose *general* behaviour was good or bad, apart from their attitude to the persecution of Christians.

Christians were not a Jewish sect, Christianity ceased to enjoy the "permitted" status of Judaism. The Empire had to decide whether this new religion should fall into the "permitted" or "not permitted" category. Rome was normally tolerant in religious matters; but if it felt that a particular religion was a threat to public morality or political stability, the authorities would suppress it. For example, they stamped out the cult of Bacchus in 186 BC because it led its worshippers into extremes of sexual depravity and violence.

The question, then, is why Rome decided that the Christians were a threat to the well-being of the Empire. And the answer lies in the exclusive truth-claims that Christians made for their faith. The other religions of the Empire were *syncretistic* (Greek for "federated", "joined in alliance") - that is, they did not make any claim to be the one and only truth. A person could "mix" his religions and follow more than one. Christianity, and of course Judaism, stood out against this pattern. The Christians and the Jews insisted that they alone had the true faith and the only way of salvation. The Roman world could tolerate such a view in the Jews, because Jews were simply following the traditional religion of their nation and ancestors, and did not go around trying to make everyone else into Jews. The Christians had no such excuses; their religion was new, unheard-of, and burning with a passion to convert all pagans. So the Church's exclusive, intolerant, missionary attitude to other religions marked Christians out and made them very unpopular. To their pagan neighbours, this evangelistic devotion to Christ as the only Saviour seemed highly arrogant and dangerously anti-social.

To make things worse, Christians refused to worship the emperor (or the *genius* of the emperor - see Chapter 1, section 1). The authorities saw this as a serious political offence. Worshipping the emperor was a sign of loyalty to the Empire; to refuse was to be a traitor. The chief test of whether someone accused of being a Christian was a real Christian, was for the magistrates to order him to worship a statue of the emperor and say, "Caesar is Lord" - that is, Caesar is a divine figure, a god. A faithful Christian would refuse, because for him or her, "Jesus is Lord", not Caesar. One could not worship both Caesar and Christ.

Another reason for the great unpopularity of Christians was that most people believed them to be guilty of all kinds of evil practices.

Pagans accused Christians of cannibalism, incest and black magic. Some of these accusations arose through a misunderstanding of genuine Christian practices. The accusation of cannibalism, for example, was probably based on the Lord's supper, where Christians spoke of eating Christ's flesh and drinking His blood; the accusation of incest arose partly from the fact that Christians called each other "brother" and "sister" and "loved each other". People were highly suspicious of Christians anyway, because Christians met in secret through fear of persecution. It was a vicious circle: because the authorities were likely to persecute them, Christians met in secret - but the more they met in secret, the more likely the authorities were to persecute them!

Until the year 250, there were no persecutions of universal Empire-wide extent. Outbreaks of persecution were local, limited to particular cities or provinces, and often short-lived. Pagans increasingly blamed and victimised Christians for any local calamity or disaster; in the words of Tertullian: "When the Tiber floods, or the Nile fails to flood, up goes the cry: Christians to the lion!"[16] The idea was that the gods were angry because Christians were drawing people away from worshipping them. So pagans blamed all local catastrophes on the Church. It became a common saying, "No rain, because of the Christians." Since Christians did not worship the gods, people even regarded them as atheists. "Away with the atheists!" was a popular anti-Christian cry.

The provincial governors were the only judges who could order the death penalty. Their sole concern was to govern their province in the political interests of Rome. Expediency rather than moral principle guided their decisions. Often the only question they would ask was, "Will persecuting the Christians please the general population and calm them down?" So whether the authorities persecuted Christians in any particular part of the Empire depended on the ups and downs of popular anti-Christian feeling. When anti-Christian feeling was high, governors would yield to it and persecute the Church.

---

16 The Tiber is the river beside which Rome is built. The Nile is the great river of Egypt, the flooding of which was actually desired by ancient Egyptians as a method of irrigation. So the flooding of the Tiber was a disaster for Rome, but for Egyptians it was the failure of the Nile to flood that was disastrous. Christians were blamed for both.

The first official government pronouncement about how Christians were to be dealt with came from the emperor *Trajan* (AD 98-117). Pliny, the governor of the province of Bithynia in Asia Minor, wrote to Trajan in AD 112 asking how he should handle people accused of being Christians (Pliny seems to have been a fussy weakling who could not act without first getting definite orders from Rome). Trajan's reply was that Pliny should not actively hunt down Christians, and must not accept anonymous accusations. If anyone accused of being a Christian could prove that he was not, by worshipping the pagan gods, the magistrates must acquit him. But anyone found guilty of being a Christian must be put to death. This became the normal policy for the next 200 years. The worst period of persecution in the 2nd Century came under the Stoic emperor *Marcus Aurelius* (AD 161-80), who had great contempt for Christians. Believers were executed in Africa, Rome and France.[17] The authorities killed a large number of Christians in Lyons and Vienne in the south of France in a particularly violent persecution in AD 177. Marcus Aurelius was not personally responsible for these persecutions, but if he knew of them we can be fairly sure he would have done nothing to stop them. The most virtuous of the pagan emperors was no help to the Church.

An eyewitness account of the persecution in Lyons and Vienne has survived, and it gives us a vivid picture of the sort of treatment Christians could expect from the Roman authorities. Let us follow the account as it tells us about what happened to a Christian slave-girl called *Blandina*:

> "The whole fury of crowd, governor and soldiers fell with crushing force on Sanctus, the deacon from Vienne; on Maturus, very recently baptised, but heroic in facing his ordeal; on Attalus, who had always been a pillar and support of the church in his native Pergamum; and on Blandina, through whom Christ proved that things which men regard as

---

17   The Romans called France *Gaul*. It became known as *France* after the Germanic tribe of the *Franks* settled there in the 5th Century (see Chapter 11). However, I will refer to it as France throughout Part One to make it easier to identify with the modern land of France.

mean, unlovely and contemptible, are by God deemed worthy
of great glory, because of her love for Him, shown in power
and not vaunted in appearance. We were all afraid, and
Blandina's earthly mistress (herself facing the ordeal of
martyrdom) was in agony in case she should be unable to
make a bold confession of Christ due to her bodily weakness;
but Blandina was filled with such power, that those who took
it in turns to subject her to every kind of torture from morning
to night were exhausted by their efforts, and confessed
themselves beaten - they could think of nothing else to do.
They were amazed that she was still breathing, for her whole
body was mangled, and her wounds gaped; they declared that
torment of any one kind was enough to part soul and body, let
alone a succession of torments of such extreme severity. But
the blessed woman, wrestling magnificently, grew in strength
as she proclaimed her faith, and found refreshment, rest and
indifference to her sufferings in uttering the words, 'I am a
Christian. We do nothing to be ashamed of, '....

"Blandina was hung on a post and exposed as food for the wild
beasts which had been let loose in the arena. She looked as if
she was hanging in the form of a cross, and through her ardent
prayers she aroused great enthusiasm in the other martyrs
who were undergoing their ordeal. In their agony, they
seemed to see in their sister the One Who was crucified for
them, that He might convince those who believe in Him that
anyone who has suffered for the glory of Christ has fellowship
for ever with the living God. As none of the wild beasts had
touched Blandina, they took her down from the post and
returned her to prison, keeping her for a second ordeal....

"On the last day of the sports they brought Blandina in again,
and with her Ponticus, a boy of about 15. Day after day the
authorities had taken them in to watch the others being
punished, and tried to make them swear by the pagan idols.
When they stood firm and treated these efforts with contempt,
the mob was infuriated with them. The boy's tender age called
forth no pity, the woman's tender sex called forth no respect.
They were subjected to every horror and every punishment in
turn. The mob tried again and again to make them swear by

the gods, but in vain. Ponticus was encouraged by his sister in Christ, so that the pagans saw she was urging him on and stiffening his resistance, and he bravely endured every punishment till he gave back his spirit to God. Last of all, like a noble mother who had encouraged her children and sent them ahead of her in triumph to the King, blessed Blandina herself passed through all the ordeals of her children and hastened to rejoin them, rejoicing and exulting in her departure as if she had been invited to a wedding supper rather than thrown to wild beasts. After whipping her, giving her to the beasts, and burning her with hot irons, the authorities finally dropped her into a basket and threw her to a bull. The beast gored her again and again, but she was now indifferent to all that happened to her, because of her hope, her firm grip on all that her faith meant, and her communion with Christ. Then she too was sacrificed. The pagans themselves admitted that they had never known a woman suffer so much or so long."

The early Church felt the highest reverence for its martyrs. It saw them as Christians who had most fully followed their Lord, by being conformed to His death. The Church therefore treated the dead body of a martyr (or what was left of it) with special respect and tenderness. For example, after the martyrdom of bishop Polycarp of Smyrna in AD 160 (see section 1 for his *Letter to the Philippians*), the Christians of Smyrna took care to preserve his physical remains: "We gathered his bones, which are more valuable than precious stones and finer than the purest gold, and we laid them in a suitable place, where the Lord will permit us to meet together in gladness and joy, to celebrate the birthday of his martyrdom." This quotation shows us that the Smyrnean believers would hold a special religious service every year on the day Polycarp was put to death, to treasure in their hearts the memory of their great bishop and martyr. Christians all over the Roman Empire did the same for their own local martyrs.

Over the next few centuries, Christians pieced together the information about the different martyrs, so that the whole Church came to consecrate many days in the year to the celebration of one or more of these heroes of the faith. This meant that (for instance) all Christians, not just those of Smyrna, would be remembering

Polycarp on the day of his death. Later, other great Christians ("saints" - outstandingly holy people) who had not died a martyr's death also had special days assigned to them, for the Church to consider their lives and deeds on that day. This practice has continued to the present time within Roman Catholicism and Eastern Orthodoxy. Protestants, however, abandoned it at the Reformation,[18] partly because so many "legends" about the martyrs and saints had crept into the stories of their lives (a legend is a grand but historically untrue tale). The early Church's reverence for the bones of its martyrs laid the basis for the "cult of relics" (see Chapter 7, section 3, under **Church worship**).

4. The apologists.

The *apologists* is a name historians give to a number of Christian writers from the 2nd Century who wrote in order to disprove the accusations that pagans made against Christians, and to show the intellectuals of the Roman world that Christianity was worthy of their attention and their belief. The name "apologist" comes from the Greek *apologia*, meaning "a speech for the defence". From this we get the term *apologetics* - defending the Christian faith from attacks against its beliefs, and exposing the falsehood of what other religions teach.

Nearly all the apologists wrote in Greek. Sometimes they addressed an apology to a particular emperor or provincial governor. The apologist would try to show that Christians were good law-abiding citizens who paid their taxes and prayed for the Empire. He would also explain to the world what Christians believed and practised. The apologists aimed other apologies more at the intellectual culture of the day, trying to demonstrate that Christianity was the best and truest philosophy.

The apologists were highly cultured and literary men, who had often practised philosophy before becoming Christians. They included:

Aristides, an Athenian who in AD 140 dedicated an apology to the

---

[18] See Part Three for the Reformation.

emperor Antoninus Pius (AD 138-61). Aristides was a converted philosopher.

Athenagoras, another Athenian who had been a Platonist philosopher before his conversion. He addressed his *Intercession on behalf of the Christians* to the emperor Marcus Aurelius and his son Commodus in about AD 177. He was especially concerned to disprove accusations of atheism, cannibalism and incest. Athenagoras was one of the clearest, most forceful and persuasive of the apologists.

Melito of Sardis, bishop of Sardis in Asia Minor, who in his own day was a famous writer of many books. He was active in the period AD 170-80. The great African theologian Tertullian admired his writings,[19] which sadly have almost all been lost. Melito wrote an apology addressed to Marcus Aurelius. We also owe to Melito the first known Christian list of books contained in the Old Testament. He made a special trip to Palestine to seek information about the Hebrew Scriptures; his list corresponds with the Jewish and Protestant Old Testament of today.

Theophilus of Antioch, bishop of Antioch, who in about AD 180 wrote his *Apology to Autolycus*, an educated pagan friend. Theophilus tried to show Autolycus that idolatry is false and Christianity true, and that Christians are good, virtuous, law-abiding citizens. He had a very negative attitude to Greek philosophy, accusing Plato of having stolen his best ideas from the Old Testament prophets.

Minucius Felix, unusual among the apologists because he wrote in Latin rather than Greek. He was probably of North African descent, and had a wide knowledge of Greek and Roman culture. He wrote an eloquent apology called *Octavius*, which sets out the arguments between Christians and pagans in the form of a dialogue, and demonstrates the superiority of the Christian faith to pagan idolatry. It is perhaps the most charming and readable of all the apologies. We do not know when *Octavius* was written - probably in about AD 230.

---

19   Tertullian was himself a great apologist. See Chapter 5, section 2.

Justin Martyr (Died AD 165)

Justin Martyr. Justin was the greatest of the 2nd Century apologists. Born of Greek parents in Palestine, he began seeking the truth in Greek philosophy, especially Platonism, which gave him an inspiring vision of eternal beauty, truth and goodness. But he was still not satisfied. He started thinking about Christianity after being impressed by the fearless way that Christian martyrs went to their deaths. Finally Justin became a Christian himself, through an unexpected meeting with an old man when he was out walking one day along a sea-shore at Ephesus. The old man talked with Justin about the meaning of life, and introduced him to the Old Testament Scriptures and Christ as providing the answer. Justin spent the rest of his life teaching philosophy as a Christian. He settled in Rome in about AD 153, and wrote two apologies. His ***First Apology*** he dedicated to the emperor Antoninus Pius; his ***Second Apology,*** dedicated to the Roman senate, was written later as a supplement to the first.

In his writings, Justin tried to show that all the truths which the Greek philosophers, particularly the Platonists, had been striving to understand were now perfectly revealed in Christianity. To demonstrate this, Justin described Christ as the ***Logos***. This is Greek for "Reason". (**John's Gospel** calls Christ the Logos in chapter 1, verses 1 and 14. English Bibles usually translate "Logos" as "Word", but it also means "Reason". The English word "logical" derives from it.) Logos was a term which Greek philosophers used to refer to the eternal principle of Reason that gives order and meaning to the universe. Philosophers saw the Logos as standing half-way between God and creation; God was too distant and perfect to have any immediate contact with the universe, but He could deal with it indirectly through His Logos. According to Justin, this eternal Logos or Reason was Christ Himself before He became flesh as Jesus of Nazareth.[20] As the eternal Logos, Justin said, Christ had been at work not only among the Jews, but in the pagan world too, instructing the minds of those philosophers who wanted to live in harmony with Reason. Justin especially admired the great Athenian philosopher Socrates, Plato's teacher, whom Justin saw as a sort of "Christian

---

[20] Later theologians did not find this philosophical understanding of the Logos satisfactory. It admitted the eternity of the Logos, but made Him inferior to God the Father. The Father was too exalted and glorious to have direct dealings with creation, but apparently the Logos was not.

before Christ". So instead of setting the Christian faith and Greek philosophy against each other, Justin believed that Christianity was the fulfilment of Greek philosophy. The philosophers had only seen parts of the jigsaw: Christianity gave the complete picture.

Justin also wrote a book called *Dialogue with Trypho*. This is a learned and polite debate between Justin and a Jew; it is relatively free from the anti-Jewish feeling that spoils so many early Christian writings. In the *Dialogue* Justin sought to prove that Christianity was the true fulfilment of Judaism and the Old Testament.

The authorities in Rome executed Justin for being a Christian in about AD 165. It is both odd and tragic that the emperor at the time was Marcus Aurelius, the Stoic philosopher, who might have been expected to be more sympathetic than other emperors to Justin's teaching.

The apologists did not succeed in persuading the Roman government to cease from persecuting Christians. Probably no emperor ever read any of the apologies addressed to him. The chief effect of the apologies was on the Church itself: they helped to develop the Church's theology, and to strengthen the confidence of believers in the truth and righteousness of the faith they confessed.

Important people:

The Church	*Political and military*
Clement of Rome (active AD 90-100)	Emperor Trajan (AD 98-117)
Ignatius of Antioch (died AD 110)	
Papias (active AD 110-30)	Emperor Antoninus Pius (AD 138-61)
Polycarp of Smyrna (AD 70-160)	
Aristides (mid-2nd Century)	Emperor Marcus Aurelius (AD 161-80)
Athenagoras (mid-2nd Century)	
Justin Martyr (died AD 165)	
The martyr Blandina (died AD 177)	
Melito of Sardis (active AD 170-80)	
Theophilus of Antioch (late 2nd century)	
Minucius Felix (late 2nd or early 3rd Century)	
Hippolytus (died AD 236)	

Justification by faith

All the Old Testament saints were honoured and glorified, not through themselves, not through their own works or righteous behaviour, but through the will of God. And we too, who have been called through God's will in Christ Jesus, are not justified through ourselves, or through our own wisdom or understanding or godliness, or through our own deeds done in holiness of heart; no, we are justified through faith. For it is through faith that Almighty God has justified all people that have ever lived from the beginning of time. To Him be glory for ever and ever! Amen.

Clement of Rome, *Letter to the Corinthians,* **chapter 32**

The glory and necessity of love

Who can describe the bond of God's love? What human being can rightly tell the excellence of its beauty? The height to which love exalts us is beyond our speech. Love unites us with God. Love covers a multitude of sins. Love bears all things. Love is longsuffering in all things. There is nothing corrupt or arrogant in love. Love allows no schisms, and gives rise to no seditions, but does all things in harmony. Love is what makes all the elect of God perfect. Without love, nothing is well-pleasing to God. In love the Lord has taken us to Himself. It was because of His love for us that Jesus Christ our Lord gave His blood for us by the will of God, His flesh for our flesh, His soul for our souls. You see, my beloved, how great and wonderful a thing is love! No-one can declare its perfection. Who can find anyone who is fit to dwell in love, except those to whom God has granted such fitness? Let us therefore pray, and beg of God's mercy, that we may live blameless in love, free from all human parties that prefer one person above another.

Clement of Rome, *Letter to the Corinthians,* **chapters 49-50**

Christ our light and our life

God hid the virginity of Mary, the birth of her Child, and the death of the Lord, from the understanding of the prince of this world. These three mysteries, which God brought about in His quietness, we must now proclaim with a shout. How were they revealed to the ages? A star shone in heaven, brighter than all other stars; its light was beyond description, its strangeness caused amazement; and all the other stars, and even the sun and moon, became a chorus for that star which outshone them all. It troubled them all to know where this strange appearance came from, so different from the other heavenly bodies. From that time onward, all sorcery and every spell were abolished; the ignorance of wickedness vanished; the ancient kingdom of Satan was overthrown: for God was displayed in human form, to bring newness of eternal life. Then what God had perfected in His purpose He began to carry out, and it stirred the whole universe, because God was undertaking the destruction of death itself.

If Jesus Christ counts me worthy, through your prayers, and if it should be His will, I intend to write you a second pamphlet in which I will proceed to expound the divine plan I have been speaking about, especially if the Lord should make some revelation to me. This plan is based on the New Man, Jesus Christ, and consists in faith and love towards Him in His suffering and resurrection. Meanwhile, meet together as one community in grace, every single one of you, in one faith and one Jesus Christ, the One Who was born of David's line in His human nature, Son of Man and Son of God. Obey your bishop and your presbyters with minds free from distraction. Break one bread, which is the medicine of immortality, our antidote against death that we might have the assurance of living in Jesus Christ for ever.

Ignatius of Antioch, *Letter to the Ephesians* chapter 29-30

Christ dying and drawing sinners to Himself

When our wickedness had reached its height, and its wages - punishment and death - were clearly hanging over us, the time arrived which God had appointed beforehand, for Him to manifest His own kindness and power. He revealed how His love had such an overwhelming regard for the human race, and that He did not hate us or thrust us away or remember our sins against us, but showed great longsuffering and patience with us. He Himself took upon Himself the burden of our transgressions; He gave His own Son as a ransom for us, the Holy One for sinners, the Blameless One for the wicked, the Righteous One for the unrighteous, the Incorruptible One for the corruptible, the Immortal One for mortals. For what else could cover our sins except His righteousness? Who else could justify wicked and ungodly people like us, except the only Son of God? O sweet exchange! O unsearchable work! O blessings that surpass all expectation! The wickedness of the many has been swallowed up in a single Righteous One; the righteousness of One has justified a multitude of transgressors! Even before Christ came, God showed us that our nature was incapable of achieving life. Now, having revealed the Saviour, Who is able to save what could not previously be saved, God has willed by these truths to persuade us to trust in His kindness, and to reckon Him as our Nourisher, Father, Teacher, Counsellor and Healer, our Wisdom, Light, Honour, Glory, Power and Life, so that we should have no anxiety about mere food and clothing.

If you desire to possess this faith, you too must receive above all things the knowledge of the Father. For God loves the human race. It was for us that He made the world, and made everything in it subject to us. He gave us reason and understanding. To us alone He granted the privilege of looking upwards to Him, creating us in His own image. And to us He has sent His only-begotten Son, and has promised us a heavenly kingdom, which He will give to all who love Him. When you have attained this knowledge, you will be filled with joy unspeakable. How will you be able to love enough the One Who has first so loved you?

The Letter to Diognetus, chapters 9-10

The Son is greater than the sun

At first, God gave the sun to be worshipped, as Scripture says (**Deuteronomy 4:19**), but you never see anyone going so far as to suffer death for his faith in the sun. However, people of every race have suffered and are still suffering through the name of Jesus, preferring to undergo any harsh treatment rather than deny Him. For the Logos of truth and wisdom is more fiery and bright than the powers of the sun; He enters into the depths of the heart and mind. This is why Scripture says, "His name shall rise above the sun"

(Psalm 72:17).... He was so bright and powerful at His first coming, though He came in humbleness and ugliness and contempt, that He has received recognition among every race; in people of all tribes He calls forth repentance from their previous sinful way of life. The demons are subject to His name, and all the principalities and powers are more afraid of this Man's name than of anyone else's in the past. And when He comes again in glory, will He not totally destroy all who hate Him, and all who have wrongly deserted Him, but give rest to His own people and grant them all the things they have been longing for? To us, then, it has been given to listen, to understand, and to be saved through this Christ, and to know all the purpose of the Father.

Justin Martyr, *Dialogue with Trypho*, chapter 121

Gloria in excelsis

Glory to God in the highest,
and on earth peace and good-will to mankind!
We praise You, we bless You, we worship You;
we glorify You, we give You thanks for Your great glory,
O Lord God, heavenly King,
God the Father almighty!
O Lord God, Lamb of God, Son of the Father,
You Who take away the sins of the world,
have mercy on us:
You Who take away the sins of the world,
have mercy on us!
You Who take away the sins of the world,
accept our prayer:
You Who sit at the right hand of God the Father,
have mercy on us!
For You alone are holy,
You alone are the Lord;
You alone, O Christ, together with the Holy Spirit,
are Most High in the glory of God the Father.

(One of the earliest Christian hymns)

Christians on trial: The letter of Pliny, governor of Bithynia, to emperor Trajan

This is how I have dealt with people accused of being Christians. I asked them if they were Christians; if they confessed, I asked them a second and a third time, threatening them with punishment. If they continued to confess their faith, I ordered them to be put to death. For I reckoned that whatever it was they were confessing, I ought to punish them anyway for their obstinacy and unbending perversity. Others were guilty of the same insanity, but they were Roman citizens, so I ordered them to be sent to Rome....

As for those who claimed they were not Christians, and never had been, I thought I should let them go. They said a prayer to the gods which I ordered them to recite, and offered worship before your statue [the statue of Trajan] with offerings of incense and wine, which I had ordered to brought into the court, along with images of the gods. They even cursed Christ. People say that real Christians cannot be made to do such things....

The accused held that their only crime or error had been this: On a certain day they used to gather before sunrise and recite, by turns, a liturgy to Christ as to a god; they bound themselves by an oath, not for criminal purposes, but swearing not to commit theft, robbery, or adultery, never to break their promises, and always to return property entrusted to them when it was demanded.... I thought I should find out more about the truth of this, by torturing two female servants who were called "deaconesses". But I discovered nothing else than a perverted and wild superstition. So I adjourned the case and referred it to you. The question seemed to me to deserve consideration, especially since so many are threatened; for many people, of every age and rank, both men and women, are in danger now and in the future of embracing this superstition. Its infection has penetrated both cities and villages and the countryside....

Pliny's *Letters to Trajan*, Letter 10

An early Church prayer for setting apart a deaconess

Eternal God, Father of our Lord Jesus Christ, Creator of man and of woman, You Who filled Miriam, Deborah, Hannah and Huldah with Your Spirit, and graciously granted to a woman the birth of Your only-begotten Son, and placed female keepers of Your holy gates in the tabernacle of testimony and in the temple: look down now also on this Your handmaid who is to be ordained to the office of deaconess, and bestow on her the Holy Spirit, cleansing her from all filthiness of flesh and spirit, that she may worthily carry out the work committed to her, to Your glory, and the praise of Your Christ, with Whom be glory and adoration to You and the Holy Spirit for ever. Amen.

From *The Apostolic Constitutions*, Book 8, chapter 19

Chapter 4.

GNOSTICS, CATHOLICS AND MONTANISTS

1. The Gnostics.

One of the most serious spiritual threats the Christian Church has ever faced arose in the middle of the 2nd Century, around AD 130-60 (roughly in the lifetime of Justin Martyr). This was the *Gnostic* movement.[1] The dangerous and divisive thing about the Gnostics was their claim that they, not the Church, were the true Christians. This created a crisis of identity for the Christian faith, and great confusion among pagans about who the real Christians actually were.

Historians argue about the origins of Gnosticism. To some extent, it may have been a movement which began before the birth of Christianity. In the New Testament we find the apostles Paul and John condemning certain Gnostic ideas (*e.g.* in **Colossians 2** and throughout **1 John**). Still, it was not until the 2nd Century that the movement became widespread and a serious menace to the life of the Church. The early Church fathers all agreed that Simon the Magician (**Acts 8:9-24**) was the source of the alternative Gnostic version of Christianity. In fact, until recently, we were completely reliant on what the Church fathers said for our understanding of Gnosticism. However, in 1945, an Arab peasant of Nag Hammadi (in Egypt) discovered a large earthenware jar buried on a mountain, containing an important collection of ancient Gnostic documents, which enable us to see from the Gnostics' own writings what they believed.

---

[1] Gnostic is pronounced "Noss-tik" - the "g" is silent.

When we speak of "Gnosticism" or a "Gnostic movement", we must not think of one single united organisation or philosophy. There was a huge and astonishing variety of different Gnostic groups: Barbelonites, Cainites, Cerinthians, Encratites, Justinians, Marcionites, Marcosians, Nicolaitans, Ophites, Sethians, Severians and Valentinians, to name a few. However, they shared a number of basic beliefs in common. They all claimed that they possessed a special knowledge or *gnosis*[2] (Greek for "knowledge") of spiritual truth which was not available to the ordinary Christian. Jesus had privately taught this secret knowledge to His apostles, they said, and it had been passed on and handed down to the Gnostics. It was impossible, Gnostics argued, to understand the Gospel correctly without this secret knowledge, and the various Gnostic sects had their own Scriptures containing their version of the *gnosis*. The most famous Gnostic Scripture is the *Gospel of Thomas*, part of the Nag Hammadi collection; it was probably written in Syria in about AD 140, and records over a hundred alleged sayings of Jesus.

Based on this secret knowledge, the great Gnostic leaders created vast schemes of philosophy and theology, which (they claimed) answered all the vital questions of human existence. The secret knowledge or *gnosis* of the Gnostics was concerned with the true way of salvation. According to Gnostics, the whole physical world of space, time and matter was evil - all Gnostics were Docetic.[3] The material world, Gnostics taught, had not been created by the supreme God, but by an inferior and foolish being called the *Demiurge* (Greek for "architect"). They identified the Demiurge with the God of the Old Testament, and therefore regarded the Old Testament as an evil and unspiritual book. The supreme God and the physical universe were completely alien to each other. The human body was part of this evil material world; salvation meant escaping from the body, and from the world of space and time in which the body holds us prisoner (there was no place for a physical resurrection in the Gnostic scheme). Gnostics had a totally negative attitude to all physical activities, particularly sex which they abstained from. The only thing

---

2   *Gnosis* is pronounced "Noh-siss".
3   See previous Chapter, section 2 for Docetism, under the heading **Church teaching**.

of any value was the soul, which was a divine spark from the spiritual world, trapped inside the body by the wicked Demiurge.

If Gnostics rejected the Old Testament and Judaism, they had a more positive attitude to Christianity. They made use of some New Testament books, especially **John's Gospel**, alongside their own Scriptures. Christianity, they said, teaches how the supreme God sent Christ into the world to save a special group of elect souls from the tyranny of the Demiurge and from the misery of existing in the world of space, time and matter. Christ was not God in person, but one of an exalted rank of spiritual beings called *aeons*; Christ was the greatest of these beings. Since physical matter was evil, Christ the Redeemer could have had no contact with it. Some Gnostics taught that the Christ descended on the man Jesus at His baptism, possessed Him, spoke through Him, and left Him at His crucifixion; others taught that Jesus was not a human being at all - He only *seemed* to have a body of flesh, but in reality He was a purely spiritual, heavenly being. Gnostics interpreted Christ as the "Heavenly Revealer" Who had come down from the spirit-world to give the elect the true knowledge of the way home. For Gnostics, humanity's great problem was not sin; the problem was our *ignorance* of our true spiritual nature and destiny. Christ solved this problem by giving us back the lost knowledge of who and what we really are, and where we belong.

In order to return to the supreme God and reach the heavenly homeland of beauty and light, the soul (according to Gnostics) had to travel after death through the spiritual realms above this physical earth, and these realms were controlled by hostile demonic stars and planets. To make the journey safely, the soul needed to possess the secret knowledge of the Gnostics. Some Gnostics viewed this knowledge in a very crude way as a series of magic passwords or spells; others saw it in a more philosophical way, as an inner awakening of the soul, an enlightenment about one's true spiritual identity and the way back to the spiritual homeland of heaven.[4]

---

4 The modern "New Age" movement has many similarities with Gnosticism, and often makes use of Gnostic sources.

There were various Gnostic leaders teaching different types of Gnosticism. Two of the most important were *Basilides*, who taught in Alexandria during the reign of the emperor Hadrian (AD 117-38), and *Valentinus* who taught in Rome from about AD 137 to 154. However, the most outstanding Gnostic leader was *Marcion*.[5] He was the son of the bishop of Sinope in Asia Minor. A wealthy shipowner, Marcion lived in Rome from AD 140 to 155, where he broke away from the Church and established a new form of Gnosticism. Unlike other Gnostic sects, which tended to be local and provincial in extent, Marcionites were a worldwide group; by the time of Marcion's death in about AD 160, they had spread all over the Empire as a sort of alternative Church, with their own bishops and presbyters. Marcionites were persecuted and martyred by the Roman authorities, who did not distinguish between different groups who claimed the name of "Christian". Orthodox Christians and Marcionites could find themselves in the same prison cell, awaiting death for their faith, but the orthodox disowned the Marcionites, calling them "Satan's martyrs".

Marcion's teaching was much less strange and complicated than that of most Gnostics. He did not speculate wildly about angels, aeons and the origin of the universe in the way that Basilides and Valentinus did. In his more sober form of Gnosticism, Marcion taught that the Old and New Testaments were in total opposition to each other. The Old Testament God was the Demiurge, a cruel and unloving Being, and Judaism was an evil religion, a religion of law and works and self-righteousness. The New Testament, by contrast, was the book of the supreme God, the heavenly Father revealed by Jesus Christ, and it taught a totally different religion of grace and faith and freedom. Marcion wrote a book called *Antitheses* in which he set out the contradictions between Old and New Testaments (as he interpreted them), in order to prove that the God of Judaism was not the heavenly Father of Jesus Christ. Marcion also produced his own version of the New Testament. He threw out everything that had a Jewish element, accepting only Luke's Gospel and most of Paul's letters. According to Marcion, Paul was the only apostle who had really understood Jesus. However, Marcion had to remove even

---

5   Marcion is pronounced "Mar-see-un".

from Luke and Paul all favourable references to Judaism. In common with other Gnostics, Marcion was Docetic; he taught that the world of space, time and matter was evil, and he was very hostile to sex and marriage. The very thought of sexual reproduction seems to have made Marcion feel sick.

Marcion became the supreme heretic in the eyes of the early Church. This was unfortunate in one sense, because in reacting against Marcion the Church may also have reacted against some true elements in his teaching, such as his emphasis on grace and faith. At any rate, his sect had a long life; it died out only in the 6th Century.

2. The response to the Gnostics: Irenaeus and early Catholicism.

The response of the Church to Gnosticism can be seen best in the writings of *Irenaeus of Lyons*.[6] Irenaeus was the first great Christian theologian of the patristic age. He was a Greek, born into a Christian family in Asia Minor early in the 2nd Century. As a boy Irenaeus was taught by the bishop of Smyrna, Polycarp, who as a young man had known the apostle John.[7] Polycarp's chief delight in his old age was to recount all the conversations he had had with John. Through bishop Polycarp, then, Irenaeus and the apostle John were closely linked: John taught Polycarp, Polycarp taught Irenaeus. Here is Irenaeus's account of Polycarp:

> "I can tell the very place in which the blessed Polycarp used to sit when he preached his sermons, how he came in and went out, the manner of his life, what he looked like, the sermons he delivered to the people, and how he used to report his association with John and the others who had seen the Lord, how he would relate their words, and the things concerning the Lord he had heard from them, about His miracles and teachings. Polycarp had received all this from eyewitnesses of the Word of life, and related all these things in accordance with the Scriptures. I listened eagerly to these things at the time, by God's mercy which was bestowed on me, and I made

---

6 Irenaeus is pronounced "I-ra-nay-uss".
7 See previous Chapter, section 1, for the letter of Polycarp.

notes of them, not on paper, but in my heart, and constantly by
the grace of God I meditate on them faithfully."

Polycarp died as a martyr in AD 156. The eyewitness account of his
martyrdom is one of the most famous that has come down to us from
the early Church. "Renounce Christ," demanded the Roman
governor. "For 86 years I have been His servant," Polycarp replied,
"and He has never done me any wrong. How can I blaspheme my
King and my Saviour?" Polycarp was then tied to a wooden stake
and put to death.

Irenaeus moved to Lyons in southern France as a young man. Lyons
was the capital of Roman France; founded by the Romans in 43 BC,
by Irenaeus's time it had become a large prosperous city, thronged
by merchants from every part of the Empire. The churches of
southern France had been planted by Christians from Asia Minor, so
a bond existed between Irenaeus's homeland and Lyons. The bishop
of the church in Lyons at this point, a man called *Pothinus*, was
himself a native of Asia Minor, and Irenaeus became one of his
presbyters. In AD 177, a storm of fierce persecution swept over the
churches in Lyons and Vienne; many Christians perished, including
bishop Pothinus (see previous Chapter, section 3, for an eyewitness
account of the persecution). Irenaeus was probably away in Rome
at the time, and so escaped the ordeal. When he returned to Lyons
he was elected bishop in place of the martyred Pothinus. Irenaeus
remained bishop of Lyons until his own death in about AD 200.

Irenaeus stands out as the most important Church father of the 2nd
Century. This is because he wrote against the Gnostics a lengthy
book usually known as *Against Heresies* (its longer title is *A
Refutation and Overthrow of Knowledge Falsely So-called*).
The book has survived, mostly in a Latin translation, and come down
to us today completely intact. It is priceless for what it tells us about
the beliefs of Christians in the 2nd Century and about the Gnostic
movement. Irenaeus also wrote a smaller work against the Gnostics
called *Proof of the Apostolic Preaching*.

We learn several things about Irenaeus from his anti-Gnostic
writings. He was well-educated, and knew both Greek philosophy
and Greek poetry. He had a thorough knowledge of the Old

Testament, and was familiar with most of the documents which we know as the New Testament (**Hebrews, James, 2 Peter** and **Jude** are the only books Irenaeus does not mention). He displays an astonishing knowledge of the various Gnostic sects and their teachings. There may have been a personal factor in Irenaeus's anti-Gnostic crusade: he had a friend called Florinus with whom he had grown up in Smyrna, both having been taught by Polycarp. In adult life, Florinus had renounced orthodox Christianity and become a follower of the great Gnostic leader Valentinus. Irenaeus addressed a long letter to Florinus, pleading with him to return to the true faith (unsuccessfully, as far as we know), and Valentinus is the Gnostic teacher whom Irenaeus chiefly attacks in the *Against Heresies*.

Irenaeus's argument against Gnosticism can be summed up as follows:

(i) He set forth in detail the doctrines of the different Gnostic sects. He felt that simply to describe them would show how ridiculous, unreasonable and unworthy of belief they were.

(ii) He argued against the Gnostics' claim that they had a special secret knowledge passed on from Jesus and the apostles. He pointed out that none of the Gnostic sects agreed with each other about what exactly this secret knowledge was! On top of this, Irenaeus also argued that there were many churches which the apostles had actually founded, or where the apostles had ministered. Yet none of these apostolic churches knew anything about a so-called secret knowledge. On the contrary, they all taught the same orthodox Gospel, which contradicted Gnostic beliefs. This line of defence, arguing from apostolic churches to the truth of the Gospel they taught, slid over very easily into the doctrine of apostolic succession (see previous Chapter, section 2, under **Church organisation**). In Irenaeus, however, it was more a case of the bishop deriving his importance from belonging to an apostolic church, rather than a church being a true church because it had an apostolic bishop.

(iii) He demonstrated by careful argument from the Bible that the God of the Old Testament, and the God of the New Testament, are the same God, and that the Creator of the universe is not some inferior "Demiurge" but the heavenly Father of Jesus Christ.

Irenaeus also argued that salvation did not come through any secret knowledge, but through the life and death of Christ. Irenaeus interpreted Christ as the Second Adam, Who by His perfect obedience had reversed and cancelled the disobedience of the first Adam.

(iv) He defended the goodness of creation: it was not the evil product of a Demiurge, but the noble workmanship of the heavenly Father. He also affirmed against Gnostic Docetism that Christ really took flesh, became a real man, really died and really rose again.

The response of Irenaeus and the early Church to Gnosticism had a great effect on the way the Christian faith developed in the patristic age. It prompted the Church to place a strong emphasis on *apostolic tradition* - the teaching of the apostles which had been handed down in those churches where the apostles themselves had been active. We can see this stress on apostolic tradition in three areas:

(i) Against the doctrines of the Gnostics, the Church pointed to its *rule of faith*. Each church had its own version of this rule, but they all taught more or less the same thing. The rule of faith was a summary of apostolic teaching; the version used in the Roman church developed into what has become well-known in the Western world as *the Apostles' Creed*:

I believe in God,
the Father Almighty,
Creator of heaven and earth.
And in Jesus Christ,
His only Son,
our Lord,
Who was born of the virgin Mary,
suffered under Pontius Pilate,
was crucified,
died and was buried.
On the third day He rose again.
He ascended into heaven
and is seated at the right hand of God the Father Almighty,
from where He will come again
to judge the living and the dead.

I believe in the Holy Spirit,
the holy Catholic Church,
the forgiveness of sins,
the resurrection of the dead,
and the life everlasting.[8]

(ii) There was also an emphasis on the churches which the apostles themselves had founded, or with which they had been historically connected. These churches, it was argued, were the guardians of the true apostolic faith, and they knew nothing of the so-called secret knowledge of the Gnostics. Yet surely it would have been to the leaders of these churches that the apostles would have revealed this secret knowledge, if it really existed. This emphasis on apostolic churches was the main reason why the Roman church and its bishop became so important in the Western half of the Empire. There was a good number of apostolic churches in the East; but only one church in the West could claim to have any connection with the ministry of the apostles - the church in Rome, where both Peter and Paul had taught. Christians in the West, therefore, tended to look to Rome for spiritual leadership. And throughout the doctrinal controversies of the early Church period, the Roman church had a remarkable record for being on the right, orthodox side. We see here the beginnings of the process by which the bishop of Rome eventually came to dominate all the other bishops and churches in the West. The process took four or five centuries to develop fully; in Irenaeus's day, the bishop of Rome was simply the "first among equals", entitled to a position of paramount respect, but not yet an absolute ruler of the Western Church.

(iii) There was a deep concern to preserve the writings of the apostles - the New Testament Scriptures, and to make sure that the

---

8   In the 5th Century another phrase, "He descended into Hades," was added after "died and was buried", but a number of great Western theologians rejected this addition. The Greek word Hades is often translated "hell" in English versions of the Creed - "He descended into hell." It really has a wider meaning, referring to "the spirit world", "the realm of departed souls". After death, Christ's human soul or spirit went into the spirit world. However it did not go into hell, but into paradise (**Luke 23:43**).

Church accepted only genuine apostolic Scriptures. The early Church had to guard against Marcion throwing out authentic Scriptures, and the other Gnostics adding on their own false Scriptures. The criterion by which the Church judged and accepted a writing as authoritative was its connection with the apostles. If it had been written or dictated by an apostle (*e.g.* Paul, John, Peter, Matthew), or by someone under apostolic direction (*e.g.* Mark, who wrote under Peter's direction, and Luke, who wrote under Paul's), it was regarded as "Scripture". The idea developed of seeing the collected writings of the apostles as a "New Testament" alongside the Old. Most of the books in our present-day New Testament were accepted in Irenaeus's time; debate lasted for several centuries, however, over **Hebrews, James, 2 Peter, Jude, 2** and **3 John**, and **Revelation**. By the 4th Century the Church had reached a consensus that these books, too, were genuine Scripture. In the East, the *39th Festal Letter* of Athanasius, bishop of Alexandria, written in AD 367, contained an authoritative list of New Testament books, corresponding to the New Testament we know today.[9] In the West, a Church council at Carthage in AD 397 agreed on the same list of authentic New Testament books. This list was called the "canon" of the New Testament, from the Greek word for "rule" or "standard".[10]

The Church acquired a new name for itself from the Gnostic controversy. It called itself the *Catholic* Church - as in the Apostles' Creed, "I believe in the holy Catholic church." It is essential not to confuse *Catholic* with *Roman Catholic*. We give the title "Roman Catholic" to that branch of the Western Church which, in the 16th Century, rejected the Protestant Reformation. It was only at that point in history that what we today think of as "Roman Catholicism" really came into being, as Rome defined its theology and practice much more clearly in opposition to Protestant views.[11] In contrast to this later term *Roman* Catholic, the early Church in both East and West called itself simply *Catholic*. The word comes from the Greek

---

9   For Athanasius, see Chapter 8, sections 2 and 3.
10 The list of authentic Old Testament books is called the canon of the Old Testament - see Chapter 9, section 2. The complete list of the authentic books of both Testaments is the "canon of Scripture".
11 We could also say that the Western Church became "Roman Catholic"

(cont.)

katholikos, which means "universal" or "throughout the world". By calling itself Catholic, the early Church was setting itself apart from Gnosticism. The different Gnostic sects had no unity - they all taught conflicting doctrines; but the true Church, founded on the faith of the apostles, taught the same doctrines "throughout the world". So the early Christians called themselves Catholics to express the unity of their common faith, and to distinguish themselves from Gnostics and other deviant groups.

The result of the Gnostic controversy was that the early Church developed a number of special features: an emphasis on orthodoxy, unity, tightly controlled church organisation and discipline, and the importance of standing in the line of apostolic tradition (which developed into the doctrine of apostolic succession). These features gave the early Church its unique identity as the Catholic Church.

3. The Montanists.

The crisis of identity created by the Gnostics about who were the true Christians was made even sharper by the rise of another movement called Montanism. *Montanus*, a young convert to Christianity, came on the scene in the region of Asia Minor known as Phrygia in about AD 170, when he started to prophesy. He was joined by two prophetesses, *Priscilla* and *Maximilla*. They claimed that the Holy Spirit (or the "Paraclete", as they preferred to call Him) was speaking in a new way to the Church directly through them, and that this was the fulfilment of Christ's promise in **John 14:16**, "I will pray to the Father, and He will give you another Helper [in Greek,

---

in 1054, through the great East-West schism, when the West broke fellowship with all Eastern Christians (see Part Two, Chapter 3, section 8). However, it could be very misleading for Protestants to think of the Western Church as "Roman Catholic" between the schism of 1054 and the Reformation which began in 1517. In Protestant thinking, the term "Roman Catholic" has acquired an anti-Protestant meaning. It is therefore better to think of the Western Church as "Western Catholic" rather than "Roman Catholic" after 1054 but before the Protestant Reformation. The Protestants of the 16th Century claimed still to be true Western Catholics, but not Roman Catholics. For the Reformation, see Part Three.

Paracletos], that He may abide with you for ever," and **John 16:12-13**, "I still have many things to say to you, but you cannot bear them now. However, when He, the Spirit of Truth, has come, He will guide you into all truth." The Paraclete, the Spirit of Truth, had now come to the Church in Montanus, Priscilla and Maximilla (they claimed), and was now leading believers into the promised fulness of truth. Montanists referred to their movement as "the New Prophecy".

In fact, the Montanist prophets offered no new doctrinal revelations. Their main message was the nearness of the second coming of Christ; as Maximilla prophesied, "After me, there will be no more prophecy, but the End." In the light of this imminent return of the Lord, Montanists taught a severe moral code: among the distinctive teachings of the New Prophecy were an absolute ban on second marriages in all circumstances, an obligation to frequent fasting and "xerophagies" (eating only dried food), the veiling of virgins, the rejection of forgiveness for serious sins committed after baptism, and commands from the Paraclete that Christians must never seek to escape persecution and martyrdom but embrace them eagerly. It was in this area of ethical behaviour, rather than theological doctrine, that Montanism produced "new revelations". As the great North African theologian, Tertullian (see next Chapter, section 2), a convert to Montanism, put it:

> "Righteousness was at first in a primitive state, with only a natural fear of God. From that stage, it progressed through the Law and the Prophets to its infancy. Then it passed through the Gospel to the enthusiasm of youth. Now, through the Paraclete, it is settling into maturity."

Visions, revelatory dreams, speaking in tongues, prophetic utterances of prediction and of divine comfort and rebuke, and other extraordinary religious experiences also abounded among the Montanists. They renamed their community of Pepuza in Phrygia "Jerusalem". They may have believed Pepuza to be the spot where Christ would descend from heaven and reign over the earth; but it seems more likely that they renamed it "Jerusalem" simply to make the point that Pepuza was a holy community, the dwelling place of the Paraclete in Montanus, Priscilla and Maximilla - a *spiritual* Jerusalem.

Montanism spread in many parts of Asia Minor, and took root in Italy, France and North Africa. In Carthage it won the support of the great Tertullian. Irenaeus, who was not a Montanist, still advised bishop Eleutherus of Rome (AD 182-89) to take a moderate, gentle attitude towards Montanists, to try to keep them within the Church as loyal Catholics. However, the Catholic Church as a whole rejected Montanism very decisively. The New Prophecy had formidable enemies, notably the apologist Claudius Apollinarius, bishop of Hierapolis in Phrygia, Asia Minor (where Montanism flourished most widely); another apologist named Miltiades (also from Asia Minor); the Christian philosopher and martyr, Apollonius; bishop Serapion of Antioch (died 211); the great Egyptian theologian, Clement of Alexandria (see next Chapter, section 1); the distinguished Roman theologian and martyr, Hippolytus;[12] and many others. Opponents of Montanism always referred to Montanists as "the Phrygians", after their place of spiritual origin. In Asia Minor, the Church excommunicated[13] all Montanists in a series of local councils of bishops — the first such councils we know of in Church history. In spite of Irenaeus's advice, Montanism was condemned in Rome as well, which sealed its fate in the West. Forced out of the Catholic Church in both Eastern and Western parts of the Empire, the Montanists lived a separate Church life of their own, surviving until the 5th Century in Africa and the 6th Century in Phrygia. They were finally persecuted out of existence, not by pagan emperors, but by Catholic ones after Christianity had become the Empire's established religion.

Montanism was the first manifestation of a particular form of Christianity which has appeared several times in the course of Church history; today it would be called "Pentecostal" or "charismatic". Many modern Pentecostals and charismatics look back to the Montanists as their spiritual ancestors. However, there are differences. Not many of today's Pentecostals and charismatics would share the Montanists' enthusiasm for fasting, celibacy and

---

12 For Hippolytus, see previous Chapter, section 2, under **Church worship**.

13 "Excommunicated" means "cut off from communion" - refused admission to the Lord's table. In the early Church, this act of discipline was equivalent to putting someone "out of the Church", stripping them of Church membership and all Christian privileges.

martyrdom; yet these were essential to Montanism, part of the New Prophecy's revelation of how true Christians were to live in the light of Christ's imminent return. And despite the Montanist emphasis on prophecy and vision, there is no evidence that Montanism taught a special "baptism in the Spirit" as a distinct second experience for all believers.

The rise of Montanism forces us to ask important historical questions about the supernatural gifts of the Holy Spirit in the age of the apostles (prophecy, tongues, miraculous healing), and whether they continued in the Church after the 1st Century AD. The evidence suggests that these gifts did continue in the Church, but that they were far less common in the 2nd Century. Montanism seems to have come as a fresh outburst of the supernatural; it would probably not have created the sensation it obviously did create, if these spiritual phenomena had been part of "the normal Christian life" among believers. The great Alexandrian theologian, Origen,[14] who was born in AD 185 and brought up in a Christian family, stated the case thus:

"There were signs of the Holy Spirit at the beginning of Christ's teaching. Immediately after He ascended into heaven, He showed forth more of these signs; but afterwards there were not so many. Still, even now there are traces of them among a few who have had their souls purified by the Gospel."

The "father of Church history", Eusebius of Caesarea,[15] writing in the early 4th Century AD, referred back to the early years of the 2nd Century AD in these terms:

"Even at that late date, many miraculous powers of the divine Spirit worked through the evangelists of the Church, so that - the first time they heard the Gospel - entire communities embraced with whole-hearted enthusiasm the worship of the Creator of the universe."

---

14 For Origen see next Chapter, section 1.
15 For Eusebius of Caesarea, see Chapter 7, section 1.

So Eusebius thought it was rather late in the day for "miraculous powers" to be still operating as a normal occurrence through the Church's evangelists at the start of the 2nd Century AD. Irenaeus, though, writing towards the end of the 2nd Century, testified:

> "We hear of many members of the Church who have prophetic gifts, speak by the Spirit in all kinds of tongues, bring men's secret thoughts to light for their own good, and expound the mysteries of God."

This makes the continuance of supernatural gifts a little later than Eusebius seemed to suggest. Even so, the way Irenaeus speaks in this passage hints that these gifts were not actually present in his own personal experience or his church at Lyons. Irenaeus does not say, "I myself speak in tongues," or, "In my church I have prophets"; he says rather more vaguely, "We hear of many who...." Eusebius's comment on Irenaeus's testimony was certainly very cautious and guarded: "Irenaeus makes it clear that even down to his own time, manifestations of divine and miraculous power had continued in *some* of the churches."(Eusebius does not consider the possibility that Irenaeus may be referring in this passage to Montanist "gifts".) It seems safe to conclude, then, that not long after the age of the apostles, the supernatural gifts of the Spirit probably ceased to be part of the ordinary life of the average church; there were still "traces of them [signs and wonders] among a few", as Origen said, but already by his time (early 3rd Century) Christians were looking back to the 1st Century AD as the great period of extraordinary spiritual gifts. This at least would explain why Montanism aroused such enthusiasm among those who believed in its divine origin; they saw it as a *fresh* outpouring of the Spirit. More than this, they interpreted it as a sign of the nearness of the Lord's return, which of course added to the excitement.[16]

---

[16] The belief in miracles as an ongoing feature of the Catholic Church's life began to become popular in the 4th Century and thereafter. These miracles were often associated with relics and the intercession of the saints in heaven. For relics and the intercession of saints, see Chapter 7, section 3, under **Church worship**.

Yet as we have seen, the Catholic Church condemned and excommunicated the Montanists. Why? The following reasons have been suggested:

(i) Broadly speaking, ordinary Christians were highly suspicious of the Montanists' prophecies, visions, speaking in tongues, cult of martyrdom, and general state of religious intensity and enthusiasm. To Catholics, Montanists seemed like spiritual drunkards. (To Montanists, no doubt, Catholics seemed like spiritual corpses.)

(ii) The claim of Montanus, Priscilla and Maximilla to be indwelt by the Paraclete in fulfilment of **John 14:16** and **16:12-13** raised serious problems. Should the Catholic Church accept the exalted status which this claim bestowed on Montanus? Here was a simple question of truth and falsehood: Montanus was either the special organ of the Paraclete, as he asserted, or he was not. Catholics decided he was not, and that his interpretation of Christ's teaching on the Paraclete in **John's Gospel** was both false and self-serving. (The Catholic view was that these verses had been fulfilled on the day of Pentecost.) Again, the various Montanist prophecies, and the authority claimed for them, seemed to conflict with the authority of the apostolic Scriptures which the Church was then collecting into the New Testament. How could the apostolic writings be the final rule for Christian beliefs and practices, if the Montanist prophecies were genuine, with their new revelations about how Christians were to live? And why should bishops devoted to maintaining the apostolic tradition be so important in Church life, if the Holy Spirit Himself was present in His Montanist prophets to lead and guide? Finally, arising out of all this, Montanism created division and controversy at the very time when the early Catholic Church and its bishops were striving for unity and stability against the Gnostics. In all these ways, we can see that there was a deep-seated clash between the claims of the New Prophecy and the growing concerns of the Catholic Church.

(iii) Many of the Montanist prophecies did not come true. For example, we remember that Maximilla prophesied, "After me, there will be no more prophecy, but the End." Maximilla died in about AD 179 and the End did not come. Such things weakened the credibility of all Montanist prophets and their utterances.

(iv) The Catholic Church fathers criticised the way that Montanist prophets were supposedly taken over by the Holy Spirit when they prophesied. For example, one unnamed Catholic leader condemned Montanist prophets for going into trances and speaking "in a state of unnatural ecstasy, after which all restraint is thrown to the winds". This experience of possession, in which the prophet lost self-control, was not how the Holy Spirit worked, he argued; it "conflicted with the practice of the Church handed down generation by generation from the beginning".[17] The Holy Spirit never bypassed or short-circuited the mind.

(v) The Montanists condemned other Christians as "unspiritual" if they would not embrace the New Prophecy, calling Catholics "prophet-killers" for their refusal to accept Montanist prophets as genuine. Montanists habitually referred to themselves as "the spiritual people", and to Catholics as "the carnal people". So it was very difficult for Catholic Christians to get on with Montanists.

(vi) Some Montanists fell into the "Sabellian" heresy, which taught that Father, Son and Holy Spirit were not three distinct persons, but only one person acting in three different ways.[18] The majority of Montanists were in fact orthodox in their doctrine of the Trinity; their greatest theologian, Tertullian, was an ardent foe of Sabellianism, and the fierce Roman enemy of Montanism, Praxeas, was a Sabellian himself![19] However unfairly, though, the Sabellianism of the minority of Montanists gave their opponents a perfect

---

17 See the fuller quotation at the end of the Chapter. The Catholic Church fathers, it should be said, did not deny that the Holy Spirit might occasionally bestow a genuine gift of prophecy on an outstandingly holy believer, in the "lesser" sense of prophecy - predicting future events, supernatural insight into someone's character or past life, *etc.* (but not new revelations about doctrine or moral conduct). What the Catholic fathers utterly denied was the truly prophetic nature of Montanist utterances, ecstasies, and new moral revelations.

18 For the Sabellian doctrine of the Trinity, see next Chapter, section 1, and the discussion of Origen's theology. The denial that God is three distinct persons is also found in present-day "Oneness Pentecostalism".

19 For Praxeas, see next Chapter, section 2 on Tertullian, who wrote against Praxeas.

opportunity to brand the whole movement as heretical in its doctrine of God.

Probably all these factors contributed to the Church's rejection of Montanism. Some think that this robbed the early Church of much of its spiritual vitality, but it is hard to see what else Catholic Christians could have done apart from bowing to Montanist claims.

Important people:

The Church
Pothinus (died 177)
Irenaeus of Lyons (active AD 175-95)
Montanus (active AD 170 onwards)
Priscilla (late 2nd century)
Maximilla (died AD 179)

Others
Gnostic leaders:
Basilides (active AD 117-38)
Valentinus (active AD 137-54)
Marcion (active AD 140-60)

Christ, true God and true man, restores fellowship between God and mankind

As He, our Lord Jesus Christ, is our only true Master, so He is truly the good and suffering Son of God, the Word of God the Father, Who became the Son of Man. For He fought and He conquered. He battled as man on behalf of His brothers, and through His obedience He cancelled our disobedience. He bound the strong enemy and set free the weak, giving salvation to those He created by abolishing sin. For He is our most holy Lord, the merciful lover of the human race.

He united humanity to God, as we have said. It had to be as a human being that He overcame humanity's enemy, otherwise the enemy would not have been overcome with justice. But He had to be God in order to bestow salvation, otherwise we would not have it as a secure possession. And if He had not united in Himself humanity with God, human beings could not have shared in immortality. For the Mediator between God and humanity had to bring both parties into friendship and harmony through His kinship with both. He had to present humanity to God, and reveal God to humanity. How else could we share in being adopted as God's sons, unless through the

Son we had received fellowship with the Father - unless the Word of God, Who became flesh, had entered into fellowship with us?....

He Who was to destroy sin and redeem humanity from guilt had to enter into the very condition of humanity, which had been dragged into slavery and was held fast by death. He had to be human so that death might be slain by a human, and so that human beings might go forth from the bondage of death. For as through the disobedience of one man - the first man, fashioned out of virgin soil - the many were made sinners, so it was necessary that through the obedience of one man - the first man to be born of a virgin - the many should be justified and receive salvation.

Irenaeus, *Against Heresies*, Book 3, Chapter 18, sections 6-7

Our Lord Jesus Christ, out of His boundless love, became what we are, that He might make us what He Himself is.

Irenaeus, *Against Heresies*, Book 5, Preface

Mary - the new Eve

Mary the virgin is found obedient, saying, "Behold the handmaid of the Lord".... But Eve was disobedient. She did not obey, even though she was still a virgin. For Eve had Adam indeed as a husband, yet still being a virgin she became disobedient and thus made herself into the cause of death, both for herself and for the entire human race. And Mary also had a husband appointed for her, but while she was still a virgin, she by her obedience became the cause of salvation, both for herself and the entire human race.... Thus Mary's obedience dissolved the knot of Eve's disobedience; for what the virgin Eve had tied up by unbelief, the virgin Mary unloosed by faith.... Just as Eve was seduced by the word of an angel [Satan] so that she fled from God, having disobeyed His Word, so Mary received good news by the word of an angel, so that she might give birth to God in obeying His Word. And if Eve disobeyed God, Mary was persuaded to be obedient to Him, so that the virgin Mary might become an intercessor for the virgin Eve. And thus, just as the human race fell into bondage to death through a virgin, so it is rescued by a virgin; the disobedience of a virgin has been balanced in the opposite scale by a virgin's obedience.

Irenaeus, *Against Heresies*, **Book 3, chapter 22, section 4, and Book 5, chapter 19, section 1**

The importance of apostolic tradition and the church of Rome

Those who want to see the truth can observe in every church the tradition of the apostles, manifested throughout the whole world. We can give a list of those who were appointed bishops in the churches by the apostles, and their successors, right down to our own day. These bishops never knew anything of the absurd notions which these heretics [the Gnostics] produce! Even if the apostles had known "hidden mysteries" and imparted them privately and secretly to "the mature", they would have especially passed on those secrets to the men into whose care they were entrusting the churches. For the apostles would have wished those men, above all others, to be mature and beyond reproach, since they were handing over to them their own office of authority as teachers. Unblemished character in those men would be the greatest blessing, lack of it the worst disaster. But it would be very boring in a book like this to give detailed lists of the bishops in all the churches. Therefore we will refute those who hold unauthorised assemblies (through false self-importance, or pride, or blind perversity) by pointing out the tradition of a very great and very ancient church, a church known to everyone, which was founded and established at Rome by the most famous apostles Peter and Paul. This church possesses a tradition that comes from the apostles, and its faith has been declared to all and has been handed down to us through the succession of Rome's bishops. For by necessity, all churches - that is, believers from all parts of the world - go to the church in Rome, because of the most powerful authority that resides there. In this church, the tradition of the apostles has been preserved by believers from all countries.[20]

Irenaeus, *Against Heresies*, **Book 3, Chapter 3, section 1**

---

[20] By "the most powerful authority that resides" in Rome, Irenaeus (cont.)

Montanism: Some Montanist prophecies

Behold, a man is as a lyre, and I move over him like a plectrum. The man sleeps, and I remain awake. Behold, it is the Lord that stirs the hearts of men, and gives men hearts. (Montanus).

I am the Lord God Almighty dwelling in man. It is neither an angel nor an ambassador, but I, God the Father, have come. (Montanus)

After me, there shall be no more prophecy, but the End. (Maximilla).

The Lord sent me to be the advocate, teacher, and interpreter of this task, this profession, this covenant; I am forced, whether I will it or not, to learn the knowledge of God. (Maximilla)

Christ came to me in the likeness of a woman, clothed in a bright robe, and He planted wisdom in me, revealing that this place [Pepuza] is holy, and that here Jerusalem descends from heaven. (Priscilla)

I am driven off as a wolf from the sheep. But I am not a wolf. I am word and spirit and power. (Priscilla)

Montanism: What Catholics thought of it

The opposition of the Montanists to the Church, and their schismatic heresy against it, came about in the following way. There is apparently a village called Ardabau near the Phrygian border of Mysia. That is where people say Montanus came from - a recent

---

probably means the imperial government. His argument is that in the Roman church "believers from all parts of the world", from all churches everywhere, have preserved the common faith of all the churches - because people from all over the world naturally congregate in the great city of Rome, the capital of the Empire, where "the most powerful authority resides". So the church in Rome is the great treasure-house and measuring-rod of the orthodox faith of all the churches: not because of any infallible authority of the bishop of Rome (Irenaeus does not teach any such idea), but simply because the Catholic faithful from all churches of all countries are, naturally, to be found in the very great and very ancient church of the Roman Empire's capital city.

convert, during the time that Gratus was governor of Syria. In his ambitious desire to be a Christian leader, he laid himself open to the enemy, became spiritually intoxicated, and fell suddenly into trances and unnatural ecstasies. He began ranting, babbling, and uttering strange sounds, delivering prophecies in a way that conflicted with the practice of the Church handed down generation by generation from the beginning.

There were divided reactions among people who heard his false utterances at that time. Some were disturbed, reckoning Montanus to be possessed by some demonic power, in the grip of some false spirit, someone who was unsettling ordinary Christians. They rebuked him and tried to stop his babbling; they remembered the distinction which the Lord made between true and false prophets, and His warning that we must be on our strictest guard against the latter. But others were overjoyed, as if the Holy Spirit or some gift of prophecy were really at work. They became puffed up with arrogance, forgot the Lord's warning, and welcomed a spirit which harmed and deceived the mind, leading people astray; this spirit enchanted and deluded them, so that it was now impossible to silence it.

By craft, or rather by the careful application of a cunning method, the devil brought about the ruin of the disobedient; they even honoured him, who deserves no honour! He secretly excited and inflamed the minds of those who were not open to the true faith, raising up two companions for Montanus: two women [Priscilla and Maximilla] whom he filled with this false spirit, so that they babbled madly, in a disorderly and wild way, like Montanus himself. This spirit granted favours to those who were overjoyed and exultant about him, swelling their heads with extravagant promises. Sometimes, to give the appearance of not being at their beck and call, the spirit rebuked them sharply and convincingly to their faces, though this trick of the Phrygians deceived few. This arrogant spirit taught them to despise the whole Catholic Church throughout the world, because the Church refused to welcome or honour the spirit of false prophecy. For the Christians of Asia Minor had come together many times to investigate the recent prophetic utterances, and pronounced them blasphemous, rejecting the movement as heresy. Then, at last, the Church threw out those who followed this error and excommunicated them....

The false prophet speaks in a state of unnatural ecstasy, after which all restraint is thrown to the winds. As we have already said, he begins with a blank mind which he himself chooses, and ends up with a complete loss of mental self-control! But the Montanists cannot point to a single one of the Old or New Testament prophets who were moved by the Spirit in this way - not Agabus, or Judas, or Silas, or Philip's daughters, or Ammia of Philadelphia, or Quadratus.... [Ammia and Quadratus were accepted Catholic prophets in the late 1st and early 2nd Century AD].

Unknown Catholic writer, quoted by Eusebius of Caesarea, *History of the Church*, Book 5, chapters 16 and 17

Chapter 5.

AFRICAN CHRISTIANITY: ALEXANDRIA AND CARTHAGE.

When the Romans spoke of "Africa", they usually meant North-West Africa, the area covered today by the modern nations of Tunisia, Algeria and Morocco. In this chapter, however, we will be using the term "Africa" in a broader sense to mean the whole of Mediterranean Africa, including present-day Libya and Egypt. In Roman times, two outstanding cities dominated this huge territory: Alexandria in the North-East, and Carthage in the North-West.

1. The Church in Alexandria: Clement and Origen

The Egyptian city of Alexandria was, after Rome, the greatest city in the Roman Empire. If Rome was the Empire's legal and administrative capital, Alexandria acted as its intellectual and cultural capital, as well as being one of its most important trading ports. It was the liveliest centre of artistic, scientific and philosophical activity in the Greek and Roman world. A deeply Hellenistic community, it also had a vast Jewish population. Religious movements and ideas of every variety met and circulated in Alexandria, influenced each other, and were influenced by Greek philosophy.

We do not know anything about the beginnings of Christianity in Alexandria, although the New Testament says that Apollos came from there (**Acts 18:24-8**). Probably the Christian faith established itself in Alexandria among Hellenistic Jews. The Gnostic movement also had strong Alexandrian roots: the influential Gnostic leaders Basilides and Valentinus both came from the Egyptian capital.

Clement of Alexandria (died 215). The first great Christian teacher in Alexandria whose writings have survived is Clement (called "Clement of Alexandria" to distinguish him from Clement of Rome). Clement appeared on the scene in around 170 or 180, and seems to have vanished in 202 after an outbreak of persecution. Scholars think he died in Asia Minor in about 215. Clement was a convert to Christianity in adult life, and travelled widely throughout the Empire to learn from various Christian teachers. The one who impressed him most was an Alexandrian called ***Pantaenus*** (died about 190). Pantaenus was a Stoic philosopher who had become a Christian. After missionary work which took him as far East as India, Pantaenus became head of a Christian school or academy of philosophy in Alexandria, where he tried to show that Catholic Christianity was better than Gnosticism at dealing with life's great intellectual questions. Clement stayed with Pantaenus and, in about 190, took over the leadership of the Christian academy.

Three main writings of Clement have come down to us:

Exhortation to the Greeks. This was an apology for Christianity which criticised pagan religion and sought to convert the reader to Christ. Like Justin Martyr,[1] Clement presented Christ as the eternal Logos Who is educating the whole human race, Jew and Gentile, into a true knowledge of God.

The Tutor. This was a sequel to the ***Exhortation***, a handbook of instruction for the new convert. Its concern was with how the Christian should conduct himself in the world. Clement examined every area of life - food and drink, the home, marriage, recreation, music, dancing - and stated how the Christian should behave in each area. He recommended a simple lifestyle, midway between luxury and poverty.

Carpet Bags. This is a strange book, in which Clement seems deliberately to wander about over a great variety of themes. In the course of his wanderings, Clement offered his ideal of the perfect

---

[1] For Justin Martyr and his view of Christ as the Logos, see Chapter 3, section 4.

Christian. He taught that faith - believing what the Bible says - was only the first step in the Christian life. After faith came knowledge (Clement used the Greek word *gnosis*): a growing spiritual knowledge of God which transformed the human mind into God's likeness. Clement described the Christian as the "true Gnostic". Gnostics claimed a special knowledge of spiritual truth, but only the Catholic Christian really possessed it. Sharing Justin Martyr's view of Christ as the Logos, Clement also agreed with Justin in holding a positive attitude to Greek philosophy. He argued that philosophy prepared the Greeks to receive Christ, just as the Old Testament prepared the Jews. The Logos had always been at work among all peoples, leading them by different paths towards the knowledge of the one true Creator God.

Clement's positive approach to Greek philosophy involved him in some controversial ideas. When he contrasted simple faith with advanced spiritual knowledge, "faith" often appeared to mean "orthodox Christianity", while "knowledge" meant "Greek philosophical knowledge". Clement freely used both Platonic and Stoic ideas and writings in his discussions of the Christian view of life. Even in opposing the Gnostics, Clement seems to have absorbed some of their attitudes; for instance, Clement defended the goodness of marriage against Gnostic criticism, but he still could not believe that the ideal Christian husband and wife would ever have sex for enjoyment, rather than for the "pure" purpose of producing offspring. This was a view repeated by many of the early Church fathers, notably Augustine of Hippo.[2]

Clement's writings shine with a happy, peaceful, optimistic spirit; reading them can be a remarkably uplifting experience. Clement's optimism came partly from his own joyful personality, and partly from his belief in the universal presence and activity of the Logos, which made him appreciate truth and goodness wherever he found them, even in pagan philosophy (he referred to "the noble and half-inspired Plato"). His books overflow with quotations from the philosophers and poets of Greece. Few Christians were better equipped than Clement to meet the pagan intellectuals of Alexandria

---

2   For Augustine, see Chapter 9, section 3.

on equal terms, and present the Christian faith to them in a way they could understand and honour. Perhaps Clement's only superior in this respect was his pupil Origen.

Origen (185-254). Origenes Adamantius, or "Origen" as he is usually called, was born in Alexandria to Christian parents in about 185.[3] From his childhood he displayed such spiritual purity of character, and such a thirst to understand the Bible, that his father Leonides often tiptoed to the young Origen's bed at night and kissed his sleeping son's breast, "where it seemed so clear that the Holy Spirit of God had made His temple". The Alexandrian authorities executed Leonides for his faith in 202. Origen himself desired to follow his father into the glory of martyrdom, and was prevented from doing so only because his anxious mother hid all his clothes! Having escaped martyrdom through modesty, Origen became a pupil of Clement in his Christian academy, devoting himself completely to the study of the Bible and Greek philosophy. Tradition says that in his youth he read **Matthew 19:12**, took it literally and castrated himself, although later in life he expressed his disapproval of such an interpretation of this verse.

The young Origen was so brilliant that his bishop, ***Demetrius of Alexandria*** (bishop from 189; died about 231), appointed him the head of a school for instructing those who wanted to be baptised. These people were called ***catechumens*** (pronounced "katta-ku-mens" from the Greek word ***katecheo***, "to teach or instruct"); the Church instructed them for a two or three year period prior to their baptism. Origen was only 17 when he became head of the Alexandrian catechetical school; it seemed a promising start, the dawn of a splendid career. However, Origen and Demetrius quarrelled bitterly when Demetrius tried to control what went on in the school. Single-bishop leadership had been fully established in Alexandria only since about 180; Demetrius was trying to increase the scope of his power as bishop by taking charge of the catechetical school, and Origen resisted, defending the school's traditional

---

3 Origen's name can be prounced either "Orri-jun" or "Orri-gun". Americans prefer "Orri-jun" to avoid confusing the Alexandrian Church father with the not very patristic American state of Oregon.

independence. He made a lifelong enemy of Demetrius in consequence. Still, the school prospered under Origen's leadership, attracting vast numbers of students, and producing some outstanding future bishops of the Eastern Church, notably Dionysius of Alexandria and Gregory Thaumaturgos (see next Chapter, section 4).

As well as teaching in Alexandria's catechetical school, Origen now started to go on journeys throughout the Empire to learn from the most distinguished Christian and pagan teachers, visiting Rome, Jerusalem, Antioch, Greece and Arabia. He soon became famous as a sort of consultant on matters of Christian doctrine, and began to exercise a far-reaching influence on the theology of the Church in the East. In 231 the church in Palestinian Caesarea ordained Origen as a presbyter, but this proved the last straw for his bishop Demetrius, who fiercely opposed this action. It was highly irregular for a man to receive ordination outside of his own bishop's jurisidiction, and Origen was in any case disqualified by Church law due to his self-castration.[4] Demetrius excommunicated him from the Alexandrian church. Origen made Caesarea his base of operations for the rest of his life, writing, travelling, teaching and preaching. Arrested during a fresh outbreak of persecution under the emperor Decius in 250, Origen was subjected to prolonged sadistic torture by the authorities, and died as a result of his injuries in 254.

Origen wrote a huge number of books, but only a few have survived. They can be divided into four main groups:

Biblical. Origen produced a new scholarly edition of the Old Testament, in which he set alongside each other the Hebrew text, the Hebrew text in Greek letters, and four Greek translations of the Old Testament. This was called the *Hexapla*. He also wrote commentaries and sermons on almost every book of both Old and New Testaments. Christians throughout the East studied these commentaries and sermons, especially in the monasteries.[5]

---

4   The growing body of Church law had laid it down that a person who had made himself a eunuch could not be a presbyter or bishop, perhaps influenced by **Deuteronomy 23:1**.

5   For monasteries, See Chapter 7, section 3, under the heading **Church life: The monastic movement.**

First Principles. This was the first known attempt in Church history to produce a "systematic theology" - a writing that deals in an orderly manner with all aspects of Christian doctrine. Origen divided the book into four sections: on God, creation, free-will and the Scriptures. For a summary of the teaching of *First Principles*, see below on Origen's theology.

Against Celsus. Celsus was a pagan philosopher, a Platonist, who attacked Christianity in the 170's in a book called *True Word*. This was the most probing criticism of Christianity ever written by a pagan. Celsus had carefully studied the Bible and Christian writings, and was well aware of the difference between the Catholic Church and the Gnostic sects. He approved of some things in Christianity, *e.g.* its belief in one supreme God, its doctrine of the Logos and some of its ethical teaching. However, he was scathing about the person of Jesus, rejecting Him as an imposter and a sorcerer, and accusing the apostles of inventing the "myth" of the resurrection. Celsus's main problem with Christians was their refusal to accept the established religion of the Empire; he condemned them for being disobedient, anti-social and divisive law-breakers. Origen wrote a response to Celsus in 248. It is one of his most important writings, and the greatest of all the apologies for Christianity produced by an early Church father. Origen answered Celsus point by point, displaying tremendous culture and learning, and writing in a calm, dignified manner. On the central question of Christian disobedience to the religious laws of the Empire, Origen insisted that God's law must come before human law. Christians did not try to overthrow the pagan rulers of the Empire by force, Origen argued, but where the Empire's laws conflicted with God's, Christians would disobey the Empire, follow God, and peacefully suffer the consequences.

Practical Writings. Origen wrote a highly influential book on prayer, containing the oldest known commentary on the Lord's prayer, and an *Exhortation to Martyrdom*, which shows that Origen had lost none of his youthful willingness to die for Christ rather than compromise his loyalty to his Lord.

Origen was a controversial figure in his own lifetime and has continued to be so. On the one hand, few Christian leaders from the patristic age can compare with Origen for his noble, humble, gentle character, or for his sheer depth and breadth of knowledge, both of Christian theology and pagan philosophy. On the other hand, Origen's own theology gave rise to the most fierce disputes. He claimed that the Bible alone, not Plato or any pagan philosopher, was inspired, and that the Bible must be the basis of all Christian thinking. But in fact, Platonism greatly shaped and coloured Origen's whole outlook. When he interpreted the Bible, he said it had three levels of meaning, which he called the *body* (the literal meaning), the *soul* (the moral or ethical meaning) and the *spirit* (the spiritual meaning). This scheme of interpretation sprang out of Origen's threefold view of human nature as body, soul and spirit, a view which may itself be rooted in Platonic philosophy. Origen regarded the literal meaning of the Bible as less important than its moral and spiritual meaning. This enabled him to build up his own theology in a way that did not tie it too closely to a literal understanding of the text.

The "deeper meaning" which Origen found in a text is usually called its *allegorical* meaning. An allegory is a statement or a story in which the words have two levels of meaning: the obvious meaning, and another secret meaning. For example, I could say: "Three men prepared a meal to feed their children." The obvious meaning is that three male human beings prepared some food to be eaten by their offspring. But I could also say that my statement has a secret allegorical meaning: the three men represent the Trinity, the meal represents the Lord's supper, and the children represent the Church. So the statement, "Three men prepared a meal to feed their children," really means, "The three persons of the Trinity brought the Lord's supper into being to nourish the Church spiritually." Origen tended to interpret the statements and stories of the Bible in this allegorical way. He did not ignore the obvious or literal meaning, but he saw the deeper allegorical meaning as more important.[6]

---

6 Interpreting the Bible "literally" does not mean failing to recognise poetic language when the Bible uses it. When David calls God "my rock and my fortress" (**Psalm 18:2**), he does not mean that God is literally a large stone or a military tower. He means that just as a rock and fortress protect a man from enemies, so God also gives protection. We realise that this is poetry and interpret it accordingly. But much of the Bible uses non-poetic language, where rocks and fortresses do literally mean large stones and military towers. Origen's allegorical

(cont.)

This way of interpreting the Bible was the method that Greek philosophers used to interpret the traditional stories of the pagan gods, *e.g.* in Homer's *Iliad* and *Odyssey*. When the obvious literal meaning of a story seemed unworthy of belief, often because it was immoral, philosophers would seek a deeper and more spiritual meaning.

When Origen interpreted the Bible, he found an understanding of life which went something like this. Creation happened in two stages. First, God created a purely spiritual world of spirit-beings. This creation did not take place in time, but was an eternal act; there never was a time when these spirit-beings did not exist. (This view is known as the "pre-existence" of souls.) God gave them free-will as their most precious possession, but they misused their freedom to turn away from their Creator. As a result of their sin, God then created the physical universe of space and time. Some of the spirits which had rebelled He then placed in physical bodies as human beings, and made them experience hardship and discipline to bring them back to Himself. Others who fell more deeply became demons. Both for humans and demons, a return to God was always possible, because spiritual beings always have free-will, no matter how badly they have abused it. Even Satan himself, according to Origen, could repent and be saved. The process of salvation would not be complete until God had brought every rebellious spirit back to Himself. This was Origen's doctrine of *universalism* - the universal salvation of all fallen humans and angels. Origen thought that hell was not a place of eternal punishment, but a place where a purifying fire cleansed souls from their sins. His belief that God had created the physical world only as a result of sin meant that Origen saw no continuing place for physical things, once redemption was complete; the resurrection body, he argued, would be a pure spirit-body, devoid of matter.

The significance of Jesus in the process of redemption, according to Origen, was that He is the Revealer of God. From before the creation

---

method of interpretation, however, would see hidden spiritual meanings where most readers would think none were intended; it would allow us (if we so wished) to see *any* mention of a rock or a fortress as referring spiritually to God.

of the world, the divine Logos had united Himself with a pre-existing human spirit. Then, in time, this Logos-spirit also took a human body of flesh, and became Jesus of Nazareth. Jesus's human life on earth belonged to the changing world of time; but His spirit was united with the Logos, and the Logos belongs to the unchanging realm of eternal truth. Salvation, for Origen, meant that a person had to penetrate through the human life of Jesus of Nazareth to the eternal truth of His divine nature as the Logos. The knowledge of the Logos in Jesus would gradually change a person into the likeness of God.

One of Origen's most far-reaching services to the Catholic Church was his insistence that the Logos and God the Father were two distinct persons. An understanding of the Trinity was circulating at this time, which came to be known as *Sabellianism*, named after an obscure Roman theologian called *Sabellius*. According to Sabellians, God's oneness - the fact that there is only one God - required Christians to believe that God was only one person. The Father and the Logos, they claimed, were really the same person; it was God the Father Who became flesh as Jesus Christ. Sabellians said this because they believed whole-heartedly in the deity of Christ, but felt that God would split apart into two Gods if Christ was a distinct person from the Father. So they argued that God was only one person, Who acted now as Father, now as Son, rather like a single human being who has two roles in life, as a parent at home and a business executive at work. (They applied the same understanding to the Holy Spirit: He too was simply God the Father acting in a different way.) Sabellianism is also called *Modalism*, because it sees the Son and the Spirit as merely "modes" or ways of the Father's acting, rather than distinct persons.[7]

Origen fought vigorously against this teaching. He insisted that God the Father and the Logos were two distinct persons Who enjoyed a

---

7   Sabellianism is also known as *Monarchianism*, because of its belief in the "monarchy" of God the Father. By "monarchy", Sabellians meant that there is only "one principle" in God (the Greek for this is *monos,* one, and *arche*, principle - hence "monarchy"). This "one principle" is the Father. The Son and the Holy Spirit are merely God the Father acting as Redeemer and Sanctifier, according to this view.

personal relationship with each other - loving each other, communing with each other, acting towards each other. In explaining and defending this concept, Origen was the first Christian theologian to teach the doctrine of the *eternal generation* of the Logos ("generation" means begetting or fathering an offspring). This doctrine meant that the distinction between the Logos and the Father was like the distinction between a human child and its father. Clearly child and father are two distinct persons. But through the natural process of conception, the child has derived human nature from its father - it shares its father's humanity. In a similar fashion, Origen taught, the Logos was born, begotten, or generated out of God's very nature or substance, and therefore shared God's divine nature. This birth or begetting did not happen at a particular moment in time; it was a timeless or eternal act. There never was a time when God was without His Logos. Origen, then, attributed a timeless existence to the Logos; but he said the same about all spiritual beings - every spirit, for Origen, was eternal. The distinctive thing about the Logos was that He was not brought into existence *out of nothing*, as other beings were; He was born or begotten *out of the divine nature*, from the very essence or substance of God. The Logos was not a created being, but the uncreated offspring of the almighty Father.

According to Origen, then, the Logos did not belong to creation; He was uncreated, eternal, divine, and a distinct person from His Father. This doctrine of the eternal generation of the Logos was very important for the development of the Catholic Church's understanding of the Trinity, and the Church was deeply in debt to Origen for insisting on it and explaining it. However, alongside his teaching on the uncreated and divine nature of the Logos, Origen also maintained that the Logos was not God in the same absolute sense as the Father is. Origen thought that the divine nature existed perfectly in the Father, but that when the Father transmitted His nature to the Logos, it became a degree less than perfect - just as light loses its brightness by a degree, after it shines forth from its source. This belief that there could be "degrees" of divinity came from Greek philosophy (from Middle Platonism[8]). Origen also applied this view to the Holy Spirit,

---

8 For Middle Platonism, see Chapter 1, section 1, under the heading **Philosophy**.

Who was a degree less divine than the Logos. For Origen, the Father possessed divinity in a full and absolute sense; the Logos, Who is eternally begotten from the Father's nature, possessed divinity in a slightly lesser, inferior sense.

Origen's theology had a profound effect on the Eastern Church. In later doctrinal disputes, especially the great Arian controversy of the 4th Century (see Chapter 8), all sides in the East would appeal to the writings of Origen and claim his authority. Despite this great reverence for Origen among Eastern Church leaders, few followed him in his more obviously unorthodox views, *e.g.* his universalism.

2. The Church in Carthage: Tertullian and Cyprian

There were two chief ethnic groups inhabiting North-West Africa (present-day Tunisia, Algeria and Morocco). The coastland peoples were descendants of the Phoenicians of Palestine, mainly from the mighty cities of Tyre and Sidon, who founded Carthage in 814 BC and spread across the whole North-West African seaboard and southern Spain. However, the more inland areas were inhabited by the Berber people, who were native to Africa. The two groups had intermarried; coastland dwellers had drunk deeply of Latin culture, and Carthage had received a strong dose of Hellenism too.

We know nothing of the origins of Christianity in North-West Africa; before 180, we have no evidence of any Christian influence. In that year, however, 12 Christians from Scillium (in modern Tunisia) were martyred in Carthage, the capital city of the Roman province of Africa. This event is a good introduction to the early Church in North-West Africa, for throughout its history it saw itself as a Church of martyrs: a separate body of Spirit-filled believers, chosen by God out of the world, and called by Him to oppose pagan culture and society which were controlled by demonic powers. The North-West African Church viewed life as a fierce struggle between light and darkness, and was marked by a powerful zeal for purity of life and doctrine. It found its centre in the huge Tunisian seaport of Carthage, the third greatest city in the Empire, after Rome and Alexandria.

Tertullian (160-225). The first great Christian writer in the Latin language was a native of Carthage called Tertullian. He was born in about 160, and received a high standard of education in Greek and Roman culture. He probably spent the whole of his life in Carthage. He was converted to Christianity at about the age of 30. Historians argue about whether Tertullian was ever ordained. Jerome[9] tells us that Tertullian became a presbyter; others think he was a lay teacher in charge of catechumens, like Origen.

Tertullian was one of the most warlike spirits ever to enlist in the army of Christ; his hawkish, fire-breathing personality perfectly expressed the uncompromising hostility of the North-West African Church towards the pagan society of the Roman Empire. He was also a talented, many-sided theologian, with a gift for winging his piercing thoughts with bold, colourful and dazzling words. In the period 196-212, he produced a series of extremely important Christian writings, which fall into three main groups, according to their theme:

(a) The relationship between Christianity and the Roman Empire.

Tertullian's first Christian book was an *Apology* which appeared in 196. He argued that the Roman government should stop persecuting the Church, because Christians paid their taxes and prayed for the emperor and the welfare of the Empire. However, he was equally insistent that no Christian could actually take part in any of the affairs of pagan society. No Christian could work for the government, the army, any educational institution, or any business which supported pagan religion, *e.g.* painting and sculpting, which often involved making idols. No Christian would ever go to any kind of public entertainment. (For the reasons behind Tertullian's attitude here, see Chapter 3, section 2, under the heading **Church and society**.) Indeed, Tertullian called the whole Roman world "the camp of darkness", as against the Church which was "the camp of light". So Tertullian advocated an almost totally negative attitude towards the Empire. He said: "Nothing could be more alien to us than the state. We Christians know of only one 'state', of which we are all citizens: the universe."

---

9   For Jerome, see Chapter 9, section 2.

Tertullian's hostility to pagan culture meant that he took a different approach to Greek philosophy from that of Justin Martyr, Clement of Alexandria and Origen. Justin and Clement saw Christianity as the fulfilment of Greek philosophy; Platonism pervaded Origen's theology. By contrast, Tertullian called Christians to be on their strictest guard against pagan philosophy; it was spiritually dangerous, always threatening to poison and corrupt the purity of Christian truth. In a famous saying, Tertullian asked: "What has Athens to do with Jerusalem?" That is, What has Greek philosophy to do with the Bible? All the truth the Christian needs to know has been revealed in the Word of God. However, despite Tertullian's thunderous warnings, Stoicism deeply influenced his own religious beliefs (*e.g.* about the nature of God and the soul).

(b) The defence of orthodoxy against heresy.

Tertullian made his most positive and lasting impact in the area of doctrinal theology. He produced an important book attacking the Gnostic leader Marcion, *Against Marcion*. But his most significant theological writing was his *Against Praxeas*. Praxeas was a Roman Christian who was putting forward a Sabellian doctrine of the Trinity. He denied that there was any real personal distinction between Father, Son and Holy Spirit; they were all the same person Who simply acted out three different roles.

Against this, Tertullian developed many of the ideas and language which the Church soon accepted as essential to the orthodox doctrine of the Trinity. He was the first Christian writer to use the word "Trinity" (in Latin, *Trinitas*) as a description of God's one-in-threeness. He also employed the Latin words *substantia* ("substance") and *persona* ("person") to distinguish between God's oneness and threeness. God, Tertullian said, is one *substance* and three *persons* (in Latin, one *substantia,* three *personae*). By *substance*, Tertullian meant something like "nature" or "being"; for example, a gold coin has the nature of gold - gold is the "substance" of which it is made. By *person*, Tertullian meant "individual", an individually existing object; for example, the coin that is made of gold is an individual object. So if we imagine a gold coin, its "substance" is the gold metal from which the coin has been made, while its "person" is the individual coin itself. According to this definition of

Tertullian's, the Trinity is one single divine nature, being or substance, which exists in three distinct individuals. The Father, Tertullian argued, shared His divine substance with the person of the Son and of the Holy Spirit, just as the sun shares its light with the sunbeams that shine out of it. The Son and Spirit, therefore, have the same divine substance as the Father - they are as much God as He is. However, Tertullian was less clear than Origen about the eternal generation of the Son or Logos. He thought that the Logos had not existed as a distinct person from the Father from all eternity, but had become distinct just before the creation of the universe. Prior to that, the Logos had existed as "Reason" in a non-personal way within the Father.

Tertullian applied the same thinking about substance and person to the relationship between the divine and human natures of Christ. Jesus Christ, he said, was one person Who united in Himself two distinct substances, a divine and human substance. The two substances were joined together but not mixed up; each retained its own distinctive properties. Christ was therefore fully and truly God, fully and truly man, at one and the same time, in one single person.

With some modifications, the whole Western Latin-speaking Church accepted Tertullian's theology of the Trinity and the incarnation. As a result, the West was to be solidly anti-Arian in its theology during the violent controversies of the 4th Century.

(c) The moral behaviour of Christians.

Tertullian had very high and strict ideals of the true Christian life. He recommended frequent fasts. He taught that a Christian could get married only once - even if one partner died, the other could not remarry. A Christian who committed a serious sin after baptism could be forgiven only once (later Tertullian said he could not be forgiven at all). Above all, Tertullian glorified martyrdom, teaching that if a Christian ran away, or bribed a magistrate to save his life, he had betrayed Christ. "He who fears to suffer," he said, "cannot belong to Him Who suffered." Tertullian's fierce moral zeal made his soul burn with sympathy for the Montanists.[10] He wrote in their

---

10 For the Montanists, see previous Chapter, section 3. There is some
(cont.)

defence, scornfully condemning Catholics for their opposition to the
New Prophecy, and leaving behind him at his death a North-West
African Montanist sect called the "Tertullianists" who survived until
the 5th Century.[11] For Tertullian, the focus of unity in the Church was
not the local bishop, but the sanctifying presence of the Holy Spirit,
revealed through holiness, prophecy and miracle.

Tertullian died peacefully in about 225; the crown of martyrdom
which he had so praised was not to be his. Nor did he receive the
recognition he deserved as a theologian; Tertullian's Montanism
made him highly suspect in the eyes of the early Church fathers who
came after him - they increasingly regarded Tertullian as a heretic.

Cyprian (200-258). Christianity spread quickly through North-West
Africa during and after Tertullian's lifetime. It was well established
when the emperors Decius (249-51) and Valerian (253-60) ordered
the first full-scale, universal, Empire-wide persecutions of the
Church (see the next Chapter for a more detailed account). The
bishop of Carthage at the time of these persecutions was Cyprian.[12]

Thascius Caecilius Cyprian was born in about 200, probably in
Carthage. Upper class and rich, he was a famous lawyer and a
professor of rhetoric (the art of public speaking) prior to his
conversion. Disgusted, however, with the corruption and immorality
of pagan society, Cyprian searched for something purer and nobler,
and found the answer in Christ. Converted in 246, he gave his entire
fortune away to the poor. Within two or three years of becoming a
Christian, his outstanding qualities of character, his gentleness, love
and peaceable spirit, led to his election as bishop of Carthage.

The greatest influence on Cyprian was Tertullian; Cyprian called him
"the master" and used to read his writings every day (the Catholic
Church had not yet consigned Tertullian into the category of despised
heretic). Cyprian himself had a fairly simple, literal understanding of
the Bible, in stark contrast to Origen. He interpreted the New

---

debate among modern historians about whether Tertullian actually
seceded from the Catholic Church and joined the Montanists. If he did,
it was in around 208.

11   It is not certain what separated the Tertullianists from the Montanists.
12   Pronounced "Sip-ree-un".

Testament in a rather Old Testament way, thinking of presbyters and bishops as priests[13] and the Lord's supper as a sacrifice. Cyprian was the first of the early Church fathers to set forth a theological doctrine of holy communion in sacrificial terms, a view which became increasingly widespread. It is easy to misunderstand Cyprian's teaching. He did not think that the eucharist was a fresh sacrifice for sins. His teaching was that through the eucharist, Christ presented Himself to God the Father as the One Who had made the once-for-all sacrifice for the sins of His people on the cross; and by eating the bread and drinking the wine, believers were united with that perfect self-offering of Christ, so that He presented both Himself and the congregation to the Father. Cyprian also taught that holy communion mysteriously benefitted the "faithful departed" - believers who have died. This idea, too, became ever more widespread.

However, Cyprian's main concern was not the doctrine of communion, but Christian unity, best expressed in his book *The Unity of the Catholic Church*. Cyprian held that this unity was found in the person and office of the bishop. "Where the bishop is," he said, "there is the Church." In Cyprian's theology, the difference between the apostles and the bishops faded away almost entirely. The apostles were the first bishops; the bishops were the new apostles - not invested indeed with apostolic infallibility, but possessing absolute disciplinary authority over their congregations, and clothed with supernatural power to administer the life-giving sacraments of baptism and holy communion. (The word "sacrament" was a Western Latin word, from *sacramentum*, meaning "oath of allegiance". The Western Church increasingly used this word to describe baptism and communion. The Eastern Church called them the "mysteries".) Here, in Cyprian's concept of the

---

13 The Church began to use the word "priest" to describe a Christian minister or clergyman at the end of the 2nd Century, although it continued to use the term "presbyter" too. For the sake of consistency, I will continue to use the term "presbyter" throughout Part One. The use of the word "priest" has no necessary connection with a strongly sacrificial view of the eucharist. It could simply highlight the minister's role as worship-leader and teacher, functions which were central to the Old Testament priesthood.

Cyprian of Carthage (AD200 - 258)

bishop, was the doctrine of "apostolic succession" in all its fulness. To belong to the Catholic Church, therefore, a person had to be in fellowship with the local apostolic bishop. Each bishop was supreme in his own church, Cyprian argued, but all bishops were equal with one another. Cyprian gave a special place of honour and dignity in the Western Church to the bishop of Rome, because Peter, the prince of the apostles, had been the Roman church's first bishop. However, Cyprian would not admit that even Rome's bishop had any actual authority over his fellow bishops. And Cyprian certainly did not believe that bishops of Rome were infallible; in the controversy over baptism given outside the Catholic Church (see below), Cyprian accused bishop Stephen of Rome of "error, arrogant claims, irrelevant statements and contradictions".

From Cyprian's doctrine of the Church, it followed that the sin of *schism* - leaving the Catholic Church and its apostolic bishops - was infinitely serious. The Catholic Church alone was the true Church of Christ; all others were false. And the Holy Spirit worked only in the Catholic Church and its ministry. Therefore, in one of Cyprian's most famous sayings, "Outside the Church there is no salvation." He stated:

> "Whoever stands apart from the Church and is joined to an adulteress [a non-Catholic church] is cut off from the promises given to Christ's Church; and he who leaves the Church of Christ does not attain to the rewards of Christ, but is an alien and an enemy. You cannot have God as your Father unless you have the Church as your mother. If anyone was able to escape the flood outside of Noah's ark, then you can escape judgment if you are outside the doors of the Church."

The persecution under the emperor Decius raised some serious problems for Cyprian's understanding of the Church. Decius had ordered all citizens to offer sacrifice to the gods and to obtain an official certificate stating that they had done this. Large numbers of Church members had either offered sacrifice, or bribed magistrates to give them a fake certificate. After the persecution was over, these people wanted to be admitted back into the Church. What should be done with these "lapsed" Christians? ("Lapsed" was the term used for those who fell away under persecution.)

There were two problems: (i) Should the lapsed be accepted back into the Church immediately? Or only after a period of time? Or never? (ii) Who had the authority to decide this question?

Cyprian presided over a local Church council at Carthage in 251 and played a leading part in its decision that the lapsed could be received back into the Church, but only after a period of time during which they would be proving their sincerity by doing "penance" (repentance) for their sin. The time period of penance was to vary according to the seriousness involved in each individual case of apostasy. Cyprian also argued that the bishops alone had the authority to settle this question. Some ordinary Church members called *confessors* had assumed the right to decide the question themselves. A confessor was a Christian who had been imprisoned but not executed for his faith - or not yet executed. Many felt that the great faith of the confessors gave them the spiritual right to determine whether the lapsed could be readmitted to the Church, and on what terms. Cyprian disagreed; only the bishops had that power.

These decisions led to schisms in the Church. Some Christians in Carthage thought that Cyprian was too strict; led by the presbyter Novatus, they broke away to form a rival church with a softer, more lenient discipline. The opposite happened in Rome, where the church took the same line as Carthage towards the problem of the lapsed. Some Roman Christians led by a presbyter called *Novatian* broke away from the Roman church, forming a new congregation with a far stricter discipline: they would never readmit any lapsed believer. The new Novatianist Church became an important movement, with congregations as far away as Spain and Carthage in the West, and Syria and Egypt in the East; they became especially numerous in Constantinople, capital of the Eastern Empire from 330. The Novatianist movement survived for several hundred years, but its congregations had probably all merged back into the Catholic Church by the 7th Century. Novatian himself was a distinguished theologian; his *Concerning the Trinity* was the first great doctrinal treatise to emerge from the Christian community in Rome (probably before 250). It defended the orthodox view of the Trinity against Sabellianism, and argued strongly for the two natures of Christ as God and man in one person.

The splits in the Church produced by Decius's persecution led to even more problems. What if someone became a Christian in the Novatianist Church, was baptised by Novatianists, and then decided to join the Catholic Church? Should he be rebaptised? Cyprian said yes. Outside the Catholic Church, no baptism was spiritually effective. (This was the traditional North-West African view, upheld by Tertullian.) But *Stephen* (died 257), the bishop of Rome from 254, said no. As long as a person had been baptised by water in the name of the Trinity, his baptism was valid. It did not matter that the baptism had been done in a schismatic Church. Stephen tried to force his view on the churches of North-West Africa. Cyprian resisted; he argued that each bishop had the right to decide the question for himself. Stephen broke off relations with the entire body of North-West African believers, together with all the churches of Asia Minor (which agreed with Cyprian's view), threatening to excommunicate them all. Cyprian's response was robust:

> "Let each bishop give his opinion in this matter without judging another, and without separating from the fellowship of those who are not of his opinion. None of us must set himself up as a bishop of bishops, nor force his brother-bishops to obey him by tyrannical terror. Every bishop has full liberty and complete power in his own church. No other bishop can judge him, and he cannot judge any other bishop. Let us all await the judgment of our Lord Jesus Christ, Who alone has the power to appoint us as governors in His Church, and Who alone can judge our conduct."

The dispute between Rome and Africa came to an end when a fresh persecution of the Church broke out under the emperor Valerian. The authorities arrested and banished Cyprian in 257, and martyred him in 258. Stephen also died, perhaps as a martyr.

Cyprian and his work had a profound influence on the Empire-wide Christian community. He helped to make it into a "Church of the bishops". However, the West rejected his stance on rebaptism in favour of Stephen's view. And Cyprian's insistence on the equality of all bishops gave way, in the West, to a belief in the supremacy of the bishop of Rome.

Important people:

The Church
Pantaenus (died 190)
Praxeas (early 3rd Century)
Sabellius (early 3rd Century)
Clement of Alexandria (died 215)
Tertullian (160-225)
Demetrius of Alexandria (active 189-231)
Origen (185-254)
Cyprian of Carthage (200-258)
Novatian (active mid-3rd Century)
Stephen of Rome (bishop from 254; died 257)

Others
Celsus (active 170-80)

A prayer of Clement of Alexandria

O Christ, Lord of the elect,
immortal Logos of God the Father,
Prince of wisdom,
Strength of the weary,
Joy without end,
Jesus, Saviour of the human race,
Shepherd, Protector, Guide, Leader,
heavenly Pathway for the flock of Your saints:
Fisher of men, You come to draw us out
from the sea of sin;
You pull Your saved fish
from the menacing waves,
and carry them along to the life of the blessed.
Guide us, Shepherd of the human flock;
reign, O Holy One, over the children You have redeemed.
Your steps, O Christ, are the road to heaven.
O eternal Logos, You are infinite time and immortal light;
You are the fountain of mercy and the source of goodness;
You are the incomparable prize of those who worship the Most High.

Clement of Alexandria, *The Tutor*, Book 3, chapter 8

The Christian attitude to money and possessions

"Why shouldn't I enjoy the things God has given, since it is within my power to do so? Didn't God make everything for our enjoyment?" If you speak like that, you are totally ignorant of God's will.... "Seek first God's kingdom and His righteousness, and all these things will be added to you" (**Matthew 6:33**). Even if God has given and handed over all things to us, and all things are lawful, yet "not all things are profitable" (**1 Corinthians 10:23**), as the apostle Paul says. God Himself brought our human race together into fellowship; He earlier shared His own goods, and placed His Logos at the disposal of all as a common possession. God made all things for all people. So all things are common to all, and the rich may not claim more than their fair share.

If you say, "It belongs to me, I have more than enough, why shouldn't I enjoy it?" - that is neither human nor social. What love says is this: "It belongs to me, so I will share it with the needy." The perfect Christian is the one who fulfils the command, "You shall love your neighbour as yourself." That is true enjoyment; that is storing up true riches. But what you spend to satisfy your foolish desires, God counts as loss, not true expenditure. For I know that God has given us the ability to make use of things, but only to the degree that we need them, and He intends the use of His creation to be common to all. O how disgusting it is that one man lives in luxury, while most live in need! But how much more glorious it is to benefit others than to live in abundance! How much wiser to spend money on people, rather than on gold and jewels! How much more useful to adorn ourselves with friends than with lifeless objects! Which brings the most benefit - owning property, or showing kindness? In the Gospel, the Lord openly calls the rich man a fool, when he fills up his barns and says to himself, "You have many goods stored up for many years. Eat, drink, be merry!" The Lord says, "This very night your soul will be required of you. To whom then will the things you have stored up belong?"

Clement of Alexandria, *The Tutor*, Book 2, chapters, 12, 119-20, 125

The eternal generation of the Logos

We are forbidden the ungodly belief that God the Father begets and sustains His only-begotten Son in the same way that one human being begets another, or one animal begets another. There is necessarily a great difference, and rightly so, between divine and human begetting, because nothing can be found in creation, or conceived, or imagined, which can compare with God. Therefore human thought cannot understand how the unbegotten God becomes the Father of the only-begotten Son. For it is an eternal and ceaseless begetting, just as radiance is generated from light. The Son is the Radiance of the eternal light, the perfect Mirror of God's activity, and the Image of His goodness.

> **Origen,** *First Principles*, **Book 1, chapter 2**

The unique sacrifice of Christ

The Greeks and barbarians have many traditional stories of times when various afflictions, such as plagues, poisonous calms or famines, have prevailed among a people, and when release has come through one man's self-sacrifice for the good of all, by which (as it were) the evil spirit is frustrated who causes their distress. And they do not scorn or reject this idea of self-sacrifice in the case of such a man. Now it is not our present aim to sift out the truth and falsehood of such tales. But no story is ever told, and cannot have been told, of someone who was able to accept death on behalf of the whole world, so that all the world should be purified. We have never heard from the pagans about the purification of a world that was doomed to perish, unless one man had accepted death on its behalf. For Jesus alone, by His great power, has been able to take upon Himself the burden of the sin of all, and to carry it to the cross, on which He hung, separated from God on behalf of us all.... The Father offered up this Jesus for our sins; because of our sins, "He was led like a lamb to the slaughter" (**Isaiah 53:7**).... In His humiliation, in which "He humbled Himself, becoming obedient unto death, even death on a cross" (**Philippians 2:8**), the judgment is taken away.

> **Origen,** *Commentary on John's Gospel*, **Book 28, chapter 19**

Every true Christian is the rock on which Christ builds His Church

Simon Peter answered, "You are the Christ, the Son of the living God" (**Matthew 16:16**). And perhaps if we say this as Peter said it, not by flesh and blood revealing it to us, but by the light of the heavenly Father shining in our hearts, we too become like Peter; we are declared to be blessed as he was, because the reason for Peter's blessing now applies also to us, that the heavenly Father (and not flesh and blood) has revealed to us that Jesus is the Christ, the Son of the living God. This revelation comes to us from the highest heavens, carrying up to heaven those who take every veil from their hearts and receive the spirit of wisdom and revelation from God, so that our citizenship may be in heaven. And if we have joined Peter in saying, "You are the Christ, the Son of the living God," not because flesh and blood revealed it to us, but by the light of the heavenly Father shining in our hearts, then we each become a Peter; Jesus might then say to us, "You are Peter," and so on. For every disciple of Christ is a rock, since we drink from the spiritual rock that follows us (**1 Corinthians 10:4**); and the teaching and organisation of the Church are all built on such rocks.

Origen, *Commentary on Matthew*, **Book 12, chapter 10**

Jesus Christ, God and man

We must ask how "the Word became flesh" (**John 1:14**). Was He transformed into flesh, or did He clothe Himself with flesh? Surely it was the second of these. We must believe that God's eternal nature cannot undergo change or transformation. Transformation involves the destruction of what first existed; the thing that is transformed ceases to be what it was, and begins to be something else. But God does not cease to be, and He cannot be anything else other than what He is. And the Word is God, and "the Word of the Lord endures for ever" (**Isaiah 40:8**), remaining in the same form. His incarnation, then, means that He comes to exist in flesh, and is revealed, seen and handled through flesh. Other reasons demand this interpretation. For if His incarnation happened through a transformation and change of His substance, Jesus would then be one substance made from two

- flesh and Spirit[14] - a kind of mixture, just as amber is a mixture of silver and gold. In that case, Jesus would end up being neither gold (Spirit) nor silver (flesh), because the one element changes the other to produce a new third thing. This view of the incarnation produces a Christ Who is neither one thing nor the other, but a third thing which is very different from either. But we see in Christ two forms of being, not confused with each other, but joined together in one person, Jesus, Who is both God and man. And the proper nature of each substance keeps its own full reality. The Spirit carried out in Jesus its own actions - the powers, works and signs; and the flesh experienced the things that belong to it - hunger during the conflict with Satan, thirst when it met the Samaritan woman, weeping over Lazarus, being troubled at the approach of death, and finally the experience of death itself.

Tertullian, *Against Praxeas*, **chapter 27**

The exile and martyrdom of Cyprian

[The soldiers of the governor of North Africa, Paternus, bring Cyprian into his presence:]

Paternus: The most sacred emperors, Valerian and Gallienus,[15] have honoured me with letters requiring all who do not observe Rome's religion to profess their return to Roman rites of worship. I have therefore asked you, By the name of what religion do you call yourself? What is your answer?

Cyprian: I am a Christian and a bishop. I know no other gods beside the one true God, Who made heaven and earth, the sea, and everything in it. We Christians serve this God; we pray to Him day and night, for ourselves, for all mankind, and for the health of the emperors themselves.

---

14 Tertullian is not using the term "Spirit" here to mean the person of the Holy Spirit, but the divine nature which is common to all three persons of the Trinity, as in **John 4:24**, "God is Spirit."
15 Gallienus was Valerian's son who ruled with him as co-emperor, then succeeded him as emperor.

Paternus: Do you persist in this purpose?

Cyprian: This good purpose, which acknowledges God, I
                cannot change.

Paternus: In obedience, then, to the command of the
                emperors, you can go into exile to the city of
                Curubis.

Cyprian: I go.

[A year later there was a new governor, Galerius Maximus. He
recalled Cyprian from exile:]

Galerius: Are you Thascius Cyprian?

Cyprian: I am.

Galerius: The most sacred emperors have commanded you to
                conform to the Roman rites of worship.

Cyprian: I refuse.

Galerius: Think about the consequences.

Cyprian: Do as you must. In so clear a case, I do not care
                about the consequences.

Galerius: Thascius Cyprian: you have long lived an ungodly
                life, and you have brought together a number of
                people bound by an illegal association, and you have
                professed yourself an open enemy of the gods and
                religion of Rome. The pious, most sacred and
                exalted emperors, Valerian and Gallienus, have
                tried in vain to bring you back to conformity with
                their customs of religious worship. Therefore, since
                you have been arrested as the chief and ringleader
                in these notorious crimes, we shall make you an
                example to those who have wickedly associated

with you. The authority of the law shall be sealed in your blood. It is the sentence of this court that Thascius Cyprian be executed by the sword.

Cyprian: Thanks be to God.

From *The Acts of Saint Cyprian*

Chapter 6.

FROM PERSECUTION
TO TOLERATION

1. The persecutions under Decius and Valerian.

In general, the first half of the 3rd Century was a time of peace and numerical growth for the Church. Many rich families became Christians. Believers began to set buildings aside specifically for Christian worship; in Rome, they built the first Christian cemetery. Some emperors showed a positive attitude towards Christianity. The emperor *Alexander Severus* (222-35) employed the great Christian scholar *Julius Africanus* (160-240) to organise Rome's public library. Africanus wrote a *History of the World* up to his own times, and a 24 volume encyclopedia which dealt with a vast range of topics. He was also a highly competent Bible scholar: he wrote a letter to Origen[1] arguing (rightly) that the story of Susanna in the Septuagint (the Greek Old Testament) could not be part of the genuine Hebrew Scriptures of the Old Testament, because its language proved it must have been written originally in Greek. He also wrote a treatise reconciling the seeming contradictions between the genealogies of Jesus in **Matthew** and **Luke**.

The emperor Alexander's sympathy towards Christians, shown by his employment of Africanus, extended to the emperor's own personal religious beliefs. Alexander's private chapel had images of Jesus and Abraham alongside pagan gods, and his mother Julia Mamaea (who was the real power behind Alexander's throne) once arranged a special meeting with Origen in Antioch to discuss religious matters with him. The emperor Philip the Arab (244-49)

---

[1] For Origen, see previous Chapter, section 1.

was also well-known for his Christian inclinations. However, in 249 there was a military coup, and Philip was overthrown by his ablest general, **Decius**, who was emperor for the next two years. In 250 Decius organised the first universal persecution of Christians throughout the Empire.

Decius believed that the Church was a deadly threat to the Empire's unity and stability. Christians had made themselves very unpopular in 247 by refusing to join in the pagan festivities celebrating the one thousandth anniversary of the founding of Rome. Then, starting in 248, a series of invasions by northern Germanic tribes called Goths shook the Empire. Origen noted that anti-Christian feeling was on the rise everywhere.

Decius shared this feeling. He blamed the Christians for the Empire's calamities; the gods were angry because the Church was drawing away so many people from worshipping them. So Decius decided that he must eliminate the Christian Church, like some cancerous growth, from the body of the Empire. He began by targetting Church leaders. The authorities executed the bishops of Rome, Antioch and Jerusalem; Cyprian of Carthage escaped only by going into hiding. Then Decius ordered that all inhabitants of the Empire must offer sacrifice to the gods and obtain an official certificate stating that they had done so. Christians who refused, such as Origen, were imprisoned and tortured. Many died. However, large numbers of Christians gave in, and either offered sacrifice to the gods or purchased a fake certificate by bribing magistrates.

Decius died fighting the Goths in 251, but after a short breathing-space the emperor **Valerian** (253-60) renewed the persecution. In 257 he prohibited all meetings for Christian worship and systematically tried to kill all the Church's bishops and presbyters. Cyprian of Carthage was his most famous victim. Many others (not just the leaders) died for the faith. But again, many gave in and offered sacrifice or bribed magistrates for a false certificate.

The persecutions came to an end when Valerian was treacherously taken prisoner at a peace conference by the Persian emperor Shapur. Valerian's son Gallienus (260-68) became the new Roman emperor; he hated his father, made no attempt to rescue him, and abandoned Valerian's policy of persecution. This was not because Gallienus had any sympathy with Christians; he and his highly refined wife Salonina were disciples of the pagan philosopher Plotinus (see next section). Gallienus believed that the only effective weapon against the Church was education, not persecution. He therefore made every effort to promote Hellenism throughout the Empire. His subjects failed to appreciate the noble enterprise and assassinated the cultured emperor in 268, massacring his entire family. Even so, for the next 44 years the Empire left Christians in peace. And yet in a sense the damage had already been done. Decius and Valerian had badly shaken the Church: so many Christians had committed apostasy to save their lives. This created lasting splits in the Church, as we saw in the previous Chapter, because of the different attitudes that Church leaders took towards lapsed Christians who wanted to return to the Church.

2. The Empire at the end of the 3rd Century.

The lack of persecution in the last half of the 3rd Century was mainly due to the tottering military situation of the Empire. Northern Germanic tribes invaded again and again, in Asia Minor, the Balkans, Greece and France. Once they even penetrated into Spain and raided North-West Africa. Meanwhile the Sassanid Empire of the Persians attacked from the East, seizing control of the Middle Eastern provinces three times and having to be forced out again. For a time it seemed that the Roman Empire would collapse under the crushing weight of its enemies. However, it fought back under two brilliant soldier-emperors, Claudius Gothicus (268-70) and Aurelian (270-75). The situation had become stable again by the time of the emperor Diocletian (284-305).

Bordering on the Empire's Eastern province of Cappadocia in Asia Minor was the independent kingdom of Armenia. In about 300, Christianity became Armenia's official national religion, through the evangelism of *Gregory the Illuminator* (240-332) - the "Illumina-tor" referring to Gregory as the one who brought the light of Christ to the Armenians. He is also often called "the apostle of Armenia". Gregory was himself an Armenian, possibly of royal descent, who grew up in Cappadocia where in later life he became a Christian.

Returning to Armenia, he converted the Armenian king Tiridates III (died 314) and the whole Armenian royal family to the Christian faith. Armenia thus became the first nation on earth to accept Christianity as its established religion. Gregory himself became the *catholicos* or archbishop of Armenia, a position passed on to his male descendants for several generations. He established his spiritual headquarters in Etchmiadzin, and to this day the catholicos of Etchmiadzin is the spiritual leader of the Armenian Church.

Three new religious movements came on the scene in this period:

Sun-worship. Pagan religious thinkers began to reorganise the traditional worship of the gods around a new cult of sun-worship. The sun became a symbol of the one supreme God, Who had long been acknowledged by philosophers, but had not, until now, had any real place in the ordinary worship of pagan people. So the cult of sun-worship showed how the old paganism itself was increasingly moving towards a belief in one God. The emperor Aurelian, in particular, tried to make sun-worship fashionable by building in Rome a great temple to the Unconquered Sun in 274. People began celebrating the 25th of December as the sun's "birthday" (from which we derive the festival of Christmas). There was also a strong link between sun-worship and the Eastern mystery cult of Mithras, god of light, which was very popular in the Roman armies.[2] The fact that sun-worship involved believing in one supreme God made it easier for many people to pass over from worshipping God through the sun, to worshipping Him through the Son. However, this had its dangers; some converts to Christianity continued to practise sun-worship as well.

Neoplatonism. A vigorous revival of philosophy took place in the 3rd and 4th Centuries. The man who inspired this movement was *Plotinus* (205-70), an Egyptian who taught in Rome.[3] Plotinus was one of the most influential philosophers humanity has ever known. He took the philosophy of Plato and, by reinterpreting it, transformed it into one of the great spiritual faiths of the world. Plotinus's philosophy is called *Neoplatonism* (from the Greek *neo*, meaning

---

2   For Mithraism, see Chapter 1, section 1, under **Eastern mystery cults**
3   Plotinus is pronounced "Plah-ty-nuss".

"new" - the "new Platonism"). In his reinterpretation of Plato, Plotinus taught that the source of all things was something he called *the One* - but the One was so high and mysterious that nothing could really be said about it. Sometimes Plotinus called the One "God" or "the Good". According to Plotinus, the One was the origin of everything else. Just as light flowed from the sun, so everything that existed flowed from the One (a process Plotinus described as "emanation"). But light became dimmer and weaker, the further away it got from its source; similarly, everything that existed became less and less real, the further away it was from the One. So, Plotinus argued, there were different levels of reality, one beneath another, and each level was less real than the one above it.

We could think of Plotinus's view of things as a kind of ladder, with the One at the top. Climbing down the ladder, the first rung we touch (the first thing to flow or "emanate" from the One) is a level of reality called *Nous*, which means Mind or Spirit. Plotinus did not mean our human minds or spirits, but something far beyond them. Mind is the image of the One; Neoplatonists even referred to Mind as "the Son of God". Mind brought the universe into existence. Then the next rung down the ladder from Mind is *Psuche* (Soul), which stands midway between Mind and the physical world. Within Soul, Plotinus included both individual human souls and a greater "World-Soul". Then the next rungs down the ladder from Soul are Nature and (at the bottom) Matter. Plotinus taught that the human soul had a sense of incompleteness because of the distance between itself and its ultimate source, the One. The soul longed for the One, as a wanderer longs for his native land. By spiritual discipline, training itself to live for spiritual rather than earthly things, the soul could climb up the ladder of reality and at last be united with the One - a glorious experience, which Plotinus claimed he had had a number of times.

Plotinus was an attractive and even captivating personality, and his teaching bore fruit in Rome's educated pagan circles. Indeed, the general ideas of Neoplatonism came to influence the outlook of many intelligent and serious-minded people in the later Roman Empire, much as the philosophy of "human rights" influences many educated people today. Neoplatonism encouraged a widespread practice of *asceticism* (rigorous bodily self-denial as an aid to spiritual growth), and a widespread acceptance of *mysticism* (a belief in the possibility of spiritual union or oneness with God). Neoplatonists were often very hostile to Christianity; the last great pagan emperor, Julian the Apostate (361-3), an uncompromising enemy of the Church, was a Neoplatonist.[4]

However, for others, embracing Neoplatonism was a stage on the way which led finally to conversion to Christianity. This was because there were many points of contact between Neoplatonist and Christian views. For example, Plotinus's three divine principles of the One, Mind and Soul had a certain resemblance to the Christian belief in Father, Son and Holy Spirit. The most famous Neoplatonist convert to Christianity was Rome's distinguished Neoplatonist philosopher *Marius Victorinus* (died some time after 362), who sent shock-waves through the ranks of Roman pagans by accepting Catholic baptism in about 350. He then devoted his great intellect to upholding the doctrine of the Trinity in the Arian controversy (see Chapter 8). The ideas and spiritual atmosphere of Neoplatonism deeply influenced many other Christian theologians, such as the Cappadocian fathers[5] in the East, and Ambrose of Milan[6] and Augustine of Hippo[7] in the West. This does not mean that they accepted all its teachings. However, they felt that much of the general Neoplatonist outlook on life fitted in with what the Bible taught. So they exploited some of the concepts and language of Neoplatonism in order to define the meaning of Christian doctrines more precisely, and to give clearer expression to them in a way that made sense to the educated classes of their own day.

Manichaeism. This was a new form of Gnosticism,[8] invented by a Persian named *Mani* (216-77). Mani called himself "the apostle of Jesus Christ", and claimed he had received a new revelation which brought together all the truths of all previous religions. Deeply influenced by the Gnostic leader Marcion, Mani taught that the whole universe could be explained as a conflict between the two equal and eternal forces of Light and Darkness. Human beings must recognise

---

4   For Julian the Apostate, see next Chapter, section 2
5   For the Cappadocian fathers, see Chapter 8, section 3.
6   For Ambrose, see Chapter 7, section 2.
7   For Augustine, see Chapter 9, section 3.
8   For Gnosticism, see Chapter 4, section 1.

that they are a mixture of these two forces, and devote their lives to purifying themselves from all Darkness. They will be helped by the agents of Light, who include Buddha (founder of the Buddhist faith), Zoroaster (founder of the Zoroastrian faith), Jesus and Mani himself. To purify themselves, people must abstain from everything that binds them to the physical material world, such as work, property, meat-eating and marriage - like all Gnostics, Mani saw physical matter as an evil force. Mani was also a typical Gnostic in rejecting the Old Testament. He placed a great emphasis on reason, and claimed he could establish all his teachings by rational proof. He divided his followers into two groups, the "elect" and the "hearers". The elect had to obey Mani's ascetic moral and religious code very strictly, and were regarded as priests; but the hearers, whose main duty was to attend to the needs of the elect, were allowed to practise a less disciplined lifestyle.

Manichaeism was a zealous missionary faith, and it spread quickly through the Empire, especially in Syria and Africa. Its followers were called **Manichees**.[9] Christians and pagans alike feared and opposed them (Plotinus and Neoplatonists especially detested Manicheaism). This last great flowering of the Gnostic movement in the early Church period also spread throughout Persia, the land of Mani's birth, and its missionaries reached as far as India and China. In southern China, Manichaeism survived until the 16th Century.

3. The final struggle: from Diocletian to Constantine.

The emperor **Diocletian**, a soldier who seized power in 284, was a great political reformer, and carried out a drastic reorganisation of the Empire. He divided it into two administrative spheres, East and West, and placed the West under the authority of a colleague, a second emperor. Each emperor was known as an "Augustus". Then, under each Augustus was a junior emperor called a "Caesar". The Augustus ruled some provinces in his half of the Empire, the Caesar ruled the others. When the Augustus died, his Caesar was to take his place. Diocletian also divided up East and West into 12

---

9 Manichee is pronounced "Manna-kee". Manichaeism is pronounced "Manna-kee-izzum".

new administrative districts (called dioceses[10]), changed the
structure of the court, civil service and army, and carried out other
economic and social reforms. These reforms were so successful,
they enabled the Empire to survive for another thousand years in the
East.

For most of his reign, Diocletian carried out a policy of religious
toleration. However, Diocletian's Caesar, *Galerius* (died 311), was
extremely hostile to Christianity. Towards the end of his reign, under
Galerius's influence, Diocletian became a less tolerant ruler. In 297
he banned Manichaeism, ordering that all Manichees must be put to
death. Then in 303 Galerius persuaded Diocletian to take action
against the Christians too. So began the last and most terrible
persecution of the Church by the Empire.

Diocletian dismissed all Christians from the government and the
army, and issued three anti-Christian edicts in 303, and a fourth one
in 304:

First edict: All church buildings were to be destroyed, all
                   Bibles burnt, and all Christian worship forbidden.

Second edict: All clergy were to be arrested and imprisoned.

Third edict: All clergy were to offer sacrifice to the gods or be
                   tortured.

Fourth edict: All citizens throughout the Empire were to
                   sacrifice to the gods and be executed if they
                   refused.

The persecution was fierce throughout the East. There were many
martyrs. In the West, persecution was bad in Italy and North-West
Africa, which were under the authority of Maximian, the West's
anti-Christian Augustus. But Maximian's Caesar, Constantius, who
controlled Spain, France and Britain, was more tolerant; he only
destroyed a few church buildings, and executed no-one. The Church

---

10 From which we get the ecclesiastical word *diocese* - the district over
    which a bishop has authority.

stood up to Diocletian's persecution far better than it had to Decius's and Valerian's. Indeed, many Christians openly courted martyrdom, and often displayed a militant hostility to the Roman state. For example, the authorities tried to force a Christian man named Andronicus to sacrifice to the gods, even stuffing into Andronicus's mouth the bread and meat of the sacrificial ritual. Andronicus's response was fierce:

> "May you be punished, bloody tyrant, both you and those who have given you power to defile me with your unholy sacrifices!" shouted Andronicus. "One day you will know what you have done to the servants of God!" "You accursed villain!" replied the magistrate. "Do you dare to curse the emperors who have given the world such a long and profound peace?" "I have cursed them, and I will curse them!" Andronicus said. "They are scourges of the public, they are drinkers of blood, and they have turned the world upside-down!"

In 305 Diocletian stepped down from power. He was ill, and he had intended himself and his fellow Augustus, Maximian, to rule only for a 20 year period. So he forced Maximian to resign at the same time. This meant that Galerius, the man responsible for the anti-Christian policy, became the new Augustus in the Eastern half of the Empire, with the result that persecution in the East became even more violent. However, the tolerant Constantius became Augustus in the West. When Constantius died in 306, his troops made his son **Constantine** (born about 280, died 337) into the new Caesar, in the northern British city of York. The West was now divided between Constantine, who controlled Britain, France and Spain, and Maxentius, who controlled Italy and North-West Africa. Constantine was tolerant, but Maxentius was anti-Christian.

In 311, Galerius finally gave up persecuting the Church in the East. He admitted he had failed to destroy Christianity, and issued a new edict of religious toleration. He was a sick man at the time, and asked the Christians to pray for him. He died soon afterwards. The East was now divided between **Licinius**, who controlled Greece and the Balkans, and Maximinus Daia, who controlled Asia Minor, Syria, Palestine and Egypt. Licinius was tolerant, but Maximinus Daia started persecuting the Church again.

The uneasy peace in the West between the tolerant Constantine and the anti-Christian Maxentius came to an end in 312. War broke out. Constantine, with a smaller army than Maxentius, invaded Italy; the two armies faced each other across the Milvian bridge on the river Tiber outside Rome. Up to this point, Constantine had been a sun-worshipper. However, on the night before the battle of the Milvian bridge, he had a dream in which the first two Greek letters of the name of Christ, Chi and Rho (in Greek, X and P) appeared, one on top of the other in the shape of a cross, producing the symbol depicted below. Constantine also saw or heard the words, "By this sign you will conquer." The following day Constantine had the Chi-Rho sign painted on the shields of his troops. (The Church has often used the Chi-Rho sign since then as a Christian symbol.) Then Constantine prayed to the God of the Christians for victory, and won an amazing and crushing triumph over Maxentius who was killed in battle. At the age of 32, Constantine was master of the West. He believed that the Christian God had granted him victory, and from now on Constantine acted as the great champion and protector of Christians.

THE CHI-RHO SIGN

The sign Constantine saw   *Another way of depicting the Chi-Rho*

What kind of person was this new young imperial friend of the Church? Constantine was a tall, strong, handsome man, whose physical presence always had a very positive and imposing impact on others. He had a sharp insight into people's characters and motives, an ability to strike swiftly and precisely in war and politics, and an overflowing energy which he devoted unselfishly to the affairs of the Empire. The brightest features of his moral character were his generosity with money, his sense of justice as a ruler, and his purity in matters of sex - all his Christian biographers gloried in the third of these virtues, so rare in politicians at that time. However, Constantine was also vain and flashy about his personal appearance, an easy prey to flattery, and increasingly tyrannical as his power increased. He could become extremely suspicious about the loyalty of relatives, friends and servants, with tragic results in the case of his son Crispus.

Constantine's acceptance of the Christian faith was the most important conversion in history, apart from that of the apostle Paul; as we will see, it altered the religious destiny of the Roman Empire. Because of his historic influence, Constantine certainly deserved the title that was given him - "Constantine the Great". Yet Christians and historians have often debated what really happened that fateful night at the Milvian bridge. Some have concluded that Constantine did not sincerely embrace Christianity at all; they point to some distinctly unChristian acts in Constantine's later life, *e.g.* his ordering the killing of a number of people for purely political reasons, or in a fit of rage. The darkest of these episodes was when Constantine had his own son Crispus put to death in 326. Constantine's wife Fausta falsely accused Crispus (her step-son) of trying to rape her; and Constantine, seething with fury, ordered Crispus's execution without giving him a chance to answer the charge. Were these the acts of a true follower of Jesus Christ, some have asked? But this is not a very fair argument, unless we can prove either that Christian rulers are sinlessly perfect, or that Constantine never repented (as some historians from the early Church period say he did repent of Crispus's judicial murder). Orthodox Christians who believe in the Trinity have also felt disturbed by the way that in his last years, Constantine began favouring the Arian heresy which denied that Christ was God in the flesh (see Chapter 8). But this does not disprove Constantine's Christian sincerity; it only calls in question his theological judgment, in a controversy which was so confusing in its earlier half that many orthodox bishops opposed those who upheld the deity of Christ.

On the other side, we can point to strong evidence of a Christian conscience at work in many of Constantine's laws and policies (see next Chapter, section 1). We must also recognise that Constantine had nothing to gain, either in the political or military sphere, by professing the Christian faith; the Roman ruling classes were almost entirely pagan in their religious loyalties, and by far the most popular religion in the army was the Eastern mystery cult of Mithraism. So whatever Constantine's motives were, his conversion cannot have been the product of a desire to win political or military favour. After his victory at the battle of the Milvian bridge, he certainly conformed outwardly to Christianity; he regularly attended Christian worship, listened to the longest sermons without murmuring, and observed Easter with great solemnity. Indeed, Constantine often made speeches to his court in which he condemned pagan idolatry and sang the praises of Christianity as the one true faith; and when his courtiers clapped and cheered him, he would always redirect their applause by pointing upwards to heaven.

No doubt the arguments over Constantine's conversion will continue to rumble on. But the simple fact is that at a distance of 1,700 years, it is impossible for us to be sure what was really going on in Constantine's heart and mind when he professed the Christian faith. All we can do is look at the effects which this crucial event had on the history of the Church.

While Constantine was triumphing over Maxentius in the West, war broke out in the East between Licinius and Maximinus. Licinius won. He now controlled the entire Eastern half of the Empire. In 313, Constantine and Licinius met in Milan, northern Italy, and agreed on a policy of freedom for all religions, pagan and Christian.[11] For the first time, the Empire gave Christianity full legal status as an officially tolerated faith. However, Licinius was still a pagan, and grew increasingly anti-Christian over the next decade. He dismissed all Christians from the army. He prohibited all meetings of bishops. In 320 he started persecuting Christians violently: his soldiers destroyed Church buildings and put bishops and presbyters to death. Licinius's motive was probably suspicion; he had become convinced that his Christian subjects were secretly loyal to Constantine, their fellow believer. The tensions between Licinius and Constantine finally broke out into open war in 324. Constantine invaded the East; he regarded himself as fighting a holy war against Licinius, to rescue the Eastern Church from persecution by an anti-Christian tyrant. Constantine defeated Licinius at the battle of Chrysopolis (in

---

[11] This agreement is often called the *Edict of Milan*. However, no edict was actually issued at the time of the agreement in Milan. A law was later decreed to make the Milan agreement officially legal, but this law was not an edict and was not issued in Milan!

Bithynia, Asia Minor), took him prisoner and executed him. Constantine the Christian was the single undisputed master of the entire Roman Empire.[12]

4. Christian leaders from Decius to Constantine.

Between the death of Origen in 254 and Constantine's conquest of the West in 312, a number of important Church leaders were active. Some of the most outstanding were:

Dionysius of Alexandria (died 265). Dionysius was bishop of Alexandria from 248 to 265. He tried to mediate between Cyprian of Carthage and Stephen of Rome over the baptism of heretics (see previous Chapter, section 2); Dionysius agreed with Stephen's doctrine of baptism, but supported Cyprian in his view that churches must not break communion with each other over the issue. When the persecutions under Decius and Valerian broke out, Dionysius escaped by fleeing, and recommended generous treatment of believers who had denied the faith to save their lives but had then repented. A pupil of Origen, Dionysius reproduced much of his teacher's theology, especially Origen's total opposition to Sabellianism. His *Refutation and Apology*, addressed to the bishop of Rome, also named Dionysius (bishop from 259 to 268), was an important and influential defence of the orthodox doctrine of the

---

12 An old tradition says that Constantine's mother Helen was born in the southern British city of Colchester. This tradition is found in an old English rhyme:

From Colchester there rose a star,
The rays thereof gave glorious light
Throughout the world, in climates far -
Great Constantine, Rome's emperor bright.

Constantine was certainly proclaimed emperor in York in Britain. If Helen was born in Colchester, the first of Rome's Christian emperors was also, on his mother's side, British by birth. There is no really solid proof of this, but British Christians of a bygone age often seized on this old tradition to back up the idea that Britain was a land specially chosen by God.

Trinity against Sabellian views. Unfortunately the book has not survived, except in quotations made from it by Eusebius of Caesarea and Athanasius.[13]

Firmilian of Caesarea (died 268). Firmilian, the bishop of Caesarea in Cappadocia (Asia Minor), was a friend and disciple of Origen, and exercised great influence in the Eastern Church. The only work of Firmilian's that has survived is a letter to Cyprian of Carthage, taking Cyprian's side against Stephen of Rome in the controversy over baptism of heretics. Stephen had broken off relations with the churches of Asia Minor for their pro-Cyprian stance; Firmilian's letter to Cyprian is remarkable for its outspoken criticisms of Stephen, and has proved highly embarrassing for the later Roman Catholic belief in the supremacy of the pope. "You Africans," Firmilian wrote to Cyprian, "may say to Stephen that having known the truth, you have rejected his erroneous custom. As for us, we possess at the same time both truth and custom; we oppose our custom against that of Rome; our practice is of the truth, for we have preserved from the beginning what Christ and the apostles have given to us.... O Stephen, what disputes, what discussions you stir up for all the churches in the world! What a grievous sin you have committed in separating yourself from so many flocks! You have killed yourself. Do not deceive yourself; the true schismatic is he who renounces communion with the unity of the Church. While you think that all others are separated from you, it is you who are separated from all others!"

Gregory Thaumaturgos (213-70). Gregory was the first bishop of the city of Neo-Caesarea in Pontus, Asia Minor, from the 240's onwards. He belonged to a wealthy and powerful pagan family in Neo-Caesarea; when his sister's husband became governor of Palestine, Gregory visited the province in 233, attended the lectures of Origen (who was then based in Caesarea), and was converted to Christianity. Gregory's description of his conversion is famous:

> "Like some spark kindled in my soul, a fire of love lit up and blazed forth, both towards Him, the holy and altogether lovely Logos, the most desirable of all for His unspeakable beauty, and also towards Origen, His friend and prophet."

---

[13] For Athanasius, see chapter 8, secions 2 & 3.

For the rest of his life, Gregory was a zealous disciple of Origen. Returning to his native Neo-Caesarea in 238, he was ordained its first bishop, and evangelised the city so effectively that by the time of his death in 270 almost its whole population had embraced the Christian faith. He also won a remarkable reputation for performing miracles, which is why he is called *Thaumaturgos* (Greek for "wonder-worker"). Among his writings were his *Panegyric to Origen*, where Gregory told the story of his conversion, and his *Creed or Exposition of Faith*, which contained an influential statement of faith in the Trinity (see the end of this Chapter).

Methodius (died 311). Little is known of Methodius's life. It used to be thought that he was the bishop of Olympus in Greece, but some modern scholars argue that he was actually bishop of Philippi in Macedonia. He wrote a vast number of treatises, few of which have survived in their original Greek (although some other works have survived in translation into Slavonic). Like Dionysius of Alexandria and Gregory Thaumaturgos, Methodius was a disciple of Origen - at least for a time; but he later abandoned his admiration for the great Alexandrian thinker and wrote against him. In his *On the Resurrection*, Methodius particularly opposed Origen's idea that human souls have existed from all eternity, and that the resurrection body will not be physical. This sort of opposition to Origen would become increasingly more widespread in the Eastern Church in the 4th and 5th Centuries, especially after the Arian controversy, and eventually led to Origen's official condemnation as a heretic by the Second Council of Constantinople in 553 (see Chapter 12, section 2). Methodius also wrote against Gnosticism in his *Concerning God, Matter and Free-will*, and in praise of celibacy in his *The Banquet - or, Concerning Virginity*.

Arnobius of Sicca (active 304-10). Arnobius was an adult convert from paganism in the important North-West African city of Sicca, in the province of Numidia (present-day Algeria). Few details of his life have come down to us. He taught rhetoric in Sicca. At the time of his conversion, he wrote a lengthy book in Latin entitled *Against the Gentiles*, which is a fantastically rich mine of information about the pagan religious beliefs and practices of Arnobius's day.

Lactantius (240-320). Lactantius may have been a native of Italy.

He studied rhetoric under Arnobius in Sicca, and became sufficiently famous to attract the attention of the emperor Diocletian, who appointed him a teacher of rhetoric in Nicomedia (in the province of Bithynia, Asia Minor). Having embraced Christianity, Lactantius resigned from his teaching position in 303 when Diocletian launched his great persecution of the Church, and lived in poverty until Constantine the Great made him the tutor of his son Crispus in 312. Lactantius was one of the most highly educated men of his day, and many have praised his Latin Christian writings as the most eloquent, clear and beautiful of all the Western fathers except Jerome.[14] His main work was his *Divine Institutes*, which he dedicated to Constantine. It was at the same time a masterpiece of apologetics, and the first systematic theology written in Latin (the Latin equivalent of Origen's *First Principles*). Divided into seven books, it dealt with "The false worship of the gods", "The origin of error", "The false wisdom of the philosophers", "True wisdom and religion", "Justice", "True worship" and "The blessed life". Among Lactantius's other writings was his *The Anger of God*, which set out to prove that Greek philosophy was wrong in denying the emotion of anger to God; divine anger, Lactantius argued, was a necessary part of God's reaction to sin - He cannot delight in good unless He also hates evil. This is probably Lactantius's most interesting treatise, and is still relevant today, since so many Christian theologians have followed the teachings of Greek philosophy on this point.

Important people:

The Church	*Political and military*
Julius Africanus (160-240)	Emperor Alexander Severus
Dionysius of Alexandria	(222-35)
(died 265)	Emperor Decius (249-51)
Firmilian of Caesarea (died 268)	Emperor Valerian (253-60)
Gregory Thaumaturgos (213-70)	Emperor Diocletian (284-305)
Arnobius of Sicca (active	Emperor Galerius (ruler of
304-10)	Eastern Empire 305-11)
Methodius (died 311)	Emperor Licinius (ruler of
Lactantius (240-320)	Eastern Empire 311-24)

---

[14] For Jerome, see Chapter 9, section 2.

Gregory the Illuminator
(240-332)
Marius Victorinus (died after
362)

Emperor Constantine "the Great"
(born about 280; proclaimed
Caesar 306; sole ruler of
Western Empire 312; sole
ruler of entire Empire 324-
37)

Others
Plotinus (205-70)
Mani (216-77)

An early confession of faith in the Trinity

There is one God, the Father of the living Logos Who is the Father's personal Wisdom, Power, and eternal Image. God is the One Who perfectly begets the perfect Begotten; He is the Father of His Only-begotten Son.

There is one Lord, the Only One from the Only One, God from God, the Image and Likeness of the Deity, the all-accomplishing Logos, the Wisdom Who embraces the fashioning of all things, the Power Who forms the whole creation, the true Son of the true Father: the Invisible from the Invisible, the Incorruptible from the Incorruptible, the Immortal from the Immortal, the Eternal from the Eternal.

And there is one Holy Spirit, Who has His personal existence from God, and is manifested by the Son to mankind. He is the Image of the Son, the Perfect Image of the Perfect; He is the Life, the cause of all living things; He is the holy Fountain; He is Sanctity, the source and leader of sanctification. In Him is manifested God the Father, Who is above all and in all, and God the Son, Who is through all.

There is a perfect Trinity, existing in glory and eternity and sovereignty, without division or separation. There is nothing created or in bondage in the Trinity; there is nothing added, as if it did not previously exist but was introduced later on. Thus the Father never lacked the Son, and the Son never lacked the Spirit, but without alteration or change the same Trinity endures for ever.

Gregory Thaumaturgos, *Creed or Exposition of Faith*.

The life of the pagan philosopher Plotinus

Plotinus, the philosopher, our contemporary, seemed ashamed of having a fleshly body. So deeply rooted was this feeling, that we could never persuade him to tell us of his ancestry, his parents or his birthplace. He also simply could not bring himself to agree to have his likeness portrayed by a painter or sculptor. When Amelius kept on urging him to let a portrait be made, Plotinus asked him, "Isn't it enough that I carry about this bodily image in which nature has enclosed us? Do you really think I must also agree to leave behind an image of this image, as a desirable spectacle for posterity?".... He refused to take any medicines which contained any substance from wild beasts or reptiles. After all, as he remarked, he did not even approve of eating the flesh of animals which were reared for the purpose of being served up to humans....

Plotinus possessed from his birth a greater gift than others enjoy. An Egyptian priest arrived in Rome, and a friend introduced him to Plotinus. The priest wanted to show off his powers to Plotinus, and offered to summon up a visible manifestation of Plotinus's guardian spirit. Plotinus gladly agreed; the ceremony was carried out in the temple of Isis, the only place in Rome (they say) which the Egyptian priest regarded as pure. At the priest's summons, it was not a mere spirit-being, but a divine being that appeared. The Egyptian exclaimed to Plotinus, "You are exceptionally gifted; the spirit-guide within you does not belong to the lower ranks - it is a God!".... Thus Plotinus had for his indwelling spirit a Being of the more divine degree, and he kept his own soul (itself godlike) constantly focused upon that inner presence. This was what prompted him to write his treatise on *Our Guardian Spirit*, an essay that explains the differences among spirit-guides....

He had a remarkable insight into people's characters. A precious necklace was once stolen from the honourable widow Chione, who was living with her children in the same house as Plotinus. The slaves were brought before the philosopher; he looked at each of them, and then pointed at one of them, saying, "This is the thief." The man was whipped, and kept on denying the accusation, but he eventually confessed and gave back the necklace. Plotinus also predicted the future of each of the children in the household. For example, when someone asked him about the character and destiny of Polemon, Plotinus replied, "He will be a great lover of women and will die young." And so it was!....

Eustochius has left us an account of Plotinus's last moments. Eustochius was staying at Puteoli and arrived late at Plotinus's house. When he finally entered, Plotinus said: "I have been waiting for you for a long time. I am striving to give back the Divine in myself to the Divine in the universe." And as he spoke, a snake crept under the bed where the philosopher was lying, and slipped away through a hole in the wall. At that very moment, Plotinus died.[15]

From Porphyry's *Life of Plotinus*

The meaning of life

No-one builds a house for the mere purpose that there should be a house, but that it should shelter and protect the person who lives in it. Likewise, no-one builds a ship just so that people can look at it, but so that people can sail in it. And no-one makes containers merely that containers should exist, but so that they can hold useful and necessary things. We must, then, believe that God made the world for some purpose. He created the world so that human beings might come into existence; and human beings come into existence so that they may recognise God as their Parent in Whom wisdom dwells, and worship Him as the source of justice. People worship God so that they may receive the reward of eternal life; and they receive the reward of eternal life so that they may serve God for all eternity. Do you see how everything is joined together, the beginning with the middle with the end? Let us now look at these statements individually and see if this scheme can survive an investigation.

God made the world for the sake of mankind. If you can't see this, you are little different from an animal. Who looks up at heaven except human beings? Who admires the sun, the stars, and all God's works, except human beings? Who cultivates the earth and reaps its

---

15 From this account, it is clear that Plotinus was the ultimate New Age guru of the 3rd Century.

fruits? Who navigates the sea? Who has the fish, birds and beasts in his power - who except human beings? Therefore God made everything for mankind, because all things are given over into mankind's use. The philosophers saw this correctly, but they did not see what follows - that God created mankind for Himself. Since God set about for humanity's sake so great a work as the creation of the world, and since He gave humanity so much honour and power that it was supreme in the world, it was necessary in consequence, and a duty, that humanity should acknowledge God as the Author of such great blessings - He Who created mankind, and the world for mankind's sake - and that human beings should give to God the worship and honour He deserves. We worship God so that through a religious life, which is itself justice, we may receive from God immortality. There is no other reward for the believing soul. The reward is unseen on earth; an invisible God suitably bestows only an invisible reward.

Lactantius, *Epitome of the Divine Institutes*, **chapters 63-64**

The heroism of Eastern and Western martyrs under Maximinus and Maxentius

Need I recall Maximinus's crimes of lust, or count the host of women he seduced? [Maximinus ruled Asia Minor, Syria, Palestine and Egypt from 305 to 313.] He was incapable of passing through a town without leaving a trail of dishonoured wives and ravished virgins. Everyone submitted to all his wishes, except Christians, who laughed at death and snapped their fingers at his vile tyranny. The Christian men endured fire, sword, crucifixion, wild beasts, drowning, hacking off of limbs, branding, stabbing and gouging out of eyes, mutilation of their whole bodies, and also starvation, chains and being forced to work down in the mines. They were ready to suffer anything for their faith, rather than offer to idols the worship that is due to God alone.

As for the Christian women, taught by God's Word, they showed themselves to be as manly as the men. Some underwent the same ordeals as the men, sharing with them the prize of courage. Others, when dragged away to be sexually abused, gave their souls up to death rather than submit their bodies to that dishonour. Alone among those whom the tyrant tried to seduce in Alexandria, a Christian woman of the greatest eminence and distinction named Dorothea won the victory over Maximinus's loose and lustful soul by her heroic spirit. Famed for her wealth, family and education, Dorothea put everything second to purity. In spite of Maximinus's constant attempts to seduce her, and her willingness to die rather than give in, he could not execute her, because his lust was stronger than his anger. So he exiled her as a punishment, seizing all her possessions. Countless other Christian women were assaulted by Maximinus's provincial governors, but they refused even to listen to any proposal of sexual intercourse, and so underwent every kind of punishment; they were racked and tortured till they died.

Wonderful as these women were, the crown goes to a Christian woman in Rome named Sophronia, who was the noblest and purest of all the intended victims of the drunken tyrant there, Maxentius, whose conduct was only too like Maximinus's. [Maxentius ruled Italy and North-West Africa from 306 to 312.] When Sophronia was told that the tyrant's pimps were at her door, and that her cowardly husband (a Roman prefect) had given them permission to seize her and take her away, she begged to be excused for a moment, as if to prepare herself for the occasion. Then she went into her own room, shut the door, and stabbed herself in the heart, dying instantly. She left only her dead body to the emperor's pimps; but by her deeds, which spoke more loudly than any words, she proclaimed to all people then living, or yet to be born, that the only unconquerable and indestructible possession is a Christian's virtue.

Eusebius of Caesarea, *History of the Church*, **Book 8, chapter 14**

Chapter 7.

CHRISTIANITY, PAGANISM AND SOCIETY IN THE 4TH CENTURY

1. Church and state under Constantine.

Constantine's conversion did *not* lead to Christianity becoming the official religion of the Empire in Constantine's lifetime (as many people think it did). But it did change the relationship between government and religion. For the first time, the Empire had a ruler who did not look favourably on paganism. After his victory at the battle of the Milvian bridge in 312, Constantine entered Rome and broke with tradition by refusing to offer thanks to the gods for his triumph. Instead, he had a statue of himself holding a cross erected in the centre of Rome, with the inscription: "By this sign of salvation, the true proof of courage, I saved and liberated your city from the yoke of the tyrant."

Constantine did various other things which made his Christian sympathies obvious. He introduced into his court a Spanish Christian bishop, *Hosius of Cordova* (257-357), as special advisor on Church affairs. In 321 he passed a law making Sunday, the Christian day of worship, into an official day of rest. He constructed church buildings at his own expense, and gave gifts of money to individual congregations. In Rome, Constantine gave to bishop Melchiades (311-14) the ancient palace of the Laterani family, henceforth known as the Lateran palace of the popes, where famous Western Church councils would meet; he also built the beautiful Church of Saint John Lateran, which is still Rome's cathedral church today.[1] He made Christian bishops into part of the Empire's legal structure,

---

[1] Many Christians today would object to calling a church *building* a church, on the grounds that the word "church" in the New Testament
(cont.)

by decreeing that in a civil law dispute, the two parties could take their case to the local bishop, if they so desired, and the bishop's decision would have all the force of law. Many of Constantine's other laws reveal an enlightened conscience at work - for example, he introduced a system of state welfare in the form of child maintainence grants for the poor, which helped to discourage the common Roman custom of killing unwanted children at birth. He forbade crucifixion as a method of punishment, and banned the practice of branding criminals on the forehead with a hot iron, "because the human face, created in the image of heavenly beauty, should not be disfigured". Constantine also tried to outlaw the bloodthirsty games of the gladiators; but old social habits die hard, and it was not until the reign of the emperor Honorius (395-423), when Christianity was widely accepted as the Roman faith, that the games finally ceased (see the end of the Chapter for how this happened).

One of Constantine's most historic decisions was to build a new capital city for the Eastern Empire at Byzantium in Thrace, just across the sea from Asia Minor. It was finished in 330. Constantine called it "New Rome", but it became known as "Constantinople" (Greek for "city of Constantine" - modern Istanbul in Turkey). Constantine ordered two magnificent churches to be built in the city, but no pagan temples: the Empire's new Eastern capital was, from the outset, to be a Christian city, in contrast to pagan Rome in the West. Constantinople was also a Christian city in its ethical standards; the games of the gladiators were never allowed there. After the collapse of the Western Roman Empire in 410, the Eastern Empire became known as the ***Byzantine Empire***, named after Byzantium, the earlier town on the site where Constantinople was built.

In spite of all that Constantine did to advance Christianity, paganism remained the religion of the majority of the Empire's citizens during his reign. The wealthy and educated classes did not follow their

refers to a congregation of believers, not the building in which they worship. When I refer to buildings as churches (such as the Church of Saint John Lateran), I am simply reflecting the way that Christians of that time or place used the word.

emperor's religious example. And Constantine allowed freedom of worship to pagans (although he did outlaw witchcraft and private sacrifices). The main effect of Constantine's conversion was the changed relationship between the emperor and the affairs of the Church.

In the ancient world, the state and religion were always joined together. There was no such thing as a "secular state" - a state that did not acknowledge some form of religion. Prior to Constantine's conversion, Roman emperors had taken it for granted that they had to uphold and maintain the worship of Rome's traditional gods if the Empire was to have peace and prosperity. So when the emperor became a Christian, it seemed obvious that he should use his authority in a similar way to promote Christianity. Constantine did exactly this. He felt he owed his position as emperor to the will of the Christian God, and that he must further the interests of God's Church if he was to continue to enjoy God's blessing. Constantine therefore intervened as a Christian emperor to try to settle two controversies that were disturbing the peace of the Christian community.

Donatism. The last great persecution under Diocletian had left the Church in North-West Africa bitterly divided. Large numbers of Christians refused to recognise the new bishop of Carthage, Caecilian (appointed in 311), because one of the bishops who ordained him had allegedly handed over the Bible to be burnt during Diocletian's persecution. The result was a split: two rival Churches came into being, each claiming to be the true Catholic Church in North-West Africa. One Church was led by Caecilian, the other by a rival bishop called *Donatus* (died 355). The followers of Donatus were called "Donatists".

When Constantine became master of the West, he ordered that all Church property which the authorities had confiscated during the persecution must be given back. In North-West Africa, the local government gave the property to Caecilian and his followers. The Donatists appealed to Constantine to recognise them as the rightful owners of the property, on the grounds that they were the true Catholic Church in North-West Africa. Constantine was reluctant to decide the issue personally; so he allowed various tribunals of bishops to investigate the matter. The decision finally went against the Donatists. This provoked turmoil and religious violence among the always hot-headed Christians of North-West Africa, which in turn prompted Constantine to order the African authorities in 316 to exile all Donatists and confiscate their church buildings. Constantine intended his decree to restore religious peace to the North-West African Christian community, but it failed to persuade Donatists to return to the Catholic Church. In 321 Constantine acknowledged his failure and cancelled the decree. For the next hundred years, the Christians of North-West Africa would be equally and bitterly divided between Catholics and Donatists.

Constantine's intervention in the Donatist controversy meant that for the first time, an emperor had used the power of the state to try to force dissenting Christians back into fellowship with the Catholic Church. Here was the seed which soon blossomed forth into a full-blooded practice of religious persecution by a Christian state of all religious nonconformists (pagan and Christian).

Arianism. Constantine's intervention in the Arian controversy had more serious consequences. (See the next Chapter for a fuller account of Arianism.) The Council of Nicaea, which met in 325 to settle the controversy, came together at the bidding of Constantine, not the bishops who took part. As well as summoning the Council, Constantine also helped the assembled bishops at Nicaea to formulate the Creed of Nicaea. So the government was intervening, not just in the Church's administrative affairs, but in its theology. The banishment of Arius for refusing to sign the Creed was the first time that the state had punished someone for being a heretic.

At first, the Church was happy to accept this new position of a Christian emperor in its affairs. Constantine's friend, ***Eusebius of Caesarea*** (263-339), put forward the most enthusiastic defence of the emperor's role in the Church. People have often called Eusebius "the father of Church history", because he was the first Christian writer who tried to put together a complete history of Christianity up to his own time. Eusebius, who was bishop of Palestinian Caesarea, had a glowingly positive view of the Roman Empire. He thought that both the Empire and the Church reflected, in different ways, the kingdom of heaven: the Empire had replaced political chaos by strong central government, an image of God's rule over the universe;

the Church had replaced the worship of many gods by the worship of the one true God. It was therefore only natural that Empire and Church should work together. The emperor's conversion to Christianity had simply brought the Empire to its perfection. So Eusebius had no reservations about Constantine's intervention in Church affairs. He saw Constantine as Christ's spiritual representative on earth; through the conversion of the emperor, Christ had adopted and sanctified the Empire. This type of thinking soon led to the emperor acting as head of the Church as well as head of the state, appointing and dismissing bishops and trying to control the Church's theology and worship.

2. Christians, pagans and the state: Constantius to Theodosius.

Under Constantine's sons, the Empire's drift away from paganism towards Christianity became stronger. The emperor *Constantius* (he ruled the East from 337 to 353, and the West too from 353 to 361) took a much more aggressive attitude to paganism than his father Constantine had done. In 356 he forbade all animal sacrifices and ordered all pagan temples to be closed down. Many people began to join the Church because it had become fashionable to be a Christian. This drift towards the public profession of Christianity was quicker in the East than in the West. The old Roman aristocratic families in the West remained deeply attached to their ancestral paganism; they saw it as part of the ancient Roman tradition which it would be unpatriotic for them to surrender.

This steady social trend towards Christianity was suddenly reversed in 361 when *Julian* became emperor. Julian had been brought up as a Christian, but as a young man he had renounced Christianity in favour of Neoplatonism. Christians called him "Julian the Apostate". Julian was extremely hostile to Christianity, and as emperor he devoted much of his energy to reviving paganism. He restricted government jobs to pagans. He abolished the official observance of Sunday and required all educational establishments to teach pagan religion. He wrote an anti-Christian book, *Against the Galileans*, built new temples, reintroduced animal sacrifices, and even tried to organise a sort of "pagan Church" on an Empire-wide basis, with himself as its head. If Julian had reigned for any great length of time, he might have succeeded in re-converting the Empire to a new paganism. However, Julian died in battle, fighting the Persians, in 363. With him perished the last hopes of paganism. An old tradition says that Julian addressed his dying words to Christ: "You have conquered, O Galilean."

Julian was the last Roman emperor not to profess the Christian faith. Under his successors, Christianity became an irresistible social force. By 380, *Theodosius I* (379-95), orthodox Christian emperor of the East, did not think he was doing anything very unpopular or revolutionary when he issued an edict in Constantinople announcing his intention to lead all citizens in his domain to accept Catholic Christianity. As ruler of the entire Empire from 392 onwards, Theodosius - usually called "Theodosius the Great" - issued a series of anti-pagan edicts: the authorities again closed down all pagan temples, government agents demolishing many of them; all sacrifices again became illegal. From now on, orthodox Christianity was to be the official religion of the Empire. In fact, magistrates did not strictly enforce the anti-pagan laws; pagan worship continued openly in some places for several generations (and in secret for a lot longer). However, as the Empire's public faith, paganism was now finished. Theodosius also passed severe new laws against the Manichees. The only non-Christian group that the new Christian Empire officially tolerated was the Jewish people.

Church-state relations were more difficult in this period. Some of the Christian emperors such as Constantius were upholders of the Arian heresy, and they used their power to advance Arian doctrine in the Church and to persecute orthodox believers. This prompted many Christians to deny that the emperor had any right to interfere in Church affairs. Athanasius, bishop of Alexandria and leading opponent of Arianism,[2] regarded the emperor Constantius as an antichrist; Constantius's support for Arianism convinced Athanasius that emperors should have no authority over internal Church matters. When in 355 Constantius ordered bishop Hosius of Cordova to accept Arians at the Lord's table, Hosius replied famously to the emperor:

2　See Chapter 8, sections 2 and 3 for Athanasius.

"Do not intrude yourself into ecclesiastical matters, and do not give commands concerning them, but learn from us. God has put into your hands the kingdom; to us He has entrusted the affairs of His Church. If anyone stole the Empire from you, he would be resisting what God has ordained; in the same way, you should be afraid of becoming guilty of a serious sin if you take upon yourself to govern the Church. 'Give to Caesar the things that are Caesar's, and to God the things that are God's' (**Matthew 22:21**). We are not allowed to exercise earthly rule, and you, your majesty, are not allowed to burn incense."

As Hosius indicated, this view of Church-state relations took **Matthew 22:21** as its text: "Give to Caesar the things that are Caesar's, and to God the things that are God's." That is, the Empire and the Church each have their own particular area of authority marked out for them by God. The Empire rules in all earthly, civil, political matters; but the Church is its own master in all matters of Christian doctrine and discipline. This view of Church and state became quite widespread in the West. The East, however, continued to accept the emperor's authority in Church affairs. The Byzantine Empire (the Eastern Empire after the Empire's collapse in the West) would almost always allow the emperor to act as virtually head of the Church, as long as he was orthodox in theology (and sometimes even when he wasn't). This may have been because there was a strong tradition in the East, rooted in Hellenistic culture, which saw kings as divine figures.

The Western doctrine of the independence of the Church came to its clearest expression in *Ambrose of Milan* (339-97). Ambrose was a Catholic provincial governor who became bishop of Milan in 374. After Rome, Milan was the most important city of Italy, and its church enjoyed great prestige. The death in 374 of its bishop Auxentius, the West's leading Arian, threw the Milanese church into a fierce power-struggle between Arians and Catholics over who should succeed him. It was Ambrose's duty as provincial governor to make sure that the election did not erupt into public disorder and violence. As he addressed the excited Church members, exhorting them to peaceful conduct, a child's voice suddenly shouted out, "Ambrose for bishop!" The whole crowd took up the cry, even though Ambrose was not a presbyter - in fact, he was only a

Ambrose of Milan (339 - 397)

catechumen, not yet baptised. Ambrose was horrified, but interpreted the event as God's will and reluctantly submitted.

As bishop of Milan, Ambrose attained to fame as a magnificent preacher, a resolute enemy of Arianism, and a pioneer hymn-writer. He introduced into his church in Milan the Eastern practice of congregational singing in worship. Prior to this in Western worship, the psalms had been chanted or sung "responsively", as we saw in Chapter 3, section 2, under **Church worship**; Ambrose replaced this by the more complex Eastern "antiphonal" singing. Antiphonal singing meant that half the congregation sang one passage of the psalm or hymn, and then the other half of the congregation sang the next passage, and so on, the song passing back and forth from one side of the congregation to the other. From Milan, the practice spread to all Western churches. Ambrose also popularised in Western worship the Eastern practice of singing *hymns*. By "hymns", I mean newly written songs of worship, as opposed to the Old Testament psalms and other songs or poetic passages of Scripture set to music (*e.g.* the *Magnificat* of **Luke 1:46-55**). Ambrose wrote his own hymns to teach his congregation the orthodox doctrine of Christ during the Arian controversy (see the end of the Chapter for one of Ambrose's hymns). Tradition says he wrote the great Latin hymn, the *Te deum*; whether or not Ambrose was its real author, it is certainly the greatest hymn of the Western Church from the patristic age (see end of Chapter).

When the emperor Theodosius the Great made Milan his Western capital, Ambrose became his close friend and advisor; but Ambrose was quite clear that the emperor was not to behave as a ruler in the Church. Ambrose wrote: "The Church belongs to God, therefore it cannot be assigned to Caesar. The emperor is *within* the Church, not *above* it." Ambrose's view led to a famous confrontation between bishop and emperor in 390. That year, in the city of Thessalonica, a rioting mob murdered Botherich, the virtuous governor of the province of Illyria, along with several of his officials. The results were explosive. Theodosius was normally a wise, generous, far-seeing ruler, admired for his Christian integrity of character; but he had one fatal weakness - he was prone to outbursts of wild fury, which so terrified everyone that his even wife and children would hide from him. When Theodosius heard about the murder of Botherich, he lost all self-control, and in a fit of wrath he sent an order to his soldiers to massacre the Thessalonians as a punishment. Almost immediately Theodosius recoiled from what he had done, and sent another order cancelling his savage decree.

But it was too late. The Thessalonian troops, eager to avenge the murder of their beloved governor, had already butchered some 7,000 people. When Ambrose heard of this outrage, he boldly excommunicated the emperor and exhorted him to deep, meaningful repentance (see the end of the Chapter for the letter Ambrose wrote to Theodosius). Theodosius turned up at the church in Milan on Sunday, as if nothing had happened, only to find Ambrose barring his way, refusing to let him enter. The emperor claimed he had repented; Ambrose informed him that words were not enough - his repentance must be as public as his sin had been. Theodosius submitted and walked through the streets of Milan doing public penance. He was banned from attending worship for eight months. When Ambrose finally allowed him to enter church again, the emperor had to kneel and beg God's forgiveness before the whole congregation, which he did with passionate sorrow, tears streaming from his eyes.

This was the first time that a bishop had used his spiritual authority to humble an emperor. Undoubtedly Ambrose's stern, steely, uncompromising personality also had something to do with the way he was able to face down the awesome Theodosius and compel his submission. "The only real bishop I know is Ambrose," Theodosius used to say afterwards.

Ambrose's relationship with Theodosius showed that the Western doctrine of the Church's *independence* of the emperor could, in practice, turn into the Church *controlling* the emperor. Just before the Thessalonian massacre, in 388 the Christians of Callinicum on the Euphrates burnt down a Jewish synagogue. Theodosius ordered the local bishop to rebuild the synagogue from church funds. Ambrose intervened, declaring that it was wrong for a Christian bishop to be forced to use his church's money to build a place for non-Christian worship. He preached a sermon against Theodosius when the emperor was actually sitting in the congregation, and refused to let Theodosius take part in holy communion unless he gave up his plan to make the Christians of Callinicum rebuild the synagogue.

Theodosius surrendered to Ambrose and the synagogue was not rebuilt. We see here how a Church leader could use his disciplinary power to force a Christian emperor into obeying his will.

3. The development of Church teaching, organisation, worship and life.

Perhaps at no time before the Protestant Reformation of the 16th Century (see Part Three) did the theology, organisation, worship and life of the Church undergo such important developments as they did in the 4th Century. All we can do in this section is give a broad outline of what Christianity came to "look like" in the complex and colourful century of Constantine and Theodosius.

Church teaching

The central feature of the Church's theology in the 4th Century was the way it hammered out its doctrine of the Trinity on the harsh anvil of the Arian controversy. We will consider this in detail in the next Chapter. Here, however, we will look at the important view of Scripture and tradition which generally prevailed among the 4th Century fathers.

We saw in Chapter 4, section 2, how the "canon" of the New Testament Scriptures was formed, a process that reached completion in the 4th Century. The Church submitted itself utterly to the New Testament because it carried the authority of the apostles; through the Scriptures which the apostles either wrote or sanctioned, their voice continued to speak in the Church. The Old and New Testaments together, the prophetic and apostolic writings, were the divinely inspired and infallible Word of God, and they contained everything the believer needed to know for his salvation. Cyril of Jerusalem[3] taught his catechumens that

> "no doctrine concerning the divine and saving mysteries of the faith, however trivial, may be taught without the backing of the holy Scriptures. We must not let ourselves be drawn aside by mere persuasion and cleverness of speech. Do not even give

3   For Cyril of Jerusalem, see later in this section under **Church worship**.

absolute belief to me, the one who tells you these things, unless you receive proof from the divine Scriptures of what I teach. For the faith that brings us salvation acquires its force, not from fallible reasonings, but from what can be proved out of the holy Scriptures."

Gregory of Nazianzus[4] saw the inspiration of the Holy Spirit behind the tiniest details of the Bible:

"We trace the careful activity of the Spirit even in the details of Scripture, and we will never admit the irreverent idea that even the most trivial historical statements of Scripture were not carefully committed to writing by their authors with a serious purpose."

This doctrine of the Bible's "inspiration and inerrancy", as we call it today, was to be the understanding held throughout the Church in East and West, down through the ages until the Enlightenment of the 18th Century (see Part Four).

In the patristic era, alongside the written apostolic witness of the New Testament went the unwritten apostolic witness of "tradition". The word tradition in Greek is *paradosis* and simply means "what is handed down". The early Church fathers could sometimes use this word in a wide sense to include both the written and unwritten teachings and practices of the apostles, which had been handed down in the Church - both Scripture and customs. However, it was more common in the 4th Century to refer specifically to the unwritten customs as "tradition". Because the fathers regarded tradition and Scripture as equally apostolic, they had a high view of the authority of tradition. The apostolic traditions, however, were not concerned with the doctrinal content of the faith; as Athanasius proclaimed, "the holy and inspired Scriptures are fully sufficient for the declaration of the truth," echoing what we have heard Cyril of Jerusalem saying, "the faith that brings us salvation acquires its force from what can be proved out of the holy Scriptures." The doctrines of salvation were treasured up in apostolic Scripture; but apostolic tradition contained other things the Church needed to know for its

---

4   For Gregory of Nazianzus, see next Chapter, section 3.

organisation and worship. Basil of Caesarea[5] put it (perhaps rather more strongly than other fathers) like this:

"Some of the beliefs and practices which have been preserved in the Church we have received from written teaching; others have been delivered to us 'as in a mystery' [**1 Corinthians 2:7**] from the tradition of the apostles. Both have the same authority for true godliness. No-one will disagree with these things, if he has the smallest experience of the Church's ordinances. If we tried to play down the value of the customs that lack written authority, claiming that they have little validity, we would unwittingly inflict serious damage on the Gospel. For example, to mention the most common custom, who gave us a written command to make the sign of the cross over those who have set their hope on the name of the Lord Jesus? What written command do we have for turning to the east in prayer? Which of the saints has left in writing the words of the invocation [praying that the Spirit will bless] when the bread of the eucharist and the cup of blessing are displayed? We do not simply limit ourselves to the written record [of holy communion] found in the apostle Paul and the Gospels, but we add on at the beginning and the end other things received from the unwritten tradition, and we regard these things as very important in the way we observe the eucharist. We bless the water of baptism, the oil of chrism, and the person being baptised - but there are no written commands to do so. We do these things on the basis of the unspoken secret tradition. And what of the anointing with oil? Which written word commanded that? Where does the custom of immersing people three times in baptism come from? As for the other rites of baptism, from what Scripture do we obtain the renouncing of Satan and his angels? Does this not come from the unwritten secret teaching?"

This passage from Basil shows us many of the worship-customs which he and the other fathers believed had been handed down from the apostles. We will look at some of these customs in the section on

---

5   For Basil of Caesarea, see next Chapter, section 3.

Basil of Caesarea (330 - 379)

Church worship. The point here is simply that these were the kind of things that belonged to the realm of "apostolic tradition": not theological teaching, but certain customs of Church worship and organisation. Later, however - in the 5th Century - the Church came to reckon the doctrinal definitions of ecumenical Councils (see next heading) as inspired by the Holy Spirit.

Church organisation

Church organisation in the 2nd and 3rd Centuries had been relatively simple. Each church had its own bishop, and all bishops were equal. In the 4th Century, Church government began to become more complex. Bishops were no longer equal, but became graded into an order of more and less important - a "hierarchy". For a start, the bishops of major cities of the Empire gained greater authority. The Council of Nicaea in 325 decreed that all the bishops of each province of the Empire should meet together twice a year in synod, and it granted the bishop of each provincial capital a special status as president of the synod. The bishop of a provincial capital (a *metropolis* - Greek for "mother city") was called a *metropolitan* bishop, or sometimes an *archbishop* (Greek for "chief bishop"). A further development was that many churches came into existence which did not have a bishop at all. This happened in cities where the congregation became too big to meet in one place. Smaller congregations were set up, still under the authority of the bishop of the city, but cared for spiritually by a presbyter who was responsible to the bishop. It soon became common for the normal pastor of a congregation to be a presbyter (a priest), and for the bishop to be pastor only of the central church of a city.

Next, a few bishops became even more powerful than the metropolitans or archbishops, owing to the outstanding spiritual or political importance of their cities and churches. These supreme bishops came to be called *patriarchs* (Greek for "fatherly rulers").[6] The Church eventually recognised the bishops of Rome, Constantinople, Alexandria, Antioch and Jerusalem as having this highest

---

6   The title "patriarch" was first used at the Council of Constantinople in
     381, when Nectarius was ordained bishop of Constantinople.

patriarchal rank; the recognition became official at the Council of Chalcedon in 451. By the 5th Century, the territories of the different patriarchs had become fairly well-defined, and all other bishops and archbishops in each territory (called a "province") were under their patriarch's authority. The patriarch of Constantinople became supremely important in the East, simply because his city was the capital of the Eastern or Byzantine Empire. In the West, the bishop of Rome was the only patriarch. The Church might have recognised the bishop of the West's second greatest city, Carthage, as a patriarch too, but Vandal[7] and Arab invasions in the 5th and 7th Centuries left Carthage in ruins. Christians tended to give their patriarchs the affectionate title of "papa" or pope, which means "father". However, the normal custom is to give the title "pope" specifically to the bishop of Rome, and the title "patriarch" to the bishops of Constantinople, Alexandria, Antioch and Jerusalem.[8] Until the great East-West schism of 1054 (see Part Two, Chapter 3, section 8), the Eastern Church held to the theory that the five patriarchs of Constantinople, Rome, Alexandria, Antioch and Jerusalem should act together as the leaders of the universal Church.

The other important structure that developed in the 4th Century was the *ecumenical Council*. This was an assembly of bishops from throughout the Empire. ("Ecumenical" comes from the Greek word meaning "the inhabited earth"). From the 5th Century, the Church regarded the decisions of a Council about doctrine and discipline as inspired by the Holy Spirit and therefore authoritative (in the West, only if the Council was sanctioned by the papacy). The first two ecumenical Councils both assembled in the 4th Century to settle the Arian controversy - the Council of Nicaea in 325, and the Council of Constantinople in 381. Christian emperors summoned both Councils; so it became an accepted principle in the East that an emperor should call together an ecumenical Council. He was not in theory supposed

---

7   The Vandals were a tribal confederacy from Germany who conquered North-West Africa in the early 5th Century. See Chapter 11, section 1.

8   In other words, "pope" and "patriarch" really mean the same thing. It would be correct to speak about the pope of Constantinople, the pope of Alexandria, *etc*. But most readers would find the idea of five popes confusing!

to control the Council after he had convened it, but in practice an emperor could exercise a powerful influence over what went on in a Council. In the West, by contrast, as the spiritual claims of the papacy grew (especially under pope Leo the Great,[9] pope from 440 to 461), the theory was that the pope should summon an ecumenical Council, or at least give it his approval, if it was to be valid.

Church worship

The worship of the Church underwent important developments in the 4th Century. Up until now, virtually all churches throughout the Empire had conducted their worship in the same language, Greek. However, in the 4th Century, the West increasingly used Latin, until by about 350 it had replaced Greek as the preferred language of Western worship. This reflected the fact that the Eastern and Western halves of the Empire were drifting apart culturally, and it contributed powerfully to the process by which Eastern and Western Christianity went different ways theologically and spiritually. Also, within the East, many Syrian churches began to use Syriac in worship, and many Egyptian churches began to use Coptic. This paved the way for Syrian and Egyptian Christians to form their own independent national Churches in the 5th and 6th Centuries, separate from the mainstream of Eastern Byzantine Christianity (see Chapter 12).

There was also an increasing emphasis in 4th Century worship on *liturgy* - a fixed, written form of worship. As we have seen, liturgies had been in use in Christian worship from the earliest times (see Chapter 3, section 2, under **Church worship**), but there was now less and less room for the bishop, who led the worship, to vary from the set pattern. Again, in the earlier centuries the different main churches had their own liturgies; but now, in the East, the liturgies of Basil of Caesarea and of the church in Constantinople came to dominate. Basil of Caesarea revised the liturgy of the church in Caesarea - it is still used in Eastern Orthodoxy today during Lent and Christmas. The rest of the time, Eastern Orthodoxy employs the shorter Constantinople liturgy, known as the liturgy of John

---

9   For Leo the Great, see Chapter 10, section 4.

Chrysostom.[10] Churches throughout the West increasingly conformed their liturgies either to the one used in Rome, or (usually) to the "Gallican" liturgy of the French churches. It was only in the 8th Century that the Roman liturgy triumphed over the Gallican in Western worship.

Other aspects of worship also underwent change in the 4th Century, *e.g.* the way Christians celebrated Easter. In previous centuries, only Easter Sunday had really been important; but the 4th Century saw the development of the 40 days of Lent and the Easter week, with Good Friday as significant as Easter Sunday. The celebration of Christmas on the 25th of December also became an established practice in the 4th Century. It is first mentioned in Western worship in the year 336. The date was the pagan festival of the birth of the sun, taken over and Christianised by the Church (for sun-worship see previous Chapter, section 2). The customs of the old Roman festival of the *Saturnalia* on 17th-21st December, when candles were lit, parties held and gifts exchanged, also became attached to Christmas. In the East, the 6th of January was for some time the preferred date for celebrating Christ's birth, but in 379 Gregory of Nazianzus introduced the Western date in Constantinople when he was bishop there. Still, it was not until 431 that Egypt accepted 25th December as the date of Christmas; Palestinian Christians did not accept it until the 6th Century; and the Armenian Church still celebrates Christmas on 6th January to this day.

4th Century worship also witnessed a powerful trend towards a greater use of ritual and ceremony. We find the clearest example of this in the church of Jerusalem during the leadership of Cyril (310-86), bishop from 350 - usually called *Cyril of Jerusalem*, to distinguish him from the 5th Century father Cyril of Alexandria.[11] It is in Cyril's Jerusalem church that we first hear of clergy wearing special vestments, the use of incense, the carrying of lights (lamps, candles, tapers), and other ceremonies. Cyril's *Catechetical*

---

10 For John Chrysostom, see Chapter 9, section 1. The Constantinople liturgy is named after Chrysostom, but there is little evidence to connect him with the writing of it.

11 For Cyril of Alexandria, see Chapter 10, sections 3 and 4.

Lectures to his catechumens, based on the Creed of Jerusalem (almost identical with the Apostles' Creed - see Chapter 4, section 2), give us a colourful picture of the baptismal ceremonies which were practised in the 4th Century.

Cyril tells us that the catechumens gathered in the vestibule of the baptistery, turned to the West, and publicly renounced "Satan, his works, his pomp and his service". Then, turning to the East, they professed their faith in the Trinity. After this the catechumens were led into the baptistery, where they took off their clothes and were anointed with oil which had first been exorcised. Then, one by one, they were immersed three times in the baptismal pool; this threefold or triple immersion signified their faith in each of the three persons of the Trinity, and Christ's three-day slumber in the tomb. They were then anointed with oil again, on the forehead, ears, nostrils and breast, in a ceremony called *chrismation* (from *chrisma*, the Greek word for "anointing"). Chrismation symbolised the gift of the Holy Spirit. Finally, the newly baptised people were clothed in white garments, given lighted tapers, and led into the main part of the church where they took part in holy communion for the first time. In the Western churches, they were also given milk and honey just before communion, to symbolise their entrance into the heavenly promised land. Catechumens throughout the Empire were all baptised at the same period, Easter and Pentecost.

Cyril's *Lectures* give us a full account of how the Catholic Church had, by the 4th Century, come to understand the meaning of baptism. Cyril called baptism "the bath of regeneration" and taught his catechumens that it had three main effects. First, it washed away the guilt of all sins committed prior to baptism. Second, it sanctified the baptised person, by conferring on him spiritual union with Christ in His death and resurrection, the gift of the Spirit, and adoption as God's child. Third, it impressed a "seal" or permanent mark on the soul, by virtue of which the baptised person was set apart as the Holy Spirit's temple. Cyril's doctrine of baptism was the view held by all Christians in the 4th Century, and indeed from the 150's onward. In assessing this patristic doctrine of "baptismal regeneration", modern readers should keep four things in mind:

(a) Cyril and other fathers insisted that it was not the *water* of baptism that bestowed these spiritual benefits, but the Holy Spirit,

Who worked inwardly in the soul at the same time that the water outwardly washed the body.

(b) *Believers' baptism* was the norm of baptismal practice in the 4th Century. Even though there is clear evidence that infant baptism was practised (and probably had been since the 2nd Century[12]), most Christian parents would still not baptise their children, precisely because they linked baptism with the washing away of sin. For example, Monica, the mother of the great theologian Augustine of Hippo (354-430), did not have Augustine baptised in infancy, because she did not want him to lose the grace of baptism by all the sins she felt sure he would commit as a child and teenager.[13] Owing to this widespread belief that baptism could deal only with sins committed *before* a person was baptised, even adult converts often delayed their baptism till the last possible moment, when they were ill and dying. The classic example of this was the emperor Constantine the Great, who was baptised only in his last moments of life.

(c) If a catechumen died before being baptised, some of the greatest of the early Church fathers taught that he or she was saved without baptism. When the godly young Western emperor Valentinian II (383-92) was murdered in 392 before his baptism, Ambrose of Milan comforted Valentinan's two sisters with the assurance that their brother's soul had gone to be with Christ. "It was enough that he desired baptism," Ambrose said. "His sincere desire for baptism was no less effective than baptism itself." Augustine taught the same: "A person is baptised invisibly, when the reason why he was not baptised in water was an unavoidable death rather than contempt for true religion."

(d) The fathers saw *acceptance of the true faith* as necessary if baptism was to be effective. The mere physical act of baptism, without true faith, was empty of value. Baptism given by heretics, *e.g.* Manichees and Arians, was therefore regarded by the early

---

12 In his treatise *Concerning Baptism*, written in about 200, Tertullian spoke about Christian parents baptising their infants. He argued against the practice, but recognised that it happened.

13 For Augustine, see Chapter 9, section 3.

Church fathers as spiritually worthless; heretics performed the outward act of baptism, but their faith was not in the true gospel, and so their baptism conferred no spiritual benefit.[14]

Along with the growth of ritual and ceremony in 4th Century worship went the expansion of the "cult" (religious honouring) of saints and relics. Christians attached an ever greater importance to the dead bodies of those who had been considered outstandingly holy in their lifetimes, especially martyrs. Chapels and shrines, and sometimes churches, were built over the tombs of saints. Believers increasingly prized "relics" of saints - things that had belonged to the saint when he was alive, *e.g.* a piece of his clothing, or even one of his bones. The idea developed (it had been present in seed-form since earliest times) that the dead saint, now in heaven, could help struggling believers on earth by his prayers. After all, "The effective, fervent prayer of a righteous man avails much" (**James 5:16**); surely a saint's prayers would be even more effective now that he was in heaven? So Christians practised - not praying *to* the saints - but asking the saints in heaven to pray *for* them. This was called

---

14 This is not to say that all the early Church fathers would have *rebaptised* a heretic who converted to orthodoxy. Opinions were divided. Athanasius of Alexandria and Basil of Caesarea practised the rebaptism of *heretics*, *e.g.* Arians. But unlike Cyprian of Carthage, they did not rebaptise *schismatics* (*e.g.* Novatianists), who held to the orthodox faith even though they were out of fellowship with the Catholic Church. (See Chapter 5, section 2 for Cyprian and the Novatianists.) However, other fathers held that *heretical* baptism was valid as an outward act, even though it conferred no inner spiritual benefit; the heretic did not need to be rebaptised, but he still needed to receive the Holy Spirit. The French council of Arles in 314 decided that as long as a heretic had been baptised in the name of the Trinity, he did not need rebaptism; but he did need prayer and the laying on of hands in order to receive the Spirit. East and West eventually went different ways on this issue. Both held that the Holy Spirit works only in the true Church. But the West concluded from this that when a baptised heretic or schismatic joined the Church, the Spirit would at that point make his baptism effective, and that rebaptism was wrong. The East, by contrast, concluded that the converted heretic or schismatic should normally be rebaptised, since baptism could not be spiritually effective outside the true Church. (Sometimes the East relaxed this rule to make it easier for heretics and schismatics to convert.)

"invocation", or "invoking" the saints (from the Latin *invocare*, "to call upon"). In popular piety, it often drifted into a custom of actually praying *to* the saints which was little different from the way that pagans had prayed to their various gods. People considered particular saints to be especially good at meeting particular needs: one could bring about a cure for childlessness, another could protect travellers, another could reveal the future, *etc.*

The great Church leaders of the time, like Basil of Caesarea, Chrysostom, Ambrose, Augustine and Jerome,[15] positively encouraged this cult of the saints, relics, and invocations. Others, however, did not like what was going on. A French presbyter called Vigilantius protested at what he saw as Christians lapsing into pagan customs and practices: "Disguised as religion, we almost see the ceremonies of the pagans being introduced into the churches. People light rows of candles in broad daylight, and in all places they kiss and adore the dust of a dead body, contained in a little pot and wrapped up in a precious cloth."

It was also during the 4th Century that believers began to adorn churches with pictures of Christ and the saints (this would include holy men and women from the Bible itself and from the history of the Christian Church). Christians in the East called these pictures *icons* - icon is the Greek word for "image". Prior to the 4th Century, Christian icons had hardly ever been used to decorate churches, although Christians had certainly used them in other contexts. For example, Tertullian spoke (disapprovingly) of cups which depicted Christ as a good shepherd carrying a sheep. Clement of Alexandria mentioned signet rings with which Christians attached their personal seal to a letter; these rings impressed a Christian symbol into the sealing wax.- a fish (Christ), a dove (the Holy Spirit), an anchor (faith - see **Hebrews 6:19**), a loaf of bread (holy communion). The fish was a favourite icon symbolising Christ. The Greek word for fish was IXΘΥΣ (in English, "ichthus"); each letter in the word stood for Ιησους Χριστος Θεου Υιος Σωτηρ – "Jesus Christ, Son of God, Saviour". The great Church historian of the 4th Century, Eusebius of Caesarea (see section 1), although himself personally opposed to

---

15 See Chapter 9, section 2 for Jerome.

icons, mentioned their widespread existence: "The features of the apostles Paul and Peter, and indeed of Christ Himself, have been preserved in coloured portraits which I have examined."[16]

Christian icons were particularly used in Rome on and around the tombs of believers. These tombs were located in secret underground passages known as "catacombs", and date back to the 1st Century AD. Early Christian art in the Roman catacombs often depicted Biblical scenes: from the Old Testament, favourite scenes were Noah's ark, Abraham sacrificing Isaac, Jonah in the fish, Daniel in the lion's den, and Shadrach, Meshach and Abednego in the fiery furnace; best-loved scenes from the New Testament were Christ being baptised, the Samaritan woman at the well, Peter walking on the water, and the raising of Lazarus. The first *church* we know about which had pictures like these painted on its walls was a 3rd Century church in Dura (in present-day Iraq).

However, it was only in the 4th Century that the adorning of churches with icons became a common practice. In part, this was because it was only in the 4th Century that church buildings themselves became the universal norm; before the conversion of Constantine, when the threat of persecution continually hung over Christians, many assemblies of believers still met in private houses. But when the fear of government persecution vanished in Constantine's reign, Christians could afford to be much more open and public in expressing their faith; and so the construction of special buildings for worship, and the adorning of these buildings with Christian art, went hand-in-hand. Even so, some of the 4th Century fathers, notably *Epiphanius of Salamis* (315-403), were violently opposed to this use of icons in churches. Epiphanius, bishop of the capital city of Cyprus, was a zealous foe of Arianism and all other deviations from orthodoxy; his book, *Medicine Chest for the Cure of All Heresies,* is our greatest single source of information about non-Catholic religious groups in the patristic period. As far as Epiphanius was concerned, icons in churches were another deviation. He once saw a picture of Christ woven into a curtain in a church in Palestine, and was so angry that he tore it down and complained to the bishop of Jerusalem.

---

[16] Eusebius's *History of the Church*, Book 7, paragraph 18.

But Epiphanius was fighting a losing battle. Other great fathers of the 4th Century, like Ambrose of Milan and Augustine of Hippo, defended the adorning of church buildings with religious icons. They became extremely popular; most churches soon displayed images of Christ and the saints, in the form of paintings, tapestries, mosaics and sculptures. Bibles, too, increasingly contained religious illustrations, which were often very beautiful. However, Epiphanius's hostility to icons never entirely died out in the Church, and it blazed up again in the Eastern Church with devastating ferocity in the great "iconoclastic controversy" of the 8th and 9th Centuries.[17]

Church life: The monastic movement

The most significant development in the spiritual life of the Church in this period was *monasticism*. Many ordinary Christian men became so disgusted with the sinful state of the Empire that they decided to "drop out" of society completely. Like John the Baptist **(Luke 1:80, Mark 1:4-6)**, they would go off into remote unpopulated regions, such as deserts, and live simple ascetic lives there, away from the corrupting influences of the world. Men who did this were called *monks* (from the Greek *monachos*, a person who lives alone). The movement began to develop in the latter half of the 3rd Century, but it became widespread only in the 4th. Its origins were in the less civilised areas of Syria and Egypt, where Hellenistic culture had not made much impact. As their name suggests, the early monks lived solitary lives, but soon three different types of monk came into existence:

(a) Some monks continued to live alone as *hermits* (from the Greek *eremia*, the desert) or *anchorites* (from the Greek *chorizo*, to separate).[18] The solitary lifestyle of the monks who lived alone is known as *eremitic* monasticism. The supreme example of the hermit was an Egyptian desert monk called *Antony* (251-356),[19] a

---

17 For the iconoclastic controversy, see Part Two, Chapter 3, section 3.

18 Later, monks applied the term "anchorite" to a special kind of hermit - one who lived not just alone, but in closely confined quarters, *e.g.* a cell in a monastery. A woman anchorite was called an "anchoress".

19 The dates of Antony's life are correct; he lived a long time!

close friend of Athanasius, the great bishop of Alexandria.
Athanasius wrote a popular biography of Antony which helped to
spread monastic ideals in both East and West. Born into a rich
Christian family, Antony withdrew from society as a young man,
giving away all his money and property to the poor. He then spent
some 20 years alone in the Egyptian desert, in a ruined fort near the
Red Sea, where he fasted, prayed, studied the Scriptures, and
engaged in dramatic struggles with demons. Emerging from his
solitude in the early 4th Century, he gathered a group of disciples and
taught them the spiritual wisdom he had learned in his lonely years.
People looked on Antony as an awesome figure, someone who
seemed on a higher spiritual plane than ordinary Christians. He had
a reputation as a miracle-worker. Probably no-one had such a great
effect as Antony in attracting others to live the monastic life.

(b) Others lived together in a community of monks. This is known as
cenobitic monasticism, from the Greek *koinos bios*, "common life".
The place where the monks lived was called a *monastery* - the word
originally meant a hermit's cave. The chief inspiration behind
cenobitic or community monasticism was *Pachomius* (290-346),[20]
a native of southern Egypt and an ex-soldier. Pachomius at first
practised the solitary life of a hermit, but in about 320 he founded a
community of monks in the Egyptian village of Tabbenisi. His monks
lived a common life, working and praying and eating together, and
sharing all property (based on the early Christians of Jerusalem,
Acts 2:44-5). They were economically self-supporting through
their manual work - *e.g.* weaving and farming. Pachomius wrote a
"rule" to govern the community life of his monks, and other monastic
communities adopted this rule. The rule laid down a sort of schedule
or timetable for the daily activities of the community - when the
monks were to work, pray, meditate, *etc*. Another important aspect
of the monastic community was its practice of strict obedience to its
leader. Monks normally called the head of a monastery an *abbot*
(from the Aramaic *abba*, father). In the East, they sometimes
referred to an abbot as a *hegumenos* (Greek for leader); the head
of an important Eastern monastery, or of a group of monasteries, was
called an *archimandrite* (from the Greek *arche*, ruler, and

---

20 Pronounced "Pak-oh-me-us".

mandra, a sheepfold). From "abbot" came the word *abbey* as a description for a monastery. Much later, monasteries were also known as *convents* and *cloisters*.

(c) Another type of monasticism which became quite popular in the East was a sort of cross between the eremitic and cenobitic, called *skete* monasticism (from the Skete region of Egypt). A skete was a small group of up to 12 monks living together with a more experienced monk, who acted as their spiritual director. They would meet together with other local sketes for joint-services on Sundays and other holy days.

The monastic movement was not restricted to men. Christian women also established communities devoted to cultivating the spiritual life; these women were called *nuns* and their communities *nunneries*. This comes from the Latin word *nonna*, which is the feminine form of the Latin word for a monk, *nonnus*. The head of a nunnery was known as an *abbess* (the feminine form of abbot) - or in the East, a *hegumena*.

All monks, whether eremitic, cenobitic or skete-type, would renounce all worldly property and pleasures, be celibate, and consecrate themselves to prayer, fasting and Bible study. This simple, disciplined style of life practised by monks and nuns was part of the general spirit of asceticism, which had become increasingly popular in Roman society since the 3rd Century, partly through the impact of Neoplatonism.[21] Even Christians who did not become monks often practised an ascetic lifestyle; almost all the leading Churchmen of the 5th and following Centuries were ascetics. An ever more popular aspect of Christian asceticism was a belief in the high spiritual worth of celibacy - *i.e.* leading a single (unmarried) life. By the end of the 4th Century, most Christians had come to accept that celibacy was better than marriage. Congregations began to insist that their bishops must be celibate men. And as Christians more and more saw the monasteries as the best training-grounds for spiritual life, churches increasingly drew their bishops from among monks who were already committed to celibacy.

---

[21] See previous Chapter, section 2, on Neoplatonism.

The early monks of Egypt had a great influence on later generations of monks, ascetics and theologians, and are often referred to as the "desert fathers". Their understanding and practice of the Christian life, which owed much to the teachings of Origen,[22] were preserved in an important body of writings known as *Sayings of the Fathers*. However, it was the writings of *Evagrius Ponticus* (345-99), a native of Asia Minor who settled in Egypt in the 380's, that best summed up, and gave a theological framework to, the spirituality of the desert fathers. Evagrius made an abiding impact on later Eastern theologians, and on the great John Cassian, who did much to promote the monastic movement in the Western half of the Empire (see below).

Syrian and Egyptian monks tended to be very cut off from society. By contrast, Greek or Hellenistic monasticism preserved many more links with the surrounding culture. It was largely shaped by Basil, bishop of Caesarea, one of the "Cappadocian fathers" (see next Chapter, section 3). Basil discouraged monks from living alone; he preferred them to live together in communities. He founded many monasteries in Asia Minor and, like Pachomius, drew up a set of rules for monks to live by (Basil's rules are still influential in Eastern Orthodox monasticism today). Monasteries which were run according to Basil's rules were not cut off from society, but educated children, nursed the sick, and gave hospitality to travellers. By the 5th Century it became an accepted principle that only a bishop could establish a monastery.

In the West, monastic communities began to spring up in the mid-4th Century. Athanasius's *Life of Antony* was translated into Latin and had great influence. Anthony's Western equivalent was the gentle ex-soldier and zealous foe of Arianism, *Martin of Tours* (335-97). Born in Pannonia (present-day Hungary), Martin founded a loose association of hermits in Ligugé in France in the 360's, and promoted monasticism after becoming bishop of Tours (north-western France) in 372. From Tours, Martin's monks streamed out through the French countryside, evangelising pagans and founding monasteries and churches. Another central figure was *John Cassian* (360-435), a Scythian who spent seven years among the desert fathers of

---

22 For Origen, see Chapter 5, section 1.

Egypt before settling in southern France and founding a monastery and a nunnery in the city of Marseilles in 415. A disciple of Evagrius Ponticus, Cassian's writings (especially his *Institutes* and *Conferences*) spread in the West the ideals of the desert fathers of Egypt, and had a vast influence on the development of the whole Western monastic movement.

From the outset, Western monasticism enjoyed the enthusiastic support of leading Churchmen - Ambrose of Milan, Jerome, Augustine of Hippo. This gave it respectability and authority. It had a more cultured spirit than in the East; in Western monasticism, the ideal of withdrawing from the world to cultivate the ascetic life came to include cultivating the mind through the study of literature. This was an old Roman aristocratic ideal, and was one of the reasons why Western monasticism tended to attract converts from the ranks of the Roman aristocracy. The great Roman noble *Cassiodorus* (477-570) was especially influential in popularising this "marriage" between asceticism and culture; he outlined his ideal in his *Introduction to Theological and Secular Studies*. After the collapse of the Roman Empire in the West, the Western monasteries acted as the guardians of Western European culture and civilisation, and became the vital centres of education in the Western Catholic world. The monks were also the great missionary force of the later patristic age and Middle Ages: free from all ties of marriage and family, disciplined to live in poverty, they carried the faith into pagan lands, planting and watering it there. England and Germany, to give two outstanding examples, were Christianised by missionary monks.

Important people:

The Church
Eusebius of Caesarea
  (263-339)
Pachomius (290-346)
Donatus (active 313-55)
Antony (251-356)
Hosius of Cordova (257-357)
Cyril of Jerusalem (310-86)
Martin of Tours (335-97)
Ambrose of Milan (339-97)
Evagrius Ponticus (345-99)

Political and military
Emperor Constantius (337-61)
Emperor Julian the Apostate (361-3)
Emperor Theodosius the Great (ruled
  the East from 379; ruled entire
  Empire 392-95)

Epiphanius of Salamis (315-403)
John Cassian (360-435)
Cassiodorus (477-570)

Eusebius of Caesarea: Constantine, the emperor whom Christ loves

The only-begotten Logos of God reigns from ages which had no beginning, to infinite and eternal ages, the partner of His Father's kingdom. In a similar way our emperor, whom He loves, derives the source of his imperial authority from above, is powerful in his sacred title, and has controlled the empire of earth for a long period of years. Again, the Preserver of the universe orders all heaven and earth, and the kingdom of the stars, in harmony with His Father's will. Even so, our emperor whom He loves guides his earthly subjects to the Only-begotten Logos and Saviour, and so makes them good citizens in his kingdom. Again, He Who is the common Saviour of mankind, by His divine and invisible power, like a good shepherd, banishes far from His flock those savage beasts, the fallen spirits, who once flew through the heavens, and swooped down on human souls. Likewise His friend, our emperor, graced by His divine favour with victory over all his enemies, vanquishes and chastises the open foes of truth in accordance with the laws of war. Once again, the eternally existing Logos, the Saviour of all, gives His disciples the seeds of true wisdom and salvation, making them truly wise to understand their Father's kingdom. Likewise our emperor, His friend, acts as interpreter of the Logos of God, and aims at calling the entire human race back to the knowledge of God, proclaiming openly in everyone's hearing, and declaring with a mighty voice, the laws of truth and godliness to all earth's inhabitants. Yet again, the universal Saviour opens the heavenly gates of His Father's kingdom to all who are fleeing from this world. Likewise our emperor, imitating the One Who sets this example, has purified his earthly realm from every stain of ungodly error, and invites all holy and godly worshippers to enter his imperial palaces, desiring with all his strength to save that mighty vessel of Empire and all its crew, of which he is the appointed pilot.

Eusebius of Caesarea, *Oration on the Thirtieth Anniversary of Constantine,* **chapter 2, sections 1-5**

The end of the gladiatorial games: Telemachus's protest and martyrdom

Honorius, who inherited the Western Empire [he reigned 395-423], put a stop to the games of the gladiators which had been held for so long in Rome. A particular incident prompted him to take this action. A man named Telemachus, who had become a monk, set out from the Eastern Empire and entered Rome. There, when the hateful spectacle of the games was taking place, Telemachus went into the stadium, stepped down into the arena, and tried to stop the men who were fighting each other. The spectators of the bloody match were outraged. Inspired by the mad fury of the demons who delight in deeds of violence, they stoned to death Telemachus the peacemaker. But when the admirable emperor heard of this, he numbered Telemachus among the army of victorious martyrs, and put an end to that ungodly spectacle of the games.

Theodoret of Cyrrhus, *Church History*, Book 5, chapter 26

A morning hymn by Ambrose of Milan

Brightness of the Father's glory,
Spread the splendour of Your light;
Radiant Fountain, Dayspring dawning,
Banish now the shades of night!

O true Sun, arise within us,
Shining with Your steady beam;
O plant deep within our senses
God the Holy Spirit's flame!

God the Father, too, we worship,
Father of all-powerful grace;
Glorious Father everlasting,
From our hearts all treason chase!

Breathe Your mighty strength within us,
Break the pride of Satan's power;
Turn our hardships into triumphs;
Grant us wisdom every hour.

Guide our minds, uphold our thinking,
Keep our limbs for service fit;
Feed our faith with love's pure burning,
Purged from malice and deceit.

Christ our Lord, be bread for eating;
Faith, our wine for drinking be:
May we taste the joyous Spirit,
Drunk with His sobriety!

May this new day pass in gladness,
Modest like the dawn's fresh bloom,
Faith like midday shining brightly,
Thoughts untouched by evening gloom.

Now the dawn with splendour rises;
Jesus is our only Dawn:
Son unveiled by heavenly Father,
Father in the Logos known.

Ambrose's letter to Theodosius the Great after the massacre of the Thessalonians

I cannot deny that you are zealous for the faith and that you fear God.
But you have a naturally passionate spirit; and while you easily yield
to love when that spirit is subdued, yet when it is stirred up you
become a raging beast. I would gladly have left you to the workings
of your own heart, but I dare not remain silent or gloss over your sin.
No-one in all human history has ever before heard of such a bloody
scene as the one at Thessalonica! I warned you against it, I pleaded
with you; you yourself realised its horror and tried to cancel your
decree. And now I call you to repent. Remember how king David
repented of his crime. Will you be ashamed to do what David did?
You can wash away your sin only by tears, by repentance, by
humbling your soul before God. You are a man; you have sinned as
a man; you must repent as a man. No angel, no archangel can forgive
you. God alone can forgive you; and He forgives those who repent.
Oh how I grieve that you - you, who were so outstanding for your
spirituality, so unwilling that even one innocent person should suffer

- how I grieve that you should not repent of the slaughter of so many innocent people! You are brave in battle, and praiseworthy in every other way, but goodness was the crown of your character. The evil spirit envied you these purest of your blessings. Conquer him while you can! I love you; I honour you from my heart; I pray for you. If you believe this, accept what I say. But if you do not believe it, forgive me for preferring God to you.

The Te deum

We praise You, O God; we acknowledge You to be the Lord.
You are the eternal Father; all creation worships You,
To You all angels, the heavens and all heavenly powers, cry aloud;
To You the cherubim and seraphim constantly cry:
Holy, holy, holy, Lord God of hosts!
Heaven and earth are full of Your glory!
The glorious company of the apostles praises You;
The worthy fellowship of the prophets praises You;
The noble army of martyrs praises You;
The holy Church throughout all the world acknowledges You:
The infinitely majestic Father,
Your adorable, true and only Son,
And the Holy Spirit, the Counsellor.
You are the King of glory, O Christ;
You are the eternal Son of the Father.
When You took human nature upon you to deliver it,
You did not abhor the Virgin's womb;
When You had overcome the sharpness of death,
You opened the kingdom of heaven to all believers.
You sit at the right hand of God in the glory of the Father.
We believe that You will come again to be our Judge.
We therefore pray that You will help Your servants,
Whom You have redeemed with Your precious blood.
Make them to be numbered among Your saints in eternal glory!
O Lord, save Your people, bless Your inheritance;
Govern them and uphold them for ever!
Day by day we magnify You,
And we worship Your name to the ages of ages.
Vouchsafe, O Lord, to keep us this day without sin.

O Lord, have mercy upon us, have mercy upon us;
O Lord, let Your mercy rest upon us, for our trust is in You.
O Lord, in You have I trusted; let me not be put to shame at the last day!

Baptism and Salvation

Brothers, baptism is truly a serious thing. You must approach it with proper caution. Each one of you is about to be presented to God in the presence of myriads of the angelic hosts. The Holy Spirit is about to seal your souls. You are about to be enlisted in the army of the Great King. Therefore, make yourselves ready; clothe yourselves - not with fine linen, I mean, but with inner piety and a good conscience. Do not look upon the mere water of the baptismal washing, but look upon the spiritual grace which will be given together with the water. When pagans bring offerings to their altars, the offerings are simply physical things, but they become spiritually defiled by prayer offered over them in the name of idols. Likewise, but with opposite effect, the simple water of baptism acquires a new power of holiness when we pray over it in the name of the Holy Spirit, and of Christ, and of the Father.

Since human beings have a twofold nature - soul and body - our purification is also twofold. It is spiritual for our spiritual part, and bodily for our bodies; the water cleanses the body, the Spirit seals the soul. Thus we may draw near to God, "having our hearts sprinkled by the Spirit and our bodies washed with pure water" **(Hebrews 9:22)**. So when you go down into the water, do not think about the mere water itself, but look for the salvation which the Holy Spirit's power bestows; for without both these things, you cannot possibly be made perfect. I am not the one who says this, but the Lord Jesus Christ, Who has power in this matter. For He says, "Unless a man is born again of water and of the Spirit" (notice the two things), "he cannot enter the kingdom of God" **(John 3:3)**. If a person is only baptised in water, but God does not find him to be a fitting vessel for the Spirit, he does not receive the fulness of grace. On the other hand, if a person is marked out by good deeds, but does not receive the seal of the Spirit by water, he too shall not enter the kingdom of heaven. This is a bold saying, but it is not mine, for Jesus declares it.

Here is proof of what I say from holy Scripture. Cornelius was a righteous man; God honoured him with a vision of angels, and his prayers and gifts of charity were set up as a good memorial before God in heaven. Peter came; the Spirit was poured out on those who believed; they spoke in other tongues and prophesied; and after the grace of the Spirit was given, Scripture says that Peter "commanded them to be baptised in the name of Jesus Christ" **(Acts 10:48)**. Why? So that when their souls had already been born again by faith, their bodies might share in the grace by the water of baptism.

Cyril of Jerusalem, Catechetical Lectures, lecture 3, sections 3 and 4.

The wisdom of the desert fathers: How God teaches us humility

We must not only give thanks to God that He has created us as intelligent beings, equipped us with the power of free-will, blessed us with the grace of baptism, and granted us the knowledge and help of the Law. We must also give thanks for those things which are bestowed on us by His daily providence. For He delivers us from the cunning of our enemies, and works with us so that we can overcome the sins of the flesh. Even without our knowing it, He shields us from dangers, and protects us from falling into sin. He helps and enlightens us, so that we can understand and recognise the help He actually gives us. By His secret influence, He kindles within us repentance for our sins and for the good things we have not done, visits us with His grace, and chastises us for our soul's health. Overcoming sometimes the opposition of our own will, He draws us to salvation. And finally, even our free-will, which is quicker to sin than to obey, He turns to a better purpose, inclining it towards the way of goodness by His prompting and suggestion.

I knew of one brother monk, whom I heartily wish I had never known, since afterwards He allowed himself to be saddled with the responsibilities of a presbyter. He confessed to a most admirable elder that he was under attack from a terrible sin of the flesh; for he was inflamed with an unbearable lust, an unnatural desire to have a shameful act done to him (rather than to commit it himself). The elder, like a true spiritual physician, at once saw the inward cause and origin of this evil. Sighing deeply, he said: "The Lord would never have allowed you to be given over to so foul a spirit, unless you had blasphemed against Him." When this was revealed, the monk fell instantly to the ground at the elder's feet; struck with astonishment, as if he saw the secrets of his heart laid bare by God, he confessed that he had blasphemed with evil thoughts against the Son of God. From this, we see that someone controlled by a spirit of pride, or who has been guilty of blasphemy against God, has offended the One Who alone can give us the spirit of purity; and such a person is thus deprived of uprightness and spiritual maturity, and is not fit for the sanctifying grace of chastity....

This clearly shows that everyone who has been possessed by a puffed-up pride is given over to the "Syrians of the soul" - that is, to spiritual wickedness. Such a person is entangled in the lusts of the flesh, and polluted by sensuality, so that he might at length be humbled by earthly faults and realise how unclean he is. When he stood erect in the coldness of his heart, he could not understand that his pride made him unclean in God's sight. So God has let him be humbled by lust, so that he may get rid of his coldness; he has been cast down and confounded with the shame of his fleshly cravings, so that from now on he may hasten more eagerly towards spiritual fervour and warmth.

John Cassian, *Institutes*, Book 12, chapters 18, 20 and 22

Appendix: John Calvin on monasticism

[Present-day Evangelical Christians will probably find monasticism very strange, perhaps repellent, and may wonder how true believers in the 4th Century could possibly have established and approved such a system. It may be helpful to listen to some of the good things that John Calvin, the great Protestant Reformer of the 16th Century, says about the early monks in his *Institutes of the Christian Religion*. He contrasts the early monks with the Roman Catholic monks of his own day:]

If anyone tries to defend present-day monasticism by arguing that it is a very ancient practice, we must note that a very different way of life once prevailed in monasteries. Those who wanted to exercise themselves in the greatest self-discipline and patience retired there.... They slept on the ground; they drank only water; their food was bread, vegetables and roots; their luxuries were oil and chick-peas. They abstained from all feasting and pampering of the body. These things might seem exaggerated, if experienced eyewitnesses - Gregory of Nazianzus, Basil and Chrysostom - had not handed them down to us. By means of these simple disciplines, the monks prepared themselves for greater tasks. For the fathers we have just mentioned give clear enough proof that monastic colleges were (so to speak) training centres for the clergy; these fathers themselves were first reared in monasteries and then called to the office of bishop. Augustine shows that in his day the monasteries usually supplied the Church with clergy.... Godly men normally prepared themselves by monastic discipline to exercise office in the Church, so that the monasteries might make them fitter and better trained for so great a ministry.... I merely wish to indicate, in passing, what sort of monks the early Church had, and what sort of monastic life then existed. Thus intelligent readers may judge by comparison how shameless those men are who try to claim the early Church to defend present-day monasticism.

When Augustine outlines for us a holy and lawful monasticism, he would not impose any rigid requirement of things which the Lord's Word leaves free to us. And yet in today's monasticism, these things are indeed harshly imposed! They reckon it an unpardonable sin to depart in the slightest from what their code lays down for the colour and appearance of their clothing, the type of food, and other trivial and lifeless ceremonies. Augustine strongly argues that it is not lawful for monks to live in idleness off what others give them. He denies that such an example exists in any well-ordered monastery in his own day. But our present-day monks consider idleness the chief part of their holiness. For if you take away idleness from them, what will become of that life of "contemplation" in which they boast that they surpass all others and become like angels? Finally, Augustine requires a kind of monasticism which trains and nurtures those duties of godliness which *all* Christians must perform. He makes brotherly love the chief and almost the only rule for monks. Are we to think he thereby praises a conspiracy of a few men to separate themselves from the whole body of the Church? Augustine intends that monks should, by their example, be a shining light to preserve the Church's unity. In both these respects, the nature of present-day monasticism is so different from the early monks that the two things are almost the opposite of each other. Our modern monks are not satisfied with the godliness which Christ requires His followers to practise with constant zeal. They instead dream up a new sort of godliness to meditate on, so that they can become more perfect than everyone else....

As to the last thing Augustine says applied among the early monks - that they devoted themselves completely to love - what need is there to say how utterly alien this is to today's monasticism? The facts speak for themselves. Those who today join a monastic community break with the Church. Why? Because they separate themselves from the lawful society of believers, adopting a ministry of their own and a private administration of the sacraments. If this is not breaking fellowship with the Church, what is? And to pursue and complete the comparison I am making, how does this resemble the early monks? They dwelt apart from others, but they did not have a separate church. They took part in the sacraments along with other Christians. They attended the gatherings for worship, where they were part of the people. But our present-day monks have set up a private altar for themselves, and have thus broken the bond of unity.

Calvin, *Institutes of the Christian Religion*, Book 4, chapter 13, sections 8-13

Chapter 8.

THE ARIAN CONTROVERSY

The Arian controversy was the greatest theological controversy in the history of Christianity. It was centred on the most fundamental of all questions: Who is Jesus Christ? Is He God in the flesh? Or is He just a created being like us? The Church had inherited from Israel its passionate belief in one God. It now had to work out how that belief in one God related to the adoring worship it offered to Jesus of Nazareth in its faith, prayers, hymns and sacraments.

1. From the beginnings to the Council of Nicaea.

When the first Christian emperor, Constantine, conquered the Eastern half of the Roman Empire in 324, he found the Eastern Church divided by a fierce doctrinal dispute. It had begun in Alexandria in 318, where an elderly, cultured and ascetic presbyter called *Arius* (256-336), a popular preacher from Libya, had started teaching that the Father alone was God. The Logos or Son, Arius said, was a created being - formed out of nothing by the Father before the universe was made. There was once a time when the Son had not existed..According to Arius, the Son was the first and greatest of all that God had created; He was closer to God than all others, and the rest of creation related to God through the Son (*e.g.* God had created everything else through Christ). But only the Father was truly God, infinite and eternal and uncreated. By teaching this, Arius thought he was defending the fundamental truth that there is only one God. A belief in the deity of Christ, he felt, would mean that Father and Son were two separate Gods, which contradicted the many statements of the Bible about God's oneness.

Arius was also unhappy with Origen's idea that there could be "degrees" or "grades" of divinity, with the Son being slightly less divine than the Father.[1] This view had become the accepted theology of most Eastern bishops, who had a tremendous reverence for Origen's life and work. But as far as Arius was concerned, there could be no degrees of divinity: an infinite distance separated God from all that was not God. Since there was only one God, Arius argued, and since the Father was clearly God, it therefore followed that the Son could not be God - so He must be a created being. (Arius's view of Christ is almost identical to what Jehovah's Witnesses believe.)

Arius was strongly opposed by his bishop *Alexander* (bishop of Alexandria from 313). Alexander was equally unhappy with Origen's idea of degrees of divinity; but he drew the opposite conclusion from Arius. Where Origen had said that the Logos or Son was slightly less divine than the Father, and Arius said that He was a created being, Alexander insisted that the Son was fully and truly God, in as absolute a sense as the Father was. The problem for Alexander was to show that this view did not lead to a belief in two Gods, as Arius maintained that it did.

As the controversy started to spread, Alexander assembled a council of Egyptian bishops in 320 which deposed Arius for heresy. Arius, however, was not ready to give up without a fight, and went to Palestine, canvassing support from other Eastern bishops. He had a ready-made network of contacts, because many of the Middle Eastern clergy had, like Arius himself, studied under the learned *Lucian of Antioch*, head of the Antiochene theological school, who had died a martyr in 312 during Maximinus Daia's persecution of the Church.[2] Arius wrote letters to Lucian's ex-students who were now presbyters or bishops, addressing them as "Dear fellow pupil of Lucian". Lucian's views of Christ seem to have been similar to Arius's; some historians have called Lucian "the father of Arianism". Arius's methods proved very successful in popularising his cause, with the result that Church leaders throughout the East

---

1   For Origen and his doctrine of the Logos, see Chapter 5, section 1.
2   For Maximinus Daia, see Chapter 6, section 3.

became caught up in the dispute, and began to take sides either with Arius or with Alexander. Of the bishops who supported Arius, only a few actually understood and believed Arius's doctrine that the Son was a created being. However, many found the controversy deeply confusing, because in some ways Arius seemed to be closer than Alexander was to the traditional Eastern theology, derived from Origen, which said that the Son was *inferior* to the Father. Alexander was challenging this Origenist tradition by saying that the Son was *equal* with the Father in possessing the full divine nature - which, according to Arius, meant a belief in two Gods. On the other hand, Arius himself was teaching that the Son was a created being, which was certainly not what Origen had said. So the Eastern Church became increasingly perplexed and divided.

Constantine felt that it was his duty as a Christian emperor to restore unity to his Empire's divided Church. He therefore summoned the first ecumenical Council of bishops from all over the Eastern Empire, and a few from the West, to settle the dispute. The Council met at Nicaea in North-West Asia Minor, in 325. About 300 bishops were present, and an even larger number of presbyters and deacons. Eusebius of Caesarea (see previous Chapter, section 1) has left us a vivid picture of the emperor's arrival at the Council:

"When the whole assembly was seated with proper dignity, silence fell on all before the emperor arrived. First, three members of his family entered in order of rank, and then others came in, heralding his own approach. These were not the soldiers or guards who usually accompanied him, but friends in the faith. Then everyone stood up as the sign was given that the emperor was about to enter; and at last, he himself made his way through the midst of the assembly, looking like some heavenly angel of God, covered in a garment which glittered as if it were radiant with light, reflecting the glow of his purple robe, adorned with the brilliant splendour of gold and precious stones. When he reached the upper end of the seats, he remained standing at first; and when a servant had brought a low chair of wrought gold for him, he did not sit down until the bishops signalled him to do so. And then the whole assembly sat down."

We can only try to imagine what the 300 bishops felt like, summoned into the presence of the ruler of the world to restore peace to a divided Church, of which the emperor regarded himself as the divinely chosen protector.

Constantine took an active part in the debates and discussions of the Council, virtually acting as its chairman. His court advisor on Church matters, Hosius of Cordova, was a Western bishop, who (like almost all Western Christians) had a strong belief in Christ's full deity. Hosius convinced Constantine that the bishops should accept a statement of faith which clearly taught that the Son was not a created being, but was eternal and divine. The emperor championed this proposal; and after much disputing, drafting and redrafting of a doctrinal statement, a confession of faith finally emerged which is known as the Creed of Nicaea. The Creed says:

We believe in one God,
the Father almighty,
Creator of all things visible and invisible;
and in one Lord Jesus Christ,
the Son of God,
begotten of the Father,
only-begotten,
that is, *from the essence of the Father,*
God from God,
light from light,
true God from true God,
begotten, not created,
of the same essence as the Father,
through Whom [*i.e.*, through Christ] all things were created
both in heaven and on earth;
Who for us human beings and for our salvation
came down and was incarnate,
was made man,
suffered and rose again on the third day,
ascended into heaven,
and is coming again to judge the living and the dead;
and [we believe] in the Holy Spirit.

The words in italics are all anti-Arian. They state that the Son is "true

God", not created out of nothing, but begotten out of the very essence of the Father. The most important word in the Creed is the Greek word ***homoousios*** (pronounced "homma-oozy-oss"), which means "of the same essence". It came from the word *ousia*, "essence" - the deepest and innermost reality of an object. We could also translate it "nature", "substance", or "being". By stating that the Son was "of the same essence" as the Father, the Creed was clearly affirming that the Son had *the same nature and being* as the Father. Therefore if the Father was divine, eternal, unchangeable and uncreated, so was the Son. This was in total contradiction to the doctrine of Arius.

The Council then added a series of "anathemas" to the Creed. The Greek word *anathema* (pronounced "an-ath-imma") means "given over"; to pronounce an anathema on someone, or to "anathematise" him, meant to declare him to be outside of the Church. It was a stronger act even than excommunicating someone. The Church could discipline a disobedient Christian by banning him from holy communion for a time; but if it anathematised someone, it meant declaring him not to be a Christian at all. The Council of Nicaea, then, pronounced the following anathemas against Arians:

> "As for those who say, There was a time when He [the Logos] was not; and, He was not before He was created; and, He was created out of nothing, or out of another essence or thing; and, The Son of God is created, or changable, or can alter - the holy, catholic and apostolic Church anathematises those who say such things."

All but two of Arius's supporters - Secundus of Ptolemais and Theonas of Marmarica - gave in and signed the Creed of Nicaea, but Arius refused. Constantine sent him, Secundus and Theonas into exile.

2. After Nicaea: Athanasius and the anti-Nicene reaction.

The Council of Nicaea seemed to have settled the Arian controversy and restored unity and peace to the Eastern Church. The appearance, however, was deceptive. The Church, especially in the East, was to be torn apart for another 50 years by the Arian dispute.

The problem was that the Eastern Church was divided into *three* parties:

(i) The *Arian* party - those who agreed with Arius that the Son was a created being. This was a small party; there were never many full-blooded Arians.

(ii) The *Nicene* party - those who believed that the Son was equal with the Father in His divine nature. This was another small party. They became known as the Nicenes because their theology was contained in the Creed of Nicaea.

(iii) The *Origenist* party - the great majority of Eastern bishops, who accepted the traditional Eastern theology of Origen. They believed that the Son was not a created being - He was uncreated and divine, eternally begotten from the Father's essence; but they held that He was inferior to the Father in His divine nature - a degree less divine than the absolute divinity possessed by the Father.

Judged by the standards of later Trinitarian orthodoxy, the Arians were the only genuine heretics in this controversy. However, the main dispute was actually between the Nicenes and the Origenists, who were both basically orthodox. This strange state of affairs came about as follows. The Nicenes were very clear on the doctrine that Christ is fully and truly God. But they expressed their belief in Christ's deity by using language which threw the Origenists into confusion. The Nicenes said that Christ was *homoousios* with the Father - that Father and Son had the same *ousia*. What the Nicenes meant was that Father and Son shared the same divine nature, being or qualities. Unfortunately, the unorthodox Sabellians[3] also used the same word, *ousia*, to mean that Father and Son were the same *person* - that it was really the Father Who took flesh and became Jesus of Nazareth. So when the Origenists heard the Nicenes saying that Father and Son had the same *ousia*, they thought the Nicenes meant that Father and Son were the same person. And Origenists hated this Sabellian view as a deadly heresy. The Origenists therefore opposed the Nicenes, thinking they were Sabellians. That

---

3   For Sabellianism, see Chapter 5, section 1, under *Origen*.

was not generally the case; most Nicenes were not Sabellians. But the Origenists thought they were. So Origenists often went along with the real heretics, the Arians, in their battle against the orthodox Nicenes.[4]

On the other hand, the Nicenes thought that the Origenists were Arians! Origenists were very clear that God the Father and Jesus Christ were two distinct persons. However, the Eastern Origenist tradition had always held that the Son was inferior to the Father - that the Son's divinity was a degree less perfect than the Father's. Origenists were not Arians; they did not think that the Son was formed out of nothing prior to the creation of the universe - He was eternal and uncreated. However, Origenists often used language about the Son's inferiority to the Father which made it seem to the Nicenes that they were unclear about the Son's true deity. So Nicenes felt that Origenists were not much better than Arians. This Nicene view of the Origenists is reflected in many older Church history books which refer to the Origenists as "Semi-Arians".

The result of this confusion of language was that the Arians, the truly unorthodox party, were able to set the essentially orthodox Nicenes and Origenists against each other for 50 years of bitter doctrinal controversy.

The Origenist party formed the majority in the East. As we have just seen, they were unhappy with the word ***homoousios***. They had

---

4   Another powerful objection the Origenists had to the word ***homoousios*** was that it could be taken to mean that the divine ***ousia*** (nature) had been split apart into two - that Father and Son had the same ***ousia*** in the sense that two coins are made of the same metal. But the divine nature is not like a lump of metal which can be split up into two coins. Of course, this was not what the Nicenes meant. They believed that there was only ***one*** divine nature which was possessed ***equally*** by Father and Son. An illustration of this would be one country shared equally by two races or tribes: not a splitting up of the country into two countries, but the two races fully and equally sharing the one country and all its wealth, political structures and social services. So Father and Son are two persons, who fully and equally share the whole of the one divine nature.

accepted it at the Council of Nicaea, largely because the presence of the great Christian emperor Constantine had intimidated them. Afterwards, however, they had serious doubts about what they had done. Some did not like the word *homoousios* simply because it was not a Scriptural word. But most did not like it because they feared it would open the door to the hated heresy of Sabellianism - that Father and Son were the same person. So after the Council of Nicaea, there was a widespread reaction in the East against the Creed of Nicaea. Only one section of the Eastern Church stood firmly behind the Creed - Alexandria, which had deposed Arius in the first place.

In 328 Alexandria acquired a new bishop, *Athanasius* (296-373). Athanasius became the outstanding champion of Nicene theology in the East, and was one of the greatest and most influential thinkers in the history of the Christian Church. According to his friend and admirer Gregory of Nazianzus,[5] Athanasius was a small thin man with a beautiful face, piercing eyes, and a mysterious aura of power which affected even his enemies. Little is known of his early life; all we can be sure of is that before becoming bishop of Alexandria, Athanasius was the senior deacon and secretary of bishop Alexander. He took part in the Council of Nicaea, where he distinguished himself by his eloquent arguments for Christ's deity, and it was on the recommendation of the dying Alexander that the Alexandrian church elected Athanasius as his successor.

Athanasius's whole theology was centred on the doctrine of salvation. In common with Eastern Christians generally, Athanasius understood salvation to mean *deification* - Christ the Saviour makes human beings divine. This did not mean that Christ actually changed the believer's human nature into God's nature, but that human nature was lifted up by grace, through Christ, to share in the glory and immortality of God. **2 Peter 1:4** was a favourite text, where Peter describes Christians as "partakers of the divine nature". How, Athanasius asked, could Christ make human nature divine if He Himself was less than God? Salvation means union with God's life - human nature sharing in the glory of God's nature. Therefore if

---

5 For Gregory of Nazianzus, see section 3.

Athanasius of Alexandria (296 - 373)

Christ is mankind's Saviour, He must be God and man in one person; in Christ the God-man, humanity has been lifted up into the very life of God. Athanasius also argued from the fact that Christians worship Christ. How can we worship Him, Athanasius asked, unless He is God? If we are worshipping a created being, we are committing idolatry.

> "No-one else but the Saviour," Athanasius wrote, "Who in the beginning made everything out of nothing, could bring what had been corrupted into a state free from corruption. No-one else but the Image of the Father could recreate human beings in God's image. No-one else but our Lord Jesus Christ, Who is life itself, could give immortality to mortal humans. No-one else but the Logos, Who imparts order to everything and is the one true and only-begotten Son of the Father, could teach us about the Father and destroy idolatry.... He became human that we might become divine; He revealed Himself in a body that we might see the invisible Father; He endured men's insults that we might inherit immortality."

Athanasius set out his understanding of the deity of Christ (and later of the Holy Spirit) in writings such as *The Incarnation of the Logos*, *Orations against the Arians* and his *Letters to Serapion*. Throughout his 45 years as bishop of Alexandria, Athanasius proved an unswerving, uncompromising enemy of Arianism in all its forms; the most celebrated of all historians of the Roman Empire, Edward Gibbon, said of Athanasius's life that it was the classic example of "what effect may be produced, or what obstacles may be surmounted, by the force of a single mind, when it is inflexibly applied to the pursuit of a single object. The immortal name of Athanasius will never be separated from the Catholic doctrine of the Trinity, to whose defence he consecrated every moment and every faculty of his being." Together with this unfaltering devotion to the deity of Christ, Athanasius combined high moral courage, a quick-thinking mind, a sparkling sense of humour, and a broad-minded tolerance of many theological differences among all who were united with him in the struggle against the Arians.[6]

---

6   Here is a typical example of Athanasius's sense of humour. When he was fleeing in a boat from the soldiers of the pagan emperor Julian the

(cont.)

In the general Eastern reaction against the Council and Creed of Nicaea, the Arians were able to build up their strength. Their leader was bishop *Eusebius of Nicomedia* in Asia Minor (died 342), a clever politician who had spun a vast web of influence in Constantine's court, and became bishop of Constantinople in 339. (He must not be confused with Eusebius of Caesarea, the father of Church history, who was an Origenist.) In 328 Eusebius managed to get Arius recalled from exile. Although Arius had sparked off the whole controversy, he was now an unimportant figure; he died in 336 in a quite horrific manner (see end of Chapter). Then Eusebius started a campaign to have supporters of the Creed of Nicaea deposed and exiled. He achieved his greatest success in 335, when he persuaded Constantine to banish Athanasius for political reasons. Eusebius accused Athanasius - falsely - of threatening to organise a dock strike in Alexandria (which would have cut off the grain supply to Constantinople), unless Arian influence at court was curbed. This was the first time Athanasius was sent into exile for his commitment to Nicene theology. He would be banished five times altogether, and spend 17 of his 45 years as bishop of Alexandria in exile.

When Constantine died in 337, the Empire was divided between his Christian sons - Constans in the West, who favoured the Nicenes, and Constantius in the East, who favoured the Arians. Athanasius returned from exile, but Constantius banished him again in 339. Athanasius and another deposed Nicene bishop, *Marcellus of Ancyra* in Asia Minor (died 374), fled to Rome. Arianism never had much support in the West; most Western bishops were solidly Nicene in their theology. Pope *Julius I* of Rome (pope from 337 to 352) reviewed the case of Athanasius and Marcellus, and at a local council in 340 declared that they had been wrongfully deposed. The Eastern bishops reacted by calling a council in Antioch in 341, where they rejected Rome's right to judge the case, and drew up a new creed which left out the word *homoousios*. Instead of the Sabellian-

---

Apostate in 362, he came to a bend in the river. He turned his boat around, and rowed back towards the pursuing boat of the soldiers. They did not recognise him (it was dark) and asked him if he had seen Athanasius. "Yes, you're quite close to him," Athanasius replied, then rowed calmly past them and escaped while the soldiers went on ahead.

sounding *homoousios*, the Origenists preferred to say that the Son was *homoiousios* (pronounced "hommoy-oozy-oss") with the Father. The difference between *homoousios* and *homoiousios* was only one letter, the letter "i". But the difference in meaning was serious. *Homoiousios* meant that the Son was "of a similar essence" to the Father: not the same, but similar.[7] The trouble was that the Arians could agree to that, but the Nicenes could not.

As a result of pope Julius's support for Athanasius and Marcellus, and the anti-Nicene pronouncements of the council of Antioch, the Arian controversy was turning into a full-scale split between the Eastern and Western branches of the Church. To kill this schism before it was born, the two emperors, Constans and Constantius, summoned an ecumenical Church council in 343 at Sardica (modern Sofia in Bulgaria), with the aim of reconciling East and West. The council, however, was a spectacular disaster. The Western bishops insisted that Athanasius and Marcellus must be allowed to take part. The Eastern bishops refused. And so the council broke up into two separate councils, Eastern and Western, which hurled curses at each other. The East-West split had become total.

This unhappy situation improved to some extent over the next few years, as Eastern and Western Christians made some concessions to each other. The West agreed to drop its support for Marcellus of Ancyra, whose theology really was as Sabellian as the East feared. The East agreed to take back Athanasius, who returned to Alexandria in 346 amid great popular rejoicing. He managed to stay there for the next 10 years, his so-called "golden decade". Dark clouds, however, began gathering in 350, when a rebel general called Magnentius murdered the Nicene emperor of the West, Constans. In 353 Constantius, Arian emperor of the East, defeated Magnentius in battle and became sole ruler of the entire Roman Empire. A new period of Arian persecution of the Nicenes began.

---

[7]   We can see the difference by writing it out like this:

HOMO - OUSIOS		*HOMOI* - OUSIOS	
|	|	|	|
SAME	ESSENCE	*SIMILAR*	ESSENCE

3. From Constantius to the Council of Constantinople.

Constantius was a vain and cruel man who liked to think he was both a great emperor and a great theologian. He was neither. His court officials and even his domestic staff dominated and manipulated him shamelessly. A pagan historian of the times, Ammianus Marcellinus, made a famous sneer about Constantius, that this was an emperor who had considerable influence with his chief butler! In matters of theology Constantius was ruled by an inner circle of Arian bishops. He used all his power as emperor to put fierce pressure on Western Church leaders to accept Arianism, silencing all argument with the crushing retort that whatever he, the emperor, believed must certainly be true, otherwise God would not have delivered the world into his hands. He sent into exile any bishops and presbyters who refused to submit. Constantius's most famous victim was *Hilary of Poitiers* (315-68), a bishop from western France, banished to Asia Minor in 356. While in exile, Hilary wrote his influential treatise *On the Trinity*. Because of his steadfast loyalty to the doctrine of Christ's deity, Hilary is sometimes referred to as the "Athanasius of the West". He is also the first of the great Latin hymnwriters; during his banishment in Asia Minor he heard the hymns that Arians were composing, and responded by writing orthodox hymns, which he put into use in Western churches after returning from exile to France in 361.

The year 356, in which Hilary was banished, was a year when everything seemed to go wrong for the Nicenes. That same year Constantius exiled the Nicene pope Liberius (pope from 352 to 366) to Berea in northern Greece. Also in 356, Constantius had the emperor Constantine's old counsellor, Hosius of Cordova, now a hundred years old, imprisoned and tortured. Both Liberius and Hosius eventually cracked under the inhuman treatment to which Constantius subjected them, and signed an Arian statement of faith (Hosius renounced it on his deathbed in 357, and confessed afresh his faith in Christ's deity). Finally, Constantius banished Athanasius again in 356; the Arian emperor sent troops into Alexandria to arrest him, but in a hair-raising chase Athanasius escaped, and went into hiding for six years in the Egyptian desert, sheltered by the desert monks. Meanwhile, Constantius's soldiers committed brutal outrages against the orthodox Christians of Alexandria. One Sunday, when a group of orthodox virgin women had gathered for prayer in a graveyard (the Arians had taken over the church buildings), imperial troops seized them and kindled a great fire. They then tried to force the women to convert to Arianism or else be thrown in the flames. When the women refused to abandon the Nicene faith, the soldiers stripped off all their clothes and beat their faces to a bloody pulp. Such were the methods of Constantius. By 360, he had terrorised most of the Church in both East and West into accepting a form of Arianism.

Full-blown Arianism now discovered two new eloquent spokesmen in the theologians *Aetius* (died 370) and *Eunomius* (died 394). The Arians ordained Aetius as a bishop without a church in the reign of Julian the Apostate; Eunomius was briefly bishop of Cyzicus in Asia Minor in 360. Aetius and Eunomius boldly taught that the Son was "unlike" the Father. Many Origenist bishops in the East, who insisted that the Son was eternal and uncreated like the Father, now found themselves being deposed and exiled alongside the Nicenes. Constantius's most famous Origenist victims were Cyril of Jerusalem, whom we met in the previous Chapter, section 3, under the heading **Church worship**, and bishop *Basil of Ancyra* (died some time after 360). Basil of Ancyra had fought hard to win Constantius over to the Origenist side; the Arians decisively defeated Basil at the council of Rimini-Seleucia in 359. Constantius then exiled both Basil and Cyril of Jerusalem in 360. These events shocked the Origenists into realising that they needed to be much clearer and stronger in their views of Christ's divine nature; they began to look more favourably at Nicene theology. In the case of Cyril of Jerusalem, it eventually led to his joining the Nicene party and acting as one of their leading spokesmen at the Council of Constantinople in 381 (see below).

Constantius died in 361. The new emperor was Julian the Apostate. As we saw in the last Chapter, Julian had been brought up a Christian, but then abandoned Christianity in favour of Neoplatonism. On becoming emperor, Julian allowed all exiled bishops to return to their churches, hoping that this would cause confusion and division among Christians. But the opposite happened. Athanasius returned in triumph to Alexandria, a popular hero. He was now convinced that he and the Origenists, whom Constantius had recently persecuted alongside the Nicenes, were fighting the same essential battle against the Arians. So in a council in 362, Athanasius suggested an alliance between Nicenes and Origenists, in the hope that the two parties would soon be able to reach doctrinal agreement and concentrate together on defeating those true heretics who taught that the Son was a created being. "Those who accept the Nicene Creed," Athanasius said, "but have doubts about the word *homoousios*, must not be treated as enemies. We will discuss the matter with them as brothers with brothers. They mean the same as we mean, and our only argument is about the use of a word." This move towards peace and unity in the Church was not what Julian the Apostate had expected. So he sent Athanasius into exile again.

Julian was killed fighting the Persians in 363. In 364 Valentinian became emperor, and he placed the East under the authority of his brother Valens - and Valens was an Arian, who started persecuting Nicenes and Origenists alike. Athanasius had come back from exile after Julian the Apostate's death, but Valens banished him again. However, the fact that both Nicenes and Origenists fell under Valens's persecuting fury helped to bring the two parties together in united opposition to Arianism. Valens soon relented on his policy of oppression, and Athanasius was allowed to return to Alexandria in 366. He spent his last six years there, carrying out his episcopal duties unmolested, and died in 373. It was Athanasius's courageous and indomitable opposition to Arianism, in spite of persecution and exile, which did more than anything else to bring about the defeat of the Arians in the Church. They never produced anyone of the same heroic moral stature as the bishop of Alexandria.

Athanasius's place was taken by a new generation of Nicene theologians. They were led by the "Cappadocian fathers" - **Basil of Caesarea** (330-79), **Gregory of Nyssa** (335-94) and **Gregory of Nazianzus** (330-90). All three were natives of the province of Cappadocia in Asia Minor. Basil and Gregory of Nyssa were brothers, born into a wealthy Christian family; the Church recognised their grandmother Macrina the Elder, their mother Emelia, and their sister Macrina the Younger, as saints, with special days dedicated to their memory. In his youth Basil went to study in Caesarea, the capital city of Cappadocia, where he met and became the intimate lifelong friend of Gregory of Nazianzus, another young Christian

Gregory of Nazianzus 'The Theologian' (330 - 390)

Gregory of Nyssa (335 - 394)

student from Cappadocia. In their warm and devoted love for each other, Basil and Gregory were the "David and Jonathan" of the patristic age (**1 Samuel 18:1, 2 Samuel 1:26**). They both immersed their minds in all the riches of pagan culture and philosophy in Athens, the cradle of European thought, but without wandering in the slightest from their Christian beliefs and commitment. Both were baptised in about 358: clear examples of individuals raised as Christians in believing families, but baptised only in their maturity (which was the prevailing 4th Century custom).

Basil then lived the life of a hermit in Cappadocia for some years, but in 364 the bishop of Caesarea, Eusebius,[8] persuaded him to accept ordination as a presbyter and help him in his battle with the Arians in the Caesarean church. In fact, Basil effectively ran the church as the presbyter in whom Eusebius placed the greatest confidence. On Eusebius's death in 370, the church elected Basil as its new bishop. In the conflict against Arianism, Basil proved a hugely effective practical Church leader, organiser and administrator, as well as a superb preacher. He was also a mighty theologian who wrote a highly important treatise *On the Holy Spirit* in 375, in which he argued for the Spirit's full deity. Many have praised Basil's sermons and treatises as the clearest, most beautiful Christian writings in Greek from the entire patristic period. We have already seen in the previous Chapter, section 3, Basil's immense contribution to the development of the Eastern liturgy and Eastern monasticism.

Meanwhile, Basil's best friend Gregory of Nazianzus became a presbyter in his home church of Nazianzus from 362, where his father was bishop. Active Church life, however, was not really to Gregory's liking; he was a sensitive, inward-looking person, who preferred writing poetry in solitude to the vicious cut-and-thrust of fighting Arians in the public arena of Church politics and theological debate. Despite this, in 379-81 Gregory was briefly bishop of the little Catholic congregation in the Eastern capital, Constantinople, where Arianism reigned supreme. Here Gregory's *Five Theological Orations* brilliantly summed up the Nicene doctrine of the Trinity, refuted Arianism, and attracted large numbers to Gregory's church,

---

8   This is yet another Eusebius, not to be confused with the *other* Eusebius of Caesarea, the Church historian, who died in 339.

winning them over to the Nicene faith. We can catch a flavour of the wild theological atmosphere of Constantinople during the Arian controversy from Gregory of Nyssa's rather amazing description:

> "If you ask a person to give you some small change for a large coin, his response is - 'What distinguishes the Father from the Son is that He is not begotten.' If you go into a shop to buy a loaf, the shopkeeper solemnly informs you that, 'The Father is greater than the Son.' If you ask your servant whether the water is hot enough for a bath, you have to be satisfied with his assurance that 'The Son has been generated out of nothing.'"

Gregory of Nazianzus's *Orations* earned him the title "Gregory the Theologian" in the Eastern Church. Together with John Chrysostom (see next Chapter), Gregory was the Eastern Church's most eloquent preacher in the age of the early Church fathers.

Basil's brother, the gentle Gregory of Nyssa, was (from 371) bishop of Nyssa, a town near Caesarea. Among Gregory's anti-Arian writings were his *Against Eunomius*, his *Sermon on the Holy Spirit against the Spirit-fighting Macedonians*, and his *Letter to Ablabius that there are not Three Gods*. The Eastern Church soon came to recognise him as one of their outstanding theologians and teachers on the spiritual life. His fame as an opponent of Arianism was so great that the assembled fathers of the Council of Constantinople (see below) asked Gregory to deliver the opening address. Gregory's overflowing admiration for Origen led him to accept Origen's doctrine of universal salvation; later theologians tried to rescue Gregory's orthodoxy by arguing that other followers of Origen had inserted into Gregory's writings the passages which teach universalism, but there is no evidence for this, and the passages are too numerous. The more realistic attitude taken by others was that Gregory of Nyssa was a holy man and a great theologian who had sadly erred on this particular point. All three of the Cappadocian fathers were in fact admirers of Origen; Basil and Gregory of Nazianzus produced an influential anthology of Origen's writings in 358 called the *Philokalia* ("Love of the Good"). However, Basil and Gregory of Nazianzus did not accept his universalism, and Basil also rejected Origen's allegorical method of interpreting Scripture (see next Chapter, section 1).

The Cappadocian fathers rank alongside Athanasius as the outstanding Eastern theologians of the 4th Century . Their writings and personal influence brought about a final union between the Nicene and Origenist parties. The Cappadocians achieved this by persuading both sides to use a new theological language. The problem centred on two Greek words, *hypostasis* and *ousia*.[9] Up till then, these two words had meant much the same thing in the Greek language. This caused great theological confusion, because when the Nicenes said that Father and Son had one divine nature or essence, they expressed it by saying that Father and Son have one *hypostasis* and one *ousia*. However, when the Origenists said that Father and Son were two distinct persons, they used exactly the same words, and said that Father and Son were two *hypostases* and two *ousiai*.

To get rid of this divisive confusion, the Cappadocians (led by Basil) made two proposals: (i) The word *ousia* should from now on refer specifically to the one divine nature or essence, as the Nicenes said; but (ii) the word *hypostasis* should refer specifically to the two distinct persons of Father and Son, as the Origenists said. We could sum up their definitions like this:

OUSIA	*HYPOSTASIS*
THE ONE NATURE, BEING OR ESSENCE OF GOD WHICH FATHER AND SON SHARE FULLY AND EQUALLY, MAKING THEM GOD.	THE PARTICULAR AND DISTINCT FORM IN WHICH THE DIVINE NATURE EXISTS IN FATHER AND SON, MAKING THE TWO DISTINCT PERSONS.

The Cappadocians also settled another dispute about whether the Holy Spirit was God. It is not surprising, after decades of controversy over whether Christ was God, that some Christians should now start arguing about the status of the Holy Spirit. Some who opposed the Arians, and accepted the deity of Christ, nevertheless denied the deity of the Spirit. They were called "Macedonians", after one of their leaders, Macedonius, who was for a time bishop of

---

[9] *Hypostasis* is pronounced more-or-less as it is spelt: "hypo-stass-is".
The plural *hypostases* is pronounced "hypo-stass-ees".

Constantinople (the Arians deposed him in 360 for his belief in Christ's deity). The Macedonians were also known as the *Pneumatomachoi* (Greek for "fighters against the Spirit"). Athanasius had already argued in 358 that the Holy Spirit must be recognised as God alongside Father and Son. The Cappadocians carried on this argument, strengthened it, and laid the basis for extending the term *homoousios* to the Holy Spirit - He too was "of the same essence" as the Father.

So what had started as a dispute about the status of Christ finally became a search for a full doctrine of the Trinity. The Cappadocians created the following formula for expressing this doctrine: **God is three *hypostases* in one *ousia*** - that is, in English, **God is three persons existing eternally in one single *being* or *nature***. An illustration of what the Cappadocians meant by this would be a mountain with three sides or faces. Whichever face of the mountain we look at, it presents the reality of the self-same mountain to us, so that we could say, "I have seen the mountain." Yet each face of the mountain is distinct from the other two. In other words, God is not three separate beings or realities; God the Father possesses one divine nature, one single reality of "Godness", which He shares completely with His Son Whom He begets from all eternity, and with His Holy Spirit Whom He eternally breathes forth. Father, Son and Spirit are therefore each fully and equally God, because they each fully and equally possess the one divine essence or nature. Yet they are distinct persons because they each possess it in a different way: the Father possesses the divine nature in and from Himself alone; the Son possesses the divine nature from the Father, as a child from a parent, by way of begetting or "eternal generation"; the Holy Spirit possesses the divine nature from the Father by "proceeding" from Him (**John 14:26**), as the everlasting Breath of His mouth.

Nicenes and Origenists rallied together around this Cappadocian formula of three *hypostases* in one *ousia*. The Origenists gave up saying that the Son was inferior to the Father in His divine nature; the Nicenes distanced themselves conclusively from the Sabellian heresy, to which some of them had been inclined. At last they could present a united front against the Arians.

The Arian emperor Valens died fighting the Goths in 378. The West had had a Nicene emperor since 375 called Gratian; Gratian now appointed a new Nicene emperor for the East, a Spanish soldier called Theodosius. Theodosius gave Arianism its death-blow by issuing an edict in 380, which recognised Nicene believers as the only ones legally entitled to use the name "Catholic" (which gave the Nicenes legal possession of all church buildings). In 381 Theodosius summoned an ecumenical Council at Constantinople. The Council of Constantinople produced a new revised form of the Creed of Nicaea, known as the *Nicene Creed*, which reaffirmed and extended the teaching of the Council of Nicaea in 325:

I believe in one God,
the Father almighty,
Creator of heaven and earth,
and of all things, visible and invisible;
and in one Lord, Jesus Christ,
the Son of God,
the Only-begotten ,
begotten of the Father before all ages,
light from light,
true God from true God,
begotten, not created,
of the same essence as the Father,
through Whom all things were created;
Who for us human beings and our salvation
came down from the heavens
and was made flesh from the Holy Spirit and the Virgin Mary,
and became man,
and was crucified under Pontius Pilate,
and suffered and was buried,
and rose again on the third day according to the Scriptures,
and ascended into the heavens,
and sits at the right hand of the Father,
and comes again with glory to judge the living and the dead,
of Whose kingdom there shall be no end;
and [I believe] in the Holy Spirit,
the Lord and the life-giver,
Who proceeds from the Father,
Who with the Father and the Son

is worshipped together and glorified together,
Who spoke through the prophets;
[and I believe] in one holy catholic and apostolic Church.
I acknowledge one baptism for the forgiveness of sins.
I look for the resurrection of the dead
and the life of the age to come.

The Nicene Creed confirmed the doctrines of the Council of Nicaea (including the word *homoousios*). It also extended Nicaea's belief in the deity of the Son to include the Holy Spirit as well, ascribing deity to the Spirit by calling Him "the Lord and the life-giver" and stating that He "is worshipped and glorified" together with Father and Son.[10] The Nicene Creed became so highly prized over the next hundred years that by the end of the 5th Century, Eastern churches had started reciting it in their worship as a public declaration of their faith. Western churches began using the Creed in worship towards the end of the 6th Century.

The Council of Constantinople brought an end to Arianism within the Catholic Church, although it lived on for several centuries among some of the Germanic tribes (see Chapter 11, Section 1). But the belief of the Catholic Church was, from now on, to be a strong and solid faith in the Trinity, Father, Son and Holy Spirit, one God in three persons.

---

10 However, the Nicene Creed does not actually call the Holy Spirit "God" and does not explicitly ascribe the term *homoousios* to Him. This was out of respect to conservative opinion in the Church, which accepted the divine status of the Spirit, but hesitated to call Him "God" directly, because there was little basis for this in the language of Scripture or tradition (but see **Acts 5:3-4**).

Important people:

The Church
Trinitarians:
Alexander of Alexandria (bishop 313-28)
Pope Julius I (pope 337-52)
Basil of Ancyra (died after 360)
Hilary of Poitiers (315-68)
Athanasius of Alexandria (296-373)
Marcellus of Ancyra (died 374)[11]
Basil of Caesarea (330-79)
Gregory of Nazianzus "the Theologian" (330-90)
Gregory of Nyssa (335-94)

Arians:
Lucian of Antioch (died 312)
Arius (256-336)
Eusebius of Nicomedia (died 342)
Aetius (died 370)
Eunomius (died 394)

The emperor speaks: Constantine on the Council of Nicaea

To attain this goal, instructed by God, I assembled at the city of
Nicaea most of the bishops, with whom I undertook to investigate the
truth, rejoicing greatly to be your fellow-servant with them.
Accordingly, all points which seemed to raise doubts or excuses for
discord, we discussed and examined accurately. May the Divine
Majesty forgive the dreadful horror of the blasphemies which some
were shamelessly uttering about our Saviour, Who is our Life and
Hope, declaring and acknowledging that they believe things contrary
to the divinely inspired Scriptures and the holy faith. More than 300
bishops, distinguished by their moderation and insight, were united in
confirming one and the same faith, which is in accurate harmony with
the truth revealed in God's decrees. Arius alone, deceived by the
subtlety of the devil, was discovered to be the propagator of this

---

11 Marcellus's Sabellianism means he was not orthodox in his views of the
    Trinity. I have put him here because he believed in Christ's deity
    and opposed the Arians.

mischief, with unholy purposes, first among you Alexandrians, then among others too. Let us therefore accept the judgment which the Almighty has presented to us; let us be re-united with our beloved brothers, from whom this shameless servant of Satan has separated us; let us go with all zeal to the common body of Christ to which we all belong. Your insight, faith and sincerity will prompt you to return to the divine favour, now that the error of Arius, the enemy of truth, has been refuted. The decision which has commended itself to the judgment of 300 bishops must surely be the judgment of God; for the Holy Spirit, dwelling in the minds of men so full of integrity and dignity, has powerfully enlightened them concerning God's will. So let no-one hesitate or linger, but let all ardently return to the clear path of truth, so that when I arrive among you, which will be as soon as possible, I may join you in rendering thanks to God, Who sees all things, for having revealed the pure faith, and restored to you the love for which you have prayed.

From a letter of Constantine to the Catholic Church in Alexandria

The death of Arius

At that time [the year 336] Alexander presided over the church in Constantinople. He was a devout and godly bishop, qualities he clearly proved by his conflict with Arius. When Arius arrived in the city, the people divided into two factions and the city was thrown into confusion. Some insisted that the Creed of Nicaea must be obeyed, others argued that Arius's views were in harmony with reason. This forced Alexander into grave difficulties, especially since Eusebius of Nicomedia had violently threatened to have Alexander instantly deposed unless he admitted Arius and his disciples to holy communion.... At his wits' end, Alexander said farewell to the resources of human wisdom, and took refuge in God, devoting himself to continual fasting and ceaseless praying. Without telling anyone, he shut himself up in the church called "Peace", went up to the altar, and prostrated himself beneath the communion table, where he poured forth his fervent prayers with weeping. He did this without ceasing for many nights and days. And he received from God what he so earnestly sought; for this was his prayer: "If Arius's views are right, may I not be allowed to see the day appointed by the emperor for discussing them. But if I myself hold the true faith, may

Arius suffer the penalty his ungodliness deserves, as the author of
these evils...."

It was Saturday, and Arius was expecting to take communion with
the church on the following day; but divine vengeance overtook his
daring crimes. As he left the imperial palace, attended by a mob of
Eusebius's followers like guards, he paraded proudly through the
city, the centre of attention. But as he approached the place called
Constantine's market, at one and the same time the terrors of
conviction attacked his conscience, and a violent seizure attacked his
bowels. He asked if there was somewhere nearby where he could
relieve himself, and someone directed him to the back of the market.
There he fainted, and his bowels came spilling out of his backside,
together with streams of blood; parts of his spleen and liver poured
out in the bloody flow. He died almost instantly. People in
Constantinople still point out where this calamity happened, behind
the meat-market in the colonnade; this constant pointing out of the
place has preserved a perpetual memorial of this extraordinary
death. The disaster filled with dread and alarm the party of Eusebius
of Nicomedia; and the news spread quickly through the city and
indeed the whole world. The emperor, growing more earnest in
Christianity, confessed that God had vindicated the Creed of Nicaea,
and rejoiced at what had happened.

Socrates Scholasticus, *Church History*, Book 1, chapters 37-38

The Son's equality with the Father

Unbelief is coming in through these men [the Arians], or rather a non-
Scriptural Judaism allied with Gentile superstition. Anyone who
holds these opinions can no longer be called a Christian, for they are
completely contrary to the Scriptures. John, for example, says, "The
Word existed in the beginning" (**John 1:1**), but these men say, "He
did not exist before He was begotten." And again John has written,
"We are in Him Who is true, even in His Son Jesus Christ; this is the
true God and eternal life" (**1 John 5:20**). But these men, as if to
contradict this, claim that Christ is not the true God, but that Scripture
only *calls* Him "God", as it also gives this title to other created beings,
on account of His participation [as a created being] in the divine
nature. The apostle Paul condemns the Gentiles for worshipping

created beings, saying, "They worshipped the creature more than God the Creator" (**Romans 1:25**). But if these men say that the Lord Jesus is a created being, and worship Him as a created being, how do they differ from the Gentiles? If they hold this opinion, is this passage not against them, and does the blessed Paul not write in condemnation of them? The Lord also says, "I and the Father are one" (**John 10:30**), and, "He that has seen Me has seen the Father" (**John 14:9**). And the apostle Paul, whom Christ sent forth to preach, says of Him, "He is the brightness of God's glory and the exact image of His person" (**Hebrews 1:3**). But these men dare to separate the Son from the Father, claiming that the Son is alien to the Father's essence and eternity; in an ungodly way they represent Him as changeable, not seeing that by speaking thus they make the Son to be *not* one with the Father, but one with created things. But who does not see that you cannot separate the brightness from the light? Brightness belongs by nature to light, and exists along with it, and does not come into existence after it.

Athanasius, *Letter to the Egyptian Bishops*, chapter 13

The deification of humanity in Christ

He took upon Himself a created human body so that He might renew it as its Creator, and deify it in Himself, and thus introduce us all into the kingdom of heaven in His likeness. For humanity would not have been deified if it had been united to a created being, or if the Son had not been truly God; nor would humanity have been brought into the Father's presence, if it had not been the Father's natural and true Logos Who had clothed Himself with the human body. And we would not have been saved from sin and the curse, unless the Logos had taken upon Himself natural human flesh, for we would have had nothing in common with any other kind of flesh. And equally, humanity would not have been deified, unless the Logos Who became flesh had been by nature from the Father, truly and properly belonging to Him. So the union was of this kind, that He might unite what is human by nature to Him Who is divine by nature, so that mankind's salvation and deification might be sure.

Athanasius, *Orations Against the Arians*, Book 2, chapter 70

The marvellous mystery of the Trinity

Whatever you think about the kind of being the Father is, you will think the same about the Son and the Holy Spirit.... Father, Son and Holy Spirit all share equally in the attributes of being "mysterious" and "uncreated". One is not more mysterious, or more uncreated, than another. But so that we can tell the difference between the three persons of the Trinity, we need to say that each person has something distinctive which He does not share with the other two. Obviously this "something distinctive" cannot belong to the divine nature itself, because the divine nature is shared in common by all three persons, with its attributes of being "uncreated", "mysterious", and so on. We need to find some particular concept which is clearly and distinctly separate from what the three persons share in common....

The Holy Spirit, the source of all creation's supply of good things, is joined to the Son, so that the Spirit is always known in knowing the Son. The being of the Spirit is also joined to the Father, from Whom the Spirit proceeds as from a Cause. So the mark of the Spirit's particular personal identity is this: *He is known after the Son and with the Son, and receives His way of existing from the Father.*

The Son, Who says that the Spirit proceeds from the Father through Himself and with Himself, is shown to be a unique person in this way: He alone *shines forth as a Son* from that Light of the Father which has no origin. As far as this particular mark of the Son is concerned, He does not share it in any way with the Father or with the Holy Spirit. The Son alone is known by His mark of being *the Only Son to be fathered by the Father.*

God the Father, Who is over all, has this as the special mark of His person: He alone is *Father.* That is, *He does not derive His person from any cause outside Himself.* This is the mark by which He is distinctively known.

When our minds see the Father as He is in Himself, we at the same time see the Son; and when we receive the Son, we do not divide Him from the Spirit. We express our faith in God with regard to all three persons, distinguishing between them to show the order that exists among them, but uniting them in their nature. If we speak about the

Spirit, we also include in our confession the One Whose Spirit He is. As Paul says, the Spirit is Christ's and God's (**Romans 8:9, 1 Corinthians 2:12**). When we take hold of one end of a chain, we pull the other end towards us. In the same way, when we draw the Spirit to us, together with Him we also draw to us both the Son and the Father at the same time. And when we truly receive the Son, we grasp Him on both sides; the Son draws His Father to us on the one side, and His Spirit on the other. For the Son, Who eternally exists in the Father, can never be cut off from the Father; and the same Son, Who brings about all things by the Spirit, can never be separated from the Spirit. Likewise, when we receive the Father, we receive in effect both the Son and the Spirit at the same time.

There can be no room in our minds for any idea of separation or division, as if the Son could be conceived apart from the Father, or the Spirit separated from the Son. In a way that we cannot describe or imagine, the three persons share a oneness with each other, and yet are distinct. The difference between the persons never tears apart the unity of their nature; and the oneness of their essence does not destroy their proper marks of distinction.

Basil of Caesarea, *Letter to Gregory of Nyssa on the Difference between "Essence" and "Person",* **chapters 3 and 4**

The glory of Christ - the glory of being a Christian

Better than others and more clearly, Paul showed what Christ is, and showed by his deeds what sort of person he must be who bears Christ's name. Paul imitated Christ so clearly that he revealed his Lord formed within himself; through a most exact imitation, the very form of Paul's soul was transformed into the One it copied, so that it seemed no longer to be Paul living and speaking, but Christ Himself living in Paul. The apostle was so beautifully convinced of his own virtues that he could say, "You seek a proof of the Christ Who speaks in me" (**2 Corinthians 13:3**), and, "It is no longer I who live, but Christ Who lives in me" (**Galatians 2:20**).

Paul makes known to us what the name of Christ means, saying that Christ is the power and wisdom of God (**1 Corinthians 1:24**). He also calls Him peace (**Ephesians 2:14**), the unapproachable light in which God dwells (**1 Timothy 6:16**), sanctification (**1 Corinthians 1:30**), ransom (**1 Timothy 2:6**), high priest (**Hebrews 2:17**), passover lamb (**1 Corinthians 5:7**), propitiation for souls (**Romans 3:25**), splendour of God's glory and image of His person (**Hebrews 1:3**), Creator of the ages (**Colossians 1:16**), spiritual food and drink and rock and water (**1 Corinthians 10:3-4**), the foundation of our faith (**1 Corinthians 3:11**), the keystone of the arch (**Ephesians 2:20**), image of the invisible God (**Colossians 1:15**), the great God (**Titus 2:13**), the head of His body the Church (**Ephesians 5:23**), the firstfruits of those who sleep (**1 Corinthians 15:20**), the firstborn from among the dead (**Colossians 1:18**), the firstborn among many brothers (**Romans 8:29**), the Mediator between God and mankind (**1 Timothy 2:5**), the only-begotten Son crowned with glory and honour (**Hebrews 2:9**), the Lord of glory (**1 Corinthians 2:8**), the ruler of all that exists (**Colossians 2:10**), the King of righteousness and Prince of peace (**Hebrews 7:2**), the universal monarch Who possesses His royal power without end (**Hebrews 1:8**).

Paul added many other titles too, almost without number. If we compare them all with one another, and the meaning of each title combines to show what is meant, they give us a certain image of what Christ's name means. They show us as much of the unspeakable greatness of Christ as our souls can understand. And our good Master has granted us fellowship with that greatest, most divine and first of names, so that those whom He honours with the name of Christ are called Christians. By necessity it follows that all the meanings expressed in this word should be seen in us too, so that our name will not be false but be proved by the way we live.

Gregory of Nyssa, *Homily on Perfection to Olympius*

Chapter 9.

JOHN CHRYSOSTOM, JEROME AND AUGUSTINE OF HIPPO

The 4th and 5th Centuries were the "golden age" of the early Church fathers. There were many outstanding Church leaders, often with strong and colourful personalities, whose achievements continue to influence people even today. We have already looked at Athanasius, the Cappadocian fathers, Ambrose of Milan, and the great monastic figures such as Antony, Martin of Tours and John Cassian.[1] In this Chapter, we are going to consider three more great Christian leaders, whose lives and works, beginning in the 4th Century and ending in the 5th, reveal a lot about the times in which they lived.

1. The preacher: John Chrysostom (344-407)

John Chrysostom[2] was one of the most glorious preachers of the early Church, or indeed of the Church in any age. He was born in Antioch some time between 344 and 345. His father, a high-ranking army officer, died when John was a child, and John was brought up by his Christian mother, Anthusa. As a young man, he at first pursued a career in law, studying under Libanius, an eminent pagan teacher of rhetoric, who regarded John as his best student. Libanius also made a famous remark in praise of the character of John's mother Anthusa: "O gods of Greece, what wonderful women these Christians have!" However, after his baptism in about 370, John abandoned his dreams of a legal career, and decided to become a monk. He went to live with other monks in a cave outside Antioch, and practised such a harsh ascetic self-discipline that he damaged his

---

1   See Chapter 7, for Ambrose, Antony, Martin of Tours and John Cassian, and Chapter 8 for Athanasius and the Cappadocian fathers.
2   Pronounced "Kriz-oss-tum".

health. Returning to Antioch in about 380, he became a deacon in 381, and in 386 bishop Flavian, the patriarch of Antioch, ordained him as a presbyter .

Over the next 12 years, John's preaching in Antioch won a matchless reputation for brilliance. Later, after his death, the Church gave him the nickname *Chrysostom*, which is Greek for "golden mouth". He preached his way verse-by-verse through books of the Bible, and was astonishingly direct and outspoken in denouncing sin among believers, especially the sin of compromising with worldly standards of behaviour. He also made hard-hitting criticisms of the way that rich Christians used or abused their wealth. Others wrote down Chrysostom's sermons as he preached them, and many have survived, *e.g.* his 58 sermons on selected **Psalms**, 90 sermons on **Matthew's Gospel**, and 88 on **John's**. Most modern students find them to be among the easiest to read and most practically helpful of all the writings of the early Church fathers.

Chrysostom's method of interpreting Scripture was the opposite of Origen's (see Chapter 5, section 1). Origen, we recall, had searched for a deeper "allegorical" meaning which did not always have much connection with the ordinary meaning of the text. By contrast, Chrysostom stuck to what scholars call the Bible's "grammatico-historical" meaning; that is, he took the words and sentences of Scripture in their normal obvious sense, according to the rules of Hebrew or Greek grammar and the historical narrative or context in which the words were found. Then he showed the relevance and application of the text's meaning to the lives of his hearers. Basil of Caesarea[3] was a great advocate of this grammatico-historical method, and explained it as follows in his sermons on the days of creation in **Genesis:**

> "I know the principles of 'allegory' from the writings of others. Some preachers do not admit the ordinary meaning of the Scriptures. They will not call water 'water', but something else. They interpret a plant or a fish according to the fancy of their own imagination; they change reptiles and wild beasts

---

3   For Basil of Caesarea, see previous Chapter, section 3.

John Chrysostom (344 - 407)

into something allegorical, just like those who interpret the meaning of dreams according to their own personal ideas. But when I hear the word 'grass', I understand that it means grass! Plants, fish, wild beasts, domestic animals - I take them all in a literal sense."

The church in Antioch was particularly committed to Basil and Chrysostom's approach to Scripture, and so theologians call it the "Antiochene" method of interpretation. Origen's method, with its quest for deeper allegorical meanings, is known as the "Alexandrian" method, since it was typical of the church in Alexandria. These two differing methods of expounding Scripture involved differing approaches to doctrine too, as we will see in Chapter 10.

Chrysostom also wrote an influential book about the ministry, *On the Priesthood*, which has been reprinted and translated into other languages more often than any of Chrysostom's other works. Another early Church father, *Isidore of Pelusium* (360-440), a presbyter-monk[4] from Pelusium in Egypt, said of this book: "No-one can read this volume without feeling his heart inflamed with the love of God. It sets forth how worthy of reverence and how difficult is the office of the priesthood, and it shows how to fulfil it as it ought to be fulfilled."

In 398, patriarch Nectarius of Constantinople died. The struggle between different factions to get their candidate elected as Nectarius's successor was fierce, highly politicised, and simmering with plots, conspiracy and intrigue. However, the emperor *Arcadius* (395-408), advised by his chief minister, the eunuch Eutropius, already had his eye on Chrysostom. Eutropius had heard Chrysostom preach in Antioch; his "golden-mouthed" eloquence had convinced Eutropius that this was the man who would bring glory to the patriarchal throne of the Eastern capital. To prevent the citizens of Antioch raising a riotous protest against the loss of their favourite preacher, emperor Arcadius sent troops to Antioch. The governor of the city then invited the unsuspecting Chrysostom to visit

---

4   A presbyter-monk (or priest-monk) is simply a monk who has also been ordained as a presbyter, often called a *hieromonk* in the East (Greek for "priest-monk").

a chapel with him outside the city walls - and there, the imperial troops virtually kidnapped Chrysostom and escorted him to Constantinople. Chrysostom protested, but (as Eutropius had forecast) the people of Constantinople were overjoyed at the thought of having the East's most famous preacher as their patriarch. Chrysostom submitted and was ordained to his new office.[5]

Chrysostom's gripping sermons at the Church of the Holy Wisdom (Constantinople's chief church) immediately won him a big popular following among ordinary people in Constantinople. But he also made dangerous enemies among the rich and powerful. The fact is that the new patriarch's personality did not fit into the corrupt and complex political world of the Eastern capital and its imperial court; Chrysostom was an intense, unworldly man, a holy ascetic who had neither taste nor talent for politics or court intrigue. The forthright criticisms of the sins of emperor Arcadius's ministers and servants which Chrysostom made from his pulpit outraged Arcadius and his young and beautiful German empress *Eudoxia* - this was not the sort of preaching they had expected! Eudoxia especially hated Chrysostom; some morally dubious conduct on her part once inspired Chrysostom to preach about the Old Testament queen Jezebel in a way that made most of his listeners sure that he was really referring to Eudoxia. Chrysostom also attracted a host of enemies from among the bishops of Asia Minor. He used his authority as patriarch to try to force them to live up to his own high ascetic ideals of the ministry, and many of them found his personality and methods harsh, cold and lacking in human sympathy. However, Chrysostom's deadliest foe was *Theophilus*, patriarch of Alexandria from 385 to 412. Theophilus resented the fact that Constantinople had become more important than Alexandria in the Christian world, and was determined to do anything he could to destroy the position of Constantinople's patriarch. He also had personal reasons for disliking Chrysostom, since Chrysostom had given hospitality to four Egyptian monks, known from their height as the "Tall Brothers", whom Theophilus had condemned.

---

5   Arcadius's actions in securing Chrysostom as patriarch of Constantinople shows how the Christian emperors of the East had started behaving as virtual heads of the Church. Arcadius had reduced the role of the people in choosing their new patriarch to merely assenting to his own imperial choice.

By 403 Chrysostom had stirred up so many enemies, Theophilus saw that his moment to strike had arrived. He came in person to Asia Minor to complain about Chrysostom's treatment of the Tall Brothers, called together a council of bishops at Chalcedon, packed it with Chrysostom's foes, and declared him deposed. Chrysostom was accused, among other things, of gluttony, drunkenness, sexual immorality, and sucking throat lozenges in church. The action of this council had no validity in Church law. The emperor Arcadius, however, jumped on the chance to get rid of the troublesome preacher, confirmed the council's verdict, and dispatched a squad of imperial troops who arrested Chrysostom and carried him off into exile. Within days, an earthquake shook Constantinople. The empress Eudoxia, terrified that this was God's judgment, ordered the troops to bring Chrysostom back. He re-entered Constantinople in triumph, the people thronging the streets and cheering. The patriarch had won his first contest with the emperor and empress.

However, Chrysostom's victory was not to last. Just a few months later in 404, Eudoxia had a silver statue of herself set up near the Church of the Holy Wisdom, and the games and festivities around the statue disturbed the services of worship. Chrysostom expressed his strong disapproval; Eudoxia was again enraged against the patriarch and began scheming for his downfall. Feeling his enemies closing in on him, Chrysostom condemned Eudoxia in bold but wild language during a sermon, comparing her to a new Herodias who was once more demanding the head of God's servant John on a platter (see **Mark 6:14-29**). For this insult to the empress, Arcadius suspended the patriarch from his duties. Chrysostom refused to obey. So Arcadius sent troops to arrest him; they marched into the Holy Wisdom during a baptismal service, seized Chrysostom and hurried him off into exile again (to Armenia). The people of Constantinople rioted in protest, and pope Innocent I of Rome (401-17) put pressure on Arcadius to recall Chrysostom, but in vain. In 407, Arcadius's soldiers moved Chrysostom to an even remoter place of exile; he was over-exposed to the sun on the journey and died as a result. Afterwards, the whole Eastern Church came to recognise Chrysostom as a great and holy man, honouring him as one of their most revered and beloved saints. In 438, emperor Theodosius II (408-50), the son of Arcadius and Eudoxia, brought Chrysostom's remains back to Constantinople, publicly begged forgiveness for the terrible sin of his parents, and had the saint's bones buried in the Church of the Apostles.

Chrysostom was the most gifted preacher and Bible commentator of the Eastern Church in the patristic age. His fate, however, showed that no bishop in the Eastern Empire could hope to stand up against the power of his emperor - in contrast to the West, where Ambrose of Milan had forced Theodosius I to bow to his will (see Chapter 7, section 2).

2. The scholar: Jerome (347-420).

Jerome was the most accomplished scholar of the early Church. Born into a wealthy Christian family in about 347 at Stridonia in Dalmatia (modern-day Croatia and Slovenia), he studied logic, philosophy and rhetoric in Rome, and was baptised in 370. In 372 he set off on a journey through the Middle East, becoming a hermit in the Syrian desert in 374. Here he learned Hebrew, which made Jerome almost unique among Christians of that time - hardly any of them knew the ancient language of the Jews. After receiving ordination as a presbyter in Antioch in 379, he travelled to Constantinople, and studied theology there for two years with the renowned Cappadocian father, Gregory of Nazianzus, who was at that point bishop of Constantinople (see previous Chapter, section 3). Jerome and Gregory became close friends. Then in 382 Jerome visited Rome, where pope Damasus (pope from 366 to 384) asked him to prepare a new Latin translation of the Bible. Jerome agreed - and it took him 23 years to complete the task. In Jerome's day, there were many Latin translations of Scripture circulating in the West, but none of them were particularly good. Jerome made an entirely fresh translation, using the Greek New Testament and the original Hebrew of the Old Testament as the basis for his new Latin version. He finished it in 405. A work of massive scholarship, it was called the *Vulgate,* and soon became the accepted translation of the Bible in the Western Latin-speaking world, a position it held until the Reformation in the 16th Century. (*Vulgate* comes from the Latin word for "common" - the common Bible, *i.e.* the one in common use.)

Jerome's knowledge of Hebrew enabled him to grasp an important fact about the Old Testament Scriptures. He realised that the Greek translation of the Old Testament, the Septuagint, contained certain books which were not found in the Hebrew Old Testament. Since almost no Christians knew Hebrew, but many spoke Greek, the Church used the Septuagint in its worship, study and preaching. Jerome argued that Christians must accept as part of the authentic Old Testament only those books which the Jews included in the Hebrew Old Testament, and must reject the extra books in the Septuagint. The Church called these extra books the *apocrypha*, which is Greek for "hidden things" (this refers to the fact that the apocryphal books were not read out in public worship, because the Church did not consider them to be on the same level as the rest of Scripture). The Old Testament which Protestants use today is the Hebrew Old Testament as Jerome defined it. The Roman Catholic Council of Trent, however, in 1546 decreed that the apocrypha was divinely inspired and part of the Old Testament, anathematising all who disagreed. (The Western Church in the Middle Ages, before the storms of the Reformation, had no clearly defined view of the Old Testament canon; different theologians argued for different positions.) The Eastern Orthodox Church has never come to a universally accepted consensus on this matter; at the present day, *Greek* Orthodox theologians accept the apocrypha as inspired, whereas many *Russian* Orthodox regard it as instructive and edifying for Christians but not on the same level as Scripture as a source of teaching.[6]

While he was in Rome, Jerome won over many members of the Roman aristocracy, both men and women, to practise the monastic life. It astounded pagans to see these eminent sons and daughters of the nobility give away all their fortune to the poor and transform their magnificent stately homes into humble monasteries. However, Jerome's scathing attacks on the low moral standards of the Roman clergy and ruling classes made him the most unpopular figure in the city - especially when he reacted to criticism and mockery by

---

6   The apocrypha consists of **1** and **2 Esdras, Tobit, Judith, Susanna, Bel and the Dragon, the Prayer of Manasses, the Epistle of Jeremiah, Baruch, Ecclesiasticus** (not to be confused with **Ecclesiastes!**), **the Wisdom of Solomon, 1 and 2 Maccabees**, and additional passages in **Esther** and **Daniel**.

criticising and mocking his enemies in return, with all the devastating power of his supremely eloquent tongue and pen. (Jerome was one of those people who find it easy to pick a quarrel and then turn a quarrel into an all-out war.) As a result, when his patron and defender, pope Damasus, died in 384, Jerome had to flee from Rome with a band of disciples, and journeyed to Jerusalem.

From 386 onwards, Jerome lived out the rest of his life in a monastery in Bethlehem, constantly writing and teaching the other monks. He opened a school for the children of the neighbourhood. He produced many scholarly commentaries on the different books of the Bible, and translated a number of important Greek theological writings into Latin; his own wonderful command of language - clear, forceful, flowing and soul-kindling - earned Jerome the supreme place for sheer literary style among the Western Latin-speaking fathers. He took part in many controversies, *e.g.* the Pelagian controversy, in which he sided with Augustine against Pelagius (see next section). This provoked the Pelagians of Palestine to bitter hostility against Jerome; in 416, a Pelagian mob attacked and burnt down his monastery in Bethlehem, forcing the aged Jerome to flee and remain in hiding for two years.

Above all, Jerome wrote powerfully and movingly in praise of celibacy and monasticism. He was convinced that although marriage was a good and noble creation of God, celibacy was a superior form of the Christian life; a celibate was "married to Christ". As we have seen, Jerome converted many to the monastic life, especially females. Indeed, he exercised an amazing spiritual influence over the aristocratic Christian women of Rome, who almost worshipped him; many of them followed Jerome to Bethlehem and lived in a nunnery there under his spiritual direction. The most notable of these nuns was *Paula* (347-404), descended from two of the most ancient and illustrious Roman families, the Gracchi and the Scipios. Paula had given Jerome hospitality in Rome; accompanying him to Bethlehem, she used her wealth to build a hospital, a monastery and three nunneries there. She even followed Jerome's rare example in learning Hebrew so that she could study the Old Testament better.

Jerome died in Bethlehem, sick and almost blind, in 419 or 420. His fame and influence among Western Christians throughout the Middle Ages were second only to those of Augustine of Hippo.

3. The theologian: Augustine of Hippo (354-430).

Many Western Christians regard Augustine as the greatest theologian to arise in the Church since the apostle Paul. He certainly had one of the brightest, deepest, most powerful minds in the history of human thought, and was also one of the most beautiful writers of Latin who ever lived. We know more about Augustine than any other man in the ancient world because of his intimate spiritual autobiography, the *Confessions*. Augustine was born in 354 in Thagaste, North-West Africa (modern-day Algeria), to a pagan father and a Christian mother called *Monica* (331-87). Monica's influence on Augustine was deep and lifelong; like John Chrysostom's mother Anthusa, Monica stands out as an example of a Christian woman whose faith helped to shape her more famous son into one of the spiritual giants of the early Church. Augustine received a good education, and could have had a great career as a lawyer or civil servant, but his father's death in 370 forced him to become a teacher to support his family. He also started living with a girl whom he never married and who bore him a son, Adeodatus.[7] In 373 Augustine moved to Carthage, where he became a professor of rhetoric. While in Carthage, he was converted to a passionate love of philosophy through reading a book by the great pagan philosopher of Rome, Cicero, who had lived in the 1st Century BC. Burning with a new thirst to understand life's great questions, Augustine then turned to the Bible - but to his dismay, he found all kinds of problems and difficulties in the Old Testament; he thought it was a cruel, violent and revolting book, unworthy of being believed by a philosopher who took reason as his guide.

This experience led Augustine to make a complete break with the Christianity of his youth, and to join the Gnostic sect of the Manichees, who also rejected the Old Testament and claimed they could prove all their doctrines by pure reason.[8] Augustine remained with the Manichees for nine years. Meanwhile his mother Monica

---

7   The relationship between Augustine and his mistress lasted until just before Augustine's conversion. He left the girl in 385 at his mother's insistence; Monica wanted Augustine to enter into a proper marriage with a suitable woman, although he never did.

8   For the Manichees, see Chapter 6, section 2.

prayed unceasingly with tears for his conversion. Once she tried to persuade a Catholic bishop, himself a converted Manichee, to prove to Augustine the errors of Manichaeism and the truth of the Catholic faith. The bishop refused, explaining that only prayer, not argument, would rescue Monica's son from the Manichees. When Monica continued, weeping, to beg for the bishop's help, he replied famously: "Go; it cannot be that the son of such tears will perish!"

In 383 Augustine moved to Rome to take up a new teaching position. By now, he had started to lose his faith in Manichaeism. In fact, for a time he seriously doubted whether anyone could know what life meant. Then in 384 he was appointed professor of rhetoric in Milan. There, two things happened which brought Augustine out of his doubts and led him back to Christianity. First, he discovered the philosophy of Neoplatonism.[9] Augustine enthusiastically read the writings of Plotinus and his disciple Porphyry. From them he learned that humanity's true destiny lies in the knowledge and love of a supreme God, and he was inspired by a new idea of God as the spiritually perfect Being Whose likeness is reflected in the human soul. During his years as a Manichee, Augustine had been unable to think of God except in physical terms, possessing a spirit-body; Plotinus and Porphyry taught him that God was a pure infinite Spirit, beyond matter, space and time, but able to be known by the human soul that bears His image.

Alongside Augustine's conversion to Neoplatonism, he fell under the influence of bishop Ambrose of Milan.[10] He went to listen to Ambrose's preaching; the eloquence of his sermons, and the way Ambrose made Christianity seem an intelligent and reasonable faith, utterly captivated Augustine's mind. Ambrose's method of handling the Old Testament also helped Augustine overcome his problems with the Hebrew Scriptures. When Ambrose came across a difficult Old Testament passage, one that seemed unworthy of God, he said it should not be interpreted literally, but understood in a spiritual or symbolic sense. (This was basically the Alexandrian method of expounding the Bible - see section 1.)

---

9   For Neoplatonism see Chapter 6, section 2.
10 For Ambrose, see Chapter 7, section 2.

Augustine of Hippo (354 - 430)

Augustine was soon convinced in his mind that the Christian faith was true. However, he had a fierce struggle submitting to it in his heart and will; the attractions of the world and sensual pleasures were still overpoweringly strong. His conversion finally came when he was meditating in a garden in Milan in 386. Augustine heard a child's voice mysteriously saying, "Take and read! Take and read!" He had a copy of the New Testament with him, so he picked it up and it fell open at **Romans 13:13-14:** "Not in orgies and drunkenness, not in sexual immorality and debauchery, not in dissension and jealousy. But clothe yourselves in the Lord Jesus Christ, and do not think about how to gratify the desires of the sinful nature." In his autobiography, Augustine said: "I did not want or need to read any further. Instantly, as I finished the sentence, the light of faith flooded into my heart, and all the darkness of doubt vanished."

Augustine's son Adeodatus was converted soon after this, and Ambrose of Milan baptised both Augustine and Adeodatus on Easter Sunday in 387. The following year, father and son returned to Africa.[11] Augustine sold all his land and possessions in his native Thagaste, and founded a small monastery there. Cenobitic monasticism was almost unknown in North-West Africa at this point; Augustine's pioneer community was like a plant that scattered the seeds of monasticism across North-West Africa. Augustine himself became increasingly well-known as he produced masterful writings against the Manichees and on other subjects. In 391, while he was visiting the Catholic church at Hippo, west of Carthage, the overwhelming popular demand of the congregation forced a reluctant Augustine to accept ordination as a presbyter. The elderly bishop of Hippo, Valerius, was a Greek who could not speak Latin very well, and had been praying for a suitable assistant for years; when he noticed Augustine standing in his congregation, he began preaching on this very topic - and the congregation surrounded Augustine, crying out that here was the man Valerius needed. Augustine submitted with tears, interpreting the will of the people as the voice of God. So began Augustine's 40 year association with Hippo (present-day Annaba in Algeria). In 396, Valerius died and Augustine succeeded him as bishop.

---

11 Adeodatus died two years later in 390 at the age of 18.

Augustine's 34 years as bishop of Hippo make him shine out as one of the brightest stars in the patristic galaxy. A preacher, a practical Church administrator, a theologian, a mystic, a man of learning, a leader of the monastic movement, a writer of many books, and a pastoral counsellor: among the early Church fathers there were few who surpassed Augustine in these roles, and none who combined them all so successfully. He had no equal at all in the way he mingled passionate religious feeling with sharp and deep doctrinal thinking. The emblem that tradition has assigned to Augustine sums up his personality: a heart on fire, pierced by two arrows in the shape of a cross. Profoundly gloomy and pessimistic about human nature and earthly life, Augustine burned with other-worldly love for Christ and the heavenly country His cross had purchased for His people. To read Augustine (especially his prayers) is to have heart and mind lit up by eternity and ushered into the presence of God; down through the centuries, no other father of the Church has had so many spiritual pilgrims come and quench their soul-thirst from the well of his writings.

As bishop of Hippo, Augustine became involved in several religious controversies. The two most important were with Donatism and Pelagianism.

Donatism. The Church in North-West Africa was still split between Catholics and Donatists (see Chapter 7, section 1). By Augustine's time, the Donatists were in the majority. Augustine tirelessly preached, wrote, and even composed popular songs against them, and his vigorous and uncompromising anti-Donatist campaign finally turned the tide back in favour of Catholicism in North-West Africa. But why did Augustine feel he had to carry out this campaign? Essentially it was because he believed so deeply in the visible unity of the Church. Augustine felt it was a wound in the body of Christ that the African Christian community was so divided; somehow, unity had to be restored. Augustine was convinced that the Catholic Church in North-West Africa was the true Church, because it was recognised by, and in fellowship with, the rest of the Catholic Church throughout the Empire; the Donatist Church, by contrast, was a local sect found only in North-West Africa. Augustine thought that the refusal of the Donatists to belong to the Catholic Church was a sin against Christian love, an act of division which proved that the Donatists lacked the Spirit.

Augustine devoted a lot of energy to defending the Catholic Church against Donatist accusations that it was an apostate Church with false clergy, whose spiritual actions (*e.g.* baptising converts) had no meaning or value in God's sight. Donatists would rebaptise Catholics who joined them, arguing that baptism was not valid when given by the presbyters and bishops of the false Catholic Church. By contrast, African Catholics did not rebaptise Donatists who joined them. Augustine argued that the validity of baptism did not depend on the personal worthiness or orthodoxy of the clergyman who baptises, but on Christ Himself. As long as Christ's command to baptise with water in the name of the Trinity was obeyed, the baptism was valid - it was really Christ Himself Who was baptising the convert through the act of the presbyter or bishop. The same reasoning applied to holy communion. In this way Augustine developed the Western theology of the sacraments of baptism and eucharist: they were something Christ did, and as long as they were correctly carried out in accordance with Christ's command, their validity as sacraments could not be spoiled by the sinfulness of the Church or its clergy.[12] However, Augustine also held that when baptism was given outside the Catholic Church, although it was objectively valid, it would never produce its spiritual fruit of salvation unless the baptised person joined the Catholic Church. Such a person did not need to be rebaptised; but he did need to become a Catholic if his baptism was to be spiritually effective. By this argument Augustine tried to preserve Cyprian's view of the Catholic Church as the only body in which the Holy Spirit worked savingly.[13]

---

12 We may see the relevance of Augustine's argument by the following illustration. Imagine that after your conversion you are baptised by your local minister, Mr Smith. Some time later, Mr Smith runs away with the wife of one of his deacons. You find out that he was committing adultery with her at the time he baptised you. Does that mean you are not truly baptised? Does the sinfulness of Mr Smith destroy the validity of your baptism? Augustine would say no. As long as Mr Smith baptised you with water in the name of the Trinity in accordance with Christ's command, it was Christ Himself Who was baptising you; Mr Smith was only His instrument. The sinfulness of the instrument cannot take away the validity of Christ's act.

13 For Cyprian's views, see Chapter 5, section 2. The East did not accept Augustine's view that baptism was objectively valid outside the Catholic Church; see footnote 14 of Chapter 7, section 3.

Augustine also criticised the Donatists for their view that the true
Church (by which they meant themselves) was a morally pure
community. Augustine argued that here on earth, the Church was
always a "mixed" community of true and false, sincere and deceitful,
wheat and tares. True Christians were still sinners; and Augustine
was much less confident than the Donatists were about telling the
difference between genuine and counterfeit Christians. The
Donatists' claims that they were a pure community did not carry any
weight with Augustine. He pointed out the faults and scandals that
disgraced the Donatist as well as the Catholic Church.

Finally, Augustine justified the use of state power against the
Donatists to force them to come back into the Catholic Church. This
was a policy which Augustine had at first opposed, but in the end he
came around to supporting it. The policy was partly in response to the
violence which some extreme Donatists called "Circumcellions"[14]
used against Catholics, *e.g.* attacking Catholic church buildings. At
one point Augustine narrowly escaped being assassinated by a band
of Circumcellions! More importantly, when the Western emperor
Honorius (395-423) started putting pressure on the Donatists to
return to the Catholic Church, by exiling their leaders and
confiscating their church property, the policy worked. Many
Donatists did return to the Catholic Church, and became good, solid,
loyal Catholics. This impressed Augustine. His main objection to
persecution had been his belief that it would not work - that it would,
at best, only produce reluctant insincere conversions, and flood the
Church with hypocrites. When he saw that persecution did seem to
work, he changed his mind and wrote in defence of the policy.
Augustine now argued that such action by the emperor was like a
father punishing his children for their own good. The emperor was
lovingly compelling the Donatists back into the true Catholic Church,
thus ensuring their eternal salvation.

Modern supporters of religious toleration have often blamed
Augustine for this policy of persecution, but in fairness to Augustine
it must be pointed out that Christian emperors had been using their

---

14 The word "Circumcellion" is of uncertain meaning. It may come from a
    Latin word meaning "around the cells" - that is, around the shrines of
    martyrs, where the Circumcellions gathered for worship.

power to punish religious nonconformists ever since Constantine the Great. Augustine actually opposed this policy at first, and then simply offered a theological argument to justify an existing practice. However, it is true that people used Augustine's arguments, and the great authority of his name, to justify the persecution of religious nonconformists throughout the Middle Ages and Reformation period in the West. What most later supporters of persecution failed to notice was that Augustine remained totally opposed to the use of violence or the death penalty against non-Catholics. Fines and banishment were the only penalties Augustine had in mind.

Pelagianism. The events and writings for which Augustine is best remembered arose out of the Pelagian controversy. *Pelagius* was a British monk of cultured mind and blameless character who came to Rome in about 383. The worldliness he found among Roman Christians shocked him to the core of his being; most of them, Pelagius felt, viewed Christianity as a set of rituals which offered bliss in the future life, without the slightest hint that it should also influence their moral behaviour in the present. In the depths of his sadness and disgust, Pelagius's mission in life dawned on him as though from heaven: he was to be an apostle of sanctity to his fellow Christians, carrying the high ascetic ideals of monastic holiness into the Church at large. Every Christian was to be a sort of monk who lived in the world instead of in a monastery or a cave. Inflamed by this thrilling and compelling vision, Pelagius gathered a group of disciples in Rome, taught them, and guided them into his own conception of a pure spiritual life. Others caught his vision, and the Pelagian movement grew.

Unfortunately for Pelagius, his ardent zeal for holy living was wedded to a rather unorthodox theology. Although his doctrine of God was Catholic enough (he believed in the Nicene doctrine of the Trinity), his beliefs about human nature sparked off a storm of controversy which ended in his condemnation for heresy. Pelagius held that all human beings were born into the world as sinless as Adam was before he fell; the apostasy of Adam had not corrupted humanity's nature, but had merely set a fatally bad example, which most of Adam's sons and daughters had freely followed. However, there were some people (according to Pelagius) who had managed to remain sinless throughout their lives by a proper use of their free-

will, *e.g.* some of the Old Testament saints like Daniel. In fact,
anyone could become sinlessly perfect if only he tried hard enough.
Pelagius admitted, of course, that human beings needed God's grace
in order to be good, but he had his own peculiar definition of grace.
For Pelagius "grace" really meant two things: (i) God's gift of natural
free-will to all human beings; (ii) God's gift of the moral law and the
example of Christ, which revealed perfectly how people should live,
and supplied strong incentives in the form of eternal rewards and
punishments. Pelagius's theology therefore made the fruits of
human goodness grow almost entirely out of human free-will and
effort; entry into heaven, in the Pelagian scheme, became a just
reward for living a good life on earth, rather than an undeserved gift
purchased for helpless sinners by the blood of an all-sufficient
Saviour.

An army of tribal Germans called Visigoths captured and wrecked
Rome in 410.[15] Among the refugees who fled to North-West Africa
were Pelagius and his most enthusiastic disciple, an upper-class ex-
lawyer named *Celestius*. Celestius, a much more extreme, logical
and consistent thinker than his master, and a far more aggressive and
vigorous personality, tried to get himself ordained as a presbyter in
the African Catholic Church; instead, a council in Carthage
condemned him for heresy. Alerted to what Pelagius and Celestius
were teaching, Augustine now began to write against them. In a
harvest of books such as *On Nature and Grace, On the Grace of
Christ and Original Sin,* and *On the Spirit and the Letter*,
Augustine explained, explored and defended the absolute sovereignty of God's grace in saving sinners. The controversy spread to
the East, where Pelagius and Celestius had gone; Jerome attacked
Pelagius, but a synod at Jerusalem acquitted the British monk of all
charges of heresy. Augustine and the North-West Africans
persuaded pope Innocent I (401-417) to excommunicate Pelagius
and Celestius in 416. Innocent died almost immediately afterwards,
and his successor, pope Zosimus (417-18), received Pelagius and
Celestius back into fellowship. However, at this point the Western
emperor Honorius stepped in. A Pelagian mob had beaten up a
Catholic who was a retired government official; Honorius angrily

---

15   See Chapter 11, section 1.

responded by banishing Pelagius and Celestius. Pope Zosimus fell into line and excommunicated the two men again. The ecumenical Council of Ephesus finally condemned Pelagianism as a heresy in 431.[16]

The Pelagian controversy left a fabulously rich legacy of writings from Augustine in which he set out his understanding of sin and salvation. Against Pelagius and Celestius, Augustine argued that the entire human race was mysteriously present in Adam, the head of mankind; when he sinned and fell, human nature itself sinned and fell in him. As a result, every human being is born into the world with a sinful nature. This is called "original sin". One of Augustine's arguments for the reality of original sin was that babies would not need baptism if they were born sinless, which shows that infant baptism had finally become the normal practice in the Church by the 5th Century. In a very real sense, Augustine said, the corruption of original sin has robbed us of our freedom. We are still free to do what we *want* to do; but until God saves us, all we ever want to do is sin. So we are not free to do what we *ought* to do. In another sense, though, Augustine held that lost sinners do still have free-will; our wills are free in the sense that even when we sin, we always sin *willingly*, with our own choice and consent - nothing forces us to sin against our wills. We could sum up Augustine's view thus: it is absolutely certain that we will always sin willingly, unless the grace of Christ saves us.

Because of their slavery to sin, then, Augustine argued that people could not become Christians by their own wills, but only by the almighty transforming power of God. Conversion was not a human achievement; it was the result of the Holy Spirit working sovereignly in the hearts of sinners to break their bondage to sin, and create in them a willingness to follow Jesus Christ. God took the unwilling and made them willing. "Grace" was therefore not natural free-will, as Pelagius maintained, and it was more than simply God's gift of the moral law and the example of Christ; it was the life-giving power of the Holy Spirit, Who created a good will in evil people, and then worked with that good will to make it bear fruit in sanctification. Augustine was fond of quoting Christ's words to the disciples in

16 For the Council of Ephesus, see next Chapter, section 3.

250 years of Christ's power

John 15:16, "You did not choose Me, but I chose you, and appointed you to go and bear fruit, and that your fruit should remain." From all eternity, Augustine said, God had chosen the sinners He would save, and predestined them to become Christians. They were "the elect". The rest God left in their own sinful desires. This was not unfair, because no-one deserved to be saved. If God chose some sinners for salvation in Christ, that was pure mercy and grace; if He left others in their own self-centred slavery to sin, that was merely justice and righteousness.

However, Augustine did not think that all Christians were elect! It was, he argued, clear from Scripture and experience that there were some believers who fell away and lost their salvation; God had granted them a *temporary* salvation, but had not elected them to *eternal* salvation. Election bestowed on a believer the extra gift of "perseverance" - staying a believer to the end of one's life. Thus no Christian on earth could be sure that he was in fact one of the elect; it all depended on whether God had granted him the additional grace of perseverance. And no-one could know that unless he actually persevered to the end. Christians therefore had to remain in a state of humble uncertainty about their eternal destiny, at the same time seeking to persevere in holiness and also praying for the grace of perseverence.

On top of this, Augustine criticised the sinless perfection teaching of Pelagius and Celestius. No-one, Augustine taught, not even the greatest saint, would ever be perfectly free from sin in the present life. The true Christian life was not sinless perfection, but a daily desperate struggle with the sin that still dwelt in human nature. It was the same point Augustine had made against the Donatists when they claimed to be a pure Church; but at least the Donatists made purity a fruit of God's grace, not human free-will.

The Pelagian controversy continued to rumble on in various ways until Augustine's death and even afterwards. Augustine filled the last years of his life with writing against *Julian of Eclanum* (380-455), an Italian bishop and the most clear-minded thinker and lively writer that Pelagianism produced. However, the controversy was not a straight fight between Augustinians and Pelagians. A small group of writers arose in southern France, usually called "Semi-

Pelagians" (the name is rather misleading - they should perhaps be called "Semi-Augustinians"). Their leader was the great John Cassian,one of the founding fathers of Western monasticism.[17] Other important Semi-Pelagians were the notable bishop, Bible scholar and preacher *Faustus of Riez* (died about 490), and the presbyter-monk *Vincent of Lerins* (died some time before 450). The Semi-Pelagians agreed with Augustine that the whole human race had fallen in Adam, and that sinners could not become Christians or do spiritual good without the powerful help of God's grace. But they insisted that although a sinner could not save himself, he could at least cry out to God for saving grace, just as a sick person might not be able to heal himself, but he could at least take himself to the doctor. Conversion was therefore a joint product of the divine and human will working together, a view known as *synergism* (from the Greek "working together"). Vincent of Lerins argued that a test of Catholic doctrine was that it had been believed "everywhere, always, by everyone" in the Church. Augustine's doctrine of mankind's helpless slavery to sin and God's sovereign predestination of some to salvation, Vincent said, failed to pass this test, because until Augustine taught it, it had been believed nowhere, at no time, by no-one![18]

Augustine wrote against the Semi-Pelagians, but treated them with mildness, gentleness and respect: the Pelagians were blasphemous heretics, but Semi-Pelagians were erring brothers in Christ. After Augustine's death, a number of his disciples took up and defended his views against the Semi-Pelagians. Leading Augustinians were the layman *Prosper of Aquitaine* (390-463), who was a scholar, poet, and (after 440) secretary to pope Leo the Great;[19] the African bishop *Fulgentius of Ruspe* (468-533); and two distinguished bishops of France, *Avitus of Vienne* (bishop from 490 to 519) and *Caesarius of Arles* (470-543). Caesarius ensured the victory of a basically Augustinian theology at the council of Orange (southern France) in 529. The council's doctrinal statement received official approval in 531 from pope Boniface II (pope from 530 to 532).

---

17 For John Cassian, see Chapter 7, section 3.
18 An Augustinian might reply that it had been believed by Jesus and the apostles.
19 For Leo the Great, see next Chapter, section 4.

The Western Church broadly accepted Augustine's doctrines of sin and salvation, with some modifications. Most of the great Western theologians of the Middle Ages were "Augustinians" in their basic understanding of human sin and divine grace. So were the Protestant Reformers of the 16th Century. The East, by contrast, followed the Semi-Pelagian (or Semi-Augustinian) "synergist" outlook which John Cassian, Faustus of Riez and Vincent of Lerins had championed in France. Because of Augustine's view of the Catholic Church, he held that the grace which saved the elect was channelled through the one true Church and its sacraments. If anyone lived and died outside the Catholic Church, that showed he was not one of the elect. This was the type of Augustinianism which prevailed in the Middle Ages in the West. Later, the Protestant Reformers rejected Augustine's doctrine of the Church, and taught that the Holy Spirit bestowed His grace directly on the elect by creating personal faith in the Gospel, written or preached. In this way the Reformers "liberated God's grace" from its confinement in one exclusive Church. The Protestant Reformation has often been called "the triumph of Augustine's doctrine of grace over Augustine's doctrine of the Church".[20]

Among his many writings, Augustine penned several truly great Christian books. The three most influential were:

Confessions. This is the story of Augustine's early life and spiritual pilgrimage to faith in Christ. It is told in the form of a prayer to God. It has always been Augustine's most popular book; the story of his journey to God has deeply moved and inspired many Christians who have not shared his distinctive theology.

On the Trinity. This contained Augustine's attempt to explore the mystery of the Trinity. It had a huge impact on later Western theology, especially on three points: (i) Augustine defined God's unity or oneness in terms of the *divine essence* shared fully and equally by the three persons of the Trinity. This was in contrast to the Eastern view, which located God's unity or oneness in the *person*

---

20 For the Protestant Reformation, see Part Three.

of the Father.[21] (ii) Augustine taught that the Holy Spirit eternally proceeds from the Son as well as from the Father. Again, this was in contrast to the Eastern view that the Spirit proceeds from the Father alone. (iii) Augustine tried to find "shadows" or "traces" of the Trinity in created things, especially in the human soul. He found a significant trace in the threefold activity of the soul in thinking, remembering and willing. Another trace was in the emotion of human love, which involved a lover, a beloved, and the love that bound them together.

City of God. Augustine wrote this after the Visigoths captured Rome in 410. Pagans blamed the disaster on the fact that Rome had abandoned its traditional gods. Responding to this charge, Augustine developed a Christian view of world-history. The human race, he said, had always been divided into two spiritual communities: the "city of the world", made up of those who were controlled by a supreme love of self and earthly things; and "the city of God", made up of those who were controlled by a supreme love of God and eternal things. The two cities were mingled with each other here on earth, but they would be finally separated into their opposite destinies when Christ returned. The city of God existed and was nurtured

---

21 We can sum up the difference between the two views like this. In Eastern thought, the divine essence is, first and foremost, the *Father's* essence, which He fully communicates to the Son and the Spirit. So for Eastern theology, the person of God the Father is the "bond of unity" in the Trinity, because He is the one source of the divine essence. However, in Augustine's thought, the divine essence *itself* is the supreme reality, in which Father, Son and Spirit exist as little more than three ways in which the essence relates to itself (or so Augustine's critics have always felt). So for Augustine, it is the divine essence which is all-important, not the person of the Father. The "bond of unity" in the Trinity is therefore not the Father, it is the divine essence itself. If Augustine saw any of the divine persons as the Trinity's bond of unity, it was the Holy Spirit, Whom Augustine viewed as the "bond of love" binding Father and Son together. This difference between the Eastern and the Augustinian view of the Trinity is very important, because it laid the theological basis on which the Eastern and Western branches of the Church finally split up into two separate Churches with very different traditions of theology and spirituality. See Part Two, Chapter 3, sections 4 and 8.

within the Catholic Church, although the Church contained tares as well as wheat; the city of the world found its most obvious expression in the state. (By this teaching, Augustine strengthened the Western sense of the profound difference, even tension, between Church and state.) The city of the world could never provide true peace and security; sinful human passions and conflicts always disturbed it. While they were here on earth, Augustine argued, not even the members of God's city were exempt from the changing fortunes and calamities of earthly life (such as the fall of Rome). Human beings could find enduring happiness only by looking beyond this sin-cursed life, and fixing their hearts on what was spiritual and eternal through faith in Jesus Christ.

Augustine died in 430, while Hippo was under siege from an invading Germanic army of Vandals. However, his theology lived on in the Western Church. He is the Christian thinker who has had by far the greatest influence on the beliefs, practices and spirituality of Western Christianity.

Important people:

The Church
Monica (331-87)
Paula (347-404)
John Chrysostom (344-407)
Theophilus of Alexandria
    (died 412)
Pelagius (active 383-417)
Jerome (347-420)
Augustine of Hippo (354-430)
Celestius (active 400-431)
Isidore of Pelusium (360-440)
Vincent of Lerins (died before 450)
Julian of Eclanum (380-455)
Prosper of Aquitaine (390-463)
Faustus of Riez (died about 490)
Avitus of Vienne (died 519)
Fulgentius of Ruspe (468-533)
Caesarius of Arles (470-543)

Political and military
Eastern emperor Arcadius (395-
    408)
Eastern empress Eudoxia (395-
    408)
Western emperor Honorius
    (395-423)

Justification by faith in the crucified Christ

"Having forgiven us all sins, having wiped out by the doctrines the handwriting which was against us, which was contrary to us, He took it out of the way, having nailed it to His cross. Having disarmed principalities and powers, He made a public spectacle of them, having triumphed over them in it" (**Colossians 2:13-15:** this is Chrysostom's version of the text). "Having forgiven us," he says, "all sins." Which sins? Those which made us spiritually dead. Did He allow them to remain? No, He wiped them out. He did not merely scratch them out, He wiped them out, so that they could no longer be seen. He did this "by the doctrines" - the doctrines of the faith. So it is enough to believe. He does not contrast works with works, but works with faith. What next? "Wiping out" is an advance on forgiveness; and now he says, "He took it out of the way." And furthermore, He did not keep possession of the handwriting that He took away, but tore it to pieces by nailing it to His cross. "Having disarmed principalities and powers, He made a public spectacle of them, having triumphed over them in it" - nowhere does Paul speak in such in an exalted tone.

Do you see how greatly in earnest Christ was to do away with the handwriting? We were all held captive by sin and punishment. He Himself, by suffering punishment, did away with both the sin and the punishment, for Christ was punished on the cross. To the cross, then, He fixed the handwriting, and afterwards tore it to pieces by His power. What handwriting was this? He means either what the Jews said to Moses, "All that God has said, we will do and be obedient" (**Exodus 24:3**); or this, that we owe God obedience; or rather this, that the devil held possession of the handwriting which God set down against Adam - "In the day you eat from the tree of knowledge, you will die" (**Genesis 2:17**). This handwriting, then, which the devil held in his possession, Christ did not hand to us, but Himself tore it to pieces, as One Who joyfully forgives.

John Chrysostom, *Sermon on Colossians 2:6-15*

Every Christian an evangelist

There is nothing colder than a Christian who does not work for the salvation of others. You cannot use poverty as an excuse; the widow who threw in her two small coins will accuse you (**Luke 21:2-4**). Peter said, "Silver and gold have I none" (**Acts 3:6**). Paul was so poor, he often went hungry and lacked even necessary food (**Philippians 4:12**). And being lower-class by birth is no excuse either. The apostles were obscure men from obscure families. Or are you uneducated? That is no excuse. The apostles were illiterate (**Acts 4:13**). Are you weak in body? That is no excuse. Timothy was a person who suffered from frequent illnesses (**1 Timothy 5:23**). Everyone can serve his neighbour if only he is willing to play his part.

Look at the trees which bear no fruit. See how strong and majestic and smooth and tall they are. But if we had a garden, we would much rather have pomegranates and fruitful olive trees. The tall fruitless trees are pleasing to the eye but they are of no practical use, or very little. They are like people who are concerned only about themselves. Such people are fit for burning! (At least the trees are useful for shelter and making houses out of them.) Such self-centred people were the foolish virgins, who were chaste, discreet and self-controlled, but did not serve others (**Matthew 25:1-13**). Therefore they were delivered over for burning. Such also were those who did not feed Christ (**Matthew 25:41-46**). Christ does not accuse them of personal sins, adultery, swearing falsely, or anything like that; He merely accuses them of not being of any practical service to others. Such a self-centred person was the man who buried his talent (**Luke 19:11-28**). His private life was spotless - but he never served his neighbour. How can such a person be a Christian? I ask you, if you mixed leaven with flour but it did not make it rise, would it still be leaven? If a perfume did not fill a room with fragrance, would we still call it perfume?

Don't tell me, "It is impossible for me to influence others." If you are a Christian, it is impossible for you *not* to influence others! Just as the elements that make up your human nature do not contradict each other, so also in this matter - it belongs to the very nature of a Christian that he influences others. So do not offend God. If you say, "The sun cannot shine," you offend Him. If you say, "I, a Christian, cannot be of service to others," you have offended Him and called Him a liar. It is easier for the sun not to shine than for a Christian not to do so. It is easier for light itself to be darkness than for a Christian not to give light. So don't tell me it is impossible for you as a Christian to influence others, when it is the opposite which is impossible. Do not offend God. If we arrange our affairs in an orderly manner, these things will certainly follow quite naturally. It is not possible for a Christian's light to lie concealed. So brilliant a lamp cannot be hidden!

John Chrysostom, *Homily 20 on the Acts of the Apostles*

The blessedness of virginity

I am about to make a comparison between virginity and marriage - and I would beg my readers not to think I am condemning marriage when I praise virginity. Nor am I dividing the saints of the Old Testament, who had wives, from those of the New who kept themselves from the embraces of women. For the Old Testament saints lived under one covenant that was suited to their times, but we live under another - we "upon whom the ends of the ages have come" (**1 Corinthans 10:11**). While that old law remained, "Increase and multiply and fill the earth" (**Genesis 1:28**), and "Cursed is the barren who does not bear children in Israel" (**Exodus 23:26**),[22] all the people married and were given in marriage, leaving father and mother and becoming one flesh. But then the apostle's voice sounded forth: "The time is short!" And he added, "From now on, even those who have wives should be as though they had none" (**1 Corinthians 7:29**). Why? Because "He who is unmarried cares for the things that belong to the Lord, how he may please the Lord. But he who is married cares about the things of the world, how he may please his wife. There is also a difference between a wife and a virgin. The unmarried woman cares about the things of the Lord, that she may be holy both in body and in spirit. But she who is married cares about the things of the world, how she may please her husband" (**1 Corinthians 7:32-34**). What, then, are you making

---

[22] This is either Jerome's mistranslation of Exodus 23:26, or else Jerome was quoting from some version of the Old Testament which rendered the verse this way.

such a noise about? What are you fighting against? It is the chosen
vessel Paul who says these things! He is the one who says, "There
is a difference between a wife and a virgin"....

"The unmarried woman cares about the things of the Lord, that she
may be holy both in body and in spirit." See, this is the purpose of the
virgin life - "to be holy both in body and in spirit". But "she who is
married cares about the things of the world, how she may please her
husband." Do you really think there is no difference between these
two: on the one hand, the virgin who consecrates her days and her
nights to fasting and prayer; and on the other hand, the woman who
makes herself ready for her husband's return, putting lipstick and
eyeshadow on her face, rushing out to meet him, wrapping herself
around him? The virgin modestly conceals the gifts of beauty which
nature has given her; she makes herself seem less attractive. But
there you see the married woman, gazing at herself in a mirror,
painting herself, trying to make herself appear more beautiful than
she was by birth - really, she is insulting her Creator.

And then from marriage come babies who scream, servants who
make a nuisance, children who hang about your neck; you get all
anxious over money and trying to protect youself against loss. Here
a band of cooks in aprons attack the meat with knives, there a gang
of dress-makers gossip away. Then a servant announces that the
master has arrived with some friends. So the wife flaps about like a
bird all over the house, looking to see if the couch is smooth, the floor
swept clean, the cups crowned with garlands, the dinner ready. Now,
tell me, tell me honestly - where in all this can you find any thought
of God? And those are the *happy* homes! In others, you have the
tambourine banging, the flute squeaking, the harp twanging, the
cymbals clashing - where, I ask you, is the fear of God in all this
noise? Then the so-called friend who lives off others drops in, and
boasts, and indulges in malicious gossip, and takes delight in harsh
remarks about those who are not present; and then the slave girls
come in, to put their bodies on display in seductive dances before the
lust-consumed eyes of male visitors. What does the unfortunate wife
do amid these scenes? She either enjoys it all, and thus inflicts
spiritual death on her soul; or she is offended by it, and thus earns the
anger of her husband! And so come quarrels, and then divorce. And
if you can find any household free from these things (they are as rare

as gold), yet the running of the house, bringing up the children, giving attention to your husband, supervising your servants - alas, alas, how all these things distract your mind from God.

Jerome, *Concerning the Perpetual Virginity of the Blessed Mary*, chapter 22

What do I love when I love God?

In loving You, O Lord, I do not just have some vague feeling; my love is positive and certain. Your Word touched my heart, and from that moment I began to love You. See how heaven and earth and all that they contain call me to love You! Their message never ceases to sound in the ears of all mankind, so that no-one has any excuse not to love You. More than all this, You will show pity to those whom You pity, and You will have mercy on those to whom You are merciful (**Romans 9:15**). For if it were not for Your mercy, the praises of heaven and earth would fall on human ears that were deaf.

But what do I love when I love my God? Not physical beauty. Not fading charm. Not the splendour of earthly light, so precious to our eyes. Not the sweet melodies of harmony and song. Not the fragrance of flowers, perfumes, spices. Not manna or honey. Not a body which we can embrace with physical delight. It is not these things I love when I love my God. And yet, when I love Him, I do love a light of a certain kind, and a voice, a perfume, a food, an embrace; but they are of the kind that I love deep in my inner being, where my soul is bathed in a light which no place can contain - where it listens to a voice that never fades away with time - where it breathes a fragrance that no gust of wind can carry away - where it tastes a food that never runs out through eating - where it clings to an embrace that does not dissolve through the fulfilment of desire. This is what I love when I love my God.

But what is my God? I put this question to the earth. It answered, "I am not God," and everything on earth said the same. I asked the sea and the chasms of the deep, and the living things that creep in them, but they replied, "We are not your God. Seek what is above us." So I spoke to the blowing winds, but the entire atmosphere and all that lives in it replied, "I am not God." Then I asked the sky, the sun, the

moon, the stars; but they told me, "We are not the God you seek."
I spoke to everything around me, all that my senses revealed to me,
and I said, "Since you are not my God, tell me about Him. Tell me
something of my God!" In a clear and loud voice they replied: *"God
is the One Who made us."* I asked these questions simply by gazing
at these things, and their beauty was the only answer they gave.

Augustine of Hippo, *Confessions*, Book 10, chapter 6

Grace and free-will

No-one will say that "free-will" actually vanished from the human
race because of the first man's sin. Yet it is true that sin robbed
mankind of "liberty", the liberty that existed in paradise - that is, the
liberty we can define as "perfect righteousness with immortality".
That is why human nature stands in need of divine grace. So the Lord
says, "If the Son sets you free, you will be really free" (**John 8:36**)
- free for a good and righteous life. Even so, free-will has not entirely
perished from sinners; for free-will is the power by which people
commit sin! This is especially the case with all who delight in sinning
and love their sin; they choose to do what pleases them. The apostle
says, "When you were the slaves of sin, you were free from
righteousness" (**Romans 6:20**). It is clear that people can become
"slaves of sin" only because they are in fact free; for the thing that
makes people "free from righteousness" is their own sinful free
choice! By contrast, however, the only thing that makes people "free
from sin" is the grace of the Saviour. The admirable teacher Paul
makes this very distinction: *free* from righteousness (**Romans
6:20**) - *set free* from sin (**6:22**). He says "free" from righteousness,
not "set free" from it; but to prevent his Christian readers from taking
any credit to themselves, he does not say they are "free" from sin,
but "set free" from it. He deliberately uses the phrase "set free" in
harmony with the Lord's statement, "If the Son sets you free". For
the children of mankind cannot live a good life unless God makes
them into His children. How then can Julian of Eclanum try to
pretend that the power to live a good life comes from our free-will?
Only God's grace gives this power through Jesus Christ our Lord.

**Augustine of Hippo, *Concerning Two Letters of Pelagius*, chapter
1, section 5**

Christ chose us

"You did not choose Me," Christ says, "but I chose you" (**John 15:16**). Such grace is beyond description. What were we, apart from Christ's choice of us, when we were empty of love? What were we but sinful and lost? We did not lead Him to choose us by believing in Him; for if Christ chose people who already believed, then we chose Him before He chose us. How then could He say, "You did not choose Me," unless His mercy came before our faith? Here is the faulty reasoning of those who say that God chose us before the creation of the world, not in order to make us good, but because He foreknew we would be good. This was not the view of Him Who said, "You did not choose Me." We were not chosen because of our goodness, for we could not be good without being chosen. Grace is no longer grace, if human goodness comes first. Listen, you ungrateful person, listen! "You did not choose Me, but I chose you." Do not say, "I am chosen because I first believed." If you first believed, you had already chosen Him. But listen: "You did not choose Me." And do not say, "Before I believed, I was already chosen on account of my good works." What good work can come before faith, when the apostle Paul says, "Whatever is not from faith is sin" (**Romans 14:23**)? What then shall we say when we hear these words, "You did not choose Me"? We shall say this: We were evil, and we were chosen that we might become good by the grace of Him Who chose us. For salvation is not by grace if our goodness came first; but it *is* by grace - and therefore God's grace did not *find* us good but *makes* us good.

Augustine of Hippo, *Commentary on John 15:16*

The depth of Scripture

There is such depth in the Christian Scriptures that, even if I studied them, and nothing else, from early childhood to worn-out old age, with ample time and unflagging zeal, and with greater intellectual ability than I possess, I would still each day find new treasures within them. The basic truths necessary for salvation are easily found within the Scriptures. But even when a person has accepted these truths, and is both God-fearing and righteous in his actions, there remain so many things which lie under a great veil of mystery. Through reading the Scriptures, we can pierce this veil, and find the deepest wisdom in the words which express these mysteries, and in the mysteries themselves. The oldest, the ablest, and the most eager student of Scripture, will say at the end of each day: "I have studied hard, but my studies are only just beginning."

Augustine of Hippo, *Letter 137*

Chapter 10.

CHRISTOLOGICAL CONTROVERSIES: FROM APOLLINARIUS TO THE COUNCIL OF CHALCEDON

1. The background: Antiochenes and Alexandrians

The Arian controversy had been about the relationship between Christ and God - the status of the Son in relation to the Father. As we saw in Chapter 8, this dispute was settled within the Catholic Church by the Council of Constantinople in 381. However, even before the Council met, a new set of questions had begun to agitate the minds of Christian thinkers. This time the issue was the relationship of the divine and the human *within* the person of Christ. (The study of this subject is usually called *Christology*.) Catholic theologians had battled against Arians to establish the doctrine that the Logos is fully and truly God, not a created being. However, the Gospels obviously teach that Jesus of Nazareth was a man. So the Church now had to struggle with the question of how Jesus Christ could be *both* God *and* man at the same time - how His divine and human natures related to each other.

There were two main ways of looking at this question. The theologians of Antioch , the "Antiochenes", favoured one way; the theologians of Alexandria, the "Alexandrians", preferred the other. We saw in Chapter 9, section 1, how these two different schools of theologians adopted different methods of interpreting Scripture: the Antiochenes emphasised the literal meaning of the text, the Alexandrians stressed its deeper allegorical meaning. So it comes as no surprise to find that Antiochenes and Alexandrians also had different interpretations of what Scripture said about Christ as God and man.

The Antiochene insistence on the literal, historical meaning of Scripture carried with it an equal insistence on the human, historical figure of Jesus of Nazareth. Antiochene thinkers - men like **Diodore of Tarsus** (died about 394), **Theodore of Mopsuestia** (350-428), **Nestorius** (381-451), **Ibas of Edessa** (died 457), and **Theodoret of Cyrrhus** (393-458) - emphasised that Christ was a real human being with a complete human nature like us, a human body, and a human soul, mind or spirit.[1] They felt that Christ's human obedience to the will of the Father was central to His work of saving humans: the One in Whom the human race is saved and recreated must Himself be human, the source of a renewed human life. The Antiochenes also emphasised the *distinction* between Christ's human and divine natures. They feared that if they did not keep the two natures apart, all the limitations and weaknesses[2] of the human Jesus which the Gospels record (His frustration, His ignorance, His growth in wisdom and grace) would be applied to His divine nature. But how can God's nature be weak or limited? If Jesus's human limitations were applied to His divine nature, they would destroy His divinity. And then the Arians would have been right after all: Jesus Christ was not truly divine! Antiochenes also feared that, unless they made a sharp separation between Christ's two natures, His divine qualities (almighty power, perfect knowledge, *etc.*) might be ascribed to His humanity, making Him super-human and thus not genuinely human like us.

---

1   The Greek word for mind or spirit is *nous*. It can be translated either way, as "mind" or "spirit". Some of the early Church fathers made a distinction between the *nous* and the soul (*psuche*). For them, the soul was the physical life-force that animated the bodies of both animals and humans. The *nous*, however, was a higher faculty of intellect or understanding, which humans possessed but animals did not. Sometimes the fathers called the *nous* "the *rational* soul" (the principle of mental or intellectual life), as distinct from *psuche* which was "the *animal* soul" (the principle of physical or bodily life). However, most of the fathers did not make any distinction between *nous* and *psuche*, and even condemned any such distinction as an "Apollinarian" error (see section 2).

2   By "weaknesses" I do not mean *sinful* weaknesses like laziness or a bad temper. I mean the sort of *natural* weaknesses that a created being has in comparison with the Creator - our puny minds, our vulnerability to disaster and death, *etc.*

To avoid these disastrous conclusions, the Antiochenes kept the human and divine natures of Christ as far apart as possible. They sometimes spoke as if the man Jesus had a separate personality from the divine Son, thus splitting Him apart into two persons. Their view of the union between divine and human in Christ seemed (to their critics, at least) to be that the divine Son chose a particular man, Jesus of Nazareth, came and dwelt in Him, sanctified Him, and spoke through Him. This sort of thinking could lead to the belief that there were two Sons in Christ: a divine Son of God (the eternal Logos) and a human Son of Man (Jesus of Nazareth). Sometimes the Antiochenes thought of Jesus as little more than the supreme example of how God could dwell in and work through a man.

The theologians of Alexandria - men like Athanasius,[3] *Apollinarius* (300-390), *Didymus the Blind* (died 398), *Cyril of Alexandria* (died 444) and *Eutyches* (378-454) - favoured the other way of approaching the question. In contrast to the Antiochenes, the Alexandrians emphasised the divine nature in Christ. They were overwhelmingly convinced that salvation, the recreation of humanity, must have God the Creator as its source: the activity of the Saviour must be the activity of God. Therefore all the words, actions and experiences of Christ recorded in the Gospels, were the words, actions and experiences, not of a human person, but of God Himself. To make sure of this, the Alexandrians insisted that the divine Logos was the supreme (or even the only) source of activity in Christ.

So instead of separating Christ's human and divine natures, as the Antiochenes tended to do, the Alexandrians united them into as close a oneness as possible - but always at the expense of the human nature. They often made Christ's humanity into just a tool or instrument which the divine Son took up and used. For the Alexandrians, Christ's human nature had little or no real agency, activity or power of its own. In fact, in their concern for the deity and unity of Christ, Alexandrians sometimes ignored or even denied the existence of a human mind or spirit in Christ. (Even the great Athanasius was not perhaps as clear as he could have been about the reality of Christ's human mind.) Alexandrians tended to feel that if Christians placed any emphasis on a human mind or spirit in Christ,

---

3   For Athanasius, see Chapter 8, sections 2 and 3.

it would break Christ up into two separate persons, two Sons, a human and a divine Son. And if there were two separate Sons in Christ, we could no longer say, "Jesus *is* the Son of God"; we could only say, "Jesus had a relationship with the Son of God."

2. Apollinarianism.

Apollinarius was an Alexandrian thinker, a friend of Athanasius and a strong opponent of Arianism. He became bishop of Laodicea in 361. In the 370's he got into trouble for teaching quite openly that Christ did not have a human mind or spirit. Apollinarius believed that the human mind was the source of all human weakness and sin. He therefore felt that Christ's sinless perfection required Him not to have a human mind. The divine and infinite mind of the Son or Logos, Apollinarius taught, took the place of a human mind in Christ: He was a divine mind in a human body. This absence of a human mind preserved Christ from the possibility of sin. Apollinarius also thought that if Christ had a human as well as a divine mind, He would split apart into two separate persons, a human Son of Man and a divine Son of God. So again, to avoid this disastrous conclusion, Apollinarius denied that Christ had a human mind.

Various theologians such as Gregory of Nazianzus condemned Apollinarius's teaching, and so did the Council of Constantinople in 381.[4] The orthodox response to Apollinarius was that if Christ is the Saviour of human beings, He must Himself be a human being; and since human beings have minds, the Saviour must have a human mind. Gregory of Nazianzus put it like this: "What has not been taken up has not been healed." (By "taken up" Gregory meant "taken up by the Son into union with His divine nature".) If the Son did not take up a human mind when He became man, it follows that He did not spiritually heal or sanctify the human mind, and therefore cannot be the Saviour of our fallen and sinful minds. What Gregory meant by this was that our spiritual renewal is sharing in the glorified human nature of Christ. So if Christ does not have a human mind, there can be no spiritual renewal for our minds.[5]

---

[4] For Gregory of Nazianzus and the Council of Constantinople, see Chapter 8, section 3.

[5] See the quotation at the end of the Chapter for Gregory's argument against the Apollinarians.

Apollinarius's extreme teaching and its condemnation shocked the Alexandrians into thinking again about the relationship between the divine Son and His human nature.

3. Nestorius and the Council of Ephesus.

The Antiochenes also reacted against Apollinarius's teaching. They re-emphasised both the completeness of Christ's human nature and its distinctness from His divine nature. Theodore, bishop of Mopsuestia (south-eastern Asia Minor) from 392 to 428, developed Antiochene theology with great brilliance. His disciple Nestorius, a famous preacher at Antioch, became patriarch of Constantinople in 428; and this sparked off a fresh controversy. Nestorius had learned from Theodore that it was wrong to call the Virgin Mary *theotokos* (Greek for "the birth-giver of God" - in other words, that Mary bore or gave birth to God the Son in His human nature). Most Christians gave Mary this title, and Alexandrian theologians like Cyril, patriarch of Alexandria from 412 to 444, defended it ardently. The Alexandrians argued that Christ is God, so if Mary gave birth to Christ, the One Who was born of her was God. Therefore Mary was the birth-giver of God. Almost all theologians who have believed in Christ's deity (including Protestants) have agreed that *theotokos* is a correct title for Mary.[6] However, the passion with which people upheld the title *theotokos* in the 5th Century may also reveal the way that Mary was beginning to become an object of popular devotion in

---

6 *Theotokos* is often translated "mother of God", a title which many Protestants have rejected. The Greek word could be translated either way, as "birth-giver of God" or "mother of God". However, to call Mary "mother of God" could be taken to mean that she still has a mother-relationship with Him even now, in heaven, and can exercise some sort of special mother's influence over Him. This could lead to the practice of praying to Mary to influence Christ in our favour - which is why many Protestants have hesitated to call Mary "mother of God". But the title *theotokos* does not necessarily imply any of this. It points to a historical fact about Mary while she was here on earth: in her womb she bore God the Son in His human nature and gave Him birth. If we understand "mother of God" in this sense, there is nothing theologically wrong with it from a Protestant stand point.

the Church. Within another few centuries, Mary had become as important as Christ in the religion of many.

Nestorius rejected the title *theotokos* for Mary. This was not because he was protesting against the exaltation of Mary, which was then only in its very early stages. He protested because he was a committed Antiochene. Nestorius made a sharp distinction between Christ's human and divine natures, and tended to speak about Jesus as a man with whom the divine Son had united Himself. According to Nestorius, Mary gave birth to the human person Jesus, not to the divine Son Who joined Himself to Jesus. Nestorius therefore rejected the title "birth-giver of God" for Mary. He suggested that Mary should be called *Christotokos*, "birth-giver of Christ".

Nestorius's utterances raised up a deadly enemy for him in Cyril, patriarch of Alexandria. Cyril was the deepest-thinking and most influential of all the Alexandrians, and theologians today continue to study his writings with great interest. Among his most important works were his *Concerning Worship in Spirit and Truth, Dialogues on the Trinity, Five Books Refuting the Blasphemies of Nestorius*, and a large number of sermons and letters. Unfortunately, Cyril's theological brilliance went hand-in-hand with an almost unlimited ability to turn doctrinal debates into personal quarrels of bitter ferocity. It was never enough for Cyril to disprove an opponent's theology; he had to destroy him as a man too. Not surprisingly, Cyril's burning hatred of Antiochene Christology injected new levels of party-spirit and intolerance into the whole Antioch-Alexandria dispute. When Cyril died in 444, his leading Antiochene opponent, the normally gentle-hearted Theodoret of Cyrrhus, wrote in transports of joy to patriarch Domnus of Antioch:

> "At last, at last the villain has gone! The Lord, knowing that this man's spite has been growing daily and harming the body of the Church, has cut him off like a plague and taken away the reproach of Israel. The living are delighted by his departure. Perhaps the dead are sorry at his arrival. Indeed, we ought to be alarmed: they might be so annoyed by his presence among them that they send him back! Great care must therefore be taken. It is your holiness's special duty to tell those in charge of the funeral to lay a very large, very

heavy stone on Cyril's grave, in case he tries to come back and show his unstable mind among us again."

It is not for us, so separated from the people and events of that time, to pass judgment. Let us simply accept that Cyril of Alexandria had one of those masterful personalities which excite either deep-hearted loyalty or seething hostility.

Cyril, then, detested Antiochene Christology. He also looked unkindly on anyone who was patriarch of Constantinople. This was because Cyril was the nephew of Theophilus of Alexandria, who had helped to bring about the downfall of John Chrysostom when John was patriarch of Constantinople (see previous Chapter, section 1). Cyril inherited his uncle's dislike of all patriarchs of Constantinople, for having taken to themselves the position of supreme importance in the Eastern Church which, Cyril felt, belonged to the patriarchs of Alexandria. When Nestorius's teaching convinced Cyril that the new patriarch of Constantinople was a heretic, Cyril had both doctrinal and personal reasons for plotting his downfall.

Cyril wrote against Nestorius, demanding that he accept the Alexandrian view of Christ, which Cyril expressed by saying that in Christ there was "one incarnate nature of the Logos". This sounded to the Antiochenes as if Cyril was denying that Christ had two distinct natures. However, like some fog descending on a battle, there was a deep confusion of language here. The Greek word which Cyril used for "nature" was *physis* (prounced "fy-siss") . Cyril said that the incarnate Son had only one *physis*. But he did not, in fact, mean to deny that Christ had both a human and a divine nature. The confusion came about because, both in Alexandria and Antioch, the word *physis* and the word *hypostasis* were used to mean the same thing. As far as the doctrine of the Trinity was concerned, the Cappadocian fathers had persuaded the Church that *hypostasis* must be understood to mean "person", not "nature". Theologians had not yet carried over this clear and precise understanding of *hypostasis* into the more misty realm of Christology. As far as the doctrine of Christ was concerned, the words *hypostasis* and *physis* could both be used to mean either person or nature.

So when Cyril said that Christ had only one *physis*, he was really using the word more in the sense of "person" than "nature". Cyril was denying that the man Jesus of Nazareth was a different person or *hypostasis* from the divine Logos. However, when Antiochenes like Nestorius said that Christ had two *physeis*, two natures, Cyril thought they meant He was two persons - which some of them did, to all intents and purposes. Nestorius's denial that Mary could be called "birth-giver of God" simply confirmed Cyril's fatal suspicion that Nestorius believed Jesus of Nazareth to be a separate person from the Son of God.

Cyril managed to get pope Celestine of Rome (pope from 422 to 432) and the Byzantine emperor *Theodosius II* (408-50) on his side, and in 431 Theodosius summoned an ecumenical Council at Ephesus which deposed Nestorius. Cyril opened the Council before Nestorius's supporters had arrived. When they did turn up, led by patriarch *John of Antioch* (died 441), they held a separate council and deposed Cyril. The emperor Theodosius, however, supported Cyril and reinstated him; he then replaced Nestorius as patriarch of Constantinople and later sent him into exile. The Church recognised the Council of Ephesus as the third ecumenical Council after Nicaea and Constantinople. As well as pronouncing against Nestorius, the Council also condemned Pelagianism as a heresy.[7] This was partly because Nestorius had given shelter and hospitality to the Pelagian leader Celestius in 429. However, there was also a theological link between Nestorianism and Pelagianism. Nestorianism separated the divine from the human in *Christ*, making His human nature into an independent person; Pelagianism, likewise, separated the divine from the human in *conversion*, making the human will independent of the divine in achieving salvation.

4. Eutyches and the Council of Chalcedon.

Cyril of Alexandria's victory over Nestorius at Ephesus in 431 did not end the Christological controversies within the Byzantine Empire. Many Syrian bishops, led by John of Antioch, continued to hold a strong Antiochene theology, and were disgusted at what Cyril and the emperor Theodosius II had done to Nestorius. In an effort to restore peace, Theodosius forced Cyril and John to sign a "Formula

---

7   For Pelagianism, see previous Chapter, section 3.

of Union" in 433. John and the Antiochenes had to accept the banishment of Nestorius and the title birth-giver of God for Mary; Cyril had to accept a statement of faith which was more Antiochene than Alexandrian in its language - it spoke of a "union of two natures" in Christ, complete deity and complete humanity. Cyril signed the Formula. Although it used different theological language (*physis* meaning "nature" rather than "person"), Cyril believed it taught the essential truth he had been fighting for, that Christ was one single person in Whom the divine and human were united. However, Cyril's action in signing the Formula lost him a lot of support at home; many of his Alexandrian followers felt that he had betrayed them by accepting the hated phrase "two natures". They continued to speak of "one incarnate nature" in Christ, not two.

This enforced peace lasted only while Cyril and John lived. When they died (John in 441, Cyril in 444), conflict broke out again. Controversy was soon raging around Eutyches,[8] an archimandrite in Constantinople whose Christology was an extreme form of the Alexandrian type. Eutyches taught that the union between Christ's human and divine natures was such a close fusion of the two, that the human nature had been swallowed up and lost in the divine, "like a drop of wine in the sea". According to Eutyches, the incarnate Son had only one nature; His deity had absorbed His humanity and transformed it into divinity (much as a piece of paper thrown onto a fire will be set alight and changed into fire).

Flavian, patriarch of Constantinople from 447-49, was a moderate Antiochene, and condemned Eutyches for his extreme Alexandrian teaching; but Eutyches had powerful friends at court, and the new patriarch of Alexandria, *Dioscorus* (died 454), strongly supported him. Dioscorus had all of Cyril of Alexandria's violent hostility to Constantinople and the Antiochenes, but none of Cyril's thoughtful mind or penetrating spiritual insight; in fact, Dioscorus was little better than a theological thug, a gangster strutting around in a bishop's robe. To settle the controversy, emperor Theodosius summoned another Council at Ephesus in 449. Dioscorus and his Alexandrians controlled its proceedings like a band of triumphant revolutionaries. In an anti-Antiochene rampage, they reinstated

---

8   Pronounced "Yu-tik-eez".

Eutyches, outlawed the Formula of Union of 433, and deposed patriarch Flavian and several other leading Antiochene bishops - notably the great Bible commentator Theodoret of Cyrrhus, and bishop Ibas of Edessa, who had tried to mediate between Nestorius and Cyril. They also refused to listen to an important statement of Western Christology which pope Leo I of Rome sent to Flavian (the statement was known as *Leo's Tome*).

History remembers pope Leo as *Leo the Great*, pope from 440 to 461. Born in Tuscany, northern Italy, in about 400, he was the most outstanding theologian who had so far occupied the episcopal throne of Rome, and in many ways was the founder of the papacy. Leo believed that Christ had appointed the apostle Peter as the senior bishop and final court of appeal for all Christians, and that the whole Church should accept all doctrinal statements by Peter's successors (the popes of Rome). This was one reason why Leo was so upset by the Council of Ephesus's refusal even to read out the statement he sent to Flavian. However, Leo was personally a very gentle and moderate man, a great preacher, and a brave spokesman for the Roman population against invading armies of Huns and Vandals - he twice saved the city of Rome from destruction by pleading with the Hunnish and Vandal chieftains.[9]

The second Council of Ephesus, then, was a total victory for the extreme Alexandrians. Once again the patriarch of Alexandria had toppled the patriarch of Constantinople. In fact, some Alexandrian monks ,whose zeal outstripped their common sense, beat up Flavian of Constantinople so badly that he died of his injuries a few days later. His replacement as patriarch of Constantinople was *Anatolius* (450-58), an Alexandrian and a friend of Dioscorus. However, the Alexandrians had triumphed at Ephesus only because imperial troops and gangs of violent Alexandrian monks had backed them. Pope Leo positively glowed with rage and thundered against the wicked Council as a "synod of robbers". The name stuck, and the Council is still referred to today as the Robber Synod.

The decisions of Ephesus were beyond remedy as long as emperor Theodosius II lived. As luck or providence would have it, he was

---

9   For the Huns and Vandals, see Chapter 11, section 1.

killed in a riding accident in 450, and the new emperor, **Marcian** (450-57), was favourable to the cause of Rome and the Antiochenes. In 451 he summoned a fresh Council at Chalcedon (near Constantinople). There were some 400 bishops present, almost all from the East, together with ambassadors of pope Leo. It proved a difficult gathering. Most of the bishops were disciples of Cyril of Alexandria, but opponents of Eutyches and Dioscorus, and they did not know how to express Cyril's Christology in a way that would exclude the teaching of Eutyches. At first, they simply agreed to a formula which stated that Christ was incarnate "from two natures", using the word *physis* for "nature". Unfortunately, Eutyches and Dioscorus could accept that; they took it to mean that "from" the two natures being united, one nature resulted in the incarnation. Yet Cyril had used the phrase "from two natures", so it seemed orthodox enough to the majority.

At this point, the ambassadors of pope Leo intervened, backed up by the representatives of emperor Marcian. They gave the bishops an ultimatum: either they reconsidered the formula, or Leo would refuse to recognise their proceedings. The formula was sent back to a committee. Eventually a compromise was reached, by replacing the phrase that Christ was incarnate "*from* two natures", which Eutyches and Dioscorus could accept, with the phrase that He was incarnate "*in* two natures", which Eutyches and Dioscorus certainly could not accept. The new formula satisfied Leo, the emperor, and most of the Eastern bishops, including Anatolius of Constantinople who shamelessly abandoned his friend Dioscorus. In fact, it pleased all parties except the Alexandrians and some of the Syrians. The Council officially published this formula as a new creed, called the **Creed, Formula** or **Definition of Chalcedon**. The Creed combined the Christologies of Antioch and Alexandria, and reads as follows (the words in CAPITAL LETTERS express the concerns of ALEXANDRIAN theology; the underlined words express the concerns of Antiochene theology):

"We all, with one voice, confess our Lord Jesus Christ, ONE AND THE SAME SON, at once complete in deity and complete in humanity, truly God and truly man, consisting of a rational soul and body; of the same essence as the Father in His deity, of the same essence as us in His humanity, like us in all things apart from sin;

begotten of the Father before all ages as regards His deity, THE SAME BORN OF THE VIRGIN MARY, THE BIRTH-GIVER OF GOD, as regards His humanity, in the last days, for us and our salvation; ONE AND THE SAME CHRIST, SON, LORD, ONLY-BEGOTTEN, to be acknowledged in two natures, without confusion, without change, WITHOUT DIVISION, WITHOUT SEPARATION; the distinction of the natures being in no way abolished because of the union, but rather the characteristic property of each nature being preserved, AND COMING TOGETHER TO FORM ONE PERSON AND ONE HYPOSTASIS. HE IS NOT SPLIT OR DIVIDED INTO TWO PERSONS, BUT HE IS ONE AND THE SAME SON AND ONLY-BEGOTTEN, GOD THE LOGOS, THE LORD JESUS CHRIST, as formerly the prophets and later Jesus Christ Himself have taught us about Him, and as it has been handed down to us by the Creed of the Fathers."

The Creed accepted the Alexandrian view that Christ was one single person, and it implied (if it did not explicitly state) that this person was "the only-begotten, God the Logos". It also affirmed the Alexandrian belief that the divine Son underwent all the human experiences of Jesus Christ, so that it was proper to say that God the Son was born of Mary - the Virgin Mary was the birth-giver of God. But the Creed also accepted the Antiochene view that Christ's human and divine natures each kept their own distinctive qualities and properties. Christ's humanity was as real and complete as ours; it was not swallowed up or absorbed by His deity. Christ had two complete distinct natures, fully and truly human, fully and truly divine. Finally, the Creed made it clear that *physis* and *hypostasis* were no longer to be understood in the same sense in the doctrine of the incarnation; *physis* meant "nature", not person, and *hypostasis* meant "person", not nature. In this way, the unclear language which had confused the whole debate between Alexandria and Antioch was decisively settled. Christ was one *hypostasis* in two *physeis* - one person in two natures.

The Council had not yet finished its work. It overthrew the decisions of Ephesus taken two years previously. It deposed and banished Dioscorus of Alexandria. It restored to office most of the Antiochenes whom the Council of Ephesus had deposed. It sanctioned a new standard of orthodoxy, made up of the Creed of

Chalcedon, the Creed of Nicaea (from the Council of Nicaea in 325), the Nicene Creed (from the Council of Constantinople in 381), two letters by Cyril of Alexandria, and *Leo's Tome*, the doctrinal statement which pope Leo had sent to patriarch Flavian in 449.

In one sense, the Council of Chalcedon was a great triumph for Leo the Great. He had forced the Eastern Church to give clearer expression to Cyril of Alexandria's Christology, in a way that ruled out the extreme views of Eutyches and Dioscorus. Yet in another sense, Chalcedon dealt a bitter blow to Leo. As well as formulating the Creed, the Council also passed a series of canons (Church laws); and canon 28, composed under the influence of Anatolius of Constantinople, declared that the patriarchs of Constantinople were virtually equal with the popes of Rome. The canon stated that the Church of Rome enjoyed its supreme status because "old Rome" had been the capital city of the Roman Empire; but now that Constantinople ("new Rome") was the new capital, its Church must enjoy equal rights with Rome in matters of Church government, and rank second in honour to Rome (and therefore higher in honour than Alexandria, Antioch and Jerusalem). Leo's ambassadors protested passionately against this canon, and Leo himself rejected it. The reason was plain: it made the status of the papacy depend purely on the political fact that it was based in the old capital city of the Empire, rather than on the spiritual succession of the popes from the apostle Peter. And if that was the case, how long would the patriarchs of Constantinople be content to rank second even in honour to the popes of Rome, now that the seat of the Empire had been transferred from Rome to Constantinople? Here was one of the seeds of division which would ultimately bear fruit in complete separation between the Eastern and Western Church.[10]

Apart from canon 28, most Christians recognised and accepted the Council of Chalcedon as the fourth ecumenical Council, and its Creed as the third ecumenical Creed. It did not, however, quench the fires of Christological controversy in the East. This was because the majority of Alexandrians rejected Chalcedon. To them, its doctrine of the two distinct natures of Christ meant that Christ was two

---

[10] For the East-West schism, see Part Two, Chapter 3, section 8.

persons - the hated error of Nestorius. They continued to hold to Cyril's formula of "one incarnate nature of the Logos". The result was that important sections of the Eastern Church condemned the Council and Creed of Chalcedon as Nestorian, and (in time) broke away to form their own independent national Churches, usually known as the *Monophysite* Churches. This term comes from the Greek *monos* (one) and *physis* (nature). The Monophysite view was that the incarnate Son had only one nature, as Cyril had said, and not two, as Chalcedon said. However, the story of the Monophysites, and the storms of controversy they continued to generate in the East, belongs to Chapter 12.

5. The Nestorian Church of Persia.

Just as the decisions of the Council of Chalcedon in 451 did not put an end to extreme Alexandrian Christology, so the decisions of the Council of Ephesus in 431, which deposed Nestorius (see section 3), had not in fact put an end to Nestorianism. The entire Christian community in the Persian Empire (modern-day Iraq and Iran) eventually became Nestorian in its theology. This came about in the following way.

Christianity was well established in Persia by the 4th Century. All Persian Christians looked on the bishop of the Persian capital city (Seleucia-Ctesiphon) as their spiritual leader; they gave him the title patriarch or *catholicos*. However, when the conversion of Constantine made Christianity into the favoured religion in the Roman Empire, the Persian emperors became suspicious of the political loyalties of their Persian Christian subjects and started to persecute them. The official religion of Persia was *Zoroastrianism*, which believed in an eternal conflict between two equal and opposite powers of good and evil - Ormuzd, the Wise Lord, and Ahriman, the Persian equivalent of the devil. The symbol of Ormuzd was fire, and so people of other faiths sometimes referred to Zoroastrians as "fire-worshippers".

During this period of persecution, Persian Christian leaders received their training in the Eastern Roman city of Nisibis, near the river Tigris on the Persian frontier. Bishop James of Nisibis (died 338) set up a theological school there; one of the great Eastern fathers,

Ephrem the Syrian (died 373), a native of Nisibis, ran the school. Ephrem wrote in Syriac rather than Greek, and was an outstanding theologian, Bible commentator, poet and hymnwriter (Syrian Christians called him "the harp of the Holy Spirit"). The school at Nisibis, strongly Antiochene in its theology, prospered until 363. Then it moved East to Edessa, near the Euphrates, when the Romans handed Nisibis over to the Persian Empire after Julian the Apostate's disastrous anti-Persian war (see Chapter 7, section 2).

A new period of freedom for the Persian Church came under the Persian emperor Yadzgard I (399-421). In 410 Yadzgard summoned a Persian Church council; 40 bishops were present. They adopted the Nicene Creed as the Persian Church's confession of faith. However, Yadzgard renewed the persecution of Christians at the end of his reign, a policy carried on by his son Vahram V (421-38). Many Persian believers fled across the borders into the Byzantine Empire, seeking asylum. Vahram demanded their return - and this led to war between Byzantium and Persia. The end result was a peace treaty in which Vahram guaranteed religious liberty for Christians in Persia, and the Byzantine emperor Theodosius II in return guaranteed a similar freedom for Zoroastrians in the Byzantine Empire. After this treaty was signed, another council of the Persian Church met in 424; the council decreed that the Persian catholicos (patriarch) was subject only to Christ - not to the patriarch of Constantinople, nor to the pope of Rome. This amounted to a declaration of spiritual independence by the Persian Church, and helped prepare the way for its acceptance of Nestorian theology.

The hostility of Monophysites (extreme Alexandrians) eventually forced the great Antiochene school of theology at Edessa to move back to Nisibis in the mid-5th Century. This was where the school had started in the 4th Century, when Nisibis had been a Roman city. However, Nisibis was now within the Persian Empire. The new Nisibis school, under its great teachers Ibas of Edessa and Narses, flourished to an amazing extent, and kept alive a powerful Antiochene theology among Persian Christians. This was one reason why in 486 a Persian Church council officially adopted a Nestorian statement of faith as the expression of the Persian Church's Christology. Another reason was the nationalistic desire of the Persian Church to have a theology of its own, distinct from Byzantine theology. In 489, the Byzantine emperor Zeno (474-91) responded by banishing all Nestorians from Edessa; they emigrated into Persia. So the doctrinal rivalry between the Chalcedonian[11] Christology of Byzantium and the Nestorian Christology of Persia now corresponded to the national rivalry between the two great Empires.

In 612 the Persian Church became even more deeply committed to Nestorianism, when it adopted the theology of one of its greatest thinkers, the monk *Babai the Great* (569-628). Babai's Christology was strongly Nestorian; he taught that there were two *physeis* (natures) and two *hypostases* (persons) in Christ. The oneness of Christ, he said, was found in the relation of Sonship: the human person of Jesus of Nazareth shared in the divine Logos's "Son-relationship" with the Father. So in Babai's terms, there were in Christ two natures, two persons, and one Sonship. To the obvious question whether believers ought to worship the human person of Jesus, Babai replied that worship should be offered to the "unity of the Sonship".

Monasticism blossomed richly within the Persian Nestorian Church, especially through the organising and reforming genius of abbot *Abraham of Kashkar* (501-86). The most famous Nestorian monk, however, was *Isaac of Ninevah* (died 700), otherwise known as Isaac the Syrian. Many of his Syriac writings on mysticism and the ascetic life were translated into Greek by Chalcedonian monks of the great Saint Sabbas monastery near Jerusalem. Eastern Christians would read and admire Isaac's writings for centuries without realising that he was a despised Nestorian heretic! On the other hand, later on in his life Isaac himself came under suspicion within the Nestorian Church for abandoning its distinctive beliefs.

A mighty missionary spirit animated the Nestorians. They planted successful churches in parts of Arabia, the shores of the Caspian sea, Malabar (the south-western coastal region of India), among the Turkish and Tartar peoples of central Asia, and even in China. The story of the Chinese Nestorian mission is particularly striking, since Christianity had never before penetrated so far eastwards. The first Nestorian missionaries reached China in 631, and established a

---

[11] By "Chalcedonian" I mean "loyal to the Creed of Chalcedon" - opposed to both Nestorians and Monophysites.

Isaac of Ninevah (Died 700)

Chinese Nestorian Church which flourished for 200 years.
However, beginning in 845, the Chinese emperor Wu Tsung
subjected the Chinese Nestorians to fierce persecution. The
persecution was in fact aimed chiefly at Buddhist monks, but the
Nestorian Church was strongly monastic, and Wu Tsung hated
monks of any sort. The result was that by the 10th Century, the
Chinese authorities had completely wiped out the Nestorian Church
in China.

Important people:

The Church	*Political and military*
Catholics:	Emperor Theodosius II
Ephrem the Syrian (died 373)	(408-50)
Apollinarius of Laodicea (300-390)[12]	Emperor Marcian (450-57)
Diodore of Tarsus (died about 394)	
Didymus the Blind (died 398)	
Theodore of Mopsuestia (350-428)	
John of Antioch (died 441)	
Cyril of Alexandria (patriarch 412-44)[13]	
Flavian of Constantinople (patriarch 447-49)	
Ibas of Edessa (died 457)	
Theodoret of Cyrrhus (393-458)	
Anatolius of Constantinople (patriarch 450-58)	
Pope Leo the Great (born 400; pope 440-61)	

Nestorians:
Nestorius (381-451)
Abraham of Kashkar (501-86)
Babai the Great (569-628)
Isaac of Ninevah (died 700)

Monophysites:
Eutyches (378-454)
Dioscorus of Alexandria (patriarch 444-54)

---

12 I have classed Apollinarius as a Catholic because of his part in the
    struggle against Arianasm. However, the Council of Constantinople
    condemned Apollinarius in 381 for his denial that Christ had a human
    mind.
13 Monophysites would claim Cyril of Alexandria as one of their own.

Complete salvation in a complete Saviour

The Apollinarians must not deceive others or themselves into thinking that "the Man of the Lord" (as they call Christ, Who is more truly called Lord and God) was without a human mind. For we do not separate His humanity from His divinity; we teach that He is one and the same person. Once He was not a man, but only God the Son, existing before all the ages, and He was not connected with a body or anything physical; but now He has become man too, taking humanity upon Himself for our salvation. He suffers in the flesh, but is incapable of suffering in His divinity; He is limited in the body, but unlimited in the Spirit; He is on the earth, and at the same time in heaven; He belongs to the visible world, and also to the eternal order of being; He can be understood, yet is incomprehensible. He combined these elements in Himself so that the whole of our human nature, which had fallen into sin, might be recreated afresh by One Who was completely human and at the same time God.

Anyone who does not admit that holy Mary is the birth-giver of God is out of touch with the Deity. Equally far from God is anyone who says that Christ passed *through* the Virgin like water through a channel, without being formed *in* her in a way that was both human and divine. He was formed in Mary in a divine way, because it was without the agency of a man; and He was formed in Mary in a human way, because it was according to the normal process of growth in the womb. Again, a person comes under condemnation if he says that a human being was first of all formed in Mary, and then later the divine nature was added to it. This would mean that the person conceived in Mary's womb was not God. Or if anyone introduces two Sons, one derived from God the Father, the other from Jesus's mother, not being one and the same Son, then he fails to share in the adoption of sons which is promised to those who believe rightly. There are indeed two natures in Christ, the divine and the human (the human including soul and body); but there are not two Sons, or two Gods, or two human beings (although Paul speaks of the inner and outer elements of our human nature as the "inner man" and "outer man").

To sum up: the Saviour is made out of two separate elements. The invisible element is not the same as the visible, nor the eternal element the same as the time-born; but there are not two separate beings -

emphatically not. Both elements are blended into one; the divinity takes on humanity, or the humanity receives divinity, or however you wish to put it.....

Have you placed your hope in a Jesus Who was a human being without a human mind? Then you yourself are truly mindless, and do not deserve a complete salvation. For what has not been taken up has not been healed. Our nature, in its different aspects, has been saved only to the degree that it has been united with God. If it was half of Adam that fell, then half of our nature might be taken up and saved. But it was all of Adam that fell; and so all of our nature is united with all of Him Who was begotten of the Father, and thus gains a complete salvation. Then let the Apollinarians not envy us this complete salvation, nor equip the Saviour with just bones and muscles, which would only be the outward appearance of humanity.

Gregory of Nazianzus, *Letter 101*

The Word became flesh

[A dialogue between two speakers, A and B:]

B. But the Nestorians maintain that if "the Word became flesh" (**John 1:14**), He no longer remained the Word, but ceased to be what He was.

A. This is nothing but folly and stupidity, the madness of a crazed mind. They seem to think that the term "became" must necessarily mean change or alteration.

B. That is what they say, and they support their argument from the God-inspired Scriptures. For Nestorius maintains that Scripture says of Lot's wife, "She became a pillar of salt" (**Genesis 19:26**), and of Moses's staff, "He threw it on the ground and it became a serpent" (**Exodus 4:3**). In all these cases, he says, a change of nature took place.

A. Well then, how does that apply when we sing in the psalms, "The Lord became my refuge" (**Psalm 94:22**) and "O Lord, You have become my refuge from one generation to the next" (**Psalm 90:1**)?

Has God stopped being God, and "become" a refuge by some transformation of His being? Has He changed His nature into something that He was not at first?

B. Such an idea is unfitting and unsuitable to One Who is God by nature. His essence is unchangeable; He remains what He was and is for ever, even if we say that He "became" a refuge for various people.

A. What you have said is excellent and perfectly true. When we are thinking about God, and we use the word "became", it is utterly blasphemous and absurd to presume that it means change; we must try to understand it in another way, by means of wisdom, and find a meaning which is more fitting and applicable to the unchangeable God.

B. If we are to continue believing that it is essential to God's nature that He is immutable and unchangeable, in what sense can we say the the Word became flesh?....

A. The only-begotten Logos, even though He was God, begotten from God by very nature, "the radiance of His glory, the exact representation of the being" of the Father Who begot Him (**Hebrews 1:3**) - it was this very Logos Who became man. He did not change Himself into flesh; He did not undergo any mixture or blending or anything like that. But He submitted Himself to being emptied (**Philippians 2:7**); He did not proudly reject taking upon Himself the poverty of our human nature, but "for the honour that was set before Him, He counted the shame as nothing" (**Hebrews 12:2**). As God, He wished to take hold of our flesh that was gripped fast by sin and death, and make it superior to sin and death. So He made that flesh His very own, and not without a soul as some have said, but animated with a rational soul; and thus He restored our flesh to its original state. He did not proudly refuse to follow the path required by His plan, and therefore Scripture says that He experienced a human birth like ours, while remaining all the time what He was in His own divine nature. He was born of a woman in a miraculous way, for He is God by nature, invisible and without a body, and only by taking a form like ours could He manifest Himself to His earthly creatures. He thought it good that He should make

Himself human, and in His own person display our humanity glorified by the majesty of His deity. So the same person was God and man at the same time; He was "in the likeness of men" (**Philippians 2:7**), for even though He was God, He was "found in fashion as a man" (**Philippians 2:8**). He was God in human guise, the Lord in the form of a slave. This is what we mean when we say that the Word became flesh, and for the same reason we affirm that the holy Virgin is the birth-giver of God.

From Cyril of Alexandria's *Concerning the Unity of Christ*

Leo's Tome: Two natures in one person

Eutyches should not have spoken so emptily in his explanation of the Word becoming flesh, as if the Christ Who was brought forth from the Virgin's womb had the form of a man but did not really have a body derived from His mother's body.... The Holy Spirit made the Virgin fruitful, but Christ's real body was derived from her body. When Wisdom built for herself a house, the Word became flesh and dwelt among us - dwelt in that flesh which He took from a human being and made alive with the spirit of rational life. Thus the qualities of each nature and essence [human and divine] were entirely preserved, and came together to form one person. Majesty took upon itself humility, strength took upon itself weakness, eternity took upon itself mortality. To pay the debt into which we had fallen, a nature which cannot be harmed was united with a nature which can suffer. Thus the man Christ Jesus, the one single Mediator between God and mankind, was able to die in His human nature, but unable to die in His divine nature; and so the conditions of our healing were fulfilled. In this way the true God was born in the full and perfect nature of humanity, complete in His own qualities, complete in ours. By "ours" I mean those qualities which the Creator formed in us at the beginning, which He took upon Himself in order to restore. For there was no trace in the Saviour of those qualities which the deceiver introduced into our nature, and which the deceived human race allowed to come in. God entered into fellowship with human weaknesses, but He did not share our sins. He took upon Himself the form of a servant without the stain of sin, exalting the human qualities without diminishing the divine.

From Leo's *Tome*

You know me

Lord Jesus Christ, King of kings,
You are sovereign over life and death;
You know our deepest secrets,
and our thoughts and feelings are all naked before You.
O make good the evil I have done in Your sight.

Lower and lower sinks my life each day,
but my sin is growing.
O Lord, God of my soul and body,
You know the great frailty of my spirit and flesh;
please give strength to my weakness,
and uphold me in my agony!

You Who are my powerful support,
You know that many have a high regard for me.
Give me a thankful heart, then,
O Lord of infinite goodness -
a heart which will not forget Your benefits.
But I pray that *You* will forget my many sins
and forgive all my infidelity.

O Lord, do not despise the prayer
of a man who is so filled with sorrow!
Preserve me in Your grace,
as You have preserved me in the past.
For I now understand the wisdom of that saying:
"Blessed are those who pass quickly through life,
for they will receive a crown of glory."

O Lord, I praise You, I glorify You,
in spite of my unworthiness,
for Your mercy towards me
has passed all limits!
You are my Helper and my Shield.
May Your name be praised without end!
To You, O Lord our God, be glory!

A poem by Ephrem the Syrian

The blessing of trials

God often allows good people to experience trial. He allows temptations to rise up against them on every side. Whether these trials come from human beings, from demons, or from the flesh, let it be a cause of thanksgiving. God cannot show His favour to a person who wishes to dwell with Him, except by sending him trials for the sake of truth, just as no-one can become worthy of this greatness apart from the grace of Christ. Saint Paul clearly calls it a gift: "For to you it has been granted on behalf of Christ, not only to believe in Him, but also to suffer for His sake" (**Philippians 1:29**). Saint Peter says the same: "But even if you should suffer for righteousness' sake, you are blessed" (**1 Peter 3:14**), for you are given to share in the suffering of Christ. The way of God is a daily cross. No-one has ever gone to heaven through an easy life.

Isaac of Ninevah, *Directions on Spiritual Training*, **text 67**

Chapter 11.

THE FALL OF ROME AND THE NEW GERMANIC KINGDOMS IN THE WEST

1. The fall of the Roman Empire in the West.

When a Visigothic army besieged and captured Rome early in the 5th Century, people at the time viewed the event as nothing less than the "fall of the Roman Empire" in the West. However, the process by which the Western Empire collapsed had already begun in the 4th Ce

The Visigoths who sacked Rome in 410 were one of various Germanic tribes who lived north of the river Danube, covering a vast area which took in not only modern Germany, but present-day Poland, the Czech Republic, Slovakia, Hungary and south-eastern Russia. From 375 onwards, the Germans came under attack from a numerous and fierce migrating people of Asia called the Huns, whose most famous leader history knows simply as *Attila the Hun* (441-53). To protect themselves against the Huns, the Germans banded together into large tribal confederacies under a single chieftain or king. The main confederacies were the Ostrogoths (Western Goths), Visigoths (Eastern Goths), Franks, Vandals, Lombards, Burgundians, Angles, Saxons and Jutes. They then sought security from the Huns by crossing over into the Roman Empire. The Empire was no strange place to them; many Germans already served in the Roman armies, and had adapted to Roman customs.

By the middle of the 4th Century, part of the Empire's civilisation which the Germans encountered was the Christian faith. However, it was Christianity in its Arian form - the heresy that denied the deity of Christ.[1] The Visigoths were the first Germanic group to convert

---

1   For Arianism, see Chapter 8.

from paganism to Arianism; an Arian bishop called Ulfilas (311-81) had evangelised many of them, and had translated the Bible into Gothic. In 376 the Visigoths crossed the Danube river into the Empire to escape from the Huns, and settled in the Roman provinces of Moesia and Thrace (present-day Bulgaria and Serbia). They felt that their settlement in the Empire involved accepting the Empire's religion, and in 376 the Church in the East was officially Arian (it was during the reign of the Arian emperor Valens). The whole Visigothic people therefore embraced Arianism. The Ostrogoths, Vandals, Lombards and many of the Burgundians also converted from paganism to Arianism before they migrated into and mastered the Western Empire. So the religion of most of the Germanic conquerors of the Empire was not paganism, but Arian Christianity. The Germans who remained pagan - the Franks, Angles, Saxons and Jutes - worshipped Wotan (or Wodin) as their chief god, together with other deities such as Thor (god of thunder), Tiwaz (god of war), Freya (goddess of fertility), and Saeter (a water-god). We derive the names of most our days from these Germanic gods: Tuesday (Tiwaz's day), Wednesday (Wodin's day), Thursday (Thor's day), Friday (Freya's day), Saturday (Saeter's day).

The first sign that the Empire was in serious trouble from the Germans was when the Visigothic army overthrew the emperor Valens, killing him and crushing his troops in 378 at the battle of Adrianople (north-west of Constantinople). The Visigoths had taken refuge in the Empire only two years previously, but rebelled when the Roman authorities treated them badly. The emperor Theodosius the Great (379-95)[2] managed to restore order, but he allowed the Visigoths to stay inside the Empire as allies of Rome. After Theodosius's death, the Visigoths under their new king, *Alaric* (395-410), became hungry for more territory, and moved into northern Italy. After several years of fighting, Alaric besieged and captured Rome itself in 410. The vast and ancient city, once the capital of the world, collapsed in flames, as the brutal Visigoths set its buildings on fire and massacred its population, sparing only church buildings. Rome's fall sent emotional shock-waves crashing through the entire Empire. Jerome in Bethlehem said, "My voice is choked, and sobs break my voice as I dictate this letter. The city which has conquered

---

2   For Theodosius, see Chapter 7, section 2.

the whole world is itself conquered!"[3] (From this point onwards it is customary to refer to the Eastern Roman Empire as the "Byzantine" Empire, after Byzantium, the name of the old town on the site where Constantinople now stood.) The Visigoths then moved out of Italy and by 419 had settled in France.

While the Visigoths were ravaging Italy, the Vandals (who had also embraced Arianism) pushed across France in 406 and migrated into Spain. Under pressure from the Visigoths, the Vandals then crossed the straits of Gibraltar into North-West Africa in 429, and under their king *Genseric* (428-77) launched a campaign of violent and bloody conquest, destroying towns and cities, slaughtering their Catholic inhabitants. The West's greatest theologian, Augustine of Hippo, died while a Vandal army was besieging his city.[4] Genseric established a mighty Vandal kingdom on the ruins of Roman North Africa; Vandal ships ruled the Mediterranean Sea. None of this was good news for the orthodox African Christians who had survived the conquest, because the Arian king Genseric persecuted them intensely, sending Catholic bishops to the island of Corsica as slave-labour to cut timber for his Vandal fleets.

The control and defence of Italy was now in the hands of a Roman army which was in fact made up entirely of Germans. The Western emperors had ceased to have any real authority; they were merely puppet kings, set up and toppled by the German generals. In 476 one of these generals, Odovaker, deposed the last of the Western emperors, Romulus Augustulus; Odovaker's troops then elected him king. The event had little impact at the time, because the Western emperors had long been powerless, but later generations came to see the year 476 as the moment when the last remnants of the Roman Empire vanished in the West. However, even though the Germanic tribes had overthrown the Roman political system in Western Europe, they continued to think of themselves as citizens of the Roman Empire, and professed their loyalty to the emperor - that is, the Byzantine emperor in distant Constantinople. The Christian city of Constantinople, after all, was the "New Rome", and real political power in the Empire had rested in Constantinople ever since

---

3   For Jerome, see Chapter 9, section 2.
4   For Augustine, see Chapter 9, section 3.

Constantine the Great had transferred the seat of imperial government there in 330.[5] Of course, it also suited the political and territorial ambitions of the Germanic kings to have their "emperor" in far-off Constantinople rather than in nearby Rome.

After many tribal movements and conflicts, the Visigoths finally settled in Spain, the Ostrogoths in Italy, the Franks and Burgundians in France, the Vandals in North-West Africa, and the Angles, Saxons and Jutes in Britain. Of these new Germanic kingdoms, the Visigoths, Ostrogoths, Vandals, and most of the Burgundians, were Arians, while the Franks, Angles, Saxons and Jutes remained pagan. However, in 496 a crucial event happened which was to transform the religious destiny of the new West. The Frankish king *Clovis* (481-511) had married a Burgundian princess called Clotilda in 493; and Clotilda was a Catholic (not an Arian, but a believer in the Trinity). Clotilda tried to persuade her husband to become a Christian. Clovis resisted. However, in 496 he found himself in serious military trouble fighting another Germanic tribe called the Alemanni. In his desperation, Clovis prayed to the Lord about Whom his wife had so often told him, promising that he would become a Christian if Christ gave him victory in battle.

> "O Jesus Christ," Clovis prayed, "You Whom Clotilda maintains to be the Son of the living God, You Who graciously give help to those in trouble, and victory to those who trust in You, in faith I beg for the glory of Your help. If You will give me victory over my enemies, if I may have proof of the miraculous power which those devoted to Your name say they have experienced, then I will put my faith in You and be baptised in Your name. I have called on my own gods, but I see all too clearly that they have no intention of helping me. I therefore cannot believe they have any power, for they do not come to the rescue of those who trust in them. I now call upon You. I want to believe in You, but first I need to be saved from my foes."

Victory came, the king of the Alemanni was killed, and Clovis kept his promise, accepting baptism into the Catholic faith. The tribe

---

5   For Constantine, see Chapter 6, section 3, and Chapter 7, section 1.

followed the religious allegiance of its chief: the Franks became the first Catholic kingdom among the new Western nations. Catholics praised Clovis as a new Constantine who had led his people out of pagan darkness into the light of orthodox Christianity. The Catholic Church soon became the richest and most powerful institution in Frankish society.

For our knowledge of early Frankish Christianity, we are indebted to bishop *Gregory of Tours* (538-94), whose *History of the Franks* tells the story of the Frankish people up to 591 (this is where we find Clovis's prayer, quoted above). Gregory was descended from the old Roman aristocracy; his family was devoutly Catholic, producing bishops in abundance (five previous bishops of Tours had been relatives of Gregory). Tours had become the religious capital of France, thanks to its being the site where the saintly Martin of Tours had laboured in the 4th Century; a constant swarm of pilgrims from all over the Christian world came to Tours to gather around Martin's tomb.[6] In 573, by the unanimous voice of clergy and people, Gregory was elected bishop of Tours. He became a high-ranking political counsellor to four successive Frankish kings, as well as a vibrantly energetic and active Church leader; the people of Tours adored Gregory for his sanctity and his fearless advocacy of justice for the poor and oppressed. Indeed, Gregory's reputation for holiness was so great that when an enemy brought a damaging accusation against him at a Frankish Church council in 580, Gregory's solemn protestation that he had not committed the offence was enough to convince everyone of his complete innocence.

Gregory's writings included a commentary on the **Psalms**, a valuable book on the lives of France's pioneer monks (*Life of the Fathers*), a treatise on the different offices in the Church, and a collection of testimonies to contemporary miracles. His *History of the Franks* makes it painfully clear that most of the Frankish people had embraced the Christian faith in a rather shallow and external way. Gregory and his fellow bishops had a hard time trying to convince their Frankish flocks that being a Christian involved a break with pagan customs and a change of moral lifestyle.[7]

---

6   For Martin of Tours, see Chapter 7, section 3, under **Church life: The monastic movement.**

7   Perhaps things are not so different in churches today.

Most of the new Germanic kingdoms in continental Europe and Africa, however, were not pagan but Arian. It took many years of patient, laborious evangelism and teaching by native Catholics to win over their new German masters to the Catholic faith. The Vandals in North-West Africa, and the Ostrogoths in Italy, never did abandon their Arianism. The Vandals had always been hostile to Catholics. The Ostrogoths under their king Theodoric (471-526) were at first tolerant, but in 518 Theodoric changed policy and became an anti-Catholic oppressor. This was Theodoric's angry response to the decree of the new Byzantine emperor Justin (518-27) that Arianism was to be treated as a crime and punished throughout the Empire. Theodoric hit back by persecuting Italian Catholics. His most famous victim was the great Western philosopher and theologian *Boethius* (480-524).[8]

Manlius Severinus Boethius was a noble-souled, high-minded Roman from one of Rome's ancient aristocratic families, a blood-relation of two previous Roman emperors. Educated in the East, in Athens and Alexandria, he was probably one of the most learned men in human history. Boethius rose to exalted heights of wealth, fame and power under Theodoric, becoming the Ostrogothic king's closest political advisor and the head of his civil service; but in a sudden fall from royal grace which was both total and final, Boethius was stripped of all political office, imprisoned, cruelly tortured and put to death in about 524 (Theodoric ordered a quite sadistic method of execution: his soldiers were to batter Boethius's head to a pulp with clubs). While he was in prison awaiting this horrific death, Boethius wrote a book called *The Consolation of Philosophy*. Philosophy appears to him as a woman and shows Boethius that he has not really lost anything that was worth keeping. Theodoric has merely deprived him of material goods, earthly pleasures, fame and power - which cannot bring real peace to the human soul anyway; but no-one can rob Boethius of goodness, the soul's true and eternal treasure, which comes from participating in God Himself, Who is the Supreme Good.

In the light of his own experience of suffering, Boethius also set forth in the *Consolation* profound reflections on God's justice and

---

8   Pronounced "Boh-eth-ee-us".

providence, and His foreknowledge of the future in relation to human decisions and actions. Regarding God's foreknowledge, Boethius tackled a serious difficulty. If God knows that tomorrow I am going to make a decision - let us say, to accept an offer of a new job - then how can it be a free decision? If God *knows* it is going to happen, surely it *must* happen. And if it *must* happen, where is my freedom? Am I just a puppet or robot in God's hands? Boethius offered what became the classic solution to this problem. He argued that God does not experience time as we do, as "past, present and future"; God does not dwell in time - He created time, just as He created space, and He is above and beyond the limits that time and space impose on us. In His own all-seeing mind, God views the whole of time in a single glance, as if it were all "present" in a sort of "eternal now". So God sees "future" things happening as we would see something happening in the present. And just as we do not *cause* someone to perform a free act merely by *seeing* him perform it, so God's foreknowledge of our future actions does not mean that He forces us to carry them out, or causes them by some kind of necessity which takes away our freedom. In His own eternal present, God simply "sees" us performing actions which, to us, are in the future.

For a thousand years, *The Consolation of Philosophy* was a much-admired book throughout the Western world; it breathes a spirit of serenity, calmness and dignity in the face of life's harshness, and an uplifting consciousness of eternity. Later theologians often wrote commentaries on it. Many, however, have expressed surprise that Boethius made no explicit mention of Christ in *The Consolation of Philosophy*. This is probably because Boethius was as much a Neoplatonist as a Christian, and felt most at home in those more general truths about God, the soul, and life after death, which Christianity and Neoplatonism shared in common.[9]

As well as writing a book hailed by the Middle Ages as a spiritual masterpiece, Boethius was also responsible for shaping the basic methods of education, derived from pagan Rome, which would dominate Western medieval Europe. This education was centred on

---

9   It is also possible that Boethius based the woman Philosophy on the female Wisdom of **Proverbs 8**, whom most theologians interpreted as Christ or a symbolic figure representing Christ.

the *trivium* and *quadrivium*. The *trivium* (Latin for "place where three ways meet") was a course in the three subjects of grammar, rhetoric and logic; the *quadrivium* (Latin for "place where four ways meet") involved the study of the four subjects of arithmetic, geometry, music and astronomy. Most of the new West's knowledge of the old Greek philosophy came from Boethius; he translated into Latin the treatises of Aristotle on logic, and the writings of the great Neoplatonist philosopher Porphyry.[10]

The Byzantine emperor Justinian the Great[11] (527-65) destroyed the intolerant Arian kingdoms of the Ostrogoths in Italy and the Vandals in North-West Africa. His successful Italian and African military campaigns were the last great attempt by the Eastern Empire to bring the West back under imperial control. However, Justinian's victories did not survive his own death. Italy, liberated from the Ostrogoths, suffered invasion and conquest by the Arian Lombards.

After the conversion of Clovis and the Franks to Catholicism in 496, the Burgundians soon abandoned Arianism, accepting the Catholic faith in 517 and becoming part of the Frankish kingdom in 532. In Visigothic Spain and Lombard Italy, the religious tolerance of the Arian rulers greatly helped the cross-over from Arianism to Catholicism. The Visigothic king of Spain, Reccared (586-601), accepted Catholicism in 587, and his people followed him into the new faith. The conversion of the Visigoths was officially proclaimed at the council of Toledo (southern Spain) in 589. In Italy, the fortunes of Arianism and Catholicism swung backwards and forwards from one Lombard king to another. The final decision for Catholicism came with king Liutprand (712-44), probably the greatest of the Lombard monarchs.

A number of important Western Christians lived through these troubled times, towering over them like spiritual giants. We have already met Leo the Great[12] (pope from 440 to 461), Boethius,

---

10 For Aristotle's teaching, see Part Two, Chapter 7, section 2. For Neoplatonism, see Chapter 6, section 2.
11 For Justinian, see next Chapter, section 2.
12 For Leo the Great, see Chapter 10, section 4.

Gregory of Tours, and Cassiodorus, aristocratic scholar and monk.[13] Another was the greatest of Latin patristic hymnwriters, **Venantius Fortunatus** (540-600), an Italian who spent his active life in France where he was bishop of Poitiers. Some of his hymns are still sung today, notably his hymn on the cross, "Sing, my tongue, how glorious battle Glorious victory became," and his resurrection hymn, "Welcome, happy morning!" However, we must now meet **Benedict of Nursia** (480-547), who for his long-term influence was more important than any of these.

Benedict was a native of the village of Nursia in northern-central Italy. As a young man, his parents sent him to study in Rome, but this heavenly-minded student fled in horror from its corrupt city-life, and became a hermit, living in a cave in Subiaco (east of Rome). Here he battled with demons and with terrible temptations to sexual impurity - which he cured by rolling about naked on thorns and nettles! Once he had mastered his passions, Benedict emerged from his solitude like some new Antony,[14] an awesomely holy man who seemed able to control the very forces of nature. In 529 he founded the famous monastery of Monte Cassino, between Rome and Naples; from here, Benedict preached, fed the poor, healed the sick (miraculously, it was believed), and attracted a growing army of disciples.

Benedict wrote his own "rule" (code of conduct) for the Monte Cassino monastery, based on previous rules, such as those of Basil of Caesarea and John Cassian.[15] Benedict divided up his monks' day into three periods: (i) collective worship, lasting four and a half hours; (ii) manual work, lasting six or seven hours; (iii) the study of the Bible and the early Church fathers, from three to five hours. Benedict expected his monks to get eight hours' sleep. The other monks elected the abbot, who held the position for life; no monk could challenge his decisions, although the rule required the abbot to

---

[13] For Cassiodorus, see Chapter 7, section 3, under the heading **Church life: The monastic movement**.

[14] For Antony, see Chapter 7, section 3, under **Church life: The monastic movement**.

[15] For Basil of Caesarea, see Chapter 7, section 3, under **Church life: The monastic movement**, and also Chapter 8, section 3. For John Cassian, see Chapter 7, section 3, under **Church life: The monastic movement**.

Benedict of Nursia (480 - 547)

consult a general meeting of all the monks in all important matters. Each Benedictine monastery was to be economically self-sufficient, and there was no leader in overall charge of the various monastic communities apart from the pope himself. The wisdom, balance and practical nature of Benedict's rule as a guide for community life soon made it the most popular and widely used of all monastic rules throughout the Western world. It is known simply as the "Benedictine rule", and people often call Benedict the "father of Western monasticism".

One disciple of Benedict who did much to promote the use of the Benedictine rule was the most illustrious of all the popes of the patristic age - Gregory the Great.

2. Gregory the Great and the papacy.

The Vandals in North-West Africa, and the Angles, Saxons and Jutes in Britain, tended to carry out a policy of what we today would call "ethnic cleansing", often expelling or massacring the native peoples. The new Germanic masters of mainland Western Europe, however, did not do this. Having conquered, they lived at peace with their Roman subjects. The Germans were always a minority of the population in their new European territories. Despite having the military strength to conquer the Western Empire, they lacked the civilisation and culture to govern it properly; so they relied heavily on their more educated subjects to supply them with civil servants and political advisors. And the Germanic rulers - the Franks and Burgundians in France, the Visigoths in Spain, and the Ostrogoths for most of the time in Italy, then their successors the Lombards - did not persecute Catholics. (The exception was the Ostrogothic king Theodoric in the last years of his reign.) So the result of the Germanic conquests in mainland Europe was a new society made up of two elements: (i) a Catholic, Latin-speaking, native population who preserved the traditions of Roman life; (ii) tolerant, Germanic conquerors, mostly Arians, who wanted to adopt, not destroy, the old Roman ways. Often the Catholic bishops undertook the secular as well as spiritual leadership of the native Latin communities.

The Catholic Church was the one great Roman institution which survived the collapse of the Empire in the West . If it was to exploit these new circumstances, it needed strong and wise leadership; and this was abundantly provided by one of the greatest of Rome's bishops, pope Gregory I - known to history as *Gregory the Great* (born 540; pope 590-604). Gregory belonged to an old Roman aristocratic family. He was, in turn, a civil servant, a monk, a papal ambassador in Constantinople, and then abbot of a Benedictine monastery in Rome, before being elected pope in 590. The Venerable Bede (see section 3) has left us the following portrait of Gregory:

"Gregory was a native of Rome, the son of Gordian, descended from ancestors who were devout members of the nobility. Among them was Felix, who was at one time the bishop of the apostolic throne [*i.e.* Felix III, pope from 483 to 492], a man of great eminence in Christ's Church. Gregory maintained this family tradition by the excellence and devotion of his religious life. By the grace of God he consecrated his natural abilities, which would have brought him success in the world, entirely to the attainment of heavenly glory. He suddenly abandoned his secular career and entered a monastery. There he entered into a life of such perfection in grace that, later, he would remember with tears how his mind had been set on higher things, rising far above all that is perishable, and how as a monk he was able to devote himself completely to thoughts of heaven. He used to be able to leave behind the limitations of his earthly body through heavenly contemplation, and he looked forward to death (which most people fear as a punishment) as the doorway to life, the reward of his labours. He would speak of these things, not to impress anyone with the way he had grown in moral and spiritual maturity, but rather in sadness over the decline he felt he had experienced after taking up his pastoral responsibilities. He once described to his deacon, Peter, what his spiritual state as a monk had been, and then sadly continued, 'My pastoral responsibilities now force me to have dealings with worldly men, and it appears to me, after the unclouded beauty of my former peaceful life, that my mind is defiled with the mud of daily affairs. After I have wasted my time in attending to the worldly business of countless people, even though I retire within myself to meditate on spiritual things, I do so with manifestly less strength than before. So if I compare what I now endure with what I have lost, and when I consider the nature of the loss, my burdens seem heavier than ever.'"

We can summarise Gregory's main areas of challenge and achievement as follows:

Political leadership. During Gregory's 14 years as spiritual leader of the Western Church, we see the papacy beginning to become the great political as well as spiritual power which would dominate Western Europe for a thousand years. When the Arian Lombards invaded Italy, they took control of north and south, thus surrounding Rome in central Italy, where a large strip of land belonged to the papacy. The papacy was by this time one of the greatest landowners in the Mediterranean, with property in Italy, Sicily, France, North-West Africa and Dalmatia; it had acquired this land from wealthy Catholics, who wished to honour God and the apostle Peter by enlarging the domain of Peter's successors, the bishops of Rome. Faced with the Lombard threat, and with no prospect of help from the Byzantine Empire which had now become almost powerless in the West, Italian Catholics turned to the pope for political leadership. Without consulting the Byzantine emperor Maurice (582-602), who still had a governor resident in Ravenna (northern Italy), Gregory made treaties of his own with the Lombard invaders, and was thus instrumental in bringing peace to Italy. No previous pope had ever dared behave with such political independence. Gregory also urged the Byzantine Empire to make peace both with the Lombards and the Franks. He established an important relationship between the papacy and the Frankish monarchy: later popes would come to rely on the Franks instead of the Byzantine emperors for political and military support. Gregory also used his papal lands to give food and shelter to many who had been made destitute by the Lombards. In all these ways, Gregory helped to make the papacy into a powerful social and political institution, governing the western-central region of Italy as an independent state.

Church leadership. Gregory made every effort to use his authority as patriarch of the West to promote Church life and strengthen the papacy's position. He oversaw Visigothic Spain's conversion from Arianism to Catholicism. He tried to stop the Frankish monarchy from taking control of bishoprics and selling them for money (the

Frankish kings frustrated Gregory in this, but the popes renewed these reforming efforts with greater success in the 8th Century). He fought hard against Manichaeism in Italy and Donatism in North-West Africa, persuading the civil authorities to punish all non-Catholics (except the Jews, whom Gregory protected). He had a famous and fierce controversy with patriarch John the Faster of Constantinople (582-95). The Byzantine emperor Maurice had officially bestowed on John the title "ecumenical" or "universal" patriarch - the spiritual leader of all Christians. Gregory protested passionately that none of the five patriarchs (Rome, Constantinople, Alexandria, Antioch and Jerusalem) could claim such an arrogant title, although Rome held a paramount place of honour among them as "first among equals", by virtue of its spiritual descent from Peter, prince of the apostles. To the constant embarrassment of later popes, Gregory declared: "Whoever calls himself universal priest, or desires that title, is by his pride the forerunner of Antichrist." Amazingly, despite Gregory's strong words, his next-but-one successor, pope Boniface III (607), was quite happy to claim the title of "ecumenical bishop". Gregory preferred to call himself "the servant of the servants of God". (Later popes have retained this title too, but not usually in the humble spirit of Gregory.)

Theology. Gregory was a devout disciple of Augustine of Hippo in his theology, but he blended Augustine's theology with other elements drawn from the popular religious beliefs and practices of his own day. He taught that all human beings are born sinful, and that Christ alone by His sovereign grace can rescue sinners from their bondage to sin. This salvation comes through baptism, in which the Holy Spirit causes the sinner (including the new-born baby) to be spiritually reborn. However, the Christian must make up for sins committed after baptism through works of love. Gregory also taught that, for believers, holy communion had the power to wash away post-baptismal sin, and that if at death a Christian had any sins left which had not been dealt with, he must pay for them by sufferings in purgatory, a place of purifying fire midway between heaven and hell. Theologians had considered belief in purgatory to be an opinion rather than a definite Christian doctrine in Augustine's time; Gregory's influence helped to make it a definite doctrine in the West (although not in the East, which has never accepted the idea). Based on this belief in purgatory, Gregory introduced the practice of celebrating special communion services for the dead; such services, Gregory thought, were effective for remitting the sins of departed souls and thus hastening their passage from purgatory to heaven. By Gregory's time, people in the West were calling holy communion "the mass", from the closing words of the Latin communion liturgy - *ite, missa est* ("go, the congregation is dismissed") - which the bishop or presbyter spoke at the end of communion. The word "mass" had first been used as a description of communion in the 5th Century; by the 6th, it was the standard term for it throughout the Western Church.

Church worship. Gregory contributed richly to the development of Western worship. He opposed the superstitious veneration of images or icons of Christ, the Virgin Mary and the saints, but approved of using them to adorn churches as teaching aids for those who could not read. Gregory's influence in this area helped to promote some division of opinion between East and West during the great iconoclastic controversy of the 8th and 9th Centuries.[16] He introduced some changes in the liturgy for holy communion, including a new collection of hymns to be sung alternately by presbyter and congregation or choir. "Gregorian chant" is also named after Gregory. Scholars think that he wrote a series of chants for use on each of the festivals of the Christian year, and that what we now call Gregorian chant arose out of this. However, since the chants were not actually written down until the 9th and 10th Centuries, we cannot be certain about the precise extent of Gregory's own contribution. The style of Gregorian chant seems to have been a return to the simpler form of chanting which had been common in the West before the liturgical reforms of Ambrose of Milan in the 4th Century.[17] The hallmarks of Gregorian chant are its musical simplicity, solemnity, unearthly beauty, and "unison" (all the voices sing the same lines and notes at the same time). No musical instruments are used.[18]

---

16 For the iconoclastic controversy, and the East-West disagreement, see Part Two, Chapter 2, section 2, under the heading **Emperor and pope**, and Chapter 3, section 3.

17 For Ambrose see Chapter 7, section 2.

18 For the use of musical instruments in Western worship, see Part Two, Chapter 4, section 10.

Gregory's writings. Theologians read these very widely in the Middle Ages. They include:

(a) Gregory's *Letters*. 838 of Gregory's letters have survived. They are addressed to bishops, missionaries and secular rulers in all parts of Europe, and tell us a lot about Gregory and the times he lived in.

(b) Gregory's *Dialogues*. These contain the lives of various Western saints, such as Benedict of Nursia (our chief source of information about him). Gregory's lives of Benedict and other believers are full of stories of supernatural dreams, visions and miracles, which shows us what people of that age thought the life of an outstanding saint should be like. From Gregory's *Dialogues*, the Eastern Church calls him "Gregory the Dialogist".

(c) Works of Biblical exposition. Gregory wrote a long commentary on **Job**, using Origen's threefold method of interpretation - literal, moral and spiritual. The all-important "spiritual" interpretation was highly allegorical in nature.[19] This emphasis on the allegorical meaning of the text became the normal way of expounding the Bible among Western theologians in the Middle Ages. Gregory also wrote homilies on **Ezekiel** and the **Gospels**.

(d) The *Pastoral Care*. This is a book in which Gregory set forth his ideals of the Christian ministry. He said that a pastor must set a personal example by the way he lives, be a servant not a ruler, meditate daily on the Word of God, love truth more than popularity, and give a high place to preaching (Gregory himself was a great preacher). The *Pastoral Care* became the standard textbook on the ministry throughout the Middle Ages in the West, and is generally reckoned to be a classic work on the subject (see the end of the Chapter for a quotation from the *Pastoral Care*).

3. The Celtic Church and the conversion of the English.

Gregory the Great was deeply committed to evangelising the Germanic tribes who were still pagan. His greatest concern was for

---

[19] For Origen and his allegorical method of interpretation, see Chapter 5, section 1.

the tribes that had conquered southern Britain - the Angles, Saxons and Jutes. Tradition says that while Gregory was still a monk, he saw some boys being sold in the slave market in Rome. He asked who they were, and was told that they were pagan Angles. Struck by the boys' great physical loveliness, Gregory replied, "They are not Angles but angels!" When he became pope, Gregory prepared a great mission to England ("England" comes from "Angle-land" - the part of Britain conquered by the Angles, Saxons and Jutes).[20] He gathered religious and political information, and decided that the kingdom of the Jutes in Kent (south-eastern England) was the best place to begin. The pagan king of Kent, *Ethelbert* (589-616), had extended his power over the whole of eastern England as far as the river Humber. Moreover, he had married a Frankish Catholic princess, Bertha, who had brought a Frankish bishop with her to England.

So in 596 Gregory sent a team of Benedictine monks, led by an Italian abbot called Augustine, to king Ethelbert and the Jutes in Kent. We must not confuse this Augustine with Augustine of Hippo, who died in 430. The Augustine who went to England lived 100 years later, and is called *Augustine of Canterbury* (died 604) - a rather dull personality who acted in all things as the servant of pope Gregory, deeply humble before his master, tactless and high-handed towards everyone else. Augustine and his monks did not exactly relish their mission; in fact, they were so afraid of what the Jutes might do to them, that their spirits failed and they turned back at one point on their journey - pope Gregory had to use all his powers of persuasion to inspire them to continue. They finally arrived in Kent just after Easter in 597. Their fears proved groundless; king Ethelbert welcomed them, giving them liberty to preach throughout his kingdom. The pagan monarch was impressed by the beauty and majesty of their

---

20 The island of *Britain* is made up of three countries, England, Scotland and Wales. At present, together with Northern Ireland, they constitute the state known as the United Kingdom. *England* comprises the bulk of the southern part of Britain, *Wales* lies to the west of it, and *Scotland* to the north. In the 6th Century, none of these countries had yet become a unified state. The territory of each was fought over by various small kingdoms with ever-changing boundaries.

worship, and their simple ascetic lives. Augustine soon won over
Ethelbert himself to embrace the Christian faith (we are not sure
when - certainly within four years), and Augustine was soon
reporting to Pope Gregory that 10,000 of Ethelbert's Jewish subjects
had been baptized.These were voluntary conversions; Augustine
taught king Ethelbert that it was wrong for him to force his people to
change their religion. Pope Gregory appointed Augustine archbishop
of the Catholic Church in England, and king Ethelbert gave
Augustine his own palace at Canterbury to be his official residence.
So Augustine became the first archbishop of Canterbury.

In addition to evangelising the pagan Angles, Saxons and Jutes, there
was another serious challenge for pope Gregory's mission to
England - the problem of the native British, or "Celts". The Angles,
Saxons and Jutes had forced the Celts out of most of England into
the extreme south-west (Devon and Cornwall), north-west
(Lancashire and Cumbria), Wales and Scotland. The Celts, who
inhabited Ireland as well as Britain, were already Christians; they
had accepted Christianity when Britain was still part of the Roman
Empire.[21] A strong and lively Celtic Church had existed in Britain
before the Germanic invasions, and now flourished in Ireland too.
Celtic Christianity had a number of unusual features. It was based
on the monastery rather than the congregation, and its leading figures
were abbots rather than bishops. It maintained for a long time a spirit
of bold independence in face of the papacy's claims to exercise
authority over all Western churches as the one patriarchate of the
West. And it fostered a rare and intense love of the natural world of
creation, beautifully expressed in Celtic prayers, hymns and poems.

Outstanding Celtic Christians included Patrick and Columba.
Obscurity veils much of the life of *Patrick* (390-461), and historians
argue about the details, but it seems that he was probably born in
Scotland, the son of a deacon and grandson of a presbyter. A band
of Irish criminals kidnapped him in his youth, and sold him into slavery
for six years in Ireland. It was during this period as a slave that

---

21 Rome's armies conquered Britain in the years 43-45 during the reign of
    emperor Claudius (41-54). To celebrate the event, Claudius named his
    son "Britannicus". Luke mentions Claudius in **Acts 11:28**.

Patrick experienced conversion; the faith he had learned in childhood became a living reality in his soul amid the harshness of a slave's existence. "After I arrived in Ireland," he said, "I fed cattle every day, and often during the day I prayed; the love and fear of God burned more and more within me, and my faith and spirit grew strong. In a single day I would pray as often as a hundred times, and almost as often during the night."

Patrick eventually managed to escape from his captors, and went to France, where he joined the monastery at Lerins and then at Auxerre (central France). But a vision called him back to Ireland to evangelise its largely pagan population. To this Patrick devoted the rest of his life (from 432 to 461), crusading against the supernatural powers of pagan religion that reigned in Ireland, and conquering all their dark magic in the mighty strength of Christ (see his poem, *Patrick's Breastplate*, quoted at the end of the Chapter, with its sense of warfare between the Christian and the demons, and its feeling that the natural forces of creation are on the believer's side in this conflict). Patrick's missionary labours were so successful that he is often called "the apostle of Ireland". In his own words, "I am greatly in debt to God Who has bestowed His grace on me so largely, that many people were born again to God through me. The Irish, who never had the knowledge of God and worshipped only idols and unclean things, have now become the Lord's people, and are called sons of God; and the sons and daughters of Irish kings are now monks and virgins of Christ."

Ireland was the only Western country to escape the Germanic invasions of the 4th and 5th Centuries. It developed a thriving Christian civilisation; monasteries, education, art, poetry and theology all flourished gloriously, and the Ireland of that era is often called "the island of saints and scholars". Among its great spiritual leaders were Brendan of Clonfert, Finian of Clonard (died 589), Ciaran of Clonmacnoise, and *Comgall of Bangor* (517-601), head of one of Ireland's greatest monasteries in Bangor (north-eastern Ireland)[22] and intimate friend of the great evangelist Columba.

If Patrick was the "apostle of Ireland", *Columba* (521-97) has been

22 Not to be confused with Bangor in Wales.

called the "apostle of Scotland". Born at Gartan in Donegal (north-western Ireland) in 521, he was a presbyter-monk who established a number of churches and monasteries in his Irish homeland before crossing over to Scotland in 563. Tall, beautiful, burning with physical energy, constantly singing the **Psalms** of David in a booming voice, fearless, and in love with travel and adventure, Columba summed up in his own person and life the essence of Celtic Christianity. His missionary expedition to Scotland followed the normal Irish pattern - 12 missionaries under the leadership of a 13th, based on the 12 apostles under the leadership of Christ. Columba and his team set up their headquarters on the tiny island of Iona, off the Scottish west coast. The monastery he founded there became one of the most successful centres of missionary work in the history of Christianity. From Iona, Columba and his disciples planted churches and monasteries throughout Scotland and northern England; Iona became the spiritual capital of the whole region. Among the northern Celtic Christians, the authority of the abbot of Iona had far more weight than the word of the pope.

Other teams of Irish missionaries went to France, Belgium and Germany. The greatest of the Irish evangelists in mainland Europe was *Columbanus* (543-615), a native of Leinster (eastern-central Ireland) and a pupil of Comgall of Bangor. In about 590 he went as leader of a band of 12 missionaries to France, and laboured in Burgundy (south-eastern France), Constance (northern Switzerland), and northern Italy where he founded the important monastery of Bobbio. Famed for the purity and simplicity of his life and his outspoken courage in denouncing wickedness in high places (for which the unworthy king of Burgundy banished him), Columbanus was also one of the most learned men of his age, educated in Greek and Hebrew when the knowledge of these languages had almost died out in the West. After his death, his disciples went on to evangelise Switzerland, Swabia and Franconia.

In Ireland, Scotland, Wales and the north of England, then, a strong and vibrant Celtic Church already existed when pope Gregory sent Augustine and his Roman missionaries to Kent in southern England in 596. Many Celtic Christians, however, did not look with favour on pope Gregory's mission to the Angles, Saxons and Jutes.

There were two reasons for this:

(i) Ethnic hatred. There had been 150 years of warfare in Britain between the native Christian Celts and the invading pagan Angles, Saxons and Jutes. These wars had forced the British Celts out of most of their homeland. In about 540, the Celtic presbyter and historian *Gildas* wrote his great tragic work, *The Destruction of Britain*, in which he described as an eyewitness the sufferings of his people at the hands of the pagan invaders:

> "The Anglo-Saxons smash down every colony with their battering-rams, and slaughter all the inhabitants along with the guardians of their churches, clergy and people alike; the sword gleams on every side, flames blaze around. How horrible to behold the blood-stained ruins - blood covering the tops of towers torn down and lying in the streets, blood covering high walls collapsed into a pile of stones, blood covering the holy communion altars, blood covering the mutilated corpses - blood everywhere, as if all these things had been crushed together in some monstrous wine-press. Of the miserable few British who escape, some flee to the hills, only to be captured and slain in heaps; some, compelled by hunger, go and surrender themselves to the enemy, and become their slaves for ever; others, weeping bitterly, flee overseas."

Most of the British Celts now found it very difficult to look upon their traditional enemies, the Angles, Saxons and Jutes, as brothers in Christ. As the Venerable Bede (see below) testified, "Even in our own day, the British have no respect for the Christian faith and religion of the Anglo-Saxons, and have no more dealings with them than they do with the pagans."

(ii) Religious controversy. The Celtic Christians did not like some of the religious beliefs and customs of Augustine and the Roman missionaries. They did not share Augustine's views of the papacy's authority, as patriarch of the West, to determine Western forms of worship and Church organisation; they certainly did not see why they should accept Augustine as their archbishop when they already had their own bishops. They were deeply offended by Augustine's rather clumsy attempt to force them to celebrate Easter according to the date used by the rest of the Church in both East and West (the Celts calculated the date differently). Further, in the Celtic Church, the abbot was a more powerful figure than the bishop, and bishops had no fixed dioceses but travelled about as the Spirit or their own inclinations led them; this conflicted with the normal Catholic tradition, where the bishop was superior to the abbot and (usually) confined his ministry to his own diocese. Finally, when a Christian became a monk, it was the custom to give him a "tonsure", a special way of shaving hair from the top of the head; the Celts gave their monks a semi-circular tonsure, while the Roman tonsure was fully circular - and this became another cause of contention.

Modern Protestants sometimes think that this conflict between Celtic and Roman practice was a battle between "Protestant-minded" Celts and Roman Catholicism, but this was not really the case. In the main point of the dispute - the date of Easter - Rome was simply championing the custom observed by the whole of the Church throughout East and West, with the Celts alone being out of step. Furthermore, "Roman Catholicism", as the Protestant Reformers knew it, did not begin to take solid shape until the great reform movement of Hildebrand (pope Gregory VII) in the 11th Century.[23] In any case, it is historically false to speak of **Roman** Catholicism until the great East-West schism of 1054; prior to this, all Christians in East and West[24] were one united Church, and did not collectively acknowledge the supremacy of the pope (as the Eastern Orthodox still do not). The theology and spirituality of Western Catholicism in the 6th Century were certainly not Protestant, but neither were they "Roman Catholic"; Gregory the Great's Church had no indulgences, no doctrine of icon-veneration or transubstantiation, no "vicar of Christ" claims for the popes, and no "immaculate conception" claims for Mary - these and other novelties emerged long after the 6th Century.[25]

---

[23] For Hildebrand's reform movement, see Part Two, Chapter 4, sections 4-6.

[24] Apart from the Nestorians of Persia and the Monophysites of Egypt, Ethiopia and Syria, all of whom rejected the Creed of Chalcedon and were therefore heretics in the eyes of the "one, holy, Catholic and apostolic Church" of East and West. For Chalcedon, see previous Chapter, section 4.

[25] For Gregory's attitude to the veneration of icons, see section 2 under **Church worship**, and the quotation at the end of the Chapter.

We must also realise that the authority claimed by Gregory the Great over the Celts was not *papal* authority as Protestants would understand the term. It was *patriarchal* authority. Gregory claimed to be the patriarch of the Western Church. There were four other patriarchs in the East, in Constantinople, Alexandria, Antioch and Jerusalem, each with their own territories. The *whole* Church was supposed to be governed jointly by the five patriarchs. If anyone in any of the other patriarchal jurisdictions had tried to celebrate Easter on a different date, they would have been dealt with by *their* patriarchs as Gregory dealt with the Celts. Finally, it is difficult to think of the Celts as "Protestant-minded" when the argument they employed to oppose the authority-claims of Rome was not the sufficiency of Scripture. It was the authority of a different tradition. For the date of Easter, the Celts took their stand on the authority of the holy Columba, and ultimately on a unwritten tradition which they claimed had been handed down from the apostle John. It is also worth bearing in mind the very unProtestant practice of monasticism dominated the entire Celtic form of Christianity, more than any other branch of the Church in history.[26]

The friction between the Celtic Christians and the Roman mission increased when the Celts themselves launched a new wave of missionary activity in the Angle kingdom of Northumbria, which covered the north-east of England and much of southern Scotland. The leader of the Celtic missionaries was *Aidan of Lindisfarne* (died 651). Aidan was an Irish monk from Iona who came to Northumbria at the request of its king, *Oswald* (633-42). King Oswald ("Saint Oswald", as he became known after his death) had been brought up as a Christian among the monks of Iona, and he wanted his people to learn the Christian faith. So at Oswald's invitation, Aidan settled on the isle of Lindisfarne as his base of operations, establishing a monastery there and becoming Lindisfarne's first bishop. The monks of Lindisfarne produced copies of

---

[26] The temptation for Protestants in studying pre-Reformation Church history is to see *anyone* who opposed the papacy as being somehow a "Protestant before the Reformation". Some groups fit into that category (notably the Waldensians, Lollards and Hussites), but others simply do not (notably the entire Eastern Church!).

the Scriptures which have become famous for their beautiful handwriting and illustrations. Encouraged and protected by king Oswald, Aidan's evangelism was so successful that many have regarded Aidan, not Augustine, as the true "father of English Christianity". The Venerable Bede (see below) has left us the following account of how Aidan and king Oswald evangelised the Angles of Northumbria:

"When Aidan arrived, king Oswald gave him the island of Lindisfarne, at Aidan's own request, to be his episcopal residence. The tide ebbs and flows there, so that the sea surrounds Lindisfarne like an island twice a day, and twice a day the dry sand joins it to the mainland. The king always listened humbly and eagerly to Aidan's advice, and with great energy devoted himself to extending the Church of Christ throughout his kingdom. Bishop Aidan did not know English very well, so when he preached the Gospel [in the Celtic tongue], king Oswald himself interpreted the Word of God to his elders and nobles - it was a delight to behold....

"Aidan never sought or cared about worldly possessions, and loved to give away to the poor what kings and wealthy people had given him. In the town and the country, he always journeyed on foot, unless necessity forced him to ride. Whomever he met on his journeys, whether nobles or ordinary folk, he stopped and spoke to them. If they were pagans, he urged them to accept Christian baptism; if they were Christians, he strengthened their faith, inspiring them by his words and his deeds to lead virtuous lives and to be generous to others....

"Aidan cultivated peace, love, purity and humility; he devoted himself not just to teaching God's laws, but to keeping them, and was committed to study and prayer. He used his presbyterial authority to restrain the proud and the powerful; he tenderly comforted the sick; he helped and protected the poor. To sum up everything I have learned of him from those who knew him, Aidan was careful never to neglect anything that the Scriptures of the evangelists, apostles and prophets taught him, and he consecrated himself to obeying these things with all his might."

Aidan of Lindisfarne (Died 651)

As well as Lindisfarne, Aidan founded a number of other monasteries, the most important of which was a community for both men and women at Whitby in Yorkshire - the monks and nuns lived in separate quarters. The head of Aidan's Whitby monastery was the abbess *Hilda* (614-80), "mother Hilda" as everyone called her, greatest of the early Anglo-Saxon nuns.[27] The study of theology and the writing of Christian literature blossomed fruitfully at Whitby; it was there that the first known English poet, the monk *Caedmon* (died 678), penned his celebrated Anglo-Saxon poems on creation, the incarnation, the cross and the ressurection. One of Aidan's greatest successors as bishop of Lindisfarne was the Anglo-Saxon monk *Cuthbert* (634-87). Cuthbert became a monk in his early youth at the monastery of Melrose (now in south-eastern Scotland), where he became a famous evangelist; using Melrose as his base of operations, he went out on preaching tours to Scottish towns and villages throughout the southern part of Scotland (which had many Anglo-Saxon inhabitants and was part of the Northumbrian kingdom). His contemporaries tell us that when Cuthbert preached, his face shone like an angel and his hearers fell under deep conviction of sin. He moved to the Lindisfarne monastery in 664. After some years as a hermit, in 685 he became bishop of Lindisfarne. By Cuthbert's time, some leading Celtic Christians had become convinced that Roman methods of Church organisation and observance (*e.g.* the Roman date for celebrating Easter) were superior to those of the native Celts. The whole of southern Ireland had by now accepted the Roman tradition, but the northern half of the island and Iona remained committed to the old Celtic forms. Cuthbert himself, who had been brought up among Celts, came round to the Roman way of thinking, and tried to introduce Roman customs at Lindisfarne, but a party of traditional-minded Celts opposed him.

---

[27] Anglo-Saxon England sometimes allowed a woman to be the head of a mixed community of monks and nuns. But Hilda was not a "priestess"; she could not baptise, ordain or preside at holy communion. See the end of the Chapter for Hilda's life. Mixed communities of monks and nuns also existed in the Roman-Byzantine world, but there they seem to have had both an abbott and abbess as joint-heads. The 20th canon of the 2nd ecumenical Council of Nicaea in 787 forbade the founding of any more of these mixed communities, because they were liable to give rise to scandals; in those that already existed, it ordered a strict segregation of the monks and nuns.

King *Oswy* of Northumbria (642-70), brother of Oswald, decided to resolve the growing Celtic-Roman controversy by summoning a synod at Whitby in 664. Rather oddly, two Anglo-Saxons who had each been nurtured in the bosom of the Celtic tradition acted as champions both of the Celtic and the Roman type of Christianity at the synod. Abbess Hilda defended the Celtic customs, as did the Irish bishop Colman of Lindisfarne (died 676); the monk Wilfred (634-709), the forceful and eloquent young son of a Northumbrian noble, trained by Aidan at Lindisfarne, upheld the Roman cause. Wilfrid's arguments won the day. He was the abbot of Ripon monastery, where he introduced the Benedictine rule, and later (669) became bishop of York; he is also remembered for successfully evangelising the Saxons of Sussex, on the southern coast of England.

King Oswy's historic decision in favour of Rome at the synod of Whitby had great and lasting consequences for British Christianity. It meant that in the English kingdoms the Celtic and Roman streams of Church life began to flow together into a single river. By 715, even Iona had acknowledged the Catholic date of Easter and the authority of the pope. In Wales, however, the Roman customs did not fully triumph over the old Celtic practices until the 12th Century, (hence Bede's comment, quoted earlier, that the British in his own day still had no respect for the faith of the Anglo-Saxons: he meant the British Celts of Wales and other Western extremities of Britain, not the Celtic mission in Anglo-Saxon England).

Meanwhile, Celtic and Roman missionaries converted the other Anglo-Saxon kingdoms one by one, until by 681 Christianity had replaced paganism as the national faith of the English people. The first archbishop of Canterbury whose position all England recognised was *Theodore* (668-90), a Greek monk from Tarsus appointed by pope Vitalian (657-72). Theodore continued the process of uniting the Celtic and Anglo-Saxon forms of Christianity. He did this in two ways: (i) by taking parts of each and blending them in the English Church - *e.g.* in the monasteries, combining Rome's Benedictine rule with the Celtic monastic practice of private confession of sins to a presbyter; (ii) by putting Celtic as well as Anglo-Saxon Churchmen in leading positions. Christian art, literature, Biblical studies and missionary work flourished with amazing vigour in the monasteries of the new united English Church.

The most famous monastic centre of learning in the English Church was the Benedictine monastery at Jarrow in Northumbria, where a presbyter-monk called *Bede* (673-735) earned the title "the father of English history". Bede wrote a complete history of the Church in England up to his own time, *Church History of the English People*, which is our main source of information about the Christian faith in England from its origins until the 8th Century. Bede was one of the most highly educated Western Europeans of his day. He knew all three of the Church's great languages, Latin, Greek and Hebrew (a rare achievement for any Westerner at that time). A dedicated follower of Augustine of Hippo, Bede was also well-versed in the writings of other early Church fathers, especially Ambrose, Jerome, and Gregory the Great, and in the ancient pagan literature of Greece and Rome. As well as his English Church history, Bede wrote many sermons, biographies (including a life of Cuthbert), letters, poems, and commentaries on books of the Bible, and translated **John's Gospel** into English. Bede's humble and holy character have made him one of the best-loved of English saints, among Roman Catholics, Protestants and Eastern Orthodox alike: "our father and master, Bede, beloved of God," as his fellow monks called him. The account of his death was a favourite scene among English Christians, and his dying words were written down and treasured - for example, "The time of my release is near, and my soul longs to see Christ my King in all His beauty"; "I am not afraid to die, for we have a God who is good beyond comparison." From the 10th Century onwards, people referred to him as *the Venerable Bede* ("venerable" means "worthy of veneration").

Important people:

The Church
Patrick (390-461)
Boethius (480-524)
Gildas (active 540's)
Benedict of Nursia (480-547)
Gregory of Tours (538-94)
Columba (512-97)
Venantius Fortunatus (540-600)
Comgall of Bangor (517-601)
Pope Gregory the Great
   (born 540; pope 590-604)

Political and military
Alaric, king of the Visigoths
   (395-410)
Attila the Hun (441-53)
Genseric, king of the Vandals
   (428-77)
Clovis, king of the Franks
   (481-511)
Ethelbert, king of Kent
   (589-616)

Augustine of Canterbury
  (died 604)
Columbanus (543-615)
Aidan of Lindisfarne (died 651)
Caedmon (died 678)
Hilda of Whitby (614-80)
Cuthbert (634-87)
Theodore of Canterbury (668-90)
Wilfrid (634-709)
The Venerable Bede (673-735)

Oswald, king of Northumbria
  (633-42)
Oswy, king of Northumbria
  (642-70)

Making decisions in a Benedictine monastery

Whenever the community needs to debate anything important, let the abbot assemble all the monks and set the business fully before them. After he has heard their opinions, and thought about the matter in a mature way, he may then decide on what he thinks is most profitable. The reason why we have ordained that the abbot must assemble the whole community is that God often reveals what is best to the young. The brothers should offer their opinions with humility and submissiveness; they should not argue passionately for their point of view, but leave everything to the judgment of the abbot, and they should together assent to what he decides is fitting. Yet as it is the disciple's duty to obey his master, it is equally the master's duty to decide in accordance with the principles of justice and wisdom. Everyone must follow the Rule [the Benedictine Rule] as his guide, and no-one should rashly turn aside from it. No member of the community should let self-centredness warp his attitudes. No-one should argue in a heated way with his abbot inside the monastery, and no-one should argue with him at all if they are outside; if he does, he must be chastised as the Rule prescribes. Even so, the abbot himself must act in all things with respect for the Rule and in the fear of God, realising that he must give an account of all his dealings to the true and impartial Judge. If the abbot has to decide something relating to community life which is not so important, he need only consult the elders, so that (as it is written), "Do everything with consultation, and you will not repent of what you have done" (**Proverbs 15:22**).

Benedict of Nursia, *The Benedictine Rule*, rule 3

A pastor must crucify the desire to be popular

The pastor must keep careful watch over himself, in case the craving to be popular assaults him. As he studies to understand spiritual things and as he ministers to his people, he must beware that he does not try to make the congregation love *him* more than they love the truth. He must take care in case his self-love puts him at a distance from his Creator, even if his good life seems to show that he does not belong to this world. For a man becomes an enemy of the Redeemer, if by his good works he covets being loved by the church instead of by Christ: just as a servant, sent by the bridegroom with gifts for the bride, is guilty of treacherous thoughts if he desires to attract the eyes of the bride to himself.

In fact, once this self-love has got possession of a pastor's mind, it sometimes carries him far away to softness, and sometimes to roughness. On the one hand, self-love can make a pastor's mind soft, so that when he sees members of his flock sinning, he does not dare to rebuke them, in case it weakens their love for himself. Indeed, sometimes he smooths down their sins with flatteries, when he ought to have rebuked them. Thus the prophet says wisely, "Woe to those who put cushions under every elbow and pillows under every head!" (**Ezekiel 13:18**, Vulgate translation). To put cushions under every elbow is to cherish with smooth flattery souls who are slipping from their uprightness and are lying down in this world's enjoyments. When a pastor holds back from giving unpleasant rebuke to one who sins, and instead offers him the smoothness of favour, that he may lie down softly in error, untroubled by any roughness of contradiction, this is as though the elbow of a reclining person rested on a cushion and his head on pillows. This is how a pastor ruled by self-love treats those whom he fears might harm him in his pursuit of worldly glory.

But others, whom the pastor sees have no power against him, he keeps down with the roughness of harsh rebuke, never warning them gently, but (forgetting all pastoral kindness) terrifying them with the power of domination. Such pastors God rightly condemns through the prophet, saying, "The weak you have not strengthened, nor have you healed those who were sick, nor bound up the broken, nor brought back what was driven away, nor sought what was lost; but with force and cruelty you have ruled them" (**Ezekiel 34:4**). Loving themselves more than their Creator, these pastors exalt themselves proudly over those who are under them; they do not think about what it is their duty to do, but what it lies in their power to do. They have no fear of future judgment, but arrogantly glory in worldly power. It pleases them to feel free to do even unlawful things, and not to let anyone under them contradict them. He who sets his mind on doing wrong things, and yet wishes everyone else to turn a blind eye and let him do them, is a witness against himself that he desires people to love him more than they love the truth - because he is unwilling that anyone should stand up for truth against his false conduct. No living soul fully avoids this sin. But a person desires the truth to be loved more than himself, when he wishes no-one to spare him if he offends against truth. This is why Peter willingly accepted Paul's rebuke (**Galatians 2:11**); this is why David humbly listened to the rebuke of Nathan (**2 Samuel 12:7**)....

Remember also that it is right for good pastors to desire to please people: not because the pastor longs to be loved himself, but because he desires, by the sweetness of his own character, to attract his neighbours to the truth. The good pastor makes affection for himself into a sort of road by which to lead the hearts of his hearers to the love of the Creator. It is very difficult for people to listen gladly to a preacher whom they do not love, however well he preaches. So he who is a pastor over others should work hard at being loved, in order that people may listen to him; but he must not seek their love for its own sake.

Gregory the Great, *Pastoral Care*, **chapter 8**

Gregory the Great to patriarch John of Constantinople on the title "universal bishop"

When the apostle Paul heard certain believers say, "I am of Paul, I am of Apollos, I am of Cephas," he reacted with horror as he saw them tearing apart the Lord's body in this way, and attaching His members to various heads. He exclaimed, "Was Paul crucified for you? Were you baptised in the name of Paul?" (**1 Corinthians 1:13**). If Paul could not endure to see the members of the Lord's body being attached here and there to other heads than Christ, even though these heads were apostles, what will *you* say to Christ? What will you say at the last judgment to Him Who is the Head of the universal Church, when by your title of "universal" you wish to bring all His members under your power? I ask you, whom are you imitating by this perverse title of yours? You are following Satan who despised his fellow legions of angels and tried to ascend to the highest place, that he might be subject to none and exalted alone above all others, saying, "I will ascend into heaven, I will exalt my throne above the stars of God, I will sit on the mount of the congregation in the sides of the north, I will ascend above the heights of the clouds, I will be like the Most High" (**Isaiah 14:13-14**).[28] What are your brothers, the bishops of the universal Church, but the stars of God? Their lives and teaching shine forth in truth, through the sins and errors of mankind, as the stars through the darkness of the night.[29] When you would exalt yourself above them by your ambitious title, and debase their title in comparison with your own, what do you say but these very words, "I will ascend into heaven, I will exalt my throne above the stars of God"?....

Peter, the first of the apostles (a *member* of the holy and universal Church), and Paul, and Andrew, and John (who were appointed as spiritual leaders of different national groups) - all of these were members under one Head alone. The saints before the law, the saints under the law, the saints under grace - they all make up the Lord's body; they are all members of the Church. Yet there is none among them who wanted to be called "universal". Let your Holiness then consider how much you are puffed up when you claim a title that none of them had the arrogance to assume.

Gregory's *First letter to John of Constantinople*

Gregory the Great on icons

We have heard that in a fire of intemperate zeal you have broken icons of the saints, under the seeming plea that people should not adore them. In fact, we entirely praise you for commanding people

---

28 Here is a good example of the allegorical interpretation of Scripture; Gregory interprets the "stars of God" in **Isaiah 14:13** as "the bishops of the universal Church".

not to adore them; but we blame you for breaking them. My brother, tell me whether anyone has ever heard of any presbyter doing what you have done? If anything else restrained you, should you not have controlled yourself so as not despise your brothers, imagining that you alone are holy and wise? To adore a picture is one thing; to learn through the story which a picture tells is another. What writing presents to those who read, a picture presents to those who cannot read but can see, for in the picture they behold what they ought to imitate - they "read" the picture, even though they cannot read words....Because ancient custom has reasonably accepted that the stories of the saints should be painted in holy places, you might easily have achieved what you were aiming at, if only you had mixed your zeal with wisdom; you might have gathered together a scattered flock, instead of scattering one already gathered. The worthy reputation of a shepherd might have marked you out, instead of the blame which now lies on you of being a scatterer. From acting intemperately on the impulse of your feelings, you have (it is said) so offended your children that the majority of them have withdrawn from fellowship with you. When will you bring wandering sheep to the Lord's fold, if you have not been able to keep those you already have?...

You must call together these scattered children of the Church, and show them by testimonies of holy Scripture that it is sinful to adore anything made with hands, for it is written, "You shall adore the Lord your God and serve Him only" **(Luke 4:8).** Then you must explain why you broke the pictures which had been made to edify an uneducated people, that although they could not read, they might see the story with their eyes and learn what they ought to do. You must make it clear that you broke the pictures because you saw people adoring them. Then tell the people, "If you want to have icons in the church for the purpose of instructing you, in accordance with the ancient customs, then I allow you to make them and have them. I was not angered by seeing the story which the pictures told, but by the adoration which you were wrongly paying to the pictures." Win them over with such words; bring them back to peace with yourself. Then if anyone wants to make icons, by no means forbid him to make them, but by every means forbid everyone to adore them.

Letter to bishop Serenus of Marseilles (Gregory's *Letters*, Book 11, letter 13).

Patrick's Breastplate

I bind to myself today
the strong name of the Trinity,
through belief in the Three,
through confession of the One,
the Creator of all.

I bind to myself today
the power of Christ in His baptism,
the power of His cross and burial,
the power of His resurrection and ascension,
the power of His coming again at the day of judgment.

I bind to myself today
the strength of the cherubim's love,
the obedience of the angels,
the worship of the archangels,
the hope of resurrection unto life,
the prayers of the patriarchs,
the predictions of the prophets,
the preaching of the apostles,
the faith of the confessors,
the innocence of the holy virgins,
the deeds of the righteous.

I bind to myself today
the strength of heaven,
the light of the sun,
the radiance of the moon,
the splendour of fire,
the swiftness of lightning,
the rushing of the wind,
the depth of the sea,
the stability of the earth,
the firmness of rock.

I bind to myself today
the sovereignty of God to guide me,
the power of God to uphold me,

the wisdom of God to teach me,
the eye of God to watch over me,
the ear of God to listen to me,
the Word of God to speak for me,
the hand of God to guard me,
the path of God to lie before me,
the shield of God to shelter me,
and the host of God to save me
from the snares of demons,
from the temptations of vices,
from the lusts of human nature,
and from everyone who wishes me harm
whether far or near,
whether in solitude or multitude.
I summon all these powers around me today
against every cruel and merciless power
which may attack my body and my soul,
against the curses of false prophets,
against the dark laws of paganism,
against the false laws of heresy,
against the deceits of idolatry,
against the spells of witches, wizards and druids,
against all knowledge that corrupts the human body and soul.

O Christ, protect me today
against poison, against burning,
against drowning, against wounding,
so that I may receive a rich reward.
Christ be with me, Christ before me,
Christ behind me, Christ within me,
Christ beneath me, Christ above me,
Christ on my right, Christ on my left,
Christ when I rest,
Christ when I ride,
Christ when I cross the waters,
Christ in the heart of all who think of me,
Christ in the mouth of all who speak to me,
Christ in every eye that sees me,
Christ in every ear that hears me.

I bind to myself today
the strong name of the Trinity,
through belief in the Three,
through confession of the One,
the Creator of all.
Salvation is of the Lord, salvation is of the Lord,
salvation is of Christ:
may your salvation, Lord, be always with me.

A hymn by Patrick, the "apostle of Ireland"

Mother Hilda of Whitby

At Whitby, Hilda established the same pattern of life according to the monastic rule as in her previous monastery at Kaelcacaestir [possibly present-day Tadcaster, near York]. She taught the monks and nuns the virtues of righteousness, mercy, purity, and (especially) peace and love. In harmony with the example of the early Church, no-one at Whitby was rich or poor, for they held all things in common, and no-one considered anything as his own private property. So great was Hilda's wisdom that kings and princes as well as ordinary people came and asked her advice in their difficulties, and obeyed her. She required those under her spiritual direction in the monastery to study the Scriptures thoroughly and devote themselves to good works; many men did this so well that the Church deemed them worthy of ordination and of celebrating divine communion. Five men became bishops - Bosa, Aetla, Oftor, John and Wilfrid - all of them outstanding for virtue and holiness....

All who knew Christ's servant, abbess Hilda, used to call her "mother" because of her wonderful devotion to God and possession of grace. She was an example of holy living, and not just to members of her own community; for people who dwelt far away from the monastery heard about Hilda's service to God and goodness of soul, and the story inspired them to change their lives and enter into Christ's salvation....

After Hilda had ruled Whitby for many years, it pleased the Author of our salvation to test her holy soul by a lengthy illness, so that Christ could make her strength perfect through weakness, as He did with the apostle Paul (**2 Corinthians 12:9**). A burning fever attacked her, raging in her body for six years. But throughout this time, she never stopped giving praise to her Creator, or instructing her flock both in private and public. For her very example instructed them all to serve God faithfully during times of trouble and bodily weakness. In the seventh year of her sickness, the agony reached her inmost parts, and her last day came. At dawn she received holy communion to help her on her final journey. Then she gathered together all the female servants of Christ in the monastery, and urged them to maintain the peace of the Gospel with one another and with all. While Hilda was still speaking, she welcomed death with joy - or rather, in the words of the Lord, she passed from death to life (**John 5:24**).

The Venerable Bede, *Church History of the English People*, **Book 4, chapter 23**

Chapter 12.

THE EAST DIVIDED: FROM THE MONOPHYSITES TO MAXIMUS THE CONFESSOR

As we saw back in Chapter 10, the Council of Chalcedon in 451 rejected the extreme Alexandrian Christology of Eutyches, who said that the divine nature of Christ had swallowed up His human nature. The Council's Creed also broke fresh ground by teaching that when the Church spoke of the incarnation, the Greek word *physis* meant "nature", not "person": Christ was one single person (*hypostasis*) in two distinct natures (*physeis*). The Western Church, led by pope Leo the Great (440-61), together with much of the East, recognised the Council of Chalcedon as the fourth ecumenical Council, and its Creed as the third ecumenical Creed.

Unfortunately, Chalcedon failed dismally in its aim of bringing peace and unity to the Eastern Church or to the Byzantine Empire.[1] In fact, a further 230 years of lively controversy lay ahead! These years were, in many ways, a time of immensely rich theological thought and spiritual achievement in the East, as well as being full of political colour and drama. The same period also sparked off the most explosive tensions thus far in the relationship between the Eastern and Western Church, and (towards the end) witnessed the coming of a fearsome new enemy for Christianity from the deserts of Arabia - Muhammad and the Islamic faith.[2]

1. The aftermath of Chalcedon.

Almost unbelievably, the Council of Chalcedon, which the emperor

---

[1] From this point onwards, as we have seen, historians refer to the Eastern Roman Empire as the Byzantine Empire.
[2] For a detailed account of the rise of Islam, see Part Two, Chapter 1.

Marcian had summoned to unite the East, left it more divided than
ever - broken up into no fewer than four religious parties. These were
the *Monophysites*, the *Dyophysites*, the *Cyrillian Chalcedonians*,
and the *Origenists*. A four-way contest began, which to the modern
student looks rather like a confused bar-room brawl between four
drunkards, two of them giants and two of them dwarfs.

(i) The first of the giants was the *Monophysite* party.[3] They formed
the biggest group in Egypt and Syria, and they utterly rejected the
Creed of Chalcedon. While most of them were ready to condemn
Eutyches as an extremist, they nonetheless held firmly to the
Christology and theological language of their great hero, Cyril of
Alexandria.[4] Cyril had taught that in Christ there was "one incarnate
nature of the Logos" - *one* nature, not *two* as Chalcedon proclaimed.
It was from this insistence on the incarnate Lord's one nature that
the Monophysites derived their name: *monos* (Greek for "one") and
physis (Greek for "nature"), hence "Monophysite" - someone who
believes that Christ has only one nature, not two. The Monophysites
held that it was simply not possible to make the kind of distinction
between person and nature that Chalcedon had set forth. Two
natures required two persons; one person required one nature.

Within this general understanding, there was a sort of moderate wing
and extreme wing among the Monophysites. The moderate wing
understood the word *physis* more in the sense of "person" than
"nature". Their passionate belief that Christ had only one *physis*
sprang out of their concern for the Saviour's oneness of person; they
were guarding against the hated Nestorian heresy that Christ was
two persons, a human Son of Mary indwelt by a divine Son of God.[5]
To oppose this Nestorian splitting-up of Christ, these moderate
Monophysites spoke of one single "divine-human nature" in the
incarnate Lord. They did not mean to deny the reality of the human
element in Christ, as Eutyches had done. But they would not accept
Chalcedon's definition of *physis* as nature rather than person - such

---

3   Pronounced "Monna-fizz-ite". Their belief, Monophysitism, is pro-
    nounced "Monna-fizza-tizzum".
4   For Cyril of Alexandria, see Chapter 10, sections 3 and 4.
5   For Nestorianism, see Chapter 10, sections 3 and 5.

language betrayed the way that their beloved master, Cyril of
Alexandria, had written.

The most important Monophysite leader of this moderate type was
Severus of Antioch (465-538), a presbyter-monk who rose to the
dizzy heights of becoming patriarch of Antioch in 512, but was then
deposed and banished by the anti-Monophysite emperor Justin I in
518. Among all four of the battling parties, Severus was the
outstandingly brilliant theologian of his times. His right-hand man
was the Persian bishop **Philoxenus of Mabbug** (440-523), a
dazzling preacher and writer of commentaries on the **Gospels**.
Another leading moderate Monophysite was an Egyptian who had
probably the weirdest name in Church history, *Timothy the Cat* [6]
(died 477). Timothy became patriarch of Alexandria in 457; deposed
and banished in 459 by the anti-Monophysite emperor Leo I, he
continued to trumpet forth the Monophysite cause in exile through a
series of influential writings. Then there was "the flute of the Holy
Spirit", *Jacob of Sarug* (451-521), a composer of beautiful Syrian
Christian poetry. If these men had not been Monophysites, history
would beyond doubt have recorded them as illustrious fathers of the
early Church.

However, alongside Severus, Philoxenus, Timothy and Jacob, there
were other Monophysites who were much closer to the extreme
teaching of Eutyches. They held that in Christ, the human and divine
natures had blended into one new nature, in a way that even other
Monophysites felt undermined the reality of the Saviour's humanity.
The most famous spokesman of these extreme Monophysites was
Julian of Halicarnassus (died some time after 518). Julian taught
that the union of natures in Christ changed His human body into
something divinely immortal and incorruptible from the moment of its
conception in Mary's womb. Severus of Antioch, the moderate
Monophysite leader, wrote against this position, condemning it
violently. Christ's body, Severus argued against Julian, received the
grace of immortality as part of His reward from the Father at the
resurrection; but during His earthly life as a baby, a boy and a man,
the Lord's human flesh was identical with ours in its mortal nature,
its openness to pain and death.

---

6   Timothy was nicknamed "the Cat" (or "the Weasel") by his enemies
    because of his small stature.

Whatever their exact shade of opinion, all Monophysites were united in rejecting Chalcedon as Nestorian for its affirmation of two natures in Christ.[7] They also rallied together around a warcry invented by one of their bishops, *Peter the Fuller* (died 488) of Antioch. One of the most famous prayers of the Eastern liturgy is the *trisagion* (Greek for "thrice holy"), which addresses God thus: "Holy God, Holy and Mighty, Holy and Immortal, have mercy on us!" Peter the Fuller inserted the words, "Who was crucified for us", so that the *trisagion* now said: "Holy God, Holy and Mighty, Holy and Immortal, *Who was crucified for us*, have mercy on us!" The *trisagion* was supposed to be a prayer to the entire Trinity; but Peter's new version changed it into a prayer to Christ alone. Peter's aim was to make it clear that the One Who died on the cross was God Himself - a divine person, not (as the Nestorians said) a human person. As Cyril of Alexandria had put it, "One of the Holy Trinity suffered in the flesh." However, if there is one thing guaranteed to provoke Christians to rage, it is tampering with their traditional forms of worship, and Peter the Fuller's new Monophysite version of the *trisagion* would almost cost an emperor his throne (see next section).

(ii) The first of the dwarfs was the *Dyophysite* party.[8] Despite their small size, they exercised a huge influence in the early years after the Council of Chalcedon, because they stood out as Chalcedon's foremost champions and the greatest opponents of the Monophysites. The Dyophysites belonged to the old Antiochene school of Ephrem the Syrian, Diodore of Tarsus, Theodore of

---

7   The more hard-line Monophysites even criticised Cyril of Alexandria himself for having accepted the Formula of Union of 433 (see Chapter 10, section 4), which spoke of Christ having "two natures". For instance, the leading Monophysite Timothy the Cat said of Cyril: "This man, having excellently expressed a wise proclamation of orthodoxy, became unreliable and must be condemned for teaching an opposite doctrine. For after first proposing that we should speak of one incarnate nature of the Logos, he destroyed the doctrine he had formulated and was caught professing two natures in Christ."

8   Pronounced "dy-a-fizz-ite". They are sometimes called the "strict" Dyophysites because of their extreme insistence on the two natures of the Saviour.

Mopsuestia, Ibas of Edessa, and Nestorius;[9] they believed whole-heartedly in the two distinct and complete natures of Christ, human and divine. This is why theologians call them Dyophysites, from the Greek *duo*, "two", and *physis* - "two natures". They were led by Nestorius's old friend, the renowned Syrian theologian Theodoret of Cyrrhus[10] (393-458), and by patriarch Gennadius of Constantinople (458-71).

The Christology of the Dyophysites contained all the strengths and weaknesses that had always marked Antiochene thinking. Very clear on the distinct reality of Christ's deity and humanity, they were still somewhat in a fog about the oneness of the Saviour's person and its relationship to His two natures. This lack of clarity came out most disturbingly (as far as the Monophysites were concerned) when the Dyophysites rejected Cyril of Alexandria's statement that "One of the Holy Trinity suffered in the flesh." The Dyophysites insisted that it was the human nature of Jesus of Nazareth, not the divine person of the Logos, that suffered on the cross. The Monophysite response was swift and crushing: how can Christ's human *nature* suffer, but His divine *person* not be involved in the suffering? Surely we cannot separate nature and person in this way. It is a person who acts, feels, and experiences, in and through his nature. So by teaching that it was only Jesus's humanity that suffered on the cross, the Dyophysites seemed to be saying that Jesus was a human person - the dreaded Nestorian heresy, condemned by the Council of Ephesus in 431. The Christology of the Dyophysites, more than anything else, convinced the Monophysites that the Creed of Chalcedon was indeed a heretical Nestorian confession of faith.

(iii) The second of the giants was the *Cyrillian Chalcedonian* party. This was the largest group in the Eastern Church, apart from Egypt and Syria. It consisted of those who accepted the basic Christology of Cyril of Alexandria, as the Monophysites did, but who understood *physis* in the sense of nature rather than person, so that Christ possessed two distinct natures within His single person, as Chalcedon had proclaimed. This, they thought, was what Cyril

---

9   For these Antiochene thinkers, and the development of Nestorianism, see Chapter 10, sections 1, 3 and 5.

10 For Theodoret of Cyrrhus, see Chapter 10, sections 1 and 4.

himself had really meant, even if he had been less than perfectly clear about it. So for this party, there was no real contradiction between Cyril and Chalcedon - hence the name modern historians have given them, the "Cyrillian Chalcedonians". Their quarrel with the Monophysites was twofold: (a) Theologically, did Christ's one person require His two natures to blend into a single divine-human nature? Monophysites said yes; Cyrillian Chalcedonians said no. (b) At the more turbulent level of Church politics and personalities, had Chalcedon betrayed the beloved Cyril of Alexandria? Monophysites said yes; Cyrillian Chalcedonians said no.

Some great Church leaders stepped forth from the Cyrillian Chalcedonian camp. *John Maxentius* (6th Century), a Scythian monk, proved that most followers of Chalcedon were not Nestorians by championing Cyril of Alexandria's formula, "One of the holy Trinity suffered in the flesh"; he persuaded both Rome and Constantinople to accept the formula. *Theodore of Raithu* (6th Century), presbyter-monk of a monastery in the Sinai peninsula, fought hard-hitting literary duels with both the moderate Monophysite Severus of Antioch and the extreme Julian of Halicarnassus; Theodore argued that the Christologies of Chalcedon and of Cyril of Alexandria were essentially the same. But by far the mightiest theologian of the Cyrillian Chalcedonians was *Leontius of Jerusalem* (active 530's). We know next to nothing about Leontius as a man, but his *Against Nestorius* was absolutely crucial in putting his party's Christology on a firm, clear and independent footing, in contrast to all the other options, whether Monophysite, Nestorian or Origenist.

(iv) The second of the dwarfs was the *Origenist* party. This was a small group of monks who based their understanding of Christ on the writings of Evagrius Ponticus - the great 4th Century disciple of Origen, who had summed up the spirituality of the early desert fathers of Egypt.[11] The Origenists differed from the other parties in holding Origen's view that Jesus of Nazareth was a human soul created by God from all eternity, who had never fallen into sin and

---

11 For Evagrius Ponticus, see Chapter 7, section 3, under the heading **Church life: The Monastic movement**; for Origen, see Chapter 5, section 1.

was united in closest union with the Logos. This led them into the highly unorthodox notion that it was not the Logos Himself, but the eternal human soul of Jesus which became flesh; some of them said that any other human soul that was united to the Logos could become a Christ just like Jesus. However, their greatest theologian was **Leontius of Byzantium** (active 520-40), whose Origenism was of a moderate variety; and Leontius contributed very richly to the development of Chalcedonian Christology through his remarkably creative thinking and writing, as we shall see in a moment. (This period is confusing enough without two of its greatest thinkers both being called Leontius, but life is rarely simple. Leontius of Byzantium was an Origenist; Leontius of Jerusalem was a Cyrillian Chalcedonian.)

The chaotic clash between these two giants and two dwarfs - Monophysites, Cyrillian Chalcedonians, Dyophysites and Origenists - tore the Eastern Church apart, with deep and lasting effects which are still with us today.

2. From Chalcedon to Justinian the Great.

After the Council of Chalcedon had deposed Eutyches's friend Dioscorus from the patriarchate of Alexandria in 451, it appointed the Chalcedonian Proterius in his place. However, the Monophysite people of Alexandria rioted in protest, and it took Byzantine troops to force them to accept Proterius. When the emperor Marcian (who had summoned the Council of Chalcedon) died in 457, the good Christians of Alexandria murdered Proterius at the holy table of his own church, and installed the Monophysite Timothy the Cat in his place. The new Byzantine emperor **Leo I** (457-74) exiled Timothy in 459. But events had made it painfully obvious that the Egyptians were fiercely Monophysite, and that imperial soldiers alone could compel them to submit to Chalcedon. A similar hostility to Chalcedon boiled over in Syria, where the largely Monophysite population of Antioch rebelled in 469 against their Chalcedonian patriarch Martyrius. They replaced him with the Monophysite Peter the Fuller - the one who inserted the words "Who was crucified for us" into the *trisagion* (see previous section). But emperor Leo banished Peter in 471.

Ominously, the Monophysite theological opposition to Byzantium was becoming blended with Egyptian and Syrian nationalism. Greece and Asia Minor, where loyalty to Chalcedon reigned, were Greek by race and language; Monophysite Egypt and Syria, however, were Semitic by race, with Coptic as the national language in Egypt, and Syriac in Syria. Egyptians and Syrians soon started referring scornfully to the Byzantine Church and its bishops as "Melkite" (imperial) - the emperor's Church, the emperor's bishops. All too clearly, the doctrinal divisions in the Eastern Church were rapidly ripping the Empire itself to pieces: Egypt and Syria were virtually rebel provinces kept loyal to Byzantium by the army alone.

The next emperor, *Zeno* (474-91), decided to try out a policy of compromise with the Monophysites. Backed by the patriarch of Constantinople, *Acacius* (471-89), Zeno offered the Monophysites a sort of spiritual peace-treaty in 482 called the *Henotikon* ("Union"), which contained the following terms:

(i) It made the decisions of the first three ecumenical Councils of Nicaea, Constantinople and Ephesus the only test of orthodoxy.

(ii) It rejected any doctrine contrary to the ones sanctioned by these Councils, "whether taught at Chalcedon or elsewhere".

(iii) It condemned Nestorius and Eutyches.

Zeno intended the *Henotikon* to be an olive branch, but it was more like a two-edged sword which cut very differently Eastward and Westward. In the East, it drew Monophysite Egypt and Syria back to a more willing acceptance of political rule from Byzantium, although it did nothing to stop the noisy theological debate. But the *Henotikon* provoked a complete schism between the Eastern and Western branches of the Church. Rome was committed to Chalcedon with all the passion of a lover. This was for serious theological reasons, but also because pope Leo the Great (440-61) and his statement of Roman Christology, *Leo's Tome*, had been crucial ingredients in the making of Chalcedon. So when Zeno's *Henotikon* dismissed Chalcedon as a test of orthodoxy, Rome could only see this as an act of apostasy: Byzantium was abandoning the truth, betraying the achievements of pope Leo, and rejecting the supreme apostolic authority of the papacy. As a result, pope *Felix II* (483-92) excommunicated both emperor Zeno and patriarch Acacius in 484. This meant that Rome and Constantinople were now officially out of communion with each other; the split lasted for 35 years (484-519), and is known as the "Acacian schism".

Rome's hostility pushed Byzantium still further into the arms of the Monophysites, especially under emperor *Anastasius* (491-518). The leading moderate Monophysite, Severus of Antioch, became Anastasius's chief advisor on Church affairs from 508. Severus persuaded Anastasius to go even further than Zeno's *Henotikon*, and explicitly to condemn the Creed of Chalcedon and *Leo's Tome*. Anastasius exiled the Chalcedonian patriarch of Antioch in 512, appointing Severus in his place. Peter the Fuller's Monophysite version of the *trisagion* rang out in Constantinople's chief church, the Church of the Holy Wisdom. It seemed as if Severus and the Monophysites were successfully converting the Eastern Church to their one-nature Christology. But appearances were a dreamlike deception; two very solid and massive stumbling-blocks barred the Monophysites' path.

First, Rome remained completely hostile to the Monophysites. It was doubtful that any lasting settlement could be made in the East without Rome's approval. Second, in the Greek-speaking parts of the East (Greece itself, Asia Minor, Palestine), the Monophysites had many powerful enemies, notably John Maxentius, and they made common cause with Rome against emperor Anastasius and patriarch Severus. The population of Constantinople was also fiercely Chalcedonian. When in 512 the Monophysite version of the *trisagion* was chanted in the Church of the Holy Wisdom, Chalcedonian worshippers tried to drown it out by chanting the orthodox *trisagion*; the service turned into a shouting match, tempers flared, fists flew. By the time the imperial soldiers had restored order, the cathedral was red with the blood of the dead and the injured. Emperor Anastasius nearly lost his throne in orthodox riots over the next few days, and saved himself only by promising to withdraw the hated Monophysite *trisagion* from public worship.

When Anastasius died in 518, his successor was *Justin I* (518-27). Justin was a blunt, illiterate, Latin-speaking, Western-thinking soldier from Thrace, popular with the army, and guided by a brilliant 36 year old nephew named Justinian. The new emperor was committed to Chalcedon and cooperation with the papacy. He deposed and banished Severus of Antioch, made peace with Rome through the ambassadors of pope Hormisdas (514-23), and cancelled the **Henotikon**. Thus ended the Acacian schism. The Creed of Chalcedon once more reigned supreme in the Eastern Church, Constantinople and Rome were once more in communion - and Monophysite Egypt and Syria were once more rebel provinces, yoked to Byzantium by imperial troops alone.

Justin was succeeded by his more famous nephew, **Justinian the Great** (born 482; reigned 527-65). Justinian, the most celebrated of all the Byzantine emperors, was a devout man who often fasted, would set aside entire nights for prayer, and enjoyed nothing better than reading and discussing theology. He also left behind him (in the memoirs of his enemies) a reputation for being hot-tempered, vain, cruel and jealous. Whatever his moral defects, Justinian was certainly one of the most dedicated and hard-working rulers in human history. Inspired by an appetite for governing which seemed boundless, his unceasing activities - planning, decreeing, supervising - earned him the nickname "Justinian the Sleepless". He began to relax his grip on government only in his old age, when (he said) he had become "cold to the things of this world, and burned with a love for the future life alone".

Yet "Justinian the Sleepless" did not rule by himself. For the first half of his reign, his clever, stunningly beautiful and strong-willed wife, the one-time actress **Theodora** (508-48), was Justinian's equal and partner in all the affairs of Empire. Indeed, in many ways, Theodora ruled over Justinian, for the emperor trusted his wife's political judgment completely. It was Theodora's courage that saved Justinian's throne during a savage riot which broke out in Constantinople in 532, leaving most of the city wrecked and in flames.[12] The rioters combined treason with violence, crowned

---

12 The rioters were sports fans. The population of Constantinople had a fierce passion for chariot races, and were divided into two hostile factions, the Blues and the Greens. Justinian managed to enrage and unite both groups against himself, thus provoking the riot, by condemning to death seven Blue and Green ringleaders of a bloody clash between the two factions.

someone else emperor in Constantinople's great sports arena, the hippodrome, and shrieked their defiance of Justinian. After five days of this terrifying anarchy, Justinian and all his male advisors lost their nerve and were preparing to flee. Only Theodora stood firm:

> "Everyone born into the light of day must die sooner or later; and how could an emperor ever let himself become someone who runs away from danger? If you, my lord, want to save your own skin, you will not find it hard. We are wealthy, there is the sea, and there are our ships too. But think first: when you reach safety, will you not regret that you chose flight rather than death? As for me, I stand by the old saying: the best clothes in which to die are the robes of monarchy."

Theodora's bold words put fresh heart into Justinian and his men. Imperial soldiers surrounded the hippodrome, and put all the rioters to the sword - some 30,000 died. The excitable Byzantine mob knew from then onward that it had an emperor whose authority it dared not defy.

Theodora, then, was Justinian's political right-hand woman. Her religious judgment was more debatable; Theodora was secretly a Monophysite, and did everything possible to advance the cause of the Monophysites without openly joining their party.

Aside from his role in the Monophysite controversy, Justinian's outstanding achievements as emperor were:

(i) He reconquered much of the West from its Germanic invaders, although hardly any of his conquests survived Justinian's own death. Still, through his two eminent and mighty generals, Belisarius (505-65) and Narses (480-574), Justinian established Byzantium's dominion over half the old Western Empire, reclaiming North-West Africa from the Vandals, Italy from the Ostrogoths, and southern Spain from the Visigoths.[13] For the last time, the Roman Empire politically united East with West again.

---

13   See previous Chapter, section 1, for the Germanic conquest of the West.

(ii) He reformed the entire system of law which Byzantium had inherited from Rome. The most important aspect of this legal reform was the "Justinian Code", first issued in 529 and in a revised form in 534, which gathered together the Empire's laws into a single body, in a new order, with all contradictions removed. It also gave a Christian foundation to imperial law; the Code began with a confession of faith, and showed a Christian influence in its enactments, *e.g.* its treatment of slavery, recognising slaves as human beings created in God's image, not mere pieces of property. Along with other legal collections authorised by Justinian, the Code formed the great *Corpus Juris Civilis* ("Body of Civil Law"), the fundamental body of Roman law; this was the basis of all Byzantine law for the next thousand years, and from the 12th Century it was increasingly important in Western civil law too. The Justinian Code also deeply influenced the growth of "canon law" (Church law) in the West.

(iii) He rebuilt the Church of the Holy Wisdom (in Greek, the *Hagia Sophia*), Constantinople's main church, which the riot of 532 had destroyed. Justinian transformed it into probably the most splendid church ever constructed in Christian history. It took nearly six years to build, was finished in 537, and is one of the main tourist attractions of modern Istanbul (the Turkish government turned Hagia Sophia into a museum in 1934). Two amazing qualities mark the inside of Hagia Sophia: it seems to defy the laws of gravity, and it shines with an unearthly radiance. The great Byzantine historian, Procopius of Caesarea (died 565), described it thus: "The huge dome does not appear to rest on solid stone, but seems to hang from heaven, covering the space with its golden sphere. One might say that the sun does not light up the interior from outside, but that the church's radiance comes into being without the sun, for such an abundance of light bathes this shrine." The radiance is in fact caused by the sunlight shining through the windows and striking the highly reflective gold and polished marble of Hagia Sophia's interior. 1,500 years after he built it, Hagia Sophia stands this day in all its majesty to remind us of Justinian.

Justinian's religious policy completed the Christianising of the Empire. He made Arianism, Manichaeism and other heresies illegal. He outlawed paganism, closing down the last great centre of pagan learning, the Platonist academy in Athens. He passed a law compelling all non-Christians to accept baptism, with the exception of the Jews; but Justinian placed even Jewish religious and civil rights under new restrictions - he commanded them to read the Old Testament in the Church's Greek Septuagint version, rather than the original Hebrew, and excluded Jews from all government positions.

This left the festering wound of the Chalcedonian-Monophysite division for Justinian to deal with. Urged on by his Monophysite empress Theodora, he organised a conference of Chalcedonian and moderate Monophysite bishops. From this meeting emerged Justinian's edict of 533, in which he declared that the person of Christ was the divine Logos, and that this divine person had suffered on the cross in the human nature which He had taken. The formula seemed to satisfy the moderate Monophysites; their leader, Severus of Antioch, was welcomed by Justinian in Constantinople, and in 535 Theodora placed friends of Severus in the patriarchates of Constantinople and Alexandria. Rome, however, was not at all satisfied. Pope *Agapetus I* (535-36), who was on an official visit to Constantinople in 536, behaved like some Old Testament prophet. He denounced the Monophysites who had come to power in Justinian's court through Theodora's influence, and boldly refused to commune with Anthimus, Theodora's new Monophysite patriarch of Constantinople. Indeed, pope Agapetus persuaded Justinian to get rid of Anthimus, and personally ordained a Chalcedonian, Mennas (536-52), in his place. Faced with this spectacular display of papal daring and zeal on behalf of Chalcedon, Justinian hastily dropped the moderate Monophysites. The pope's opinion was more important even than Theodora's, especially when the pope was actually present in Constantinople and in such a militantly orthodox mood.

Justinian's next move was to take out the small Origenist party from the dispute. A violent quarrel had broken out between them and Chalcedonian monks in Palestine. The head of the great Saint Sabbas monastery in the Jordan valley, *Sabbas* himself (439-532) - "Sabbas the Sanctified" - was a champion of Chalcedon against both Monophysites and Origenists, and had appealed personally to Justinian to settle the dispute. Justinian used the occasion to launch a general attack on Origenism. This came to a head in 543, when Justinian summoned a local council in Constantinople which condemned a number of Origenist doctrines - the existence of human souls from all eternity, the purely spiritual nature of the resurrection body, the final salvation of all sinners, and the Origenist view of the incarnation.[14] Ten years later the second ecumenical Council of Constantinople (see below) probably confirmed this rejection of Origenism, and also put the name of Origen himself on the list of officially condemned heretics, alongside Arius, Eunomius, Macedonius, Apollinarius, Nestorius and Eutyches. It was a tragic fate indeed for Origen, whose writings (despite their many unorthodox ideas) had once been accepted as a fountain of deepest wisdom in the Eastern Church.[15]

Having sacrificed the Origenists, Justinian's next victims were the Dyophysites. The last representatives of the old Antiochene school which had produced Nestorius, their presence among Chalcedon's defenders was the biggest obstacle to a settlement between the Monophysites and the Cyrillian Chalcedonians. To crush the Dyophysites, Justinian issued an edict in 544 which condemned all the writings of Theodore of Mopsuestia, and those writings of Theodoret of Cyrrhus and Ibas of Edessa which had been aimed against Cyril of Alexandria. (Theodore, Theodoret and Ibas were three leading Antiochenes and strict Dyophysites of the 4th and 5th Centuries[16]). Justinian's edict was known as the *Three Chapters*. The Eastern Church accepted the edict, but the West rose up in rebellion; the ambassadors of pope *Vigilius* (537-55) in Constantinople indignantly refused to sign the edict, and most of the bishops of Italy, France and North-West Africa rejected it. Many Western bishops suspected that the *Three Chapters* was Monophysite in its tendencies, and they felt especially outraged by its condemnation of the anti-Cyrillian writings of Theodoret and Ibas. The Council of Chalcedon, almost idolised in the West because of Leo the Great's contribution, had restored these renowned Antiochenes to office, after the heretical "Robber Synod" of 449 had deposed them. The censure of some of Theodoret's and Ibas's writings now, by the

---

14 For the Origenist doctrine of the incarnation, see section 1.
15 See Chapter 5, section 1 for Origen's influence in the 3rd and 4th Centuries. Some historians think the condemnation of Origen was added later to the documents of the Second Council of Constantinople.
16 For Theodore of Mopsuestia, Theodoret of Cyrrhus and Ibas of Edessa, see Chapter 10, sections 1, 3 and 4.

Three Chapters, seemed to many Westerners to defile the holy name of Chalcedon.

The East-West split over the *Three Chapters* resulted in some of the most amazing and even comical scenes in the history of the papacy. Justinian virtually kidnapped the inconstant and volatile pope Vigilius, brought him to Constantinople, and bullied him into putting out an official statement in 548 approving of the *Three Chapters*. If Justinian thought this would intimidate the Western Church into submission, he was wildly mistaken; instead, a council of North-West African bishops scornfully excommunicated the pope himself! Vigilius, who should probably be remembered as the pope who changed his mind most often, withdrew his assent to the *Three Chapters*, and took refuge from Justinian's wrath in Constantinople's Church of Saint Peter and Saint Paul. When Justinian's soldiers tried to drag him out, Vigilius (a huge man) clung so stubbornly to the base of the vast and beautiful holy table that the whole thing came crashing down, almost landing on his skull. At this point, a compassionate congregation forced the soldiers to spare the humiliated pope.

To resolve the issues raised by the Monophysite controversy in general and the *Three Chapters* affair in particular, Justinian eventually summoned on his own authority an ecumenical Council, the Second Council of Constantinople, in 553. Despite pressure from Justinian, pope Vigilius refused to preside over the Council; 165 bishops attended, only 12 of whom were Western.

The Council made a number of far-reaching decisions in the area of Christology. It affirmed that the single person of the incarnate Lord was none other than the divine Logos, a point not made explicit by the Creed of Chalcedon. This needed to be cleared up. The whole Christological debate had become even more confused by the mind-boggling suggestion, made by some Monophysites, that the one person of Christ was a fusion of a divine and a human person into a single new divine-human person. The Council set its face against this not very helpful idea in favour of the far simpler notion that the single person of Christ was the second person of the Trinity, God the Son, Who took a human nature upon Himself. The moderate Origenist theologian, Leontius of Byzantium, had portrayed this view most effectively. He argued that the Saviour's human nature never existed as a human person, but became personal by existing "in" the divine person of the Son. In other words, there never was a moment when Jesus's human nature existed independently of the divine Son; the person of the Son incarnated Himself *as* a human soul and body, which were always personally His, and had no reality apart from Him.[17] The Council's adoption of these views meant that it had expressed the oneness of Christ in a far more successful way than the Dyophysites had ever managed.

The Council went on to give its approval to Cyril of Alexandria's statement, so hateful to the Dyophysites, that "One of the Holy Trinity suffered in the flesh". This confession of faith in the deity of the suffering person of Christ was, from now on, chanted in every Eastern service in the hymn "The only-begotten Son of God". Furthermore, the Council confirmed Justinian's *Three Chapters* edict of 544 - another grave blow to the Dyophysites. And finally, turning this time to the Monophysites, the Council taught that in Cyril of Alexandria's most famous utterance, "one incarnate nature (*physis*) of God the Logos", the word *physis* was to be understood as meaning person, not nature. This was to vindicate Cyril from any suspicion of being a Monophysite in his theology, even though he had used Monophysite-sounding language.

Apart from these Christological decisions, the Council also sanctioned the title *aeiparthenos* ("ever-virgin") for Mary. The view had by now prevailed throughout the Church that Mary had given birth to no other children after Christ; her womb was a temple sanctified by God and fit for none but Him to dwell in. Therefore

---

17 Leontius's view is called *enhypostasia* (Greek for "in-personal"). The human nature of Jesus was personal, not in itself, but in the person of the Logos. As we might put it today, the person we meet in the man Jesus of Nazareth is the divine person of God the Son. Jesus's human body, mind and feelings are the human body, mind and feelings of the Logos Himself, and not of some independent human person in whom the Logos merely dwelt. This doctrine of *enhypostasia*, that Christ's human nature was in-personal, was Leontius's attempt to avoid the less satisfactory view known as *anhypostasia*, which said that Christ's human nature was simply non-personal.

Mary had been a virgin throughout her life - she and Joseph never had sexual intercourse. This doctrine is known as the "perpetual virginity" of Mary. Eastern Bible commentators interpreted the "brothers" of Jesus, mentioned in the **Gospels** (*e.g.* **Matthew 12:46-47**), as the children of Joseph by a previous marriage; the West interpreted them as Jesus's cousins.[18]

The Second Council of Constantinople (the fifth of the ecumenical Councils) witnessed the complete and enduring victory of the Cyrillian Chalcedonians over the Dyophysites. The Byzantine Church was now clearly committed to the Creed of Chalcedon as interpreted in the light of Cyril of Alexandria's Christology. It had swept aside the Origenists and Dyophysites. The way seemed more open than it had ever been for Justinian to bring about reconciliation between Chalcedonians and Monophysites, and reunify the Eastern Church.

Nothing of the kind happened, for two reasons:

First, the West failed to offer whole-hearted support to the Council. Pope Vigilius boldly refused to give his consent, but changed his mind again after Justinian banished him to a small island for six months. Large sections of the Western Church disowned their fickle-minded pope's action, as they had done in 548 when he approved the *Three Chapters*. In particular, the great Italian archbishops and churches of Milan and Aquileia angrily broke off communion with Rome (the schism lasted for years). Even so, the West did come to recognise the Second Council of Constantinople as the fifth ecumenical Council, mostly through the sweeping use of papal authority by pope Pelagius I (556-61), chosen by Justinian as Vigilius's successor.

Second, and far more serious, the Monophysites themselves were, by now, losing all interest in spiritual reunion with Byzantium. At the beginning of Justinian's reign, there were Monophysites in Syria and Asia Minor who would not accept the ministry of Chalcedonian

---

18 This is not a peculiarly "Catholic" or "Orthodox" view. Many Protestants, *e.g.* the great Reformers Martin Luther, Ulrich Zwingli and Heinrich Bullinger, have believed in Mary's perpetual virginity. See Part Three for the Reformers.

clergy; the great Monophysite leader, Severus of Antioch, supplied them with Monophysite presbyters and bishops of their own. The man who mostly carried out the ordination of Monophysite clergy throughout Syria and the southern coastlands of Asia Minor was a Syrian Monophysite monk named *Jacob Baradaeus* (died 578). Jacob was a sort of Monophysite "secret agent", who travelled throughout the Middle East, disguised as a beggar ("Baradaeus" means "dressed in rags") to escape being arrested by Byzantine troops. Almost single-handed, he established a separate Syrian Monophysite Church, with its own patriarch based in Antioch, and its own bishops, presbyters, monasteries and liturgy.[19] The Syrian Monophysites took their name from Jacob and were called "Jacobites". Their use of their own native Syriac tongue as the language of worship and theology widened the gulf separating the Jacobites from the Greek-speaking Church of Byzantium. Another Jacob, the monk *Jacob of Edessa* (640-708), perfected the independence of the Jacobite Church. Jacob was a gifted preacher, poet, theologian, Church historian, writer of liturgies, Bible commentator well-versed in both Hebrew and Greek - the list goes on. The light of Jacob of Edessa's genius lit up the whole Jacobite Church with a lasting splendour; his mighty labours left Jacobites strong and self-confident, devoutly believing that they (rather than the Chalcedonian West or East) were the true successors of the Catholic Church prior to Chalcedon.

This growth of an independent Syrian Monophysite Church sounded the death-knell for any realistic prospect of reunion between the Syrian Monophysites and the Eastern Church.[20] They have remained separate to the present day. Until the First World War of 1914-18, the Jacobites mostly lived to the north of the Tigris and Euphrates rivers (modern Turkey), with smaller communities in Kurdistan and East India. During the First World War, the Turkish Jacobites were forced by the hostility of the Muslim Turks to flee and re-settle in modern Syria and Lebanon.

---

19 Since 1239, the Jacobite patriarchs of Antioch have always taken the name "Ignatius".

20 I will refer to the Eastern Chalcedonians simply as the "Eastern Church" before the great East-West schism of 1054; thereafter I will call them the "Eastern Orthodox Church". For the East-West schism see Part Two, Chapter 3, section 8.

A twin movement for Monophysite spiritual independence developed in Egypt. From about 575, a separate Monophysite patriarch of Alexandria led the majority against the Chalcedonian patriarch in an independent Monophysite Church of Egypt. It was known as the "Coptic Orthodox Church". Like the Syrian Jacobites, the Coptic Orthodox had their own clergy, monasteries and liturgy; they too abandoned the Greek language, and used their native Coptic in worship and theology. So again, this growth of an autonomous Egyptian Monophysite Church spelt the end of any realistic outlook for reunion between Egyptian Monophysites and Byzantine Chalcedonians. The Coptic Orthodox Church remains the prevailing form of Christianity in Egypt today.

Monophysite missionaries from Syria and Egypt ensured that the Ethiopian Church also evolved along Monophysite lines. Aedesius and Frumentius, two Christian brothers from Tyre, who were shipwrecked on the coast of the Red Sea in the early 4th Century, had planted Christianity in Ethiopia (or the kingdom of Axum, as it was then called). Taken captive by the king of Axum, the two brothers won his favour and converted the royal family to the Christian faith. The great Athanasius of Alexandria himself ordained Frumentius as the first Ethiopian bishop in 340.[21] These deep spiritual links with Alexandria, plus the geographical nearness of Ethiopia to Egypt, explain why the Ethiopian Orthodox Church became Monophysite.

The Armenian Orthodox Church, which at that time was already nationally based and independent of Byzantium, also tended towards a Monophysite Christology.[22] No Armenian delegates were present at the Council of Chalcedon, and in about the year 500 the Armenian Church officially rejected the Creed of Chalcedon.

By the time of Justinian's death in 565, then, and despite the Second Council of Constantinople, the process was almost complete by which independent, national, Monophysite Churches were born in Syria, Egypt, Ethiopia and Armenia, enjoying no ecclesiastical

---

[21] For Athanasius, see Chapter 8, sections 2 and 3.
[22] For the conversion of Armenia, see Chapter 6, section 2.

fellowship with Byzantium, and developing apart from the central tradition of Eastern and Western Christianity.

3. Pseudo-Dionysius and the "negative way".

The theology and spiritual life of Greek-speaking Byzantine Christianity developed very differently from the Western Latin tradition. One of the main differences was a particular Eastern way of approaching the whole realm of doctrine and spirituality. We can see this special approach most clearly in a very important body of writings which had a deep influence on the Eastern Church in the days of Byzantium, and have continued to influence Eastern Orthodox thinking right up to the present day. Strangely, no-one knows who the real author of these writings was. He claimed to be *Dionysius the Areopagite*, one of the apostle Paul's converts in Athens (see **Acts 17:34**); in reality, he was probably a Syrian monk who lived during the reign of Justinian. However, for over a thousand years the Church accepted his writings as the genuine work of Dionysius, and therefore as coming from the age of the apostles. This gave them great authority. Christian scholars did not question the apostolic origin of the Dionysian writings until the 15th Century, and disproved it only in the 19th. Today, historians refer to the author as *Pseudo*-Dionysius (from the Greek for "false").

Four main writings of Pseudo-Dionysius have come down to us: *The Divine Names, Mystical Theology, The Celestial Hierarchy* and *The Ecclesiastical Hierarchy.* In these works, Pseudo-Dionysius presented an understanding of the Christian faith which drew heavily on the language and ideas of Neoplatonism.[23] This comes across most obviously in his *Mystical Theology*, a masterpiece of "mysticism". People often wonder what mysticism is; one way of finding out is to read this short book. Here, Pseudo-Dionysius taught that God is utterly above and beyond anything the human mind can understand. We cannot say what God *is*; we can only say what He is *not*. We cannot even say that God "exists", for He is beyond what our limited minds understand by existence. In order to approach God, Pseudo-Dionysius held that the soul must pass through a threefold

---

[23] See Chapter 6, section 2, for Neoplatonism.

discipline of **purification, illumination** and **union**. (This parallels
the three stages by which Neoplatonist philosophers had taught that
the soul ascends to "the One"). We have to purify our understanding
of God from everything our senses and our logical reason suggest to
us. This will lead to spiritual illumination by what Pseudo-Dionysius
called "the ray of divine darkness". In this divine darkness, the soul
learns to give up all activity of its own, and surrenders to God, Who
then brings the soul into union with Himself by **His** activity. Pseudo-
Dionysius stressed the importance of love in this union: through love
for God, the soul knows God's love for itself, and is united with Him
in love. This union brings about the soul's **deification** - a sharing in
God's glory and immortality (a favourite Eastern theme).

Pseudo-Dionysius's approach to theology and spirituality is known
as the **apophatic**[24] or "negative" way, because of its emphasis on
the mysterious and incomprehensible nature of God, Who can be
known only by the soul that confesses its inability to know Him. This
both reflected and strengthened the East's distrust of relying too
much on human reason in understanding God, emphasising instead
prayer and corporate worship as channels for the mystery of divine
knowledge. We find this approach in the Eastern fathers before
Pseudo-Dionysius, *e.g.* in Athanasius and the Cappadocians.[25] But
Pseudo-Dionysius gave a uniquely clear and forceful expression to
this way of "doing" theology and spirituality. At first, however, the
East looked with some suspicion on Pseudo-Dionysius, because
Monophysites like Severus of Antioch appealed to his writings to
support their views. But Maximus the Confessor[26] and John of
Damascus[27] vindicated Pseudo-Dionysius's orthodoxy and drew his
theology into the mainstream of Eastern Christian thought.

Pseudo-Dionysius also had a great impact on Western theology. In
fact, he was the only Eastern Christian thinker whose writings were
widely known and loved in the West (the great Irish theologian, John
Scotus Erigena, translated them into Latin in the 9th Century).[28]
Pseudo-Dionysius's apophatic or negative way of doing theology

---

24 Pronounced "appo-fat-ik". It comes from the Greek word for "denial".
25 For the Cappadocians, see Chapter 8, section 3.
26 See next section for Maximus the Confessor.
27 For John of Damascus, see Part Two, Chapter 1, section 4.
28 For Erigena, see Part Two, Chapter 2, section 4.

had considerable influence on some Western Latin Christians, especially mystics, but it was more his doctrine of angels and of the Church that really made an impression on the West. Pseudo-Dionysius taught that the whole of creation mirrored the Trinity by being organised into *triads* or groups of three. The angels, he said, were organised into three groups of three; in descending order of importance, these were: (i) seraphim, cherubim and thrones; (ii) dominations, virtues and powers; (iii) principalities, archangels and angels. The organisation of the Church was also triadic, *e.g.* the threefold clerical order of bishop, presbyter and deacon; the three non-clerical ranks of monk, layman and catechumen; the three sacraments of baptism, eucharist and confirmation;[29] and so on. Pseudo-Dionysius applied this "Trinitarian" principle very widely. It became the normal way of understanding angels and the Church in both East and West.

4. The Monothelete controversy and Maximus the Confessor.

The Byzantine Empire was to make one last attempt to heal the (by now) gaping rift between Chalcedonians and Monophysites. After Justinian the Great's death in 565, the emperors and patriarchs of Constantinople mostly persecuted the Monophysites. Policy changed, however, under emperor **Heraclius** (610-641), best known for his amazing military exploits against the Sassanid Empire of the Persians. Indeed, Heraclius's anti-Persian wars played a central part in motivating him towards a fresh search for religious peace within the Empire. This was because the Monophysite populations of Egypt and Syria were now so hostile to Byzantium that they were welcoming the pagan armies of Persia as blessed liberators (see Part Two, Chapter 1, section 2, for a fuller account of this).

Heraclius took his theological lead from patriarch **Sergius of**

---

[29] Confirmation was the ceremony in which a bishop, or in the East a presbyter too, laid hands on a newly baptised person to complete his reception of the Holy Spirit. Much later, the Western Catholic and Eastern Orthodox Churches decided that there were seven sacraments (or "mysteries", as the East called them); but Pseudo-Dionysius, writing in the 6th Century, said there were only three.

Constantinople (610-38), who suggested that Chalcedonians and Monophysites could unite around the formula of a "single energy" in Christ. When patristic theologians spoke of "energy" (in Greek, *energeia*), they meant the action, activity, work or operation which reveals a thing's distinctive nature. For example, the energy of the sun is its shining forth with heat and light - which reveal its distinctive "sunny" nature. And the energy of a human being is the unique set of human activities (thinking, feeling, choosing, speaking, relating to others, *etc.*) which manifest a human being's distinctive nature.

We might wonder what this has to do with the quarrel between Chalcedonians and Monophysites. It is, in fact, very deeply involved with it. The whole controversy raged around the question of how Christ could be *one* person, if He had *two* natures, a human and a divine nature. Chalcedonians distinguished between nature and person, arguing that Christ's two natures dwelt *in* each other without becoming confused *with* each other, rather like a man's body and soul, united by Christ's one single divine person. Monophysites retorted that it was wrong to make this distinction between nature and person; if Christ was only one person, this required His two natures to become one single divine-human nature. But energy was a third factor in the equation - something different from nature and person. If Chalcedonians and Monophysites could agree that Christ had only one single energy, perhaps both parties could accept the Saviour's "single energy" as the explanation of His oneness.

Sergius of Constantinople, then, argued that energy really belonged to person rather than to nature. Since Chalcedonians and Monophysites were agreed that Christ was one person, they could (Sergius suggested) see His two natures being united in the single energy of His person. In other words, the Saviour exercised His one personal energy *through* His two natures, so that one single divine-human activity pervaded them. One could not look at Christ and say *this* was a human action, but *this* was a divine action; all His actions were divine and human at the same time. Here, then, was Sergius's Christ: a Saviour Who had two natures in theory, but Who for all practical purposes, in His energy and activity, was not two but utterly one.

Emperor Heraclius championed Sergius's "single-energy" formula, and it met with some success, bringing about local church unions between Chalcedonians and Monophysites in Egypt and Armenia. However, the reunion ran into serious trouble in Palestine. The Chalcedonian monks there opposed the single-energy formula with passion; they were led by the elderly and theologically sharp-minded *Sophronius of Jerusalem* (560-638), who was elected patriarch of Jerusalem in 634. Sophronius argued that energy did not belong to person (as Sergius said), but to nature (as in the traditional patristic understanding). Christ's divine and human natures each had their own distinctive ways of acting: His divine nature operated in the divine works of creation, providence and grace; His human nature operated in the human works of birth, growth, hunger, thirst, tears and sufferings. Thus there were in Christ two distinct sets of activities, human and divine, revealing the two distinct natures of the Saviour. Sophronius outlined these views in an important circular letter to the other patriarchs (Rome, Constantinople, Alexandria and Antioch).[30]

Sophronius's forceful and influential opposition to the single-energy

---

30 Above all else, Sophronius's position was based on the orthodox understanding of the Trinity. For if energy belongs to person, as Sergius held, it would follow that Father, Son and Holy Spirit must have three different energies - the work, activity and operation of each divine person would be purely personal, arising from His own distinct individual personhood. But if that is indeed the case, the three persons of the Trinity have split apart into three gods! We would have three Creators of the universe, three Rulers of providence, and three Saviours of mankind. The whole point of the orthodox doctrine of the Trinity, hammered out by Athanasius and the Cappadocian fathers in the 4th Century (see Chapter 8), was that energy and activity belong to nature, *not* to person. So when we see Scripture ascribing the activity of creation to Father, Son and Holy Spirit, this proves that they must all be the one true God, because it shows that all three have the one single divine nature which alone possesses the power to create. To put it simply: if energy belongs to person, the Trinity performed three acts of creation as three distinct Creators; but if energy belongs to nature, the Trinity performed one act of creation as one single Creator. (We see that crucial issues were involved in the controversy about "single-energy". It may seem rather abstract and academic at first; but if we think through its implications, they affect fundamental doctrines of the faith. This is often the case in theology.)

formula prompted emperor Heraclius to try and enlist the support of the pope - *Honorius I* (625-38). It was the worst thing he could have done. Honorius plunged the quarrel into even darker and stormier waters. He professed himself unhappy with all the talk about energies - where does the Bible ever use such language? he asked; but then, like some ticking time-bomb, he threw in the explosive suggestion that Christ had a single *will* rather than a single energy. "Will" was certainly a Biblical word. Honorius thought that Chalcedonians and Monophysites could find common ground in confessing that the Saviour's human and divine natures were united by His single divine will - which, of course, meant denying that He had a human will. Emperor Heraclius seized on this idea and, in 638, issued an official theological statement, the *Ekthesis teis Pisteos* ("Exposition of the Faith"), usually known simply as the *Ekthesis*. The document forbade all further mention of energies, and decreed that Christ had only a single divine will: this was to be the new imperial orthodoxy. Those who supported the *Ekthesis* were known as *Monotheletes*,[31] from the Greek for "single will", *monon theleima*.

The Monothelete position aroused mighty enemies among orthodox Chalcedonians. The mightiest were pope *Martin I* (649-55) and the Greek monk *Maximus the Confessor* (580-662), who maintained that Christ had two wills, a human will alongside a divine one. Maximus thought this out most fully. The question itself was simple: did "will" belong to nature or to person? The Monotheletes held that it belonged to person; a human being's will (his capacity for desiring and choosing) was part of his individual personhood, not his human nature. Therefore, since Christ was not a human person, but a divine person incarnate in a human soul and body, He did not have a human will. He had only the divine will of the Logos. Maximus disagreed with this with every fibre of his being. He maintained that will was distinct from person, and belonged to nature. Just as our ability to think (our mind) is part of our human nature, Maximus argued, so also our ability to desire and choose (our will) is part of our nature. Will is just as essential to human nature as mind is. For Maximus, the

---

31 Some textbooks spell the word "Monothelites", but the correct spelling is "Monotheletes". It is pronounced "Monna-thel-eets". The doctrine itself, Monotheletism, is pronounced "Monna-thella-tizzum".

Maximus the Confessor (580 - 662)

human **person** is the subject or ego - the "I" - who acts through the mind and will of his human nature.

So far, this may sound very remote from the New Testament and Christian life. Why did Maximus get so worked up about all this? The answer actually lies in his overwhelming concern for the doctrine of salvation. The human will, Maximus pointed out, is the source of sin, the very seat of our corruption which needs to be rescued, sanctified and healed. Therefore, if there is to be any salvation for our fallen wills, the Son of God had to take up a human will into Himself in the incarnation. The only way our wills can become holy is by receiving holiness from the perfectly holy human will of Christ the God-man. But the Monotheletes were saying that Christ had no human will. Where, then, asked Maximus, does the sanctification of our sinful wills come from? Maximus's controversy with the Monotheletes was very similar to Gregory of Nazianzus's dispute with Apollinarius in the 370's; Apollinarius had denied that the Logos took up a human mind - the Monotheletes were denying that He took up a human will.[32] The response was the same in both cases. In Gregory's words, "What has not been taken up has not been healed." It was essential to our salvation, Maximus insisted, that the divine person of the Logos took up a human will; for by taking it, He flooded it with the energies of His divine will, thus making His human will sinlessly perfect, free from the very possibility of sin, and the source of liberation and salvation for our sinful wills.[33]

Maximus, then, had the strongest reasons for attacking

---

[32] For Apollinarius see Chapter 10, section 2.

[33] Maximus had a special name for the sinful human will. He called it the **gnomic** will (from the Greek **gnomei**, "judgment, opinion, intention"). He drew an important distinction between "gnomic will" and "natural will". Our natural will, said Maximus - that is, our basic human capacity for desiring and choosing, as created by God - is inclined by its own natural energy towards what is good. Before they sinned, all Adam and Eve had to do in order to be good was follow the natural direction of their natural wills. But once the human person has perverted his natural will away from good towards evil, as we have all done in Adam, this personal perversion of the natural will produces a new kind of will, the gnomic will. A gnomic will is a fallen human will which is tossed and turned by conflicting ideas and desires - by truth and error, good and evil, having
(cont.)

Monotheletism. Its denial of a human will in Christ threatened the entire doctrine of salvation, in Maximus's judgment. Of course, it also meant that Christ was not fully human; for if the capacity of will belongs to our human nature, and if (as Monotheletes said) Jesus Christ had no human will, it followed that He was not a genuinely human being.

It was not a good sign for emperor Heraclius and the Monotheletes that they had raised up for themselves such an enemy as Maximus the Confessor. For Maximus was a theologian and spiritual writer of towering eminence; he ranks with Athanasius, the Cappadocian fathers, Cyril of Alexandria and John of Damascus as one of the truly outstanding minds of the Eastern Church in the patristic age. The records of his life reveal a man adorned with humility, gentleness and heavenly-mindedness, calm in adversity, unswerving against government-backed heresy. Born in Constantinople to a rich family, Maximus began his adult life as a civil servant in the court of Heraclius. This did not prove to be to his taste; after three years, he renounced secular life and entered the monastery of Chrysopolis (near Constantinople), where he became abbot. He then moved to another monastic community at Cyzicus, a hundred miles south-west; but when Persian troops invaded the whole area in 626, he fled to the island of Crete, and from there in 628 to North Africa, where he remained for the next 20 years. When the Monothelete controversy broke out through emperor Heraclius's *Ekthesis* in 638, Maximus vigorously fought this latest attempt at reconciling Chalcedonians with Monophysites, and rallied the West against the *Ekthesis*. As we have seen, he regarded Monotheletism as a destructive heresy which assaulted the very heart of human salvation in Christ.

When Heraclius died in 641, his successor was his grandson *Constans 11* (641-68) - a cruel dictator who knew nothing of theology and cared even less. Constans tried to quench the

---

to choose between them. Maximus said that Christ did not have a gnomic will; He had only a pure natural will, like innocent Adam and Eve, inclined towards truth and goodness alone. Indeed, Christ's human will was superior even to innocent Adam's, because the divine person of the Son was clearly incapable of perverting His natural human will as Adam did.

controversy by silencing all parties; his edict of 648, the *Typos*, prohibited all Byzantine citizens from ever again mentioning wills and energies in Christ, on pain of severe punishment. It was a useless gesture. It amounted to an imperial command to the orthodox that they must tolerate heresy in the Church; and some of the orthodox were not willing to obey. One of them was the new pope, Martin I, who ascended the papal throne in July 649. Martin was a close ally of Maximus, and impressed everyone with his radiant sanctity, deep learning and (apparently) by being the most handsome man in Rome. In the Church of Saint John Lateran in October that year, pope Martin summoned a council of the Roman Church which condemned the *Typos* and Monotheletism, and affirmed that the Lord Jesus Christ had both a human will and a divine will. Maximus was present and played a leading part in this Roman council. Martin then sent copies of the council's decisions throughout East and West, together with a circular letter warning all faithful Christians against the dangerous heresy of the Monotheletes.

Such intrepid defiance of emperor Constans sealed the fate of both Maximus and pope Martin. Byzantine troops seized them in 653, carried them off to Constantinople, and imprisoned them for a lengthy period in horrific conditions which shattered Martin's already poor health. Constans eventually put them on trial (separately) for treason in 655. Martin was found guilty and sentenced to death; soldiers tore his papal robes from him, flogged him, and dragged him off to the prison cells where murderers were confined. In an unexpected touch of mercy, Constans then softened Martin's sentence to banishment, exiling him to the Crimea in the Black Sea. There, worn out by his physical and emotional ordeal, the pope died six months later, a martyr for his faith in the full humanity of Christ.

The trial of Maximus was then held. Maximus had spearheaded the doctrinal opposition to Monotheletism; Constans was determined to make a public spectacle of him. Day after day, the Byzantine magistrates hurled accusations of treason and heresy at the elderly monk - he was now 74 years old. But Maximus was completely unmoved, rejecting all the charges of treason (which were quite false), and boldly denying that an emperor had any right to interfere in theological matters: such conduct was the state laying unholy hands on the Church's independence. Although the whole might and majesty of a hostile Byzantine Church and Empire were arrayed against him, Maximus serenely stood his ground throughout the trial. Constans was not impressed; Maximus was beaten and banished to Bizya in Thrace.

From his place of exile, Maximus continued to speak and write against Monotheletism; so in 662, an enraged Constans put him on trial again. The judges pressed Maximus with the argument that everyone else in the Eastern Church had submitted to the *Typos*. How dare he, a lone monk, defy the voice of the Church? Maximus had his answer: "Even if we, or an angel from heaven, should preach any Gospel to you other than what we have preached to you, let him be accursed," he quoted from **Galatians 1:8**. Was only Maximus in the right, then, and everyone else wrong about Monotheletism, the judges asked? Did he think he alone was saved? Maximus's response echoes down the centuries: "May God grant that I do not condemn anyone, nor say that I alone am saved. But I prefer to die rather than violate my conscience by defecting from what I believe about God." Europe was not to see so heroic a sight again, until John Huss stood alone before his persecutors at the Council of Constance in 1415.[34] This time Maximus's punishment was more brutal: soldiers ripped out his tongue and chopped off his right hand, that he might speak and write no more. Constans then banished him to Lazica, on the south-eastern coast of the Black Sea, where Maximus died a few months later. It was for his unbending confession of faith amid these cruelties that the Church later hailed Maximus as "the Confessor".

5. The Third Council of Constantinople.

Constans was murdered in 668 - assassinated in his bath by a discontented servant. His son *Constantine IV* (668-85) turned out to be a very different kind of emperor from his father: a wise, moderate, popular statesman, and the first Christian ruler to crush the forces of Islam in battle (see Part Two, Chapter 1). Once he had finished saving the Empire from Muslim attack, Constantine concentrated on restoring religious peace in the Church. Acting in harmony with pope *Agatho* (678-81), a loyal disciple of pope Martin and Maximus the Confessor, Constantine summoned the sixth of the

---

34 For John Huss, see Part Two, Chapter 10, section 5.

ecumenical Councils in November 680 - the Third Council of Constantinople (it continued in session until September 681). The Council was a total triumph for the foes of Monotheletism, vindicating the belief in Christ's full humanity for which Maximus and Martin had suffered. The Council's confession of faith stated:

> "We declare that in Christ there are two natural wills and two natural energies, without division, without change, without separation, without confusion, according to the teaching of the holy fathers. And these two natural wills are not contrary to one another (God forbid!), as the ungodly heretics assert, but His human will follows His divine will, not resisting or reluctant, but subject to His divine and all-powerful will.... We glorify two natural energies, that is, a divine energy and a human energy, without division, without change, without confusion, without separation, in the same Lord Jesus Christ, our true God."

The Council also named and condemned those who had taught the single-energy and single-will doctrine, especially patriarch Sergius of Constantinople and pope Honorius, calling them instruments of Satan, heretics and blasphemers. This condemnation of a heretical pope by an ecumenical Council was later to be a favourite weapon of Eastern Orthodoxy and Protestantism in their conflict with the papacy and its claims to infallibility.

The Third Council of Constantinople brought an end to the centuries of controversy about the relationship between the human and the divine in Christ. It was also the last of the ecumenical Councils which received recognition by all three of the great branches of the professing Church - Roman Catholic, Eastern Orthodox and Protestant. Roman Catholics and Eastern Orthodox were together to acknowledge one more council, the Second Council of Nicaea in 787, but Protestants generally have rejected this Council for theological reasons.[35]

One interesting offshoot of the Monothelete controversy was a small

---

[35] For the Second Council of Nicaea, see Part Two, Chapter 3, section 3. The Second Council of Nicaea in 787 was the last of the ecumenical Councils in the view of Eastern Orthodoxy. Roman Catholics, however, have had further "ecumenical" Councils of their own.

sect in Lebanon known as the **Maronites**. They were named after their leader, the abbot *John Maron* (died 701). When the rest of the Eastern Church accepted the Third Council of Constantinople, the Maronites rejected it, remained Monothelete in their Christology, and established their own independent clergy, monasteries and Syriac liturgy, with John Maron as their first patriarch. In the 13th Century they entered into ecclesiastical union with Rome, abandoning their Monotheletism but keeping their own liturgy and the Eastern custom of allowing the lower clergy (below the rank of bishop) to marry. Today the Maronites are still the dominant Christian group in Lebanon.

The East-West unity which the Third Council of Constantinople displayed in theology fell apart a few years later over questions of Church government. Emperor Justinian II (685-95, 704-711)[36] summoned a council in 692 to deal with a host of practical matters not settled by the fifth and sixth ecumenical Councils. The council of 692 became known as the Quinisext Council (from the Latin for "fifth-sixth"), or the Trullan Council (from the *trullus*, the domed roof of the banqueting hall in the imperial palace, where the Council met). The Council was made up exclusively of Eastern bishops, and their proceedings horrified the papacy. Among other things, they proclaimed that the patriarch of Constantinople was equal to the pope of Rome, and condemned the Western Church for not allowing presbyters and deacons to marry. Pope Sergius I (687-701) protested, but to no avail. East and West were developing different attitudes and practices in all sorts of areas; without realising it at the time, they were on diverging paths which would lead ultimately to the great schism of 1054.[37]

6. Other great figures of this era.

---

[36] Justinian II was deposed and exiled between 695 and 704 by two usurpers, Leontius (695-96) and Tiberius III (698-704), but regained his throne in 704.

[37] Today's readers may be interested to know that the Quinisext Council also passed various laws relating to moral conduct; one of these laws - canon 111 - condemned abortion, demanding that doctors and pregnant women who aborted a child must be treated as murderers. This is one of the clearest indications of the patristic attitude on the subject.

The period of the Christological controversies was rich in great Christian thinkers, writers, preachers and politicians. Two who did not play any real part in the controversies of the time were Romanos the Melodist and John Climacus.

Romanos the Melodist (died 556) was one of the greatest hymn-writers of the Eastern Church. Originally from Emesa in Syria, he became a deacon in Constantinople's Church of the Theotokos during the reign of emperor Anastasius (491-518). Here Romanos began composing his hymns - *kontakia*, as the East calls them. A *kontakion* was a sort of sermon in poetic form which was chanted rather than spoken, partly by a preacher, partly by a choir or congregation. Romanos is supposed to have written about a thousand *kontakia*, but of the 90 that have survived, modern scholars accept only 60 as genuine. The Eastern Orthodox Church still chants verses from these *kontakia* on almost every major festival of the Christian year. According to tradition, Romanos received his poetic gift directly from the Virgin Mary who visited him from heaven in a dream. See the end of the Chapter for an example of Romanos's hymnwriting.

John Climacus (579-649) was abbot of the great Eastern monastery on mount Sinai. His massive influence on Eastern spirituality came through his famous book, ***The Ladder of Divine Ascent***; the Greek for ladder is *klimax*, from which John's name "Climacus" (pronounced "Klimma-kus") was taken. The *Ladder* was a handbook of teaching for monks in how to attain spiritual perfection, divided into 30 steps (like the steps of a ladder). Each step described a different virtue or vice and how the monk could acquire it or rid himself of it. Climacus offered a wealth of shrewd and sometimes remarkably frank advice, *e.g.* about sexual temptations. He also outlined in the *Ladder* one of the earliest forms of *hesychasm* - the practice of the "Jesus prayer"; we will look at this in some detail in Part Two, Chapter 9. Here let us simply notice the way that Climacus stressed the important Eastern theme of the superiority of inner mental prayer over spoken prayer. Climacus's *Ladder* became highly popular in the East; its greatest admirers in the West were to be the Jansenists of France in the 17th Century.

Important people

The Church

Chalcedonians:

Acacius of Constantinople
    (patriarch 471-89)
Pope Felix II (483-92)
John Maxentius (6th Century)
Theodore of Raithu (6th Century)
Pseudo-Dionysius the Areopagite
(6th Century)
Sabbas the Sanctified (439-532)
Leontius of Jerusalem (active 530's)
Pope Agapetus I (535-6)
Leontius of Byzantium (active 520-40)
Pope Vigilius (537-55)
Romanos the Melodist (died 556)
Sophronius of Jerusalem (560-638)
John Climacus (579-649)
Pope Martin I (649-55)
Maximus the Confessor (580-662)
Pope Agatho (678-81)

Political and military

Emperor Leo I (457-74)
Emperor Zeno (474-91)
Emperor Anastasius
    (491-518)
Emperor Justin I (518-27)
Empress Theodora
    (518-48)
Emperor Justinian the
    Great (518-65)
Emperor Heraclius
    (610-641)
Emperor Constans II
    (641-68)
Emperor Constantine IV
    (668-85)

Monophysites:

Timothy the Cat (died 477)
Peter the Fuller (died 488)
Julian of Halicarnassus (died 518)
Jacob of Sarug (451-521)
Philoxenus of Mabbug (440-523)
Severus of Antioch (465-538)
Jacob Baradaeus (died 578)
Jacob of Edessa (640-708)

Monotheletes:

Sergius of Constantinople (610-38)
Pope Honorius I (625-38)
John Maron (died 701 - founder of the Maronites)

The joy of Christmas

Today the Virgin gives birth
to the One Who is above all existence,
the earth offers a cave[38]
to the One Whom no-one can approach;
angels join with shepherds in giving glory,
and magi journey in the company of a star.
For to us is born a little Child -
the eternal God.

Come and see! Bethlehem has opened Eden!
We have found a hidden delight;
O come, let us receive the joys of paradise in a cave!
For in this cave, the root in dry ground has appeared
whose blossom is forgiveness;
in this cave, we have found the well no man has dug
from which David once longed to drink;
in this cave, a Virgin has given birth to a babe,
quenching the thirst of both Adam and David.
O come let us hasten to the place,
where there has been born to us a little Child -
the eternal God.

The mother's Creator has chosen to become her Son;
the Saviour of infants is laid as an infant in a manger.
As the one who gave Him birth gazes on Him, she says:
"Tell me, my Child, how were You sown or planted in me?
I look at You, my flesh and blood, and I am amazed;
for I give You my milk, yet I am not married.
I see You in swaddling bands,
and I know that the flower of my virginity is also sealed;
for You guarded it when You chose to be born
as my little Child -
the eternal God."
"O Saviour, save the world! This is why You came.
Make Your entire universe right again!

---

38 Eastern commentators think that the "stable" in which Christ was born
    was a cave.

This is why You shone forth on me, and on the magi,
and on all creation.
Look, the magi to whom You have revealed the light of Your face
bow down before You,
offering useful, beautiful, highly desirable gifts.
I need these gifts,
for I am about to flee with You and for You to Egypt,
my Guide, my Son, my Creator, my Redeemer,
my little Child -
the eternal God."

Romanos the Melodist, *Kontakion on the Nativity,* **verses 1,2,3 and 24**

The soul of a mystic: Pseudo-Dionysius on knowing God

We must not dare to speak or think about the hidden all-surpassing God with any words or ideas, except those revealed in Scripture. In the Scriptures, the Divine Being has lovingly taught us that we cannot understand or directly contemplate It, because It surpasses even existence itself. Many of the writers of Scripture will tell you that the Divine Being is not only invisible and incomprehensible (**1 Timothy 6:16**), but also unsearchable and beyond tracing out (**Psalm 145:3, Romans 11:33**). Anyone who would try to reach into the hidden depths of this Infinity will find no trace of It. And yet, at the same time, it is not the case that the Good cannot be communicated in any sense. From Itself, It graciously sends forth a firm and all-surpassing beam of light, bestowing suitable degrees of enlightenment on created beings, and thus drawing holy minds upward to contemplate It (as far as they are allowed), and to become partakers of It, and be made like It. Here is what happens to those who devote themselves to this communion in a right and proper way. They do not rush towards an impossibly daring vision of God, beyond what He fittingly grants them. Nor do they tumble downwards to where their own natural desires would pull them. No, God lifts them firmly and unswervingly upward towards the divine ray which illuminates them. With a love that matches the degree of light bestowed on them, they soar up, with reverence, wisdom, and all holiness.
We go where we are summoned by those divine decrees which govern all the holy ranks of the different heavenly levels. Our minds

having been made wise and holy, we offer worship to What lies hidden beyond thought, beyond existence. With a wise silence we honour What we cannot express. The enlightening beams of the holy Scriptures raise us up; and thus illuminated, with our beings fashioned to songs of adoration, we behold the divine light, in a way suited to us, and our praise sounds forth to the gracious Source of all holy enlightenment, the Source that has revealed Itself to us in the holy words of Scripture. From Scripture we learn that It is the Cause of all things: it is Origin, it is Being, it is Life. To those who fall away, It is the Voice crying out, "Come back!" - and It is the Strength that raises the fallen up again. It renews and restores the image of God which has become corrupted within us. It is the holy Rock of Peace which is there for us, when the oceans of unholiness are surging all round us. It is the Place of Safety for those who make a stand. It is the Guide that carries upward those lifted towards It. It is the Enlightenment of the enlightened. It is the Source of Perfection for those who are being perfected, the Source of Divinity for those who are being deified, the Principle of Simplicity for those who are turning towards simplicity, the Point of Unity for those who are being unified. Surpassing everything, beyond all that exists, It is the Source of every source. Graciously, as far as we can receive, It gives out a share in what is hidden. In short, It is the Life of the living, the Being of beings, the Source and Cause of all life and all being. For out of Its goodness, It both commands all things to be, and keeps them all in being.[39]

Pseudo-Dionysius the Areopagite, *The Divine Names*, Chapter 1

Actions speak louder than words

The man who has lost his spiritual feeling is a mindless philosopher, a commentator who condemns himself, a bag of wind who contradicts himself, a blind man who teaches others how to see. He talks about how to heal a wound, and does not stop inflaming it. He complains about sickness, and carries on eating what is harmful. He prays against his sin, and immediately goes and commits it. And

---

[39] Pseudo-Dionysius constantly refers to God as "It" to make the point that the divine nature is above and beyond the created level of personality and gender. (This seems to sit uneasily with his emphasis on describing God in the words of Scripture.)

when he has committed it, he is angry with himself, and the miserable man is not ashamed of his own words. "I am sinning!" he cries, and eagerly continues to do so. His mouth prays against his passion, and his body longs for it. He speaks philosophically about death, but behaves as if he were going to live on earth for ever. He laments over the separation of soul and body, but stumbles along half-asleep as if he were eternal. He talks about temperance and self-control, but lives for gluttony. He reads about God's judgment and breaks into a smile. He reads about conceit, and is conceited as he reads about it. He repeats what he has learned about keeping watch, and falls asleep on the spot. He praises prayer, but avoids practising it like the plague. He speaks highly of obedience, but is the first to disobey. He praises detachment from earthly things, but isn't ashamed to be spiteful and to fight over a mere rag. When he is angered, he becomes bitter, and then becomes angry about his bitterness, and does not feel that he is suffering one defeat after another. He eats too much, repents, and then goes and eats again. In an endless stream of babbling words, he praises the beauty of silence. He teaches meekness, and gets himself into a rage while teaching it. He wakes up from a lustful dream, sighs and shakes his head over it, and surrenders to it again. He condemns laughter and praises spiritual sorrow, with a grin on his face. He confesses his sin of vainglory to others, but wants to gain glory from his confession. He lectures about chastity while gazing passionately at the faces of women. He lives in the world and praises those who live in silent contemplation, thus shaming himself without realising it. He praises those who give charitable gifts, and curses beggars. In all this, the man is his own accuser, and he does not want to come to his senses (I will not say he cannot).

John Climacus, *The Ladder of Divine Ascent*, Step 18, paragraph 3

The Beatitudes: Pure motives

The world contains many who are "poor in spirit", but not in the right way; many who mourn, but they are mourning over their financial affairs or because children have died; many who are meek, but they meekly submit to impure lusts; many who hunger and thirst, but only to steal the goods of others and make an unjust profit. There are many who are merciful, but only towards the body and physical wants; many who are pure in heart, but pride is their motive; many peacemakers, but they put the flesh before the soul; many who suffer persecution, but it is their own fault because they behave so awkwardly; many who are reviled, but on account of shameful sins. In contrast to all this, the only people who are blessed are those who do and suffer these things for Christ, following His example. What is the nature of their blessing? "For theirs is the kingdom of heaven, for they shall see God," and so on. So it is not merely because they do and suffer these things that they are blessed, for the worldly people we mentioned do the same things; no, they are blessed because they do and suffer them for Christ's sake and in imitation of His example. In everything we do, God looks at our intention, as I have frequently said, seeing whether we are doing it for Him, or from some other motive. So when we wish to do something good, we must not think about the praise we might win from other human beings; we must think only of God, so that we always have Him before us and do everything for His sake. Otherwise we will do all the work and yet lose our reward.

Maximus the Confessor, *The Four Hundred Chapters on Love*, Third Hundred, sections 47 and 48

You alone save me

O my Saviour,
grant that this difficult labour of my salvation
may come to a blessed end!
May the rain that lashes down,
and the fierce torrents rushing from the mountains,
and the violent storm
not be able to shake the house I am building.

Please help me, O Lord, with Your triumphant hand!
Come to my aid, preserve my soul,
so that I may praise You:
You, the Giver of all precious gifts,
the Lord of mankind's salvation.

Without You, almighty Master,

no good work, plan, idea, suggestion, or safety
could even exist,
nor anything that could help us
to arrive at our final destination.

But You are the One Who created me;
You are the One Who gave me both my body and my soul.
You are the One Who lifted me up when I had fallen;
You are the One Who showed me the way back to heaven.
Yes, and without any worthiness of my own,
You are the One Who will bring me into Your house
to dwell with You for ever,
where I will sing hymns to Your glory
in the company of all Your blessed ones!

A hymn by Maximus the Confessor

GLOSSARY

Abbess
The head of a community of nuns. The word is the feminine form of "abbot".

Abbey
The dwelling place of a community of monks led by an abbot, or a community of nuns led by an abbess.

Abbot
The head of a community of monks. From the Aramaic *abba*, "father".

Alexandrian
A term describing the particular approach to the Christian faith which was common among the theologians of Alexandria and their followers, *e.g.* their emphasis on the deity and oneness of Christ, and their allegorical method of interpretation of Scripture.

Allegorical method of interpretation
The approach to Scripture, common among theologians of the Alexandrian type, which tended to downplay the literal and historical meaning of Scripture in favour of what were thought to be deeper, more spiritual meanings. Contrasted with the grammatico-historical method of interpretation.

Anathema, anathematise
When the early Church pronounced an "anathema" on someone, it meant declaring him to be outside the Christian faith and salvation.

The Creed of Nicaea anathematised Arians. Anathematising was stronger than excommunication, since the latter could be applied to a Christian who was under discipline. Anathema comes from a Greek word meaning "to give over to destruction".

Anchoress
A female hermit. The feminine form of "anchorite".

Anchorite
Another word for a hermit. From the Greek *chorizo*, "to separate".

Antiochene
A term describing the particular approach to the Christian faith which was common among the theologians of Antioch and their followers, *e.g.* their emphasis on the humanity of Christ, the distinction between His human and divine natures, and their grammatico-historical interpretation of Scripture.

Apocrypha
A group of books not found in the Hebrew Old Testament, but found in copies of the Septuagint, the Greek translation of the Old Testament. Some Christians accepted some or all the apocrypha as divinely inspired. Most believers, who did not accept the inspiration of the apocrypha, still placed a high value on them as instructive and edifying books written by godly Jews in between the Old and New Testament periods. The apocrypha consists of **1 and 2 Esdras, Tobit, Judith, Susanna, Bel and the Dragon, the Prayer of Manasses, the Epistle of Jeremiah, Baruch, Ecclesiasticus** (not to be confused with **Ecclesiastes**), **the Wisdom of Solomon, 1 and 2 Maccabees**, and additional passages in **Esther** and **Daniel**. The word "apocrypha" is Greek for "hidden things"; this refers to the fact that the apocryphal books were not read out in public worship, because the Church did not generally consider them to be on the same level as the rest of Scripture.

Apollinarians, Apollinarianism
After Apollinarius (330-390), bishop of Laodicea from 361. Apollinarius held that in the incarnation, the Son of God did not have a human mind; His infinite divine mind took the place of a finite human mind. He was thus a divine mind dwelling in a human body.

This doctrine was condemned by the Council of Constantinople in 381. See Chapter 10, section 2.

Apophatic
The "negative way" of understanding God, which says that we cannot know what God *is* - we can only know what He is *not*. Apophatic theology was given its most lucid expression by Pseudo-Dionysius the Areopagite. See Chapter 12, section 3.

Apostolic fathers
A name given to the first generation of early Church fathers, roughly in the period AD 95-140. See Chapter 3, section 1.

Apostolic succession
In the early Church, because a bishop alone could ordain another bishop, this gave rise (from the end of the 2nd Century) to the doctrine of "apostolic succession". According to this understanding of Church government, the apostles ordained the first bishops by the laying on of hands; these bishops then ordained their successors, transmitting apostolic authority to them by the laying on of their hands; and so on. Therefore, a true bishop could trace his authority directly back to the apostles through this "family tree" of ordinations. However, this view of apostolic succession did not give any kind of absolute authority or infallibility to bishops in the early Church. If bishops fell into heresy (as many did during the Arian controversy of the 4th Century - see Chapter 8), it became the duty of all orthodox Christians not to recognise them any longer. Apostolic succession included *holding the faith which the apostles had taught*, as well as being ordained by bishops who could trace their own ordination back to the apostles.

Archimandrite
In the East, the head of an important monastery or group of monasteries. Archimandrite means "ruler of a sheepfold".

Arians, Arianism
Arianism was the doctrine which in the 4th Century denied the deity of Christ, teaching that before the incarnation, as the Logos, He was not God but the first and greatest of created beings. It was condemned as a heresy by the Council of Nicaea in 325 and the

Council of Constantinople in 381. The father of the doctrine was Arius (256-336), a presbyter in the Alexandrian church. See Chapter 8.

Asceticism
The practice of rigorous bodily self-denial as an aid to spiritual growth.

Benedictine
After the Italian monk, Benedict of Nursia (480-547). Benedict wrote a guide or "rule" for monastic life, the Benedictine rule. Its wisdom, balance and practical nature as a guide for community living made it the most popular and widely used of all monastic rules throughout the Western world.

Bishop
From the Greek *episcopos*, "overseer". For the first three Centuries, this was more-or-less the equivalent of today's Protestant term "pastor" or "minister" - the leader of a local church. The bishop was the man who conducted the services of worship, oversaw church discipline, and had the sole power to ordain, baptise and preside at the Lord's supper (although he could delegate to his presbyters the act of baptising and celebrating communion). In his own church, he became bishop through a two-part process: (i) he was elected by the votes of the congregation; (ii) he was then ordained by other bishops through the laying on of hands. Until the 4th Century, every local church had its own bishop, and no bishop had authority over any other church. The 4th Century saw the rise of "metropolitan" bishops and "patriarchs" who exercised authority over the other bishops in their territory, and the development of local churches run not by a bishop, but by a presbyter who was accountable to the bishop of the main city church in his region. See Chapter 3, section 2, and Chapter 7, section 3, under **Church organisation**.

Byzantine Empire
The name which historians give to the Eastern Roman Empire after the fall of Rome in 410. The capital of the Byzantine Empire was Constantinople, built by emperor Constantine the Great on the site of an older town, Byzantium. Constantinople was finished in 330; some date the Byzantine Empire from that year.

Canon
From a Greek word meaning "rule". The canon of Scripture is the official list of books recognised by the Church as being divinely inspired and therefore binding on the Church's beliefs and practices. The canon of the New Testament was finally settled in the Eastern Church by the middle of the 4th Century; in 367, the 39th Festal Letter of Athanasius, bishop of Alexandria, listed the 27 books of the New Testament as we have them today. In the West, a Church council at Carthage in AD 397 agreed on the same list of genuine New Testament books.

Canon law
Church law, touching on matters of discipline, morality and doctrine. The first recorded enactment of canon law is **Acts 15:23-29**.

Cappadocian fathers
The great 4th Century fathers Basil of Caesarea (330-79), Gregory of Nyssa (335-94) and Gregory of Nazianzus (330-90). All three were natives of the province of Cappadocia in Asia Minor. They were the key figures in the final defeat of Arianism in the Church. See Chapter 8, section 3.

Catechumen
From the Greek *katacheo*, "to teach". A catechumen was a person whom the Church was preparing for baptism by instructing him in the Christian faith.

Catholic, Catholicism
From the Greek *katholikos*, "universal". Early Christians called themselves Catholics to distinguish them from unorthodox groups like the Gnostics. In early Church usage, a Catholic was simply a member of the universal Church of Christ, believing the same doctrines as all other true Christians throughout the world. The later term "Roman Catholic" is quite different; it can be used to describe either (a) the Western Church after the great East-West schism of 1054, or (b) that part of the Western Church which rejected the Protestant Reformation in the 16th Century.

Cenobitic
The type of monasticism which was based on community life. Cenobitic comes from the Greek *koinos bios*, "common life".

Chalcedon, Chalcedonian
This refers to the doctrine of the incarnation defined and proclaimed by the Council of Chalcedon in 451. The Creed of Chalcedon has normally been accepted by orthodox or conservative theologians as setting out the limits within which a Biblical understanding of the incarnation must operate. In the early Church period, Chalcedonians occupied the middle ground between the equal and opposite heresies of Nestorianism (condemned by the Council of Ephesus in 431) and Monophysitism (ruled out by the Creed of Chalcedon in 451). We can sum up the differences thus: Chalcedonians held that Christ was one person with two distinct natures, divine and human; Nestorians held that Christ was two distinct persons, divine and human, with two corresponding natures; Monophysites held that Christ was one person with one nature, a combined divine-human nature. See Chapter 10, section 4.

Christology
That branch of theology which deals with the doctrine of the incarnation - the divine and human natures of Christ and how they relate to each other.

Confessor
A Christian arrested and perhaps tortured for his faith, but not executed.

Convent
A Western Latin word for a monastery, from the Latin *convenire*, "to come together." Today it usually describes a monastery for females (a nunnery).

Cyrillian Chalcedonians
A party in the Eastern Church after the Council of Chalcedon, opposed to both the Monophysites and Dyophysites. They accepted the Creed of Chalcedon, but interpreted it in such a way as to make it harmonise with the Christology of Cyril of Alexandria (or at least, with what they believed Cyril had taught). See Chapter 12, sections 1 and 2.

Deacon
In the early Church, deacons were responsible for visiting the sick
and distributing food, clothing, and other necessities of life to the
poorer members of the congregation. They also assisted the bishop
in the service of worship, especially the Lord's supper, where they
distributed the bread and wine. Both men and women could be
deacons.

Deification
"Becoming divine". This was the accepted understanding of
salvation in the Eastern Church. It does not mean that human beings
are gods by nature or become God by nature. It means that through
union with Christ, believers share by grace in the glory and
immortality of God, and in that sense become divine - "partakers of
the divine nature" (**2 Peter 1:4**). In many ways, "deification" in
Eastern theology is the equivalent of "sanctification" in Western
theology.

Docetism
From the Greek   *dokeo*, "to seem". The belief that Christ only
seemed to be human, that He did not really have a body of human
flesh. Docetism stemmed from the view that flesh and physical
matter were evil, or the source of evil; therefore the Saviour could
have had no contact with it. All Gnostics were Docetic.

Donatists, Donatism
A dissenting movement in North-West Africa in the 4th and 5th
Centuries, named after Donatus (died 355). The Donatists refused
to accept the ministry of bishop Caecilian of Carthage (appointed in
311), on the grounds that one of the bishops who ordained him had
handed over the Bible to be burnt during the persecution under
emperor Diocletian. Thus the Church in North-West Africa split into
two rival Churches, the Catholics and the Donatists. Donatists held
that moral impurity in a clergyman rendered his ministry invalid - he
could not baptise, ordain or celebrate communion. They also held that
they alone were the one true Church. See Chapter 7, section 1, and
Chapter 9, section 3.

Dyophysite
From the Greek *duo*, "two", and *physis*, "nature". The Dyophysites

were a party in the Eastern Church after the Council of Chalcedon.
They held very strongly (against the Monophysites) that Christ had
two distinct natures, human and divine, but were rather weak and
unconvincing in their attempts to explain how the two natures were
united. See Chapter 12, sections 1 and 2.

Eastern Orthodox
A title often given to the Eastern Greek-speaking Chalcedonian
Church of the Byzantine Empire and its daughter Churches in
Russia, the Balkans and elsewhere. Strictly speaking, we should only
refer to it in this way after the great East-West schism of 1054; it was
only at that point that Eastern and Western Chalcedonians separated
into two mutually hostile Churches.

Ecumenical Council
A conference of bishops from all parts of the Christian world to
decide questions of doctrine and discipline. There were seven
ecumenical Councils recognised by both East and West - Nicaea
(325), Constantinople (381), Ephesus (431), Chalcedon (451),
Second Constantinople (553), Third Constantinople (680-81), and
Second Nicaea (787). The Western Church had other Councils it
regarded as ecumenical after 787, but these were not recognised by
the East. Most Protestants have not accepted the 2nd Council of
Nicaea for theological reasons (rejecting its doctrine of the
veneration of icons). "Ecumenical" comes from the Greek for "the
inhabited world"; when used in the phrase "ecumenical Council", it
has nothing to do with the modern "ecumenical movement".

Episcopacy
Government of the Church by bishops, who are seen as having a
higher office than presbyters. From the Greek *episkopos*,
"overseer".

Eremitic
The hermit's way of life. From the Greek *eremia*, desert.

Eucharist
Word commonly used in the early Church period for the Lord's
supper or holy communion. From the Greek *eucharisteo*, "to give
thanks".

Eutychians, Eutychianism
After the extreme Alexandrian theologian Eutyches (378-454). He taught that Christ's human nature was swallowed up and lost in His deity, "like a drop of wine in the sea". See Chapter 10, section 4.

Excommunication
Act of church discipline, barring a disobedient or lapsed Christian from holy communion.

Gnostics, Gnosticism
A movement divided into many sects, all claiming to be the true Christians, but holding basic doctrines which contradicted Catholic teaching. Gnostics maintained that the universe of space, time and matter was evil, created not by God but by an inferior being called the "demiurge". They denied the incarnation and physical resurrection, and usually abstained from meat-eating and sex. Gnosticism as a pseudo-Christian movement probably began in the 1st Century AD and became a serious rival to Catholic Christianity in the 2nd.

Grammatico-historical method of interpretation
The approach to Scripture, common among theologians of the Antiochene type, which emphasised the literal and historical meaning of Scripture, in contrast to the deeper, more spiritual meanings favoured by the allegorical method of interpretation.

Hegumena
Eastern word for abbess.

Hegumenos
Eastern word for abbot.

Hermit
From the Greek *eremia*, "desert". A monk who lives alone.

Homoousios
Greek for "of the same essence". Key word in the Arian controversy. The opponents of Arius adopted this word to describe the Son's relationship with the Father. If the Son was "of the same essence" as the Father, it meant that the Son possessed the same

nature and attributes as the Father; therefore, the Son was as eternal, uncreated, all-powerful, all-knowing, and divine as the Father - in direct contradiction to Arius's teaching. See **Ousia**.

Hypostasis
Greek word which, before the Arian controversy, could mean either "essence" or "person". The Cappadocian fathers defined it more closely to mean "person" as distinct from "essence". For "essence", see **Ousia**.

Icon
A religious image - of Christ, an angel, a saint - popular and fashionable from the 4th Century onwards. An icon could be a statue, a low-relief carving, a mosaic, a painting or a drawing. They usually adorned churches; paintings and drawings were found in Bibles. The East tended to reject statues as too much like the icons of pagan gods.

Jacobites
Syrian Monophysites, named after their leading figure Jacob Baradaeus (died 578). See Chapter 12, section 2.

Liturgy
Written form of worship. It includes hymns, prayers, exhortations, greetings, benedictions and doxologies. Christians used liturgy in worship from the earliest times.

Logos
Greek for "word" and "reason". The apostle John uses it as a title for Christ as a divine person in **John 1**, verses 1 and 14. Greek philosophers also used the term *logos* to refer to the cosmic principle which mediates between God and creation, giving order and purpose to the universe. The early Church often described Christ as the Logos, with reference to His divine nature.

Manichees, Manichaeism
Important Gnostic sect founded in the 3rd Century by the Persian Mani. See Chapter 6, section 2.

Marcionites, Marcionism
Important Gnostic sect founded in the 2nd Century by Marcion. See Chapter 4, section 1.

Maronites
A Christian offshoot of the Monothelete controversy in Lebanon in the 7th Century. The Maronites remained Monothelete in their Christology, after the rest of the Eastern Church had either returned to orthodoxy or else become fully Monophysite. Named after their first leader John Maron (died 701). In the 13th Century the Maronites entered into ecclesiastical union with Rome, abandoning their Monotheletism but keeping their own liturgy and the Eastern custom of allowing the lower clergy (below the rank of bishop) to marry. Today the Maronites are still the dominant Christian group in Lebanon. See Chapter 12, section 4.

Mass
Western Latin word for holy communion. It comes from the closing words of the Latin communion liturgy - *ite, missa est* ("go, the congregation is dismissed") - which the bishop or presbyter spoke at the end of communion. The word "mass" had first been used as a description of holy communion in the 5th Century; by the 6th, it was the standard term for it throughout the Western Church. It has no necessary connection with the later medieval doctrine of transubstantiation.

Medieval
Relating to the "Middle Ages", between the patristic period and the Protestant Reformation of the 16th Century.

Metropolitan
From the Greek for "mother-city". A metropolitan was a bishop of a "metropolitan" city in the Roman Empire. A metropolitan city was the chief city of a Roman province.

Middle Ages
See Medieval.

Monastery
The word originally meant a hermit's cave, but was then applied to the place where a community of monks lived.

Monasticism
The discipline and practice of being a monk.

Monk

A Christian man who lived either alone as a hermit, or with other Christian men in a monastery, devoting the day to worship and to the study of Scripture and the writings of the early Church fathers. Manual labour was also a central discipline in monasteries, which were economically self-supporting. The basic aim of the monk was to distance himself from the corrupting influences of an ungodly society, so that he could the more effectively pursue the salvation (sanctification) of his own soul and life. Outstanding monks often went on to become bishops. The word "monk" comes from the Greek *monachos*, "one who lives alone", but was later applied to those living in communities too. See Chapter 7, section 3.

Monophysites, Monophysitism

From the Greek *monos*, "one", and *physis*, "nature". Monophysites believed that in the incarnation, the divine and human natures of Christ blended into one single divine-human nature. Monophysites therefore rejected the Creed of Chalcedon in 451, which taught that Christ had two distinct natures. The Monophysites were strongest in Egypt, where they formed the Coptic Orthodox Church, and Syria, where they formed the Jacobite Church. The Ethiopian and Armenian Orthodox Churches also embraced Monophysitism. See Chapter 12, sections 1, 2 and 4.

Monotheletes, Monotheletism

From the Greek *monon theleima*, "one will". Monotheletes believed that the incarnate Saviour had only one will, the divine will of God the Son, but no human will. Monotheletism was condemned as a heresy by the 3rd Council of Constantinople in 680-81. See Chapter 12, section 4.

Montanists, Montanism

A "charismatic" movement of the 2nd Century, named after its leader Montanus. Montanists held that Christ's promise to send the Spirit of Truth had been fulfilled in the ministry of Montanus. The Catholic Church rejected his claims and excommunicated all Montanists. See Chapter 4, section 3.

Mystics, mysticism

This has always been a hard term to define. Mysticism is rooted in the belief that a person can enter into a state of spiritual "union" with God, and that this union - the ultimate experience - can be pursued by certain disciplines or techniques. But there are seemingly endless varieties of mysticism: Christian, Muslim, pagan, and others.

Neoplatonists, Neoplatonism
Neoplatonism means "the new Platonism", and is the name given to the philosophy of the great 3rd Century pagan thinker Plotinus (205-70). It had a significant impact on the Church. See Chapter 6, section 2.

Nestorians, Nestorianism
After Nestorius (381-451), patriarch of Constantinople from 428 to 431. Nestorians believed that in the incarnation, Christ not only had two distinct natures, but was two distinct persons - a divine Son of God indwelling a human Son of Mary. The Council of Ephesus in 431 condemned Nestorianism as a heresy. The national Church of Persia became strongly Nestorian in its Christology. See Chapter 10, sections 3 and 5.

Nicene creed
Confusingly, this is the Creed sanctioned by the Council of *Constantinople* in 381. The Creed which the Council of Nicaea formulated in 325 is not called the Nicene Creed, but "the Creed of Nicaea".

Novatianists, Novatianism
In the aftermath of the persecution under emperor Decius (249-51), some Christians in Rome, led by a presbyter called *Novatian,* broke away from the official Roman church, forming a new congregation with a far stricter discipline: they would never admit back into church membership any believer who had lapsed under persecution. The new Novatianist Church became an important movement, with congregations as far away as Spain and Carthage in the West, and Syria and Egypt in the East; they became especially numerous in Constantinople, capital of the Eastern Empire from 330. The Novatianist movement survived for several hundred years, but its congregations had probably all merged back into the Catholic Church by the 7th Century.

Nun
A female monk. The word comes from the Latin *nonna*, the feminine form of *nonnus*, "monk".

Nunnery
The place where a community of nuns lives.

Origenists, Origenism
(i) In the 4th Century, the Origenists were the largest party in the East during the Arian controversy. Following the theology of Origen (185-254), they held that Christ was eternal and uncreated in His divine nature, but inferior to the Father Who alone possessed divinity in an absolute sense. According to Origenists, when the Father generated the Son by an eternal act, the divine nature was transmitted from Father to Son, but was diminished by a degree in the process. Most Origenists eventually abandoned this view and accepted the Nicene belief in the full and absolute deity of the Son. (ii) In the 6th Century, the Origenists were a small party who believed in the existence of human souls from all eternity, the purely spiritual nature of the resurrection body, the final salvation of all sinners, and a view of the incarnation which saw Christ as an eternal human soul eternally united with the Logos. The Second Council of Constantinople in 553 condemned these doctrines.

Ousia
Greek for "essence", "substance", "nature", "being". A thing's *ousia* is its deepest and most basic reality - what makes it the kind of thing it is. The Councils of Nicaea (325) and Constantinople (381) declared, against Arius, that the Son was of the same *ousia* as the Father. This meant that Father and Son were identical in essence, substance, nature and being. Therefore the Son was just as much God as the Father was.

Papacy
From the Latin *papa*, "father". The office of Roman bishop, understood as being founded by the apostle Peter and enjoying first place of honour and dignity above all other bishops. The claims of the Roman bishops became ever more exalted, but the papacy as we know it today, claiming to be the "vicar of Christ" on earth, came to its maturity only in the Middle Ages, in the reign of pope Innocent III (1198-1216).

Patriarch, patriarchate

From the Greek for "fatherly ruler". The title of patriarch was given from the end of the 4th Century to the bishops of Rome, Constantinople, Alexandria and Antioch, and then in the 5th Century to the bishop of Jerusalem too. All other bishops were subject to the authority of the patriarch in whose territory their church was situated. A "patriarchate" is the office and jurisdiction of a patriarch.

Patristic

Relating to the early Church fathers. From the Greek and Latin *pater*, "father". There are various ways of defining the patristic period; I take it as covering the first six centuries of Church history (roughly the period of the first six ecumenical Councils). For the end of the patristic period and the beginning of the Middle Ages, see Part Two, Chapter 1, section 1.

Pelagianism

Named after Pelagius (active 383-417). Pelagius held that all human beings were born into the world as sinless as Adam was before he fell; the apostasy of Adam had not corrupted humanity's nature, but had merely set a fatally bad example, which most of Adam's sons and daughters had freely followed. Pelagius defined God's grace, not in terms of the inner renewing power of the Holy Spirit, but as the moral law, the example of Christ, and the persuasive power of rewards and punishments. Human free-will therefore became the chief source of salvation in the Pelagian scheme. Pelagianism was fought vigorously by Augustine of Hippo (354-430) and condemned by the Council of Ephesus in 431. See Chapter 9, secton 3.

Physis

In the dispute between the Christologies of Alexandria and Antioch in the 5th Century, this Greek word was used with differing shades and stresses of meaning. Cyril of Alexandria employed it to mean something like "person"; Antiochenes used it more in the sense of "nature". The Council of Chalcedon in 451 fixed its meaning as "nature": the incarnate Lord had two distinct *physeis*, two natures, human and divine. Most Alexandrians interpreted this statement to mean that Christ was two persons, and therefore rejected the Creed of Chalcedon as Nestorian.

Platonism
The philosophy of the Greek thinker Plato (427-347 BC) - in terms of influence, the world's greatest philosopher. Many of the early Church fathers were converted Platonists. See Chapter 1, section 1, under **Philosophy**.

Presbyter
From the Greek *presbuteros*, "elder". Important office in the early Church, second to the office of bishop. The presbyters of a church helped the bishop to provide collective leadership and discipline. They were elected by the people, and the bishop could delegate to them the power to baptise and celebrate holy communion. From the 4th century, it became common for the leader of a smaller church to be a presbyter, accountable to his bishop who was directly in charge of the main church in that area. The English word "priest" comes from "presbyter".

Purgatory
A place between heaven and hell where Christians are purified from sins which they failed to wash away on earth through holy communion and works of love. Some of the early Church fathers teach a form of this doctrine, but not in any developed way; it was Gregory the Great (540-604) who brought the idea to its maturity in the Western Church. The East rejected it.

Sabellians, Sabellianism
After Sabellius (early 3rd Century), an obscure Roman theologian. Sabellius taught that God is only one person, Who acts now as Father in creating the universe, now as Son in redeeming sinners, now as the Holy Spirit in sanctifying believers. These are simply three different roles acted out by one divine person, much as one human person might be a husband, a father, and a bus-driver. Sabellianism of one sort or another was quite popular in the early Church, because it offered a way of believing in the deity of Christ while preserving the oneness of God. However, the Church as a whole rejected it decisively. What Sabellianism failed to preserve was the personal relationships between Father, Son and Spirit, making a nonsense of the prayer-life of Jesus in the Gospels. Sabellianism is also known as Modalism and Monarchianism.

Sacrament
A Western Latin word meaning "an oath of allegiance". It was applied to baptism and holy communion. In the East, these were called "the mysteries".

Schism
The act of breaking fellowship with the Catholic Church.

Semi-Pelagians, Semi-Pelagianism
A theological position midway between Pelagianism and the teachings of Augustine of Hippo regarding the origins of the experience of salvation. Pelagianism placed salvation in the power of human free-will; Augustine ascribed salvation (regeneration, the new birth) wholly to God's grace; the Semi-Pelagians held that salvation was initially prompted by God's grace, but depended for its effect on human cooperation. See Chapter 9, section 3.

Skete
A small group of up to 12 monks who lived under the spiritual direction of a more experienced monk and met with other sketes for worship on holy days. Named after the Skete region of Egypt.

Syncretism
From the Greek for "federated", "joined in alliance". The belief that a person can follow more than one religion at the same time - that all religions are basically valid. The religious culture of the Roman Empire was syncretistic.

Synergism
Greek for "working together". This is the Eastern understanding of the relationship between God and human beings in salvation. It is similar to the Western "Semi-Pelagianism", with a strong emphasis on God's grace as lying behind all human spiritual effort, and a stress on the visible Church and its "life of grace" (especially holy communion) as the normal channel of God's sanctifying power.

Synod
A local Church council - as distinct from an ecumenical Council of the whole Church.

Theotokos
Greek title for the Virgin Mary. Literally "birth-giver of God", often translated "mother of God" by Roman Catholics and Eastern Orthodox, and "God-bearer" by Protestants. See Chapter 10, section 3.

Universalism
The belief that all human beings, and perhaps the demons too, will finally be saved.

Vulgate
Jerome's Latin translation of the Bible. "Vulgate" comes from the Latin word for "common" - the common Bible, *i.e.* the one in common use. See Chapter 9, section 2.

Bibliography

Here is a selection of some of the books I have found most useful, and which the enthusiastic non-specialist reader should (with diligence and a dictionary, in some cases) be able to enjoy and profit from. I have highlighted a few of the books in bold print; these, I think, are especially helpful for those coming to the study of Church history for the first time.

A. Books dealing with Church history in general

John Baillie, John McNeill & Henry Van Dusen (editors),
    The Library of Christian Classics (26 volumes)
Geoffrey Barraclough (editor), *The Christian World*
Henry Bettenson, *Documents of the Christian Church*
Louis Berkhof, *The History of Christian doctrines*
Thomas Bokenkotter, *A Concise History of the Catholic Church*
Henry Chadwick and G. R. Evans, *Atlas of the Christian Church*
Gregory Dix, *The Shape of the Liturgy*
R. S. Franks, *A History of the Doctrine of the Work of Christ*
J. Derek Holmes and Bernard W. Bickers, *A Short History of the
    Catholic Church*
J. N. D. Kelly, *The Oxford Dictionary of Popes*
Tony Lane, *The Lion Concise Book of Christian Thought*
Kenneth Scott Latourette, *History of Christianity* (2 volumes)
The Lion Handbook on the History of Christianity
Bernard Lohse, *A Short History of Christian Doctrine*
John McManners (editor), *The Oxford History of Christianity*
**William D. Maxwell, *An Outline of Christian Worship, its
Development and Forms***

Stephen Neill, *A History of Christian Missions*
J. Neuner and J. Dupuis, *The Christian Faith in the Doctrinal Documents of the Catholic Church*
The New International Dictionary of the Christian Church
The Oxford Dictionary of the Christian Church
Jaroslav Pelikan, *The Christian Tradition: A History of the Development of Doctrine* (5 volumes)
Philip Schaff, *History of the Christian Church* (8 volumes)
    Creeds of Christendom (3 volumes)
Williston Walker, *A History of the Christian Church* (4th edition, revised)
Timothy Kallistos Ware, *The Orthodox Church*

B. Books dealing with the early Church period
Pier Franco Beatrice, *Introduction to the Fathers of the Church*
The Venerable Bede, *Ecclesiastical History of the English People*
Henry Bettenson, *The Early Christian Fathers*
    The Later Christian Fathers
Peter Brown, *Augustine of Hippo*
    The World of Late Antiquity
Norman Bull, *The Rise of the Church*
Henry Chadwick, *The Early Church*
Eusebius of Caesarea, *The History of the Church*
Frederick Farrar, *Lives of the Fathers*
Robin Lane Fox, *Pagans and Christians*
Edward Gibbon, *Decline and Fall of the Roman Empire*
Gregory of Tours, *History of the Franks*
    The Life of the Fathers
Réné-francois Guettée, *The Papacy: Its Historic Origin and Primitive Relations with the Eastern Churches*
J.N.D. Kelly, *Early Christian Creeds*
    Early Christian Doctrines
Diana Leatham, *They Built on Rock: The Story of the Men and Women of the Early Celtic Church*
Ivar Lissnar, *Power and Folly: The Story of the Caesars*
John Meyendorff, *Christ in Eastern Christian Thought*
John Julius Norwich, *Byzantium: The Early Centuries*
Oxford History of Classical World
Elaine Pagels, *The Gnostic Gospels*

Aimé Peuch, *Saint John Chrysostom*
G. L. Prestige, *Fathers and Heretics*
Johannes Quasten, *Patrology* (4 volumes)
J. Stevenson, *A New Eusebius*
   Creeds, Councils and Controversies
Hugh Trevor-Roper, *The Rise of Christian Europe*
J. F. Webb and D. H. Farmer, *The Age of Bede*
Herbert Workman, *Persecution in the Early Church*
Frances Young, *From Nicaea to Chalcedon*

And finally, for the true enthusiast:

Philip Schaff (editor), A *Select Library of Ante-Nicene, Nicene and Post-Nicene Fathers* (38 volumes) - the writings of the early Church fathers in English. Unfortunately it is stilted 19th Century English. If you can't stomach it, you will find edited extracts in modern English in Henry Bettenson's *Early* and *Later Christian Fathers*, and J. Stevenson's *A New Eusebius* and *Creeds, Councils and Controversies*. Better still, try Henry Chadwick's recent translation of Augustine of Hippo's *Confessions*: the best introduction to the fathers, and one of the best introductions to what it means to be a Christian.

INDEX to NAMES

Page numbers in *italic* refer to illustrations. Subheadings relate firstly to the person's life, then major controversies where appropriate, followed by other comments about them.

INDEX to SUBJECTS